MANORIAL ACCOUNT ROLLS AND RENTALS
OF WALSHAM LE WILLOWS 1327 TO 1559

MANORIAL ACCOUNT ROLLS AND RENTALS OF WALSHAM LE WILLOWS 1327 TO 1559

Edited by
THE LATE AUDREY McLAUGHLIN
Revised with an Introduction by
MARK BAILEY

The Boydell Press

Suffolk Records Society
Volume LXVIII

A Suffolk Records Society publication
First published 2025
The Boydell Press, Woodbridge

ISBN 978-1-91693-140-4
ISBN 978-1-73980-963-8 (members)

Issued to subscribing members for the year 2025

The Boydell Press is an imprint of Boydell & Brewer Ltd
PO Box 9, Woodbridge, Suffolk IP12 3DF, UK
and of Boydell & Brewer Inc.
668 Mt Hope Avenue, Rochester, NY 14620–2731, USA
website: www.boydellandbrewer.com

The publisher has no responsibility for the continued existence or accuracy of
URLs for external or third-party internet websites referred to in this book, and
does not guarantee that any content on such websites is, or will remain, accurate
or appropriate

A catalogue record for this book is available
from the British Library

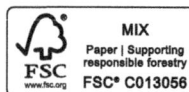

MIX
Paper | Supporting
responsible forestry
FSC
www.fsc.org   FSC® C013056

Printed and bound in Great Britain by
TJ Books Limited, Padstow, Cornwall

CONTENTS

MAPS AND TABLES

ACKNOWLEDGEMENTS

I was delighted when the Suffolk Records Society asked me to revise and prepare Audrey McLaughlin's translations of the Walsham accounts for publication. In the 1980s and 1990s Audrey and I had met on numerous occasions in and around the Suffolk Record Office at Bury St Edmunds, and later she sent me copies of her translations of the fifteenth-century Walsham court rolls with some material from South Elmham: in her words, 'you can put these to good use'. Therefore it is especially apt that this volume will enable many other historians to 'put to good use' the very rich Walsham material. I thank Bridget Hanley, senior archivist, and Emily Tillett, archives assistant, at Suffolk Archives, for help with access to the documents. Nick Amor helped me decipher one fascinating but troublesome section of the account for 1449–50. John Watts answered a query about the national events of the 1440s. Mike Durrant kindly recast an existing sketch map of Walsham by Rob Barber, which was among Audrey's papers, for publication here, and David Sherlock compiled the index of people and places. It is our hope that the final product is an appropriate commemoration of Audrey's life and work in local history. Audrey had translated and had begun the process of editing all of the accounts. I have checked them against digital copies of the originals, due to the significantly reduced service at the Bury St Edmunds Record Office, revised the editing, and written the Introduction.

Audrey's enthusiasm and encouragement made the Walsham History Group a successful and lasting legacy for the village. She would be the first to admit that her research team was a constant source of support to her and that she could not have produced the books, exhibitions, village tours and much else without their help. Those who served on the history committee or were members of the palaeography group were Rob Barber, Richard Belson, John Champion, Ann Daniels, Margaret Hey, Jean Lock, Ray Lock, Bryant Maitland, Diana Maywhort, Jean Sheehan, Mary Jane Toulson, Brian Turner, James Turner and Maureen Turner.

The Suffolk Records Society is grateful to Walsham Parish Council and to the Walsham History Group for financial assistance towards the cost of publishing this volume.

Mark Bailey
Waldringfield,
October 2024

AUDREY McLAUGHLIN
(15 NOVEMBER 1931 TO 7 JULY 2010)
AN APPRECIATION

Audrey Battlebury was born in Hackney where her father was a confectioner. At the outbreak of the Second World War, the family was evacuated to East Anglia, first to Bardwell in Suffolk, then to East Harling in Norfolk, and finally to Sweffling in Suffolk. After the war the family settled in Dunstable and Audrey worked for a time as a florist. She married and had two children, Rod and Deirdre, but the marriage did not last and she raised the children on her own. In order to support her family, she worked as an unqualified teacher which in turn led to formal training as a teacher at Putteridge Bury College of Education, Cambridge Institute of Education. She qualified in 1968. Although she first specialised in art, she soon came to realise that her passion lay in educational provision for those with special needs. She held various posts of responsibility in schools in Houghton Regis, Bedfordshire, before moving back to Suffolk in 1972. Audrey always felt that her roots were in Suffolk, as she had spent much of her childhood there. She ran a special needs department in a Stowmarket primary school until retirement in 1989.

Audrey McLaughlin's interest in history was first stirred in Dunstable. A young Deirdre had joined the Manshead Archaeological Society, but needed her mother to drive her to various meetings and digs, which led to Audrey's own direct involvement in the society's activities. It was Audrey's move in 1978 to Walsham le Willows, however, and her meeting with Stanley West, the county archaeologist, which inspired her to devote a great deal of her time to local history. In the late 1970s Stanley had proposed a programme to field walk the whole of Walsham le Willows, and he and Audrey worked under the umbrella of the Walsham le Willows Community Council to involve the local community. Audrey was responsible for, and notably successful at, gaining the trust and goodwill of local farmers, as a result of which the research group was able to cover over four-fifths of the area of the parish. She helped to map the location of Roman and medieval homesteads, revealing a settlement pattern strikingly different from the modern village. The field-walking project evolved into the Walsham History Group, with Audrey as its driving force. The collaboration yielded an important monograph, *Towards a landscape history of Walsham le Willows* (East Anglian Archaeology 85, 1998), which combined archaeology, field walking, documentary sources and landscape history to trace Walsham from its prehistoric roots to the landscape of the present day. The book became recommended reading for the history degree course at Suffolk College.

Once Audrey had discovered local history, it became her life's passion and the primary focus of her busy and productive retirement. She joined David Dymond's class in 'Documentary Studies', which introduced her to medieval documents and her first attempts at transcription. Between 1982 and 1985 she studied for a Certificate in English Local History with the University of Cambridge Board of Extra Mural Studies, writing a dissertation entitled 'The three surveys of Walsham le

Willows, their uses and limitations'. Her main interest was medieval history and in particular the prospect of working on the extant primary sources of Walsham. Not only did she teach herself to decipher and transcribe medieval handwriting, but also to translate the Latin. In this she was encouraged and supported by John Ridgard through his Medieval Latin class which was held at the Suffolk Record Office in Ipswich. Audrey was a much respected and longstanding member of the class, who quickly established a reputation as a strong palaeographer and a supportive and witty friend to fellow researchers.

For a passionate historian and able palaeographer, there was no better place to reside in the 1980s than Walsham le Willows. K.M. Dodd had already edited and published the parish's Elizabethan Field Book in the Suffolk Records Society series, and Ray and Jean Lock, residents of nearby Pakenham, were in the process of translating the superb collection of fourteenth-century court rolls of the manors of Walsham and High Hall. These also appeared in two Records Society volumes, and provided the inspiration for John Hatcher's 'docudrama' of the Black Death: *The Black Death. An intimate history* (2008). Audrey pressed ahead with the translation of the post-1400 court rolls, which are as voluminous as the fourteenth-century archive, and also the extant account rolls and surveys for Walsham manor. The court rolls have been published in typescript, and deposited at Suffolk Archives, although most of the edited translations of the account rolls never progressed beyond Word files. The one exception is a typescript of the accounts for 1402–3 and 1406–7, produced in 2002, with an eight-page introduction to the landscape and economy of medieval Walsham.

In 2007 Audrey published *Who lived in your house? People at home in early Walsham le Willows, Suffolk*, which was a culmination of thirty years of study and transcription of local documents including court rolls, manorial accounts, wills and inventories, surveys and other accounts, and also drew on her understanding of timber-framed buildings. The village trail around Walsham, for which she wrote the text, was also an exemplar of its kind. After exhausting the medieval Walsham material, Audrey turned her attention to Redgrave where she introduced the Redgrave history group to Stanley West, who guided their work in field walking all the accessible fields in the parish. Audrey transcribed from the Latin the Redgrave Field Book of Sir Nicholas Bacon, together with other medieval Latin documents, serving as both inspiration and guide to the group. In 2005 she moved from Walsham to Halesworth, where she commenced work on the manorial records of South Elmham and helped to rejuvenate the South Elmham and District Local History Group.

For three decades Audrey McLaughlin provided inspiration, leadership and strong technical knowledge to local historians and amateur archaeologists, and her legacy is ensured through their publications. The irony is that Audrey was very unassuming and would reject any notion of possessing any kind of academic standing or competence, yet the quality of her work is axiomatic. She was determined to make it openly available to local people, reflecting her generosity of spirit. Just before her death, she made her Word files of the accounts available to me in the expectation that I might make some use of them. Our hope is that this volume constitutes a fitting use. It is intended as tribute to her outstanding personal and academic qualities.

Based on an appreciation which was published soon after her death in 2010 by the Suffolk Local History Council.

The Audrey McLaughlin collection of material from Walsham le Willows

SA/I HD3157:16126

Extracts and transcripts of wills of persons from Walsham le Willows, 1396–1700, also photocopies of some wills (3 files)
Transcripts of Walsham le Willows court rolls, 1501–1699 (4 files)
Transcripts of Walsham Church House court rolls, 1501–1699 (1 file)
Dissertation by Audrey McLaughlin, 'The three surveys of Walsham le Willows, their uses and limitations', 1985
File of oddments, in chronological order, 14th–17th century
Folders re. secondary source information on Walsham le Willows, 13th, 14th, 15th (2), 16th, 17th century, 15th-century enclosures, population, poverty and charters
1577 Roll of conjectural maps for 'Towards a landscape history'
Transcript of Walsham le Willows rentals, 1327–1868 (1 file)
Details re. accounts and expenses (1 file)
Photocopy of 1695 survey held at Bury Record Office, HA504/5/13 (1 file)
Transcript of the 1695 survey (1 file)
Envelope of notes for 'Towards a landscape history'
Photocopies of Walsham Accounts, HA504/3/various

Typed or printed publications

Towards a landscape history of Walsham le Willows (with S.E. West, East Anglian Archaeology, No. 85, 1998)
Who lived in your house? People at home in early Walsham le Willows, Suffolk (diss., 2007)
Malting, brewing, ale and beer in Walsham le Willows
Walsham le Willows, a brief history
A short history of Walsham le Willows
Some 15th-century benefactors of St Mary's Church
Bills and receipts of the parish constables of Walsham le Willows, 1708–1821, by the Walsham Village History Group
The court rolls of Walsham le Willows, 1399–1500, typed translation
Two accounts of Walsham Manor, 1402/3 and 1406/7, typed translations and introduction
The Beeches, Walsham le Willows, an example of information available when researching the history of a house
Assorted photocopy extracts from printed sources
30 colour slides of houses in Walsham le Willows, 20th century
Reader Printer copy of Bury Record Office document J529/3, 1581 landholdings

Index cards

5 – Place name index A–M
6 – Place name index N–Z
7 – Subject index A–Z
8 – Court rolls index, 15th century
9 – Court rolls index, 15th century
10 – Court rolls index, 16th century
11 – Court rolls index, 17th century

EDITORIAL METHOD AND ABBREVIATIONS

The conventions for editing and abbreviating the text are those laid down by the Suffolk Records Society:

\ / for insertions

< > for deletions which are legible in the original

[*sic*] for all editorial insertions, italics within square brackets

[*illeg.*] illegible words or sections

[*blank*] empty spaces in the text

[*deleted*] for deleted and unreadable sections

[*damaged*] ... for damaged and unreadable sections

[*?*] for a reading which is not certain

qr for one quarter, a measure of grain by volume

bus. one bushel, there being eight bushels to one quarter

The use of capital letters has been modernised. Modern punctuation has been introduced to help the reader, but not where it might impose a questionable reading. Obvious abbreviations have been extended without comment. Less obvious abbreviations have been included and ended with an apostrophe, replicating the original. Original layouts have been retained for the most part, although new line and paragraph breaks have been introduced to relieve solid blocks of text.

Audrey McLaughlin had converted all surnames, field names and localities to modern spelling. I have included the original spelling of field names and localities in italics when they first occur in the first three sections of the volume.

The following abbreviations have been used in the Introduction and footnoting:

SA/B   Suffolk Archives, Bury St Edmunds office

Dodd, *Field book*   K.M. Dodd, ed., *The field book of Walsham-le-Willows 1577*, Suffolk Records Society 17 (1974)

Lock, *Walsham I*   R. Lock, ed., *The court rolls of Walsham le Willows 1303–50*, Suffolk Records Society 41 (1998)

Lock, *Walsham II*   R. Lock, ed., *The court rolls of Walsham le Willows 1351–99*, Suffolk Records Society 45 (2002)

PSIAH   *Proceedings of the Suffolk Institute of Archaeology and History*

VCH II   W. Page, ed., *Victoria History of the County of Suffolk*, volume II (London, 1907)

Map 1. The location of Walsham le Willows

INTRODUCTION

In two volumes for the Suffolk Records Society published in 1998 and 2002 Ray Lock translated and edited the extant fourteenth-century court rolls for the manors of Walsham le Willows and Walsham High Hall. These manorial courts provide exceptional insights into the life of the community around the time of the Black Death, which struck East Anglia in the first half of 1349 and killed half its population. The material inspired John Hatcher, Professor of Economic and Social History at the University of Cambridge, to use Walsham to recreate an intimate social history of what it must have been like to live through this terrifying pandemic. Hatcher combined the evidence of real people and events from the court rolls with his own academic knowledge of the Black Death to create an informed 'docudrama' of life in Walsham between 1345 and 1350.[1] An unlikely bestseller was born. Since then, various television documentaries on the Black Death have used the Walsham material to illustrate the pandemic's devastating passage. Furthermore, professional historians have been quick to recognise the intrinsic quality and the wider potential of the Walsham court rolls, using them to investigate subjects as diverse as law-making in village communities, agricultural systems and the decline of serfdom.[2] Ray Lock's work and the Suffolk Records Society have planted rural Walsham firmly and proudly on the historical map.

What, then, might justify the publication of yet more material from medieval Walsham? The most obvious reason is that the surviving manorial accounts and rentals complement the court roll material in painting a more textured picture of life in late medieval Walsham through furnishing further details of its society and economy. They provide insights into its agricultural practices, including woodland management for the production of fuel, the balance of crops and livestock, the disposal of produce, the remuneration of workers, the consumption habits of harvest workers and local lords, and the management of the manorial estate. We learn of the sale of wool and the purchase of cloth and clothing.

The importance of the Walsham rentals and accounts is enhanced by the structure and status of the manors that generated them, relatively small manors held mostly by lower status lords, from which few records have survived. Although a vast and unique archive has survived from the manors of medieval England, its bulk derives from the estates of the greatest aristocratic (barons and earls) and ecclesiastical (monastic and episcopal) landlords. The estates of these high status lords were scattered across whole regions and managed through bureaucracies which, by their nature, produced and kept written records. These estates were dominated by large classical manors, generating in excess of £50 per annum and containing a sizeable demesne of hundreds of acres and a high proportion of unfree peasants.

---

[1] J. Hatcher, *The Black Death. An intimate history* (London, 2008).
[2] L. Eldridge, *Law and the medieval village community. Reinvigorating historical jurisprudence* (Abingdon, 2023); J. Belcher, *The foldcourse and East Anglian agriculture and landscape, 1100–1900* (Woodbridge, 2020), pp. 95–8; M. Bailey, *The decline of serfdom in late medieval England. From bondage to freedom* (Woodbridge, 2014), pp. 104–18.

As a consequence, the economic and social history of medieval England has been largely written through the manorial records of these fabulously wealthy landlords, but neither these manors nor these lords were representative of the norm. The typical manorial lord held merely a couple of manors within close proximity of each other, was resident on one of them, and possessed an income of between £10 and £50 per annum: one recent estimate suggests that there were around nineteen hundred of these lesser landlords in early fourteenth-century England, compared with just five hundred of the great landlords. The manors of these lesser lords tended to be structured very differently from the classic manor, being much smaller and containing a higher proportion of free tenures.[3] The largest manor in Walsham was valued at around £30, and the next largest less than £10.[4] They were held by middle to low status lay gentry lords. Hence the manorial records and lords of fourteenth-century Walsham are reasonably representative of the archetypal English lord and manor, which are mainly hidden below the historical radar. This greatly enhances their importance.

Another reason for publishing the accounts is that they cover a period of great significance in the history of landownership and tenure in Walsham, involving changes characteristic of those occurring in many villages in late medieval and early modern Suffolk, but for which little or no documentation has survived. In the two centuries after the Norman Conquest the fission of landholding and proliferation of manorial units was commonplace in East Anglia, due to the pressure of demographic expansion and the emergence of a buoyant land market. After the Black Death, however, demographic retrenchment and a subdued land market encouraged the fusion and engrossment of manorial units, bringing the ownership of more land into fewer hands in every village.[5] A recent detailed case study of Laxfield provides an excellent example of how the original manor recorded in the Domesday Book of 1086 fragmented into a number of smaller manorial units over the next two centuries, and how thereafter a determined and acquisitive lord could acquire and reassemble them through a combination of inheritance and purchase.[6]

The Walsham accounts reveal a similar process. At the beginning of the fourteenth century, landholding in Walsham had become fragmented into four manorial units held by different lords, namely Walsham Hall, High Hall, Church House and Burchards (further details of each are provided below). In the 1380s and 1390s the new lord of Walsham Hall, Sir William de Elmham, acquired control of all four manorial units through purchase of Walsham High Hall and Burchards, and long-term leasing of Church House. In a short period he had fused all of Walsham's manorial units back into single control. This process of manorial fusion and engrossment was commonplace in rural England between c. 1350 and c. 1700, but the mechanics of how and when it occurred are less well documented. Walsham offers an excellent case study.

3   B.M.S. Campbell and K. Bartley, *England on the eve of the Black Death: an atlas of lay lordship, land and wealth, 1300–49* (Manchester, 2006), pp. 69–96, 251–68; B.M.S. Campbell, 'The agrarian problem in the early fourteenth century', *Past and Present* 188 (2005), pp. 10–24.

4   E. Powell, *A Suffolk Hundred in the year 1283* (Cambridge, 1910), p. 92; for the income from High Hall, see documents 2 and 3.

5   M. Bailey, ed., *The English manor c. 1200 to c. 1500* (Manchester, 2002), pp. 11–18; M. Bailey, *Medieval Suffolk. An economic and social history 1200 to 1500* (Woodbridge, 2007), pp. 27–31, 255–61.

6   J. Fisk, 'The lordship, structure, and evolution of the manor of Laxfield in Suffolk, 1066 to 1410' (University of East Anglia, MA by Research thesis, 2022).

The accounts contain many other points of unusual and specific interest. One is the highly active role of the wife of the lord of the manor in the daily management of the estate during the 1390s and early 1400s. Aristocratic and monastic landlords had little direct involvement in the running of individual manors, delegating this responsibility instead to their estate stewards and bailiffs, whereas lesser landlords were more likely to have a closer personal interest in the running of their smaller, and more geographically compact, estates. Not only do the Walsham accounts confirm the latter, but they also reveal the routine involvement of a woman in authorising payments, deciding where produce should be sent, and even organising the collection and sale of the wool clip from the entire estate. Gentry women are usually only visible in the sources when running their estates as widows, and it is rare to have explicit references to the highly active agency of one, very hands-on, married woman in estate management (documents 6 to 8).

Another point of interest is the tangential insights cast by the later accounts and their associated indentures from the 1440s and early 1450s into the running of the East Anglian estates of William de la Pole and his wife, Alice Chaucer, who were the Duke and Duchess of Suffolk. William had acquired Walsham in 1441 as part of the Westhorpe estate (see below) and following his acquisition the recorded payments of money from the manor to various individuals add to our knowledge of the men within de la Pole's East Anglian affinity, such as John Squire and John Belley. The significance of this information is heightened by the exceptional political events of the late 1430s and 1440s, a period of mounting political instability and crisis when de la Pole rose to become the central figure in English government under the inept Henry VI. East Anglia in particular became increasingly unstable as de la Pole vied with the other prominent regional magnate, John Mowbray, Duke of Norfolk, for power and control. Their respective supporters, who were prominent members of the local gentry, sought to dominate royal office-holding and to pursue their own interests against the backdrop of weakened royal authority and the breakdown of order, including the recourse to corruption and murder.[7] De la Pole's affinity was firmly in the ascendancy by the time he acquired Walsham, and the fate of some of its members (including tenants of Walsham) when de la Pole himself was murdered in May 1450 can be gleaned from the accounts.

Medieval Walsham le Willows

Walsham lies a dozen miles north-east of Bury St Edmunds in Blackbourne Hundred (see Map 1), a parish of 2,817 acres. Its topography is dominated by the stream which flows westwards through the centre of the parish, creating a long shallow valley characterised by meadows, damp soils and the willows which became attached to the parish's name in the sixteenth century. Boulder clay dominates the north and east of the parish, with outcrops of loamier soils elsewhere. In the Middle Ages some of these patches of lighter soils supported small areas of heathland, which is implied by the existence of a small rabbit warren (document 7) and the clearing of bracken from arable land (document 8).

---

[7] For the regional background see R. Virgoe, 'The murder of James Andrew: Suffolk faction in the 1430s', *PSIAH* 34 (1980), pp. 263–8; and C. Richmond, 'East Anglian politics and society in the fifteenth century', in C. Harper-Bill, ed., *Medieval East Anglia* (Woodbridge, 2005), pp. 183–208.

The medieval landscape and settlement pattern of Walsham were complex.[8] From the tenth century settlement of the parish was both intensified and expanded, continuing in phases until the end of the thirteenth century, a process which created a dispersed pattern of hamlets and greenside settlements. Audrey McLaughlin's work with the Walsham field-walking group has enabled an unusually accurate reconstruction of the distribution and layout of the medieval settlement, which is shown in Map 2.[9] The two main clusters of housing were to the north and south of the church, where the main manor house of Walsham was located; and around Cranmer green in the centre of the parish, where houses were located along its southern and northern fringes. There were smaller hamlets around the manor of Walsham High Hall at East End, at Upstreet in the south and at West End, the latter situated near the Great or Mickle Meadow. Meadow was distinguished from ordinary pasture, because it was capable of yielding a hay crop. The manorial accounts in this volume provide regular details about the cropping of hay from the demesne meadows, because some of the tenants of Walsham had to provide haymaking labour services as part of their rent package to the lord. The meadows were reinvigorated by regular flooding during the winter, although the accounts also provide information about any disruption to this process due to extreme weather conditions (document 10). Permanent pasture was tightly regulated as an essential supply of grazing land for livestock. Cow common and Cranmer green provided some communal grazing grounds, but the main source was Allwood green at the eastern end of the parish, containing 900 acres, over which the residents of Walsham shared rights to graze their livestock with residents of other nearby parishes.[10]

The names of fields in the eastern area of the parish, such as All(old)wood and Nether Haugh, are suggestive of the clearance of woodland around the periphery of the parish for arable cultivation, probably occurring in one of the later phases of colonisation.[11] Some parcels and groves of woodland survived this process of assarting, although the largest remnants were located on the peripheries of the parish (Map 2). Lady's Wood lay on the southern boundary with Badwell Ash and was part of the demesne of Walsham manor, as was North Haugh wood to the north of the manor house itself: together they covered around fifty acres in the 1280s.[12] The next largest was High Hall wood at the north-eastern extremity of the parish. The court rolls reveal that some of Walsham's peasants also held small patches of woodland, such as Hulkes wood, Bondes wood and Wardes wood.[13] All of these woods contained mixed species (mainly oak and hazel), which were carefully managed for their mature timber (for constructing buildings) and coppiced underwood (a major source of fuel). The use of woodland produce to create wattle hurdles to pen livestock, to construct buildings, to plug gaps in hedges and, especially, to supply hearths and ovens with fuel is an under-rated and under-researched aspect of medieval life, yet the Walsham accounts provide regular and rich information about its value and careful husbandry.

---

[8] E. Martin and M. Satchell, *Where most enclosures be. East Anglian fields, history, morphology and management*, East Anglian Archaeology 124 (2008), pp. 170–1.

[9] S.E. West and A. McLaughlin, *Towards a landscape history of Walsham le Willows, Suffolk*, East Anglian Archaeology 85 (1998).

[10] Dodd, *Field book*, pp. 49–50; West and McLaughlin, *Towards a landscape history*, pp. 1, 23–39.

[11] Martin and Satchell, *Where most enclosures be*, pp. 178–9.

[12] Powell, *A Suffolk Hundred*, p. 92.

[13] Lock, *Walsham I*, pp. 56, 280, 324; Lock, *Walsham II*, pp. 60, 74, 82–4, 86, 92–3, 144–6, 203–4.

The rising tide of colonisation and the expansion of settlement between the tenth and thirteenth centuries were driven principally by demographic expansion, which peaked in the early fourteenth century. In 1283 the ninety (mainly adult male) taxpayers recorded in Walsham are indicative of a relatively dense and wealthy population, which by one estimate reached 1,500 inhabitants.[14] Put another way, early fourteenth-century Walsham had more residents than at any time in its documented history, including the nineteenth century.[15] Such severe demographic pressure placed a premium on the production of cereals as the principal source of energy for humans and livestock, and consequently the vast majority of the surface area of the parish was ploughed for arable cultivation. The fields were not organised in the classic two- or three-field system, however, but instead laid out in a mixture of small hedged enclosures, over which no common rights pertained, and larger areas of irregular open fields containing small strips and subject to some communal pasturing. For example, in 1327 around one-third of the High Hall arable demesne lay in enclosed crofts and the remainder in 'furlongs' of open blocks of arable (document 2). Some peasant arable land was enclosed, but most lay interspersed in these irregular open fields in small strips of typically half an acre. The open fields were made available for some communal pasturing of livestock, usually for a few weeks after the harvest, but few other communing rights existed over the arable.[16]

The reduced population after the Black Death, and the rising living standards of the lower orders of society in the late fourteenth and fifteenth centuries, undermined the demand for grain and stimulated the consumption of meat and dairy products. The importance of dairying is indicated by the size and the value of the herd of cows on the Walsham demesne, which was leased to local people rather than exploited directly by the manor, and the continued importance of its sheep flock (documents 5 to 8). The majority of the residents of late medieval Walsham were directly involved in agriculture, practising semi-commercial mixed farming. Local peasants were unquestionably keeping more cows and pigs per head, as evidenced by their regular appearance in the post-plague court rolls of Walsham.[17] The general swing from cereal to livestock production is especially evident in the fifteenth century through the piecemeal engrossment of open field strips – the acquisition of abutting strips into single ownership – their enclosure with hedges and ditches, and their conversion to pasture.[18] The fifteenth-century court rolls of Walsham, translated by Audrey McLaughlin and available in typescript at Suffolk Archives, are full of such examples of a piecemeal process which transformed the local landscape and its agriculture. The reversion of former arable land to pasture, and the generally reduced rental levels of land, are evident in the details supplied about the leases of land in the account for 1470–1 (document 22).

---

[14] R. Lock, 'The Black Death in Walsham le Willows', *PSIAH* 37 (1992), pp. 316–36.

[15] Lock, *Walsham I*, p. 1.

[16] Bailey, *Medieval Suffolk*, pp. 108–12; Belcher, *The foldcourse*, pp. 95–8.

[17] Lock, *Walsham II*, pp. 232–3.

[18] West and McLaughlin, *Towards a landscape history*, p. 14; M. Bailey, 'The form, function and evolution of irregular field systems in Suffolk, 1300 to 1550', *Agricultural History Review* 57 (2009), pp. 24–9; Martin and Satchell, *Where most enclosures be*, pp. 178–9. For pasturing arrangements in Walsham see Belcher, *The foldcourse*, pp. 95–8.

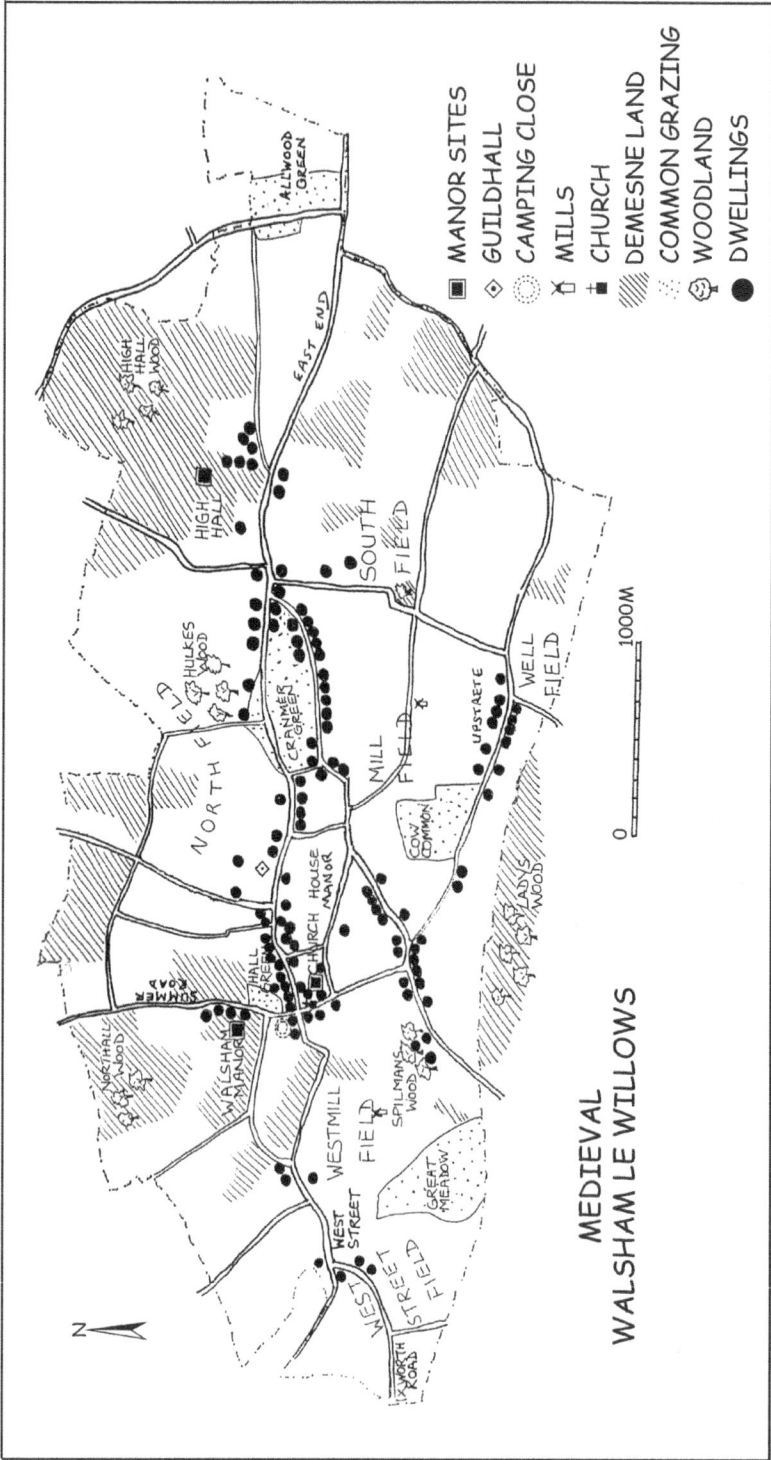

MEDIEVAL
WALSHAM LE WILLOWS

MANOR SITES ■
GUILDHALL ◇
CAMPING CLOSE ◌
MILLS ⚒
CHURCH ⛪
DEMESNE LAND ▨
COMMON GRAZING ▨
WOODLAND ✿
DWELLINGS ●

ALLWOOD GREEN

EAST END

HIGH HALL WOOD
HIGH HALL

SOUTH FIELD

HULKES WOOD

NORTH FIELD

CRANMER GREEN

MILL FIELD

UPSTREETE

WELL FIELD

COW COMMON

SLADES WOOD

CHURCH HOUSE MANOR

HALL FREEN

SOMMER ROAD

WALSHAM MANOR

NORTHHALL WOOD

SPILMANS WOOD

WESTMILL FIELD

WEST STREET

GREAT MEADOW

WEST STREET FIELD

NORTH ROAD

N

0   1000M

Map 2. Medieval Walsham le Willows

Walsham Hall

The main manor of Walsham, or Walsham Hall, was held by Lady Rose de Pakenham until her death in 1353, after which it passed through the hands of various members of the de Ufford family until the death of Robert de Ufford, Earl of Suffolk, in 1375. The lordship over the next decade or so is obscure: it was held by a succession of co-trustees until eventually acquired by Sir William de Elmham, although exactly when is unknown. In 1389 William claimed to be the lord of Walsham, yet the court of 30 March 1391 pronounced it to be the first court of seven co-trustees as joint lords of the manor, among whom were Edmund de Lakenheath and Sir John de Wingfield. As late as 1396 William appears to have been in dispute with an unknown party over the ownership.[19] The 1396–7 account (document 6) noted that the steward of estates had deputised for the lord 'at the first court' instead of stating the date of the court, which was the conventional formula, a curious choice of wording which suggests that this was the first court following the reversion of the manor to William.

The contemporary accounts do not state explicitly the identity of Walsham's lord, but their contents do provide a clear indication. Both the 1390–1 and 1396–7 accounts (documents 5 and 6) refer repeatedly to the lady of the manor, who was prone to spending periods of time in London, and to the dispatch of produce to what was clearly her main residence at Westhorpe, four miles east of Walsham. Hence throughout the 1390s Walsham manor was part of, and tightly integrated into, the administration of a landed estate centred on Westhorpe, which was held by Sir William de Elmham and his wife, Elizabeth.[20] The 1390–1 account also refers to a visit by Sir John and Lady Wingfield to the manor on the Thursday in Easter week (30 March 1391), which we know from the extant court roll was the date of the 'first court' of the new joint lords, and Sir John also attended the very next court, held on 29 June 1391.[21] John was married to Elizabeth de Elmham's sister. Furthermore, Edmund de Lakenheath, another of those co-trustees, served as steward of William's estates. The 1396–7 account documents the dispatch of a cart from Walsham to London when the lord was 'at the parliament held after Christmas', i.e. in January 1397: William de Elmham was one of Suffolk's MPs in 1397.[22]

These oblique details confirm that in the 1390s the manor of Walsham was an integral and actively managed unit within the Suffolk estate of Sir William de Elmham, although between 1391 and late 1396 the manor was transferred temporarily into the hands of seven trustees. These trustees were close associates of the de Elmhams with no practical claim over the estate, because the nominal change in lordship had no impact on the day-to-day running of the manor. The implication is that for five years the de Elmhams were playing some kind of tactical game in their dispute over the ownership of Walsham, by ostensibly transferring the lordship elsewhere while continuing to run the manor as if nothing had changed.

William de Elmham had been an active diplomat and military commander in royal service throughout the last quarter of the fourteenth century, and an MP for

---

[19] Lock, *Walsham II*, pp. 10–11, 170.

[20] W.A. Copinger, *The manors of Suffolk: volume III* (London, 1909), pp. 326–7.

[21] Lock, *Walsham II*, pp. 171–5.

[22] Although he was never a JP in Suffolk. See N. Amor, *Keeping the peace in medieval Suffolk* (Stanningfield, 2021), table 4.1. Amor also identifies one Ralph de Walsham, who was an active gentry JP between the 1360s and 1380s, who might possibly have been the unidentified lord of Walsham after 1375 (pp. 80–1, 98).

Suffolk in 1393, 1394 and 1397. During the 1380s he had amassed a considerable fortune, partly through the sale of landed inheritances in Yorkshire, which presented him with the financial means and liquidity to extend and consolidate his estate around Westhorpe through the acquisition of proximate manors, such as Walsham.[23] William died early in 1403, and some produce from Walsham was forwarded to Westhorpe for his funeral feast (document 7). Elizabeth continued to hold the manor until her death in 1419. Thereafter, it again descends into obscurity, although in May 1426 the manor was vested in seven co-feoffees.[24] In February 1441 the Duke of Suffolk, William de la Pole, and Alice his wife became lords of the manor, and the roll of their first court as lords records the expenses of Robert Lester, the bailiff, travelling by horse to Norwich to collect the court rolls of Walsham, Wattisfield, Westhorpe and Wyverstone, which were all part of the former de Elmham estate.[25] After William's murder in May 1450 Alice continued to hold the manor in her own right.[26] Hence throughout the first half of the fifteenth century, and long after the deaths of the de Elmhams, Walsham remained part of an estate centred on the principal residence and administrative hub of Westhorpe. Ironically, after decades in the hands of gentry lords, in 1441 it came to be held by a high status landlord, with profound implications for the future organisation of the manor and the tenurial structure of Walsham (see below).

The manor house of Walsham was located in the west of the parish, just north of the church (see Map 2). The accounts routinely include an 'upkeep of buildings' section, detailing the cost of repairs of the demesne buildings, which reveals that the manorial curtilage was enclosed and entered through an imposing gate and tower, and it contained a hall, kitchen and knight's chamber alongside a barn yard with a granary, stable, longhouse, dovecote and other agricultural sheds.[27] The principal resources of the demesne were the woods of North Haugh and Lady's Wood, amounting to around fifty acres, meadows and 387 acres of arable demesne.[28] A further c. 200 acres of land was held by free tenants and an indeterminate but sizeable area of land held by unfree tenants. The demesne arable lay in a number of consolidated parcels concentrated to the north-west of the site of the manor, with a few outlying parcels interspersed among the strips of tenants in the open fields.[29] In 1390–1, 60 per cent of the arable (237 acres) was sown with grain, mainly wheat, barley and oats (document 5). The annual sale of underwood from the demesne woods to local people for fuel, and the occasional provision of mature timber to effect repairs to the lord's buildings, are a notable feature of the accounts.

The manor originally possessed two windmills, imaginatively labelled West Mill and East Mill (their locations are marked on Map 2).[30] Only one is recorded in the accounts, probably the East Mill as the other must have fallen into disuse soon after the Black Death. The surviving mill was substantially rebuilt in 1402–3 from second-hand materials (document 7). It was initially leased to a local miller for

---

[23] For a biography, see https://www.historyofparliamentonline.org/volume/1386-1421/member/elmham-sir-william-1336-1403

[24] SA/B HA504/1/12.3; Dodd, *Field book*, p. 12 fn. 5a. Likewise, the ownership of Westhorpe is unknown for the two decades after Elizabeth's death: Copinger, *Manors of Suffolk, 3*, p. 327.

[25] SA/B HA504/1/12.23.

[26] SA/B HA504/1/12.23.

[27] See also SA/B HA504/1/13.8.

[28] Powell, *A Suffolk Hundred*, p. 92.

[29] Martin and Satchell, *Where most enclosures be*, figure 14.

[30] West and McLaughlin, *Towards a landscape history*, p. 47.

'multure', i.e. an agreed quantity of ground grain, which the manor then used to feed its full-time servants (known as the *famuli*), but from 1426 it was leased for an annual cash sum of 33s. 4d. (document 9). Its value gradually declined during the 1430s, falling to 20s. in 1440 (document 14), at which point it was absorbed within the lease of the entire manor. The costs of its upkeep continued to rest with the lord, however, which in 1446 were especially heavy (document 19), and in 1451 its nominal value was 17s. but no lessee could be found (document 21). It fell into permanent disuse soon after, because it is described as ruined and decayed in the 1470–1 account (document 22). A Walsham court roll from 1475 notes the grant of 'le millemont' with a surrounding ditch to a local tenant and in 1577 residents were aware of a mound where a windmill once stood.[31]

Textbooks on medieval England usually identify suit of mill as one of the onerous burdens of unfreedom, whereby all villeins were required to mill their grain at the demesne mill and to pay a toll above the market rate for the privilege.[32] Yet the lord of Walsham seldom enforced suit of mill, which meant that the commercial viability of the demesne mill was dependent on its ability to attract business in the open market. Clearly by the mid-fifteenth century it had lost that ability. The fact that the lord had the right in legal theory to impose mill suit on his villeins, but did not do so, reflects the significant gap that often existed between the theory and practice of serfdom. Indeed, by the end of the fourteenth century most of the key incidents of unfreedom had ceased to be enforced at Walsham. The main survivals – evident in the accounts – were some labour services, the requirement to act as reeve, and the payment of heriot on the post-mortem transfer of villein land.[33]

Walsham High Hall

The origins of High Hall manor are obscure, although it was carved out of the main manor of Walsham. It probably emerged sometime in the first half of the thirteenth century with the growth of settlement around East End, as part of the colonisation of the poorer soils at the eastern end of the parish, whereby woods such as Nether Haugh and Allwood were reduced in size through conversion to arable and open grazing land.

In 1325 Nicholas de Walsham acceded to the manor of High Hall, which he held until his death in 1347. It was then held by a succession of lords, including John de Brinkley between the mid-1360s and mid-1370s, who at that time was also the abbot of Bury St Edmunds. The High Hall account of 1373–4 (document 4) states explicitly that John was lord of the manor, presumably in a personal capacity: the manor had not become part of the abbey's estate. The court of Walsham held in March 1391 states that 'Wyldcattes', the alternative name for High Hall, was now held by the lords of Walsham, and the account of 1390–1 (document 5) covers both manors. Thus sometime between the mid-1370s and 1390 the manor of High Hall had been purchased by William de Elmham and amalgamated into the main manor. Upon its acquisition, High Hall was administered jointly with the main manor and its court was fully absorbed within the business of Walsham's court, although there-

---

[31] SA/B HA504/1/15.7; West and McLaughlin, *Towards a landscape history*, p. 47.

[32] For example, H.S. Bennett, *Life on the English manor. A study of peasant conditions 1150–1400* (Cambridge, 1937), pp. 129–35.

[33] The extent and decline of serfdom on the manor is explored in Bailey, *Decline of serfdom*, pp. 104–15.

after the accounts were always at pains to identify separately the lands and services associated with High Hall.[34]

The original site of High Hall was in the east of the parish (see Map 2), and the curtilage was enclosed and contained basic living quarters and agricultural buildings. The accounts refer explicitly to its hall, bakehouse, ox-shed, stable, poultry house and dovecote, and record the purchase of locks and keys to secure the various buildings (documents 3 and 4). Nicholas de Walsham clearly spent some time on the manor, although John Brinkley would not have done. After its acquisition by de Elmham the domestic range would have been either demolished or used for agricultural purposes. The manor contained a modest arable demesne of 111 acres in twelve discrete parcels of land (document 2), which was mainly concentrated to the north-east of the site of the manor.[35] The manor generated revenues of barely £10, and a profit of around £5 annually. Rents accounted for around 40 per cent of revenues, paid by around two dozen tenants. Of those tenants swearing fealty to the new lord in 1325, 46 per cent were unfree: a relatively high proportion for a manor of this size and status.[36]

Walsham Easthouse or Church House

Walsham Church House was held by Ixworth priory, which had been founded in about 1100 by the Blunt family who had been the lords of Walsham manor for most of the twelfth and thirteenth centuries.[37] This implies that the land had once been part of the original Walsham manor, but was later carved out as a separate holding and donated to the priory to augment its endowment. We do not know exactly when the priory was founded, or whether Church House was part of the original foundation. Certainly, the manor must have existed in the thirteenth century.

The manor is first mentioned in the Walsham archive in the 1396–7 account (document 6), which records the payment of 40s. to the prior of Ixworth 'for lands and tenements called Easthouse'. This was an alternative name for Church House. The 1406–7 account (document 8) notes that the lease had been renewed for another ten years for the same annual rent. William de Elmham could not purchase the manor, because it was perpetually endowed to Ixworth priory, but he had evidently managed to persuade the canons to keep renewing the lease so that he enjoyed *de facto* control of the manor. In turn, the lord of Walsham sublet most of the Easthouse lands to tenants, thereby recovering around 30s. of the head lease, and deployed the remaining land to graze the demesne's livestock. Church House was probably leased by the lords of Walsham for much of the fifteenth century, and therefore managed as if it was a permanent element of Walsham manor. Some of the manor's court rolls survive from the early fifteenth century enrolled within, but always separate from, those for Walsham.[38]

Ixworth priory was dissolved in 1538 and its site and possessions acquired by Richard and Elizabeth Codrington.[39] The freehold to Church House was acquired by the lord of Walsham sometime between 1538 and 1558 (document 23). In 1581

---

[34] Lock, *Walsham I*, pp. 12–14.
[35] Dodd, *Field book*, p. 13; Martin and Satchell, *Where most enclosures be*, pp. 178–9.
[36] Lock, *Walsham I*, p. 96.
[37] *VCH II*, p. 105.
[38] SA/B HA504/1/21A, HA504/1/21B, and HA504/1/22.
[39] *VCH II*, pp. 106–7.

it comprised a total of around 125 acres of land held by nineteen tenants, with little to indicate that it had ever contained much if any separate demesne land for the use of the lords.[40] Audrey McLaughlin's research ascertained that the building immediately south of Walsham church, now called The Priory, comprised part of Church House's holdings.

Burchards

In the 1270s Adam Burchard held freely a messuage, a small demesne consisting of thirty-six acres of arable land, two acres of pasture and three acres of wood in Walsham from the abbot of St Edmund, owing suit to Blackbourne hundred, plus six acres of arable land from the fee and Honour of Eye, with a total of eight tenants holding directly from him.[41] This was a very small lay manor, of a type not uncommon in Suffolk, and Adam stood on the social cusp between a high status freeman and low status gentry lord. The 1390–1 account mentions the payment of a standing fine in lieu of performing suit for Burchards at the hundred court, and the leasing of a parcel of land called Burchards Close to a tenant: a note attached to the latter states that the lord had recently purchased this parcel of land (document 5).

Hence Burchards was the fourth manor in medieval Walsham, which Sir William de Elmham had purchased in the late 1380s as part of his targeted acquisition of manors in the locality to construct a compact estate. The lease sections of the 1390–1 and 1396–7 accounts (documents 5 and 6) provide fragmentary details about the composition of the manor. Burchards wood is mentioned, along with the aforementioned Burchards Close leased for 12s. There is also a mention of Burchards Croft, containing eighteen acres of land, which, according to the wheat account for 1390–1, was situated near High Hall.

So the modest manor house and lands of Burchards were located somewhere east of Cranmer green; it comprised no more than sixty acres of land, including the holdings of its dependent peasants; around two-thirds of its total area had comprised arable demesne situated in two closes; and upon acquisition of the manor, de Elmham chose to lease its resources rather than utilise them as part of his Walsham demesne. Its annual value to Adam Burchard was probably around £2.

The rentals

Medieval manorial rentals, extents and surveys survive in a variety of forms, although their basic purpose is to record the people holding land from the manor, the tenure of the land, and the package of rent due from each annually. Surveys, also known as custumals, tend to be lengthy documents, describing in some detail first the demesne, then the size of each tenant's holding, its terms of tenure, and the breakdown of its rent, with particular emphasis on the unfree or customary holdings. Extents provide valuations of the various categories of rents and services due from the manorial tenantry, and usually details of the demesne too. Rentals are abbreviated lists of the tenants of the manor and their annual dues, although the amount of

---

[40] Dodd, *Field book*, pp. 17–19; Martin and Satchell, *Where most enclosures be*, p. 171.
[41] F. Hervey, ed., *The Pinchbeck Register relating to Bury St Edmunds abbey, volume II* (Brighton, 1925), pp. 203–4.

information they contain about the size of the holdings and forms of tenancy can be perfunctory.[42]

The dependent peasantry of a manor were broadly categorised into free tenants and unfree (also known as villeins, customary, bond or servile) tenants. In the early fourteenth century the proportions of free and unfree tenants across England were broadly equal, although there were prominent regional differences in distribution: in East Anglia, for example, free tenures tended to dominate.[43] Free tenants could appeal the title of their land in the royal courts and their attendance at their lord's own manor court tended to be light. The land was held heritably. Unfree tenants had no such right of appeal and were required to attend each session of the manor court: they were also liable to a heavier burden of labour services on the lord's demesne and to a wider range of additional incidents, such as death duties (heriot), marriage licences (merchet), the requirement to grind grain at the lord's mill (mill suit) and tallage (an annual or occasional levy).[44] Unfree land was usually held heritably. In the early fourteenth century it was also held on a 'service tenancy', meaning it rendered a mixed rent package payable in instalments throughout the year comprising labour services, fixed cash payments, and renders in kind (such as hens, eggs, and grain).

Service tenancies were the dominant form of tenure on unfree land in pre-plague England. The head rent on a service tenancy was ossified by custom, and was not adjusted according to fluctuations in the demand for land, which is reflected in the way the Walsham accounts record the liability for the same quantities of eggs and labour services year after year. The lord of the manor could not vary the terms of a service tenancy unilaterally and respected the customary rights of heirs, but if no heir wished to hold the land then it reverted into the hands of the lord (*in manibus domini*), at which point the lord could grant the land on the old service tenancy to a non-heir, or more likely converted the land either to a straight money rent, with no labour services or renders in kind, or to a short-term leasehold for cash. In the case of the monetary tenure (also known as a fee farm), the annual cash rent was set at the prevailing market rate at the time of the grant and held heritably. In the case of the leasehold (also known as a farm, *firma*), the cash rent was set at the market rate on first grant for a stipulated number of years and the land reverted to the lord on expiry of the lease: the lessee then renegotiated or the lord found a new tenant. Monetary tenancies and leases rapidly supplanted the old service tenancies after the Black Death.

Just two short rentals survive from fourteenth-century Walsham (documents 1 and 2). They are written on two sheets of parchment in the same hand, with faint additions above some entries in a later hand. The first sheet is headed 'Walsham' and is undated, but superscripts within the documents refer to Nicholas de Walsham and Edmund de Welles, both of whom were lords of High Hall. The second sheet of parchment is dated to the first year of Edward III's reign, i.e. 1327, and includes

---

[42] For manorial documents in general, including rentals, see P.D.A. Harvey, *Manorial Records* (British Records Association, Archives and the User, No. 5, 1984). An introduction to the structure of the medieval manor and its records, with some translated examples, is offered as Bailey, ed., *The English manor c. 1200–c. 1500*, with rentals and surveys at pp. 21–95.

[43] Campbell, 'Agrarian problem', pp. 24–44, maps 1 and 2.

[44] For a study of the day-to-day management of villeinage in Suffolk in the early fourteenth century see M. Bailey, 'Villeinage in England: a regional case study', *Economic History Review* 62 (2009), pp. 430–57. For unfree tenancy in Walsham see Lock, *Walsham I*, pp. 14–17.

a breakdown of the demesne land of High Hall manor. Thus both relate to High Hall: they were compiled around the same time in a very similar hand, and the later additions date to the 1340s.

The contents of the two rentals are brief, offering little more than the names of the tenants, organised into free and unfree, and their annual rent package. They reveal that the manor contained around two dozen tenants, about half of them unfree. The rentals do not include the size of the holdings, simply their rent packages and due dates. The rent on the vast majority of holdings was a mixture of fixed and low cash renders at set feast days, labour services and various quantities of hens (at Christmas) and eggs (at Easter). The rent packages were not obviously standardised, indicating that the holdings themselves were not of a fixed and regular size. The free tenants carried the lightest burden of labour services, usually confined to a day of ploughing on the lord's demesne and a day of reaping in the harvest, for which the lord provided food. The unfree tenants were more heavily burdened, owing more days in the harvest (again, with food) plus light weeding works, and some works during the winter. In total, from all of the tenantry, the lord of High Hall had access to eighty days of work in the winter and 130 days in the harvest each year (document 3). This represents a relatively light load of labour services. The accounts document how they were actually utilised in any given year. We know from the court rolls that the unfree tenants of High Hall were not heavily burdened with servile incidents.[45]

The structure and contents of the High Hall rentals indicate that these were working documents for the benefit of both the manorial officials tasked with collecting the rents and the auditors tasked with ensuring their collection. They provided a ready checklist of the cash, renders and labour services due from each tenant. One curious element is the addition at the foot of the second document of all the parcels of demesne arable land on the manor. This information would usually be included in a survey or extent (where the value per acre would be stated), but not often in a short rental. Although no monetary valuations are provided in this rental, detailed breakdowns of the arable demesne of small lay manors such as High Hall are exceptionally rare.

The Accounts

From the mid-thirteenth century many lords began to draw up and keep annual accounts of the flow of money and goods through their manors, partly because many manors were being exploited directly (rather than leased in their entirety) and partly because of the professionalisation of estate management and the associated spread of record keeping. After *c.* 1280 their format had become standardised throughout England, irrespective of the type of landlord, and for the next century they were usually long, detailed and informative. Their main focus was on the exploitation of the demesne, i.e. the land within the manor dedicated primarily for the use of the lord, comprising arable and pasture lands, and often other resources such as mills, woods, fisheries, dovecotes and even rabbit warrens. From the end of the fourteenth century many landlords began to lease components of their demesne manors to

---

[45] Bailey, *Decline of serfdom*, pp. 115–16.

different people, or even the entire manor in a single lease, and consequently the accounts become more akin to rent rolls and hence less informative.[46]

The purpose of the annual account was to record, supervise and authorise the activities of the local agents of the lord who were running the manor on a day-to-day basis. The most prominent officials were the bailiff or sergeant, usually a paid administrator with responsibility for more than one manor, the reeve (elected annually from the unfree tenants of the manor) and the hayward, who ran the harvest (and was also elected from the unfree tenantry). The bailiff or the reeve was responsible for the account, and therefore had to maintain a careful running record of the flows of money, stock and produce throughout the year, and at the end of the accounting year (which usually ran from Michaelmas (29 September) to Michaelmas) to attend the 'view of account' with the lord's auditors. The reckoning at the view of the account – effectively the audit – involved verifying claims for expenditure, explaining why some rents had not been collected, justifying unusual decisions and handing over any remaining cash: consequently, the accounts often contain scribbles, notes, additions, deletions and marginal comments from the auditors, either accepting or rejecting the accountant's claims. Many claims were verified through the use of tallies – a system of matching notches on wooden sticks – or through written bills or schedules issued by the leading estate administrators.[47] One of the unusual features of the Walsham archive is the survival of a roll of indentures from the 1440s, which are written confirmations drawn up by key figures within the de la Pole administration of monies received from manorial officials (Section Five).

Manorial accounts were invariably handwritten in Latin on parchment: paper began to be used in the fifteenth century (such as document 20). The front of the account (*recto*) detailed financial charges and discharges against the official whose account it was, beginning with the receipts, continuing with payments and expenditure, and finishing with the outstanding balance owed to the lord (or owed to the accounting official). The back of the account (*verso*, dorse or reverse) recorded the flows of grain, then livestock, and finished with a 'works' account. The latter comprised a detailed statement of all the labour services due from the unfree and free tenantry of the manor and how these had been expended during the course of the year. The requirement for peasants to perform labour services on the lord's demesne, especially during the all-important harvest season, as part of their rent package was one of the defining features of lord-peasant relations in medieval Europe, and the burden of services fell heaviest on the tenants of unfree (villein, serf, customary or bond) land. The inclusion of a 'works' section in many manorial accounts presents detailed information about the weight and composition of labour services and how they were actually deployed by the lord. As such, it offers important insights into the nature of local lord-peasant relations and changes over time.

The accounts repeatedly highlight the responsibilities of the key manorial officials in running the manor on a day-to-day basis: collecting rents, directing the full-time manorial servants in their tasks, organising the work to be done by customary

---

[46] It is not the intention here to provide a detailed exposition of the nature and workings of manorial accounts. The magisterial work of reference is P.D.A. Harvey, ed., *Manorial records of Cuxham Oxfordshire, c. 1200–1359*, Oxfordshire Records Society 50 (1976), supplemented by his 'Agricultural treatises and manorial accounting in medieval England', *Agricultural History Review* 20 (1972), pp. 170–82. An introduction with some translated examples is offered in Bailey, *English manor*, pp. 97–166.

[47] For a summary of this system see Bailey, *English manor*, pp. 100–4.

labour services, and managing the grain harvest. The key figures were the reeve and the hayward (also known as the messor), both of whom were elected on rotation from the unfree tenants of the manor on an annual basis. Both received remission of their rent for their year of office. The division of duties between them is often stated on the accounts, which, for example, note that certain rents 'were the responsibility of the reeve' and others of the hayward. The reeve was the senior official and the hayward's primary responsibility was the supervision of the harvest. Not surprisingly, neither position was very popular among the tenants, who frequently paid a fine to avoid office for the year of their election. Under these circumstances, their duties fell onto the bailiff, who was a salaried official answerable directly to the steward of the estate for more than one manor. The payment of the bailiff's wages, with allowances of clothing and fuel, is recorded in the accounts. The steward of estates, who was directly responsible to the lord for a cluster of (or perhaps all) manors, visited occasionally for supervisory purposes, usually coinciding with a session of the manorial court. Again, the steward's expenses are included in the accounts. These key officials were also supported by two full-time shepherds of the manor, who took responsibility for different flocks and liaised with other estate officials on the transfer of stock to other manors (documents 5 to 8). A woodward was also elected to oversee the management of the demesne woods, including the sale of underwood and the maintenance of suitable protective hedging around the woods, each year.[48]

In this volume the accounts are organised into three sections. Section Two covers the two extant accounts of Walsham High Hall from 1327 and 1373–4. No separate accounts of High Hall were produced after the acquisition of the manor by William de Elmham in the 1380s. Section Three covers the four full accounts of Walsham manor, with the manor of High Hall now subsumed within it for administrative purposes. Although this was a joint account for Walsham and High Hall manors, the accounting procedure is careful to maintain a clear separation between the Walsham and the High Hall elements. Sections One and Two feature what Harvey has categorised as Type Two accounts, in which the demesne was being directly exploited by the lord's officials, and so these include full details of stock and labour services. These are the most informative, varied and interesting type of accounts. Section Four covers Walsham accounts, including High Hall, for the period 1426–52, and these are all Type Three accounts. The demesne was now leased to a third party, so no information about the direct exploitation of its arable and livestock resources is provided, and the labour services are mainly commuted for cash. Type Three accounts tend to be repetitive and less informative than Type Two, and are more akin to annual rent rolls: in order to save space and avoid repetition, not all of these extant accounts have been produced here, although the key financial information has been extracted and presented as Tables 1 and 2, contained within Section Four. These accounts do still provide useful information about woodland management and building costs. In particular, the record of the transfers of cash during the course of the year and the allowances granted for expenses and other purposes, documented at the foot of the account, can provide interesting insights into the people involved in the wider management of the estate.

---

[48] See, for example, an amercement on William Fuller in 1464 for failing in these specific duties while serving as woodward: SA/B HA504/1/14.6.

Walsham High Hall (Section Two)

Two accounts survive, a part-year account from 1327 and a full-year account from 1373–4 (documents 3 and 4), both written on parchment. As stated in the introductory section, very few manorial accounts from small gentry manors have survived, which greatly enhances the importance of the two accounts for High Hall contained in Section Two. Indeed, survivals are so few that some historians initially doubted whether minor medieval landlords, such as held High Hall, kept detailed records at all. However, a seminal article by Richard Britnell, based on East Anglian records, confirmed that lesser lords did indeed draw up manorial accounts and court rolls in the manner of the greater landlords: the records have just not survived.[49] Their manors were smaller, often between one and five hundred acres of land, and less dependent on labour services than the manors of the aristocratic landlords and wealthy monasteries. Eugeny Kosminsky argued that these characteristics forced minor lords to be more commercial in the management of their estates, in particular using more hired labour and gearing production to the market in order to generate much needed cash.[50]

In 1327 High Hall was exploited directly and overseen by Nicholas de Walsham, the resident lord of the manor. The account contains some personal touches, such as Nicholas travelling to Thetford on business and ordering clothes from local tailors. His was a modest household and operation, judging by the small size of the permanent staff on the manor, two men and a woman. Manorial revenues barely exceeded £10 per annum, and Nicholas consumed little of the produce: most of the grain, for example, was used to feed the manorial servants and livestock, and the remainder was sold. Nearly half of the revenue of the manor was generated by sales of produce. The demesne livestock was confined to beasts of traction, with few cows and no sheep. Very similar patterns are evident in 1373–4. In 1327 fifty-eight acres of grain were harvested, and in 1373 fifty-two acres, approximately half the available area of arable demesne. Curiously, the area sown for the 1374 harvest was 106 acres, almost the entire demesne, although most of this was devoted to peas, oats and bullimong, which were all principally fodder crops and therefore livestock could eat them on the ground (document 4).

Although the quantity of labour services available to the manor was relatively modest, in 1327 the lord utilised them all directly on the demesne arable with the principal purpose of harvesting the grain (document 3). In 1373–4 around one-half of these labour services were no longer available, because following the Black Death and population decline the land either had been abandoned or converted to annual leaseholds for cash: this major change in the tenurial form of around one-half of the unfree land on the manor reflected the preference of tenants for flexible cash leases and an aversion to performing labour services.[51] One-quarter of the remaining winter works were not deployed on the demesne, but commuted for a cash sum, although all the available harvest works were utilised and were sufficient to reap the harvest without having to hire additional labourers for cash (document

[49] R.H. Britnell, 'Minor landlords in England and medieval agrarian capitalism', in T.H. Aston, ed., *Landlords, peasants and politics in medieval England* (Cambridge, 1987), pp. 227–8.

[50] E.A. Kosminsky, *Studies in the agrarian history of thirteenth-century England* (Oxford, 1956), pp. 260–77.

[51] M. Bailey, *After the Black Death. Economy, society and the law in fourteenth-century England* (Oxford, 2021), pp. 86–102.

4). Thus the management of High Hall was cash orientated and very dependent on labour services for its harvest, which conforms to Kosminsky's expectations for this type of manor.

Kenneth Dodd offered some remarks about what he believed were substantial changes to the management of High Hall between the mid-1370s and mid-1380s, having contrasted the contents of the 1373–4 account (document 4) with another dating from 1385–6.[52] The latter was originally in the Ipswich Record Office (catalogue reference V5/6/3.2) and described as an account of Walsham, then transferred to the Bury St Edmunds branch (new reference HA504/3/2) and still described as an account of Walsham for the 9th and 10th years of the reign of Richard II. On inspection, however, the heading clearly reads 'Wylasham' and its internal contents reveal without doubt that this is the manor of Willisham, some eighteen miles to the south-east of Walsham. Its management was also focused on the estate centre at Westhorpe, so it too was held as part of the de Elmham estate, which explains its survival among, and the confusion with, the documents of Walsham. While Dodd's error is understandable, his comments on High Hall in the 1380s must be discounted.

Walsham Hall (Sections Three and Four)

The first extant account from the main manor dates from 1390–1, by which date it had been amalgamated with High Hall. In the last quarter of the fourteenth century many English landlords were turning away from managing their manors directly, as agrarian profits were squeezed by a post-plague pincer movement of sagging prices for produce and shortages of labour. The challenge of turning a profit in such adverse conditions, together with the fixed overheads of running an estate bureaucracy and the unwillingness of tenants to perform their traditional labour services, encouraged them to lease more and more of their demesne resources to third parties. This transferred the risk of directly exploiting the arable and rearing livestock to the lessee, and greatly simplified the management of the manor. By about 1400 the majority of English manors were leased in part or in their entirety.

The four extant accounts between 1390 and 1407 (Section Three) reveal that Walsham was an exception to this general trend, because most of the manor's resources continued to be directly exploited. Consequently, they contain a rich variety of detail and information about agricultural life to a degree which is unusual for accounts for this period. The reason why Walsham bucked the trend is because the lord of the manor, William de Elmham, lived at Westhorpe Hall just four miles from Walsham, and sought to provision his household directly from his local manors (see Map 1). Hence the accounts record the dispatch from Walsham of large quantities of produce to Westhorpe for consumption at the seigniorial table – wheat for bread, barley to make malt, and meat, poultry and eggs – and also large quantities of wool to the 'woolhouse' there. Furthermore, the close proximity made direct control straightforward to exercise. A notable feature of these accounts is the frequent and active involvement 'of the lady', Elizabeth de Elmham, in directing affairs and authorising decisions, even when her husband was still alive. The accounts are explicit in distinguishing the agency of the lady (*domina*) from that of the lord (*dominus*). In 1396–7, for example, she personally authorised the payment of a bonus of four bushels of barley to someone called Alice, ordered the transfer of various grains to one Edmund Knight of Wyverstone, and even confirmed a decision

---

[52] Dodd, *Field book*, p. 13.

to provide cart horses with additional fodder when they were sent to pick up barley from the wharves at Santon Downham (document 6). Furthermore, the wool clip that year was described as 'sent to the lady at Westhorpe', implying her personal involvement in its collection and sale. The Walsham accounts are very unusual in revealing explicitly the highly active and influential role of Elizabeth in the running of the estate. When reading the accounts, it is difficult not to be impressed by her energy and engagement.[53]

The willingness of the de Elmham household to consume quantities of grain, eggs, pigeons, and deadstock produced on the amalgamated demesnes of Walsham and High Hall did not, however, prevent the generation of some ready cash from the same. Short-term leases of parcels of the demesne and of unfree land, which could not be tenanted on the old hereditary service tenancy, yielded over £8 each year. A herd of around sixteen cows had been built up and leased to a local person. The steady flow of money to Westhorpe over the course of the year is recorded in the section headed cash/payments delivered (see document 5). The most striking feature of the 1390–1 account is the large sheep flock kept on the manor, comprised of around 300 ewes and 400 lambs, a breeding flock operating within an estate-wide enterprise. The size of the flock had been reduced by 1402–3, and the risks of sheep farming were brutally exposed in 1406–7 when almost all the ewes and yearlings were killed by a particularly unpleasant ovine epizootic (document 8).

Nor did the close supervision of the manor by Elizabeth de Elmham prevent tensions with the tenants or ease the difficulties of finding willing workers. The demesne ploughmen were in regular receipt of additional payments to encourage them to work well, such as the 5s. 11d. paid in 1406–7 (document 8). Grain supplements were given to the people hired to winnow the demesne grain and were thinly disguised as 'sales', so in reality they were perks to attract and retain workers in an era of pressing labour shortages. For example, in 1390–1 Thomas Hereward and his unnamed wife received six bushels of wheat in addition to their wages for threshing and winnowing, and various other cash bonuses were distributed after the harvest (document 5). Nor could the de Elmhams depend on the supply of labour services from their unfree tenants to work their demesne. By 1390–1 (document 5) they no longer utilised most of the weeding and carrying services, and one-fifth of the number of winter services available before the Black Death were no longer collectable, because the holdings were now either untenanted or had been converted to cash leaseholds instead. They were eager to continue utilising the remaining ploughing, winter and harvest labour services, however, although a cryptic entry in the 1390–1 account indicates that not all the tenants shared their eagerness: thirty-four harvest works were 'sold', i.e. commuted for cash in lieu of performing the work, at a higher rate than was customary, because the tenants had been 'summoned'. In other words, the lord did not want to commute these works and the hayward had informed the tenants that they were required to work on the demesne, but the latter still did not appear on the appointed day. The inflated rate was effectively a punishment for the passive refusal.

No accounts are extant between 1407 and 1426, by which time the lordship of the manor had changed. We do not know who had acquired the manor, but the

---

[53] For reasons which are obscure, the burgesses of Dunwich sought Elizabeth's favour long after the death of her husband and on 17 December 1419 sent a gift of herring 'to the Lady Elmham'. See M. Bailey, ed., *The bailiffs' minute book of Dunwich 1403 to 1430*, Suffolk Records Society 34 (1992), pp. 83, 101. Elizabeth had made her will on 1 December: Copinger, *Manors of Suffolk, 3*, p. 326.

demesne was no longer exploited directly and was leased in parcels instead (document 9). Hence there are no details relating to the cultivation of grain, the rearing of livestock, or the purchases of petty items, and instead the accounts record the annual fluctuations in the leasing of parcels of land and the sale of labour services. The manorial administration continued with the same policy, which is reflected in the long and rather repetitious 'rental' format nature of the accounts in the late 1420s and throughout the 1430s. The acquisition of Walsham by the de la Poles in February 1441 resulted in an immediate change in the management of the manor. At the beginning of the next accounting year, they abandoned the existing policy of recording and managing every one of the manifold leases of lands, including the demesne; of managing the separate leases of the mill, the woods and the dairy each year; and of negotiating and documenting the annual commutation of all of the labour services. Instead, from Michaelmas 1441 the whole manor was leased in its entirety for five years for £44 per annum to a single lessee (or 'farmer'), a local named John Robwood (documents 14 and 15). Repairs remained with the landlord, whose steward continued to preside over the sessions of the manor court.

The reason for the change in managerial policy can be readily surmised. As the de la Poles possessed extensive estates across southern England, and as their principal residence was the Chaucer seat at Ewelme (Oxfordshire), they were unlikely to make much use of the residence at Westhorpe and, by extension, had no use for the produce of the Walsham demesne. Similarly, the policy of hands-on management of individual parcels of land and of the separate components of the demesne in dozens of separate agreements might suit a local landlord with the time and inclination to attend to such matters, but this was too time-consuming and unrewarding for a distant aristocrat with regional estate administrators. Hence leasing the whole manor in a single lease for a lump sum was the obvious option, because it greatly simplified the administration and generated cash with limited effort. The day-to-day hassle of exploiting a distant manor such as Walsham was best left to a local person with local knowledge and presence. Indeed, the lessee, John Robwood, was an established tenant of villein land at Walsham, who had just performed fealty to de la Pole as the new lord of manor. The lease included all the rents and resources of the manor, including the proceeds of the manor court, and the demesne.

The switch to a single lease for the manor was not, however, an obvious success. By Michaelmas 1444 Robwood already owed over £11 in arrears and had relinquished the lease, to be replaced by William Fuller, another prominent local tenant (documents 16 and 17). Normally, such leases would be for a stipulated term of years, but the length of his lease was left blank in the account. This might have been an administrative oversight, yet it is also possible that no term had been agreed and Fuller was keeping his options open while he tested the viability of the farm. In the event, Fuller maintained the lease for the rest of the decade and kept up with the full payment of his lease until 1450 (documents 17 to 20).

The accounts of the 1440s, when the manor was under the de la Pole lordship, are short (documents 15 to 19) and provide few details about life in Walsham. The transfers of instalments of the £44 lease from either Robwood or Fuller as lessee to de la Pole's administrators are the most dynamic element of these accounts, and these provide some useful information about the characters within the de la Pole affinity at the time when they were effectively governing East Anglia. Historians are divided on the extent of the corruption and violence perpetrated by de la Pole's affinity, although Colin Richmond is characteristically direct. In his words, they

were a thoroughly bad lot who 'governed' East Anglia for a decade or so entirely for
their own advantage ... whether the de la Pole group acted illegally or simply 'leaned'
on people to get what they wanted, they ignored both law and conventional morality.[54]

In 1441 de la Pole authorised the payment of a handsome annual annuity for life
of 20 marks (£13 6s. 8d.) from the revenues generated by Walsham manor to one
John Belley, who was designated an 'esquire' and probably hailed from Wingfield
where de la Pole held Wingfield castle (documents 15, 18, 25 and 29–31). Belley
was a lesser member of the de la Pole affinity, who must have recently performed
some act which had attracted de la Pole's favour and patronage: he had also been
awarded the sinecure of the office of parker of Huntingfield, which paid another
60s. 8d. per annum (document 24). The last recorded payments to him are in 1450.
In the 1440s there are also regular references to payments of cash to John Squire,
described as the receiver general of the de la Pole estates (documents 15 to 19).
In the 1430s Squire had served as personal chaplain to William, and in the 1440s
he was the rector of Alderton in east Suffolk while managing the Duke's Suffolk
estates. Squire was murdered in August 1450 by a mob from Alderton, Sutton and
Ramsholt during the political crisis of 1450, following the fall of de la Pole and
during the disorder of Cade's rebellion. The targeting of Squire and his summary
execution exemplified the unpopularity of the Duke and of his affinity within the
county over the previous decade.[55]

The Walsham account of 1449–50 contains some tantalising details of the
lawlessness in Suffolk during the summer of 1450 (document 20), by recording the
expenses incurred in defending the manor and its tenants from provocation and legal
action by men who were most likely members of the Duke of Norfolk's affinity:
the latter are documented elsewhere as harassing the Duchess of Suffolk's estates
following the murder of her husband, and in particular poaching deer and rustling
cattle.[56] The damage and deletions to the 1449–50 account render some words hard
to grasp, but the gist is clear enough. A shadowy figure named Robert 'Walsam'
had served a writ for debt on a group of Walsham tenants, then had apparently
come to Walsham and driven off some of their livestock to the Duke of Norfolk,
presumably claiming the beasts as a distraint for the debt. In response, two members
of the county gentry, members of the de la Pole affinity, travelled to Walsham to
support the tenants and to lead the response: they initiated a legal counter action by
making representations to the sheriff of Suffolk at Bury St Edmunds. No court rolls
survive for Walsham from 1450 to verify these sketchy events, although the court
of November 1449 had amerced seven 'drovers' a total of 7s. for driving a herd of
cattle through Walsham, breaking hedges, destroying footbridges and trampling the
grain of the locals.[57] The protagonists were all named, and included three Middleton
and two Flet brothers, none of whom were residents of Walsham. The timing makes
this an unlikely coincidence: this act of bucolic vandalism was an initial act of
political provocation sponsored by Mowbray's affinity as de la Pole's standing at
the centre of national government became increasingly precarious. Once de la Pole
had fallen, members of the rival affinity of the Duke of Norfolk began to harass

---

[54] Richmond, 'East Anglian politics', p. 186.
[55] I.M.W. Harvey, *Jack Cade's rebellion of 1450* (Oxford, 1991), p. 120; Richmond, 'East Anglian
      politics', pp. 189–90.
[56] Harvey, *Jack Cade's rebellion*, p. 121.
[57] SA/B HA504/1/13.13.

his estates and tenants openly. The name 'Walsam' is suspicious and the debt claim probably spurious.

The events of 1450 had a lasting impact on the management of the manor. The lessee, William Fuller, had not accumulated any arrears in the second half of the 1440s, but in 1449–50 he slipped into arrears of £7 (document 20), then surrendered the lease soon afterwards. From Michaelmas 1451 he was described as the bailiff of the manor, responsible for collecting all its rents, farms and perquisites, so he had transitioned from the single lessee of the entire manor to becoming the salaried administrator of all its component parts on the lady's behalf, while the demesne arable and the site of the manor were leased separately for £6 to John Bene. In effect, this returned the manor to the system of detailed management of multiple leases that had operated throughout the 1430s to 1441.

At the end of the accounting year 1452–3 there had occurred a major change in the status of the Walsham demesne. In the October court of 1453 Alice de la Pole granted most of the demesne arable to twenty-one local tenants in diverse parcels.[58] For example, John Robwood junior, whose father had been the first lessee of the manor a dozen years earlier, obtained over seventy acres of demesne arable in nine parcels, rendering in total 36s. 8d. rent per annum. Likewise, Richard Page received a grant of part of the site of the manor, including the barn yard, the grange, the garret, stables and the 'longhouse', all buildings which were essential for the running of the demesne as an agricultural unit. Crucially, all these grants were not on the standard fixed-term lease, whereby the land would revert back to the control of the lord after a stipulated term of years. Instead, they were all granted on heredi-tary fee farms, which were unfree tenures for a fixed annual cash rent bestowing customary rights of inheritance. In other words, for as long as an heir survived the tenant and was willing to take on the land, the lord could not restore the demesne to direct management to supply his or her household, or for a commercial operation.

In effect, Alice was dispensing with the hassle of having to manage and rene-gotiate a succession of short-term leases of the Walsham demesne in preference for the long-term security and administrative simplicity of permanent grants to local tenants. The flip side was that Alice was foreclosing the option of taking the demesne back into cultivation at some future point: this was a permanent break-up and alienation of the Walsham demesne to local tenants. Now that the demesne could not be actively and directly exploited by its lord, the management of the manor hardly extended beyond the collection of rents and holding of the court. The effects of this change in policy were long-lasting. The Walsham field book of 1577 notes that the site of the original manor did not belong to the lord, but instead was still split into two parcels of land on customary tenure (and the old manor house had been long decayed), and that the only remnants of the manorial demesne still in the direct control of the lord were the two woods.[59] The Walsham demesne had been transferred to the peasant sector, to the major benefit of its leading inhabitants.

The reasons for this significant and profound change in managerial policy are not stated, but they are readily deduced. The first is the prevailing political and economic conditions, which were at best uncertain and at worst dire. After the death of de la Pole in 1450, the country was politically unstable and sliding into civil war

---

[58] SA/B HA504/1/13.18.
[59] Dodd, *Field book*, pp. 142–3.

under the hapless leadership of Henry VI.[60] The political uncertainty was exacerbated by a severe economic recession, characterised by low prices, high costs and subdued levels of international trade, a combination which threatened the welfare of landlords and merchants more than that of ordinary people.[61] Under these circumstances, many landlords sought to lease their manors or demesnes for a fixed annual rent, transferring the economic risk to a tenant and removing the administrative burden involved in running the manors directly. Second, Alice possessed estates throughout southern and eastern England and increasingly spent her time in Oxfordshire, so her lifestyle was suited to simplifying and minimising the administration of her more distant demesne lands rather than arranging for them to be exploited directly or for their rent to be regularly renegotiated. The permanent alienation of demesne arable into tenant hands in the middle of the fifteenth century is an underrated phenomenon across England. Thus the initial phase of manorial engrossment at the end of the fourteenth century and the subsequent break-up of the demesne arable and its permanent transfer to local tenants in the 1450s were major influences on landholding in Walsham in subsequent centuries.

Indentures (Section Five)

The concluding section contains ten short indentures written on nine separate pieces of parchment and paper, and bound together in a single roll. They all date from a short period, 1447 to 1451, during the de la Pole ownership of the manor, and they relate to transactions between the lessee/bailiff of Walsham and members of de la Pole's East Anglian entourage. Four were written confirmations from John Belley that he had received instalments of his annual annuity from the proceeds of the Walsham revenues (documents 25, 29–31), and three confirmed the transfer of cash from the lessee to one of the central administrators of de la Pole's East Anglian estate (documents 26–8). Two were claims for receipts of expenses dating from the two years following de la Pole's death, and indicate that Alice Chaucer visited her East Anglian estates briefly in the summers of 1451 and 1452 (documents 32–3).

During the fifteenth century the use of written indentures, often on paper rather than parchment, to verify receipts and payments of money between key manorial and estate officials increased. These supplementary documents were an essential element in the accounting process, and their importance increased with the shift to rentier management.[62] However, their survival is patchy, for the obvious reason that they lost their purpose once the account had been audited and so could be destroyed: the modern equivalent is disposing of paperwork supporting personal income tax submissions once Inland Revenue has processed and accepted the tax return. Since indentures were an important part of the accounting process, but do not survive in great numbers, the extant indentures from Walsham have been included here.

This is the fourth volume produced by the Suffolk Records Society relating to Walsham le Willows. Yet even these hardly scratch the surface of its surviving archive. In addition to the published fourteenth-century court rolls, there is a long

---

[60] G.L. Harriss, *Shaping the nation: England 1360 to 1461* (Oxford, 2005), pp. 599–628.
[61] J. Hatcher, 'The Great Slump of the mid fifteenth century', in R.H. Britnell and J. Hatcher, eds, *Progress and problems in medieval England. Essays in honour of Edward Miller* (Cambridge, 1996), pp. 237–72.
[62] Bailey, *English manor*, p. 104.

run of court rolls from 1399 through to the early twentieth century.[63] Besides the 1577 field book many other early modern surveys, rentals and accounts are extant.[64] Indeed, Walsham may reasonably claim to be one of the best documented places in England between 1300 and 1900.

---

[63] SA/B HA504/1/18 to 53; HA504/2/1 to 21.
[64] See the entries in the Manorial Documents Register, https://discovery.nationalarchives.gov.uk/details/c/F250376

Section One

Rentals of Walsham High Hall, 1327
Documents 1 and 2[1]

Document 1: Rental of Walsham High Hall, no date

SA/B HA504/5/1 (1)

Walsham.   Customary tenants

The heirs[2] of Geoffrey Kembald render at the Feast of St Michael 11d., at Christmas 6½d. and one hen, at Easter 6½d. \and four eggs/ and they shall weed for half a day, and reap in the harvest for three days and they shall have food etc.

The household [*domus*] Kembald[3] at the Feast of St Michael 13d., at Christmas 6½d. and eleven hens, and every second year one hen, and at Easter 13d. and two eggs, and in the harvest five days with food from the lord, and he shall weed for half a day.

The household Payn[4] at the Feast of St Michael 2d., at Christmas 3d. and one hen, at Easter 1d. \and/ five eggs. And he reaps in the harvest for eight days and he shall weed for half a day.

The household Grennard[5] at the Feast of St Michael 2d., at the Feast of All Saints 2d., at Christmas 2d. and one hen, at Easter 3d. and four eggs. In the harvest he reaps for 16 days with food from the lord. And he makes 40 winter works. And he shall weed for half a day.

John le Wodebite[6] at the Feast of St Michael 7d., and at the Feast of St Edmund 5½d., at Christmas 1d. and two and a half hens, and at the Feast of All Saints 1d. and a quarter and half a quarter, at Easter 6½d. and two and a half eggs, at Pentecost 5¼d. and he shall weed for half a day. And he reaps in the harvest for eighteen days with food. And ten winter works.

William le Wodebite at the Feast of Michaelmas 9½d., at the Feast of All Saints 2d., at the Feast of St Edmund 3d., and at Christmas 1½d. and five and a half hens and a quarter part of one hen, at the Feast of the Purification 6d. and at Easter 10½d. and five eggs. And at Pentecost 13¼d. And he shall weed for half a day. And he reaps in the harvest for twenty two days with food from the lord. And fifteen winter works.

---

1   See Introduction, pp. xxiii–xxv.
2   Superscript, very faint in a later hand, 'in the hands of the lord'. It appears that a later scribe was using this rental to keep track of the tenurial upheaval in the wake of the Black Death, which struck Walsham around April 1349: Lock *Walsham I*, pp. 318, 325.
3   Superscript, very faint in a later hand, 'in the hands of the lord'.
4   Superscript, very faint in a later hand, 'in the hands of the lord'.
5   Superscript, very faint in a later hand, 'in the hands of the lord'.
6   Superscript, very faint in a later hand, 'in the hands of the lord'.

John Paccard[7] at the Feast of St Michael ½d. And at <Christmas> the Feast of All Saints, ½d. and a quarter part of one quarter. At Christmas ½d. and a quarter part of one hen and at Easter ½d. and five eggs, and at Pentecost ¼d. And he shall weed. And he reaps for two days \in the harvest/ and he shall have as above. And he makes five winter works.

John and Adam de Angerhalle[8] at the Feast of St Michael, 7d. At the Feast of All Saints, 1¼d. and a half of one quarter and at the Feast of St Edmund, 6d. At Christmas 1d. and half a hen. And at Easter 7d. and at Pentecost ½d. and he shall weed as above and he reaps for twelve days in the harvest and he shall have as above. And he makes ten winter works.

Gilbert Helpe[9] at the Feast of St Michael, 6d. and at the Feast of St Edmund, 6d. and at Christmas one hen. And at Easter 6d. and at Pentecost ½d. And he reaps for eight days in the harvest.

Gilbert Helpe[10] junior at the Feast of St Michael, 6d. and at the Feast of St Edmund, 6d. And at Easter 6d. And he reaps for eight days in the harvest and he shall have as above.

John and Peter Goche[11] at the Feast of St Michael, 10d. At the Feast of St Edmund, 9d. And at Easter 9d. And he reaps for twelve days in the harvest and they shall have as above.

Ralph Isabel[12] at the Feast of St Michael, 2d. at the Feast of St Edmund 2d. and 6s. 8d. And at Easter 2d. And he reaps eight days in the harvest and he shall have as above.

Sarra Prede[13] gives the lord per annum 4d. rent and one hen at Christmas for half an acre of land he holds in villeinage in Cottonefeld.

John le Chapman at the Feast of St Michael, 2½d. And at the Feast of St Edmund, 2d. And at Easter, 2½d. And at Christmas two hens. And he reaps four days in the harvest and \he shall have/.

Walsham. Free tenants

The heirs of John Stronde at the Feast of St Michael, 6d., at Christmas, 6d. At Easter 7d.

William Kembald at the Feast of St Michael, 2d. at Christmas one hen. And he reaps one day in the harvest \at boonwork/ and he shall have [*food*].

---

7   Superscript, very faint and largely illegible, but finishing with 'by the charter of lord Edmund de Welles'. Welles had succeeded Nicholas de Walsham as lord of High Hall in 1347. See Lock, *Walsham 1*, pp. 299, 308. John Packard survived the Black Death and in 1350 was described as a freeman holding customary land, Lock *Walsham 1*, p. 332.
8   Superscript, very faint in a later hand, 'now held by John ate Cherche'.
9   Superscript, very faint in a later hand, 'Hugo de Cockefeld'.
10 Superscript, very faint in a later hand, 'in the hands of the lord'.
11 Superscript, very faint in a later hand, 'now in the hands of the lord'.
12 Superscript, very faint in a later hand, 'in the hands of the lord'.
13 Superscript, very faint in a later hand, 'granted by Nicholas de Walsham, lately the lord, etc. that is William de Gippswyc'.

Robert Kembald at the Feast of St Michael, 2d. at Christmas one hen. And at Easter twenty eggs. And he reaps one day in the harvest \at boonwork/ and he shall have.

William de Cranmere at Christmas 2d. \and one hen/ and he ploughs for one day and at Easter twenty eggs and one day in the harvest.

Walter Osbern at Easter 2d. \and twenty eggs/, at Christmas one hen and he ploughs for one day and he reaps one day in the harvest and he shall have as above.

The household Peleniam at Christmas 1d., and one hen.

The heirs of Peter Pynfulg at Christmas half a pound of pepper.

William Deneys at the Feast of St Katherine 4d., at Christmas one hen, at Easter twenty eggs. And he reaps for one day in the harvest.

[*This side of the rental continues with tenants of Westhorp then of Cotton.*]

[*Reverse*]
Ancient [*vetus*] customary tenants of Walsham

[*Blank*]

New Increments[14]

Item Gilbert Helpe for four acres of land purchased from William Dun, one hen.

Item the same Gilbert for four acres of land purchased from William Kembald, one hen.

Item the same Gilbert for six acres of land purchased from Bartholemew Elmham, 1d. rent.

Item the same Gilbert for one acre of land purchased from William Evisson, ½d.

Item the same Gilbert for two acres of land purchased from John Mercator, 1d.

Item the same Gilbert for one acre of land purchased from Robert Brown, ½d.

Document 2: Rental of Walsham High Hall, 1327

SA/B HA504/5/1 (2)

Rental

Free tenants. Walsham

William de Cranmere[15] owes at the Feast of St Edmund the King 2d., and at Christmas one hen. And at Easter twenty eggs. And one ploughing per annum. And one boonwork in the harvest. And suit [*of court*].

---

[14] Increments of rent relate to more recent rents which have been added to the long-established or assize rents of the manor. They might relate to recent purchases of land from other manors, which the lord has rented out to his own tenants, or to newly colonised arable land ploughed from the pastures or woods around the peripheries of the manor. They were more likely to render a straight money rent than the mixed rent package of the traditional service tenancy: see Introduction, p. xxiv.

[15] Superscript, very faint in a later hand, 'in the hands of the lord'.

Walter Osborn at Easter 2d. And at Christmas one hen and twenty eggs. And one boonwork in the harvest and one ploughing and suit.

Robert Kembald[16] at the Feast of St Michael 2d. And at Christmas one hen and at Easter twenty eggs. And one boonwork in the harvest and ploughing, and he makes suit at all courts.

William Deneys at the Feast of St Katherine 4d., and at Christmas one hen, and at Easter twenty eggs, and one boonwork in the harvest, and he makes suit at all courts.

Emma Stronde renders at the Feast of St Michael 6d., and at Christmas 6d. And at Easter 7d. And two suits per annum.

John Pynful[17] renders at Christmas half a pound of pepper and two suits.

Christina Gilbert at the Feast of St Michael 2d., and at Christmas one hen, and one boonwork in the harvest, and suit at all courts.

[*The rental continues with short lists of free tenants at Westhorpe, Fingham and Cotton ...*]

Customary tenants

Katherine Payn[18] and her sister Mabel render at the Feast of St Michael 2d., and at the Feast of St Edmund 2d., and at Easter 3d. And at Christmas 2d. and one hen and in the harvest 16 works and two boonworks. And she [*sic*] makes 40 winter works. And he shall weed for half a day. And five eggs.

John Wodebite[19] at the Feast of St Michael 2½d. At the Feast of St Edmund 5½d. At Christmas 1d. At the Feast of All Saints 1d. and a quarter and at Easter 6½d. And at Pentecost 5½d. And at Christmas two and a half hens. And in the harvest 16 works and two boonworks. And 10 winter works and he shall weed for half a day and renders two and a half eggs.

William le Wodebite[20] for himself and for the tenement of Roger Aparil 9½d. at the Feast of St Michael 2½d. At the Feast of All Saints 2d. At the Feast of St Edmund 3d. At Christmas 1½d. and five and a half hens and a quarter part of one hen. And at the Feast of the Purification 6d. And at Easter 10½d. And at Pentecost 13¼d. And he reaps in the harvest 22 works and two and a half boonworks. And he makes 15 winter works and he shall weed for half a day and he gives ten and a half eggs.

John Paccard[21] at the Feast of St Michael ½d. And at the Feast of All Saints ¾d. and at Christmas ½d. and a quarter part of one hen. And at the Feast of the Purification 6d. And at Easter ½d. and five eggs and at Pentecost ¼d. and he shall weed. And he reaps for two days and two boonworks. And he makes 5 winter works.

John and Adam Angerhalle brothers[22] render at the Feast of St Michael 7d. and at the Feast of All Saints 1¼d. and half a quarter. And at the Feast of St Edmund 6d. At

---

16 Superscript, very faint in a later hand, 'in the hands of the lord'.
17 Superscript, very faint in a later hand, 'in the hands of the lord'.
18 Superscript, very faint in a later hand, 'in the hands of the lord'.
19 Superscript, very faint in a later hand, 'in the hands of the lord'.
20 Superscript, very faint in a later hand, 'in the hands of the lord'.
21 Superscript, very faint in a later hand, 'in the hands of the lord'.
22 Superscript, very faint in a later hand, 'in the hands of the lord'.

Christmas 1d. and half a hen and at Easter 7d. And at Pentecost ½d. and they shall weed. And they reap in the harvest 12 days and one and a half days at boonworks. And they make 10 winter works.

Gilbert Helpe[23] renders at the Feast of St Michael 6d. And at the Feast of St Edmund 6d. And at Easter 6d. And one hen at Christmas and he reaps in the harvest 8 days works and one boonwork.

[*Reverse*]

Gilbert son of Adam Helpe[24] renders at the feast of St Michael 6d. At the feast of St Edmund 6d. And at Easter 6d. And he reaps in the harvest 8 days and one boonwork.

John and Peter Goche brothers[25] render at the Feast of St Michael 10d. and at the Feast of St Edmund 9d. And at Easter 9d. And he reaps in the harvest 12 days and one boonwork.

Ralph Isabel[26] at the Feast of St Michael 2d. At the Feast of St Edmund 2d. and 6s. 8d. At the Feast of St Edmund 3d. And at Easter 2d. And he reaps in the harvest 4 days and one boonwork.

Richard Godelarde[27] at the Feast of St Michael 3d. At Christmas 3d. and a quarter of a hen. At Easter 1d. And he reaps in the harvest 8 days and one boonwork.

John le Chapman[28] renders at the Feast of St Michael 2½d. At the Feast of St Edmund 2½d. And at Christmas two hens. At the Feast of St Edmund 3d. And at Easter 6d. And he reaps 4 days and one boonwork.

Matilda and Alicia Kembald[29] pay at the Feast of St Michael 11d. At Christmas 6½d. and one hen and at Easter 6½d. and five eggs, and they shall weed for half a day and reap for 3 days and one boonwork.

The house Kembald[30] pay per annum at the Feast of St Michael 13d. and at Christmas 6½d. and 11 hens. And at Easter 13d. and \2/ eggs. And reaps in the harvest 5 days and one boonwork and he shall weed \for/ half a day.

Oliver Bercarius[31] at the Feast of St Michael 1½d. And at Christmas ½d. and four hens, and every three years one hen, and at Easter 1½d. and \5/ eggs. And he reaps in the harvest for one day.

Measured lands of the demesne of the manor of Nicholas de Walsham in the first year [1327–8] of Edward [III] after the Conquest

Item in the croft called St Katherine 10 acres 1 rood 31 perches.

Item in the furlong abutting on *Ulnysrowe* 17 acres 3 perches.

---

23 Superscript, very faint in a later hand, 'in the hands of the lord'.
24 Superscript, very faint in a later hand, 'in the hands of the lord'.
25 Superscript, very faint in a later hand, 'in the hands of the lord'.
26 Superscript, very faint in a later hand, 'in the hands of the lord'.
27 Superscript, very faint in a later hand, 'in the hands of the lord'.
28 Superscript, very faint in a later hand, 'in the hands of the lord'.
29 Superscript, very faint in a later hand, 'in the hands of the lord'.
30 Superscript, very faint in a later hand, 'in the hands of the lord'.
31 Superscript, very faint in a later hand, 'in the hands of the lord'.

Item in the croft of the sheepcote of *Aldewode* 12 acres 1 rood 17 perches.

Item in the furlong called *Threttiakris* 23 acres 3 roods 22 perches.

Item in the croft *Ducedeu* 6 acres 3 roods 33 perches.

Item in the furlong called *Hamstale* 5 acres 3 roods 25½ perches.

Item in the furlong called *Hordisawecroft* 8 acres 3 roods 4½ perches.

Item in the same furlong under the pightle of Nicholas Franceys on *le Thwerswente* 5 acres 2 roods 8 perches.

Item there in the furlong on *le Overwente* called *Hangerhallefeld* abutting on the park towards the south 24 acres 1 rood 17½ perches.

Item in the furlong called *le Hewen* towards *Hangerhalle* 9 acres 2 roods 12 perches.

Item in the furlong called *Netherhawe* on the wood of the manor with the land *le Hulnyr* 48 acres 22 perches, of which the *frisce*[32] land abuts on the Mere under the wood, 3 roods 27 perches and on *le Hulnyr* 9 acres 2 roods and 24 perches.

Item in the furlong called *Netherhawe* in two pieces 12 acres half a rood 24 perches, of which above *le Nothwente* 2 acres 2½ roods 4 perches.

Total acreage, 111.

---

[32] *Terra frisca* is arable land lying uncultivated for more than a year. Like modern set-aside, it would have soon returned to low grade pasture.

Section Two

Accounts of Walsham High Hall
Documents 3 and 4[1]

Document 3: Walsham High Hall, part year manorial account
from 20 October 1327 to 28 September 1328

SA/B HA504/3/1b

Walsham, in part[2]
Account of Gilbert Helpe reeve[3] there from Tuesday next after the Feast of St Luke the Evangelist in the first year of Edward until [*illeg.*].

Rents of assize The same answers for \37s. 1¼d. from rents of assize p.a./[4]
<from 9¼d. received from rents of assize for the term of All Saints.
And from 9s. 10d. received from rents of assize for the term of St Edmund.
And from 4d. received from rents of assize for the term of St Katherine.
And from 2s. 8½d. received from rents of assize for the term of Christmas.
And from 22½d. received from rents of assize for the term of [*illeg.*].
And from 9s. 6d. received from rents of assize for the term of Easter.
And from 20¾d. received from rents of assize for the term of Pentecost.>
Sum 37s. 1¼d.

Fines and perquisites The same answers for 11s. 7d. received from one court held at the Feast of St Martin.[5] And for 17s. 4d. received from one court held on [*illeg.*].
Sum 28s. 11d.[6]

Pasture leased And from 5s. received from sheep pasture leased this year.
And from 10d. received from pasture leased at *Hamstal*.
And from 14d. received from pasture leased at *Brokesmde*.

---

1   See Introduction, pp. xxviii–xxix.
2   The internal details of this account indicate that it extended from 20 October 1327 to 28 September, the eve of Michaelmas, 1328, i.e. around forty-nine weeks.
3   Gilbert Helpe was amerced 3d. at a court held in April 1327 (SA/B HA504/1/3.1) because he failed to present the book of the account of his office.
4   A breakdown of the individual components of these fixed rents is not provided here, but the rental of the same date listing the names of free and customary tenants with their rent and services (documents 1 and 2) would have been available for the reeve's scrutiny. The rents do not total 37s. 1¼d., because the principal term for paying rent, Michaelmas 1327, was not covered in this account.
5   The surviving court rolls from fourteenth-century Walsham are translated in Lock, *Walsham I* and *II*.
6   The average court income on lay manors in the pre-plague era was 16s.: Campbell and Bartley, *England on the eve*, p. 271, so in this year, and in 1373–4 below, the income from High Hall's court was relatively high.

And from 7s. 10d. received from the pasture of 11 acres 3 roods of frisce land [*terra frisca*] land and upon two pieces of land called *Netherhagh* leased for 8d.

And from 21d. received from pasture of 7 acres of fallow [*terra warecta*] land[7] in the furlong [*cultura*] called *Nether Wente* upon *Angerhalefeld* leased for 2d. per acre.

Sum 16s. 7d.

Sales of corn And from 21s. 8d. received from 5 qrs of wheat sold around Christmas, per qr 4s. 4d.

And from 23s. 4d. received from 5 qrs of wheat sold in Lent, per qr 4s. 8d.

And from 30s. received from 5 qrs of wheat sold at Easter, per qr 6s.[8]

And from 10s. 2½d. received from 2 pecks of barley sold, per qr 3s. 4d.

And from 5s. received from 1 qr 4 bus. of oats sold, per qr 3s. 4d.

Sum £4 10s. 2½d.

Sales of poultry The same answers for 3s. 9d. received from 30 hens sold, per hen 1½d.[9]

Sum 3s. 9d.

Farm of the dairy[10] The same answers for 5s. 4d. received from the milk of two cows from the Feast of St Luke the Evangelist to the Feast of St Botulph for 34 weeks to Richard [*illeg.*], and no more because they were expended for the use of the lord for the remainder of the year, for one cow without a calf 2s. 8d. And from 2s. received from the farm of eight hens for the said time aforesaid, per head 3d.

Sum 7s. 4d.

Sale of pepper The same answers for 7d. received from ½lb of pepper sold.[11]

Sum 7d.

Minute sales The same answers for 3d. received from brushwood [*bruscalla*] in Hamstal sold.[12]

Sum 3d.

Foreign receipts The same answers for 13s. 10d. received from the lord for various adjustments below by a tally against him.[13]

Sum 13s. 10d.

---

7   *Terra warecta* is arable land lying fallow earmarked for cultivation in the next year.

8   Wheat was an important cash crop in medieval England. The timings of sales are not always provided in manorial accounts, and the addition of such detail here reveals the tendency for grain prices to rise in the period before the harvest, reflecting increasing scarcity. Sales of grain are also recorded in the stock account, on which see below.

9   Most tenants, both free and villein, gave a hen at Christmas as part of their rent package. The receipt and disposal of the hens is also recorded in the stock account. See below, pp. 14–15.

10 Farm, from *firma*, meaning lease.

11 The ½lb of pepper was paid by one Peter Pinfold as part of the rent for the land he held from the manor. See document 1.

12 Hamstall was an arable field of about six acres, so presumably this was collected from the hedgerows.

13 Tallies – often sticks with a sophisticated system of notching – were used extensively in the auditing of accounts, providing officials with proof of their various transactions over the course of the year for the auditors' approval. Exactly how the system worked is unclear, because the accounts merely refer to the tallies and shed no light on their operation. See D. Oschinsky, ed., *Walter of Henley and other treatises on estate management and accounting* (Oxford, 1971), pp. 222–4; Bailey, *English manor*, pp. 101–4.

Various additions at the audit From various additions sold at the audit, 5s. 7½d.
Sum 5s. 7½d.

Sum of all money received £10 4s. 2¼d.

Expenses

Rent resolute with rents in decay He accounts for rent resolute for the hall of Walsham for the term of Michaelmas last past, 4d. Item in allowance to Gilbert Helpe for the terms of Michaelmas, St Edmund and Easter 18d., per term 6d.[14]
Sum 22d.

Cost of ploughs In hiring a smith for forging iron of one plough for one whole year and for shoeing four stots, front and back, from iron p.a., 10s. 6d.
In making a new plough and fitting it with timber shaped for it, 11½d.
In four collars of ?plaited rush [*glegell'*] bought, 3d.
In making two new ox yokes, 3d.
Sum 11s. 11½d.

Expenses of ploughs for boonworks and customary works In the expenses of six ploughmen with three ploughs by custom, together with the expenses of eighteen ploughmen with nine ploughs from boonworks at the sowing of wheat, 3s.[15]
Item in the expenses of four men with two ploughs from boonworks sowing barley, 6d.
Sum 3s. 6d.

Cost of carts In seven clouts bought for the carts 6d. In grease bought for the carts, 2d.
In making one new pair of wheels for the cart from the lord's timber by contract, 20d.
In one carpenter hired for one day mending a cartwheel, putting in nine new spokes, 3d.
Sum 2s. 7d.

Stipend of the manorial servants [*famuli*] In gifts to two manorial servants and one maid [*ancella*] for the days of Christmas and Easter, 3d.
In the stipend of two manorial servants for the terms of the Purification and Pentecost 2s., per term 6d.
In the stipend of the same for harvest 6s. 8d., to each 3s. 4d.
In the stipend of John Dokelyng for watching the bullocks during the harvest, 16d.
Sum 10s. 3d.

---

14 Customary tenants were required to serve as reeve as part of the rent for their land and the liability to serve was rotated among them. In the year of office, the reeve was remitted elements of the rent due from their holding: hence Gilbert Helpe was allowed 18d. off his rent.

15 The lord used the labour services due from both free and unfree peasants to sow wheat and barley on the demesne arable. The number of works owed, and how they were expended, are documented on the reverse of the account. See below, p. 15.

Threshing and winnowing In 19 qrs 1 bus. of wheat threshed by task[16] [*ad taścham*] <9d.> \4s. 4½d./, per qr <3d.> \2¾d./
In 15 qrs 7 bus. of barley threshed by task [*illeg.*]
In 4 qrs 1½ bus. of peas threshed by task 8¼d. per qr 2d.
In 25 qrs 2 pecks of oats threshed by task [*illeg.*]
In all the aforesaid corn winnowed by task 2s. 1¾d., per 5 qrs 2d.
Sum 10s. 9¼d.

Corn bought In 5½ bus. of wheat bought for the expenses of the lord after the view[17] in the summer, 4s. 1½d., per bus. 9d.
In 2½ bus. of oats bought [*illeg.*], per bus. 6d.
Item in 1 qr 4 bus. of oats bought after the view for the same 6s., per qr 4s.
Item in 3 qrs 2 bus. of oats bought in summer 17s. 4d., per qr 5s 4d.
Item in 3 qrs 2 bus. of mixture bought for the same at the said time 17s., per qr 5s. 6d.
Sum 46s. 10d.

Cost of the buildings In handles and hinges bought for the door of the ox-shed and the stable, 10¼d.
In one carpenter hired for four days hanging a new gate at Outgoing [*le Howtgong*] and for making a rack for fodder for the horses in the stable 10d., per day 2½d.
In iron latches bought for the hall shutter, 2d.
In one lock [*illeg.*] bought for the pantry door, 2d.
In fifty-six oak trees for beams <bought> for the sheep-house <5s. 2d.>.
In one carpenter hired for six days for certain [*illeg.*] repairing certain [*illeg.*] of studs[18] and for making a bench [*scannus*] in the hall and a trestle for the lady's visit and for making necessaries in the bake-house 18d., per day, 3d.
In one lock with a key bought for the sheep-house door, 2d.
In one lock with a key bought for the bake-house door, 1½d.
In repairing a lock [*illeg.*], ½d.
In handles and hinges bought for the shutters of a room in the hall, 1d.
In one handle and hinge bought for the poultry-house door, ½d.
Sum 4s. 3¾d.

Minute and necessary expenses In salt bought for pottage for the manorial servants, 2d.
In making one clay pot for pottage for the manorial servants, 2d.
In one ladle bought, ¼d.
In two shovels and one fork for carrying manure, 3d.
In one man hired for six days digging the garden 9d., 1½d per day.

---

[16] Threshing and winnowing the lord's grain was usually undertaken by hired labour, as here, although occasionally some of this work was performed by the *famuli*, who were the full-time manorial servants.

[17] 'The view' or 'the view of the account' was a formal inspection as part of the annual accounting process, at which manorial officials, such as the reeve and the granger, justified expenditure and accounted for receipts of money, often using the evidence of tallies or bills.

[18] The building expenses are tantalisingly brief, but do show that in 1327 the manorial messuage of High Hall included an ox-shed, stable, sheep house, bakehouse and poultry house. The hall was timber-framed, because its wall studs were repaired. The provision of a bench and table for the lady's visit implies she was not normally resident. The expenditure on locks and keys underlines the importance of security.

In one [*illeg.*] making drainage furrows [*sulca aquatica*] for the wheat <4d.>, for 20 perches, 1d.

Sum 16d.

Costs of mowing In mowing all the meadows of the lord this year by William Woodbite by task as contracted, 2s. 9d.

In stacking the said hay, nothing in money because [*undertaken*] by the manorial servants this year. In ale bought and expenses around collecting the said hay, 2d.

Sum 2s. 11d.

Costs of harvest In various expenses of reaping above by boonworks and by customary works, nothing in money because they are [*accounted*] in the expenses of the household this year.

In three manorial servants and the lord's groom [*garcio*] for the harvest, 7d.

In all grain reaped, tied and stacked, nothing in money because by works and boon-works this year.

Sum 7d.

Foreign and supervisors' expenses In the wages of Robert the lord's groom being here for one week looking after the lord's horses, 10½d., by tally against the same.

In three ells of woollen cloth bought to make saddle cloths [*husis*] for the lord's horses, 2s. 1d.

In expenses of the lord at Thetford [*Theff'*], 12d. without tally. \the lord confirms/[19]

Item in allowance to Ralph the smith for delivering [*illeg.*] by order of the lord, 1½d.

Item to Gilbert Salwetayl[20] for linen cloth bought from him for the lord, 2s. 4½d. \the lord confirms/

Item in thread and [*illeg.*] bought for the lord, 3d.

Item to the same Gilbert for making a doublet for the lord, price to the lord 8d. \made/

Item in shoeing the lord's horses, 2d.

In one ell of hemp[21] bought for making the lord's stockings [*calig'*], 1¾d.

Item in expenses of the same [*illeg.*] making <4d.>

Item in payment to John Sutor of Stowe[22] procurer of the lord for acquiring shoes on three occasions, <5s.> \made/ 3s. 6d.

Item to William Hawes for quittance of debt to the lord, 12d. \confirmed/.

Sum 12s. 2¾d.

[23]**Expenses of the lord** In expenses of the lord on occasions before the lady's visit, 35s. 2¾d. by three sealed tallies.

In cheese bought for expending on hospitality on the day of [*illeg.*], 8d.

In 60 eggs <bought> for the same <2½d.>

Sum 35s. 10¾d.

---

19 The production of a tally or a bill at the view of account was the most common way for an official to authenticate a claim, but in their absence the auditors sought other means of confirmation: in this case, the verbal testimony of the lord.

20 The only mention of Gilbert Salwetayl in the court rolls was in 1331 (SA/B HA504/1/3.15) when he was amerced for selling ale in breach of the assize.

21 Hemp was used to make cloth of varying quality.

22 The surname Sutor indicates a cobbler, who was probably from Stowmarket about eleven miles from Walsham.

23 Marginal note, in English in a later hand: 'to be joined to those that be examined'.

Money delivered The accountant delivered to the lord from various sales above on various occasions, £4 18s. 1½d.

Item to the same lord for rent for the term of Easter in his hall upon the bench [*scanum*] on the Feast of St Ambrose <6s. 8d.> because [*torn*].

Item to the same lord from 5 quarters of wheat sold above, 30s. by tally.

Sum £6 8s. 1½d.

Sum of all expenses and payments £13 12s. 11¼d.

And thus [*torn*] … and owes clear 68s. 9d. And acquitted by the lord from all [*torn*].

[*Reverse*] Stock account there in part in the first year of Edward III

Wheat 6 qrs 4 bus. 1 peck of wheat remain.

And [*he answers*] for 18 qrs 1 bus. of wheat received from issue[24] by tally against the threshers and it was threshed by task [*ad taseham*]. And for 1 qr wheat received from issue by a tally against John Woodbite the granger and threshed by work. And bought for the lord's expenses in summer, 5½ bus.

Sum 25 qrs 2 bus. 3 pecks

From which, in seed upon 17 acres 3 perches of land in the furlong [*cultura*] abutting upon *Wlinsrowe*; upon 19 acres 3 roods 2 perches in the furlong called *Threttiakris*, beyond 2 acres 3 roods 20 perches [*sown*] with peas [*as stated*] below; and upon 11 acres 2 roods 24 perches in the furlongs called *Holner* and *Nether Hagwe*, the residue [*of those furlongs were sown*] with barley and oats below beyond the land which lies frisce.

And so the sum of sown acres is 48 acres 2 roods 9 perches of land, 7 qrs 2 pecks of wheat by tally against Ralph Isabel the sower and the residue of seed sown by John Woodbite, recently the reeve, this year, that is 6 qrs 1 bus. of wheat.

Item baked for the lord's horses on occasions as shown at the view of account, 1 qr 1 bus. 3 pecks of wheat by tally against Robert the lord's groom.

Item baked for the same horses after the view of account on occasions, 1 bus. 2 pecks of wheat by tally before the aforesaid.

Item delivered to William le Groom, Peter de [*illeg.*] Agnes de Cleye maid [*ancilla*] of the manor to bake for the lord's visit, 1 qr of wheat.

In sales as within, 15 qrs of wheat.

In sales at the audit [*super compotum*] by the accountant 2 bus. of wheat, because thus witnessed at the recent view of account.

Sum as above.   It balances.

Barley From increment of the same, 6½ bus. He answers for 12 qrs 4 bus. of barley received from issue by tally against the thresher and it was threshed by task, of which 2 bus. is chaff [*cor'*]. And for 3 qrs 1 bus. of barley received from issue by two tallies against John Woodbite the granger and it was threshed by task, of which 3 bus. is barley chaff.

Sum 16 qrs 7½ bus.

From which, in seed upon 10 acres 1 rood 31 perches of land in the furlong *St Katerine*; and upon 6 acres 3 roods of land in the furlong called *Holner* and the

---

[24] *De exitus*, meaning the grain from the most recent harvest.

residue sown with oats as below, 6 qrs 5 bus. of barley by tally against Ralph Isabel, sown at 3 bus. per acre of barley plus in total 1 bus. 1 peck of barley.

In sustaining young livestock, 5 bus. of barley chaff.

Item delivered to Agnes de Cleye maid of the manor to make malt, 1 qr 4 bus. of barley by tally.

Item baked for the lady's visit, 4 bus. of barley by the said tally.

In livery of the manorial servants as below, 3 qrs 4½ bus. of barley.

In sales as within, 3 qrs 2 pecks of barley.

In sales at the audit, 6½ bus.

Sum as above.   It balances.

Peas He answers for 4 qrs 1½ bus. of peas received from issue by tally against the threshers and it was threshed by task.

Sum shown.

From which, in seed upon 3 acres 3 roods 20 perches of land in the furlong called *Threttiakris* and the residue sown with wheat as above; and upon 6 acres 3 roods 33 perches in the croft called *Ducedeux*; and upon 5 acres 3 roods 25½ perches in the furlong called *Hamstal*. And thus the sum of sown acres is 17 acres 2 roods 38½ perches, 4 qrs 1½ bus. of peas by tally against Ralph Isabel the sower, at 2 bus. per acre of peas.

Sum as above.   It balances.

Oats He answers for 23 qrs 1 bus. of oats received from issue by tally against the threshers and it was threshed by task. And for 1 qr 7½ bus. of oats received from produce by tally against John Woodbite the granger and it was threshed by task. From increment of the granger 1 qr 1½ bus. of oats. And bought for feed for the lord's horses, 1 qr 6½ bus. of which 1 qr 4 bus. [*allowed*] at the view.

Sum 28 qrs 2 pecks of oats.

From which, in seed upon 9 acres 3 roods 11 perches of land in the furlongs called *Netherhagwe* and *le Holner*, except for 3 roods 27 perches there which lie frisce and 19 acres which lie fallow, and except for 18 acres 1 rood 24 perches which are sown with wheat and barley; and upon 9 acres at [*illeg.*], 12 perches in the furlong called *le Hewen* towards [*versus*] *Hangerhale*; and upon 7 acres 1 rood 16½ perches upon *le Hoverwente* [*illeg.*]-feld abutting upon the meadow towards the south and the residue there, that is 7 acres of land, are frisce. And thus the sum of sown acres is 26 acres 2 roods 39½ perches, 10 qrs of oats by tally against Ralph Isabel the sower, at 3 bus. an acre of oats minus in total 1 peck of oats this year.

In meal made for pottage for the manorial servants and visitors [*superveniens*] at the time of this account, 7 bus. of oats and no more this year because the residue is with the expenses for the hospitality of the lord.

In feed for the lord's horse on occasions, 2 qrs 2 bus. 3 pecks of oats by tally against Robert the lord's groom.

Item in feed for the same, 2 qrs 1 peck of oats by sealed tally.

In sustenance of small livestock, <3 bus.> of oats.

In feed for four stots from the day of St Martin up to the Feast of the Finding of the Holy Cross, first and last nights included, so 175 nights, 10 qrs 7½ bus. of oats, per night ½ bus.

In sales as within, 1 qr 4 bus. of oats.

In sales at the audit, 3 bus.

Sum as above.   It balances.

13

In the livery[25] **of the manorial servants** [*famuli*] From barley above received for the mixture delivered to the manorial servants, 3 qrs 4½ bus. And bought for the same, 6 qrs 4 bus.

Sum 10 qrs 2 pecks

From which, in the livery of two manorial servants from the Feast of St Michael last past up to the same Feast next coming by one whole year except for three weeks, when one [*of them*] stood at the lord's table at the harvest, and five weeks when the other stood at the lord's table at the said time, 8 qrs of mixture, taking one qr each twelve weeks.

Item in the livery of certain men creating furrows [*spargentur sulc'*] for the wheat for three weeks, 1 bus. of mixture.

Item delivered to one maid making pottage for the manorial servants from the Feast of Clement up to the Feast of the Finding of the Holy Cross for 23 weeks, 1 qr 3½ bus., per week ½ bus.

Item delivered to John Woodbite for bread at the harvest last year and this year, 4 bus. of mixture of which 2 bus. are for last year.

Sum as above. And nothing remains.

Malt From barley malt upon making and brewing, nothing in the account here because it was all delivered to the lady by the hand of Agnes de Cleye maid at the manor, nil increment of the same in the lady's visit. It balances.

Stots 4 remain	Sum 4.	And 4 stots remain.
Oxen 4 remain	Sum 4.	And 4 oxen remain.
Bullocks 2 remain	Sum 2.	And 2 bullocks remain.
Cows 2 remain	Sum 2.	And 2 cows remain.

Calves From the issue of the cows, 2 calves. And from the heriot of Ralph Isabel, one. Sum 3. And 3 calves, of which one is male.

Geese 6 remain, of which 2 are female [*quorum ij mar[iole]*]. From issue, 14 geese.

Sum 20.

From which, in tithe 1 goose.

In expenses of the lord and for the visit of the lady by tally, 2 geese.   And 17 geese remain in the lady's custody.

Capons 16 remain.

From which in expenses of the lord before the lady's visit, 7 capons by tally against the lord.

And 9 capons remain.

Hens 9 hens remain, of which one is a cock. From rent at Christmas 36 hens, of which one cock.

---

[25] The *famuli* were full-time employees of the manor and were paid in a mixture of cash and kind, mainly a food livery as documented here.

From which, in expenses of the lord as shown at the view of account, 4 hens. In sales, 30 hens.   And 11 hens remain, of which one is a cock. [*illeg.*], nil because hens are at farm for money as within.   It balances.

Eggs [*illeg.*] nil because aforesaid. And from rent at Easter 110 eggs. And bought for the lord's expenses 60 eggs. And expended in provisions of the household on the occasion of the visit of the lady, by tally against Robert the lord's groom. It balances.

Pepper For rent at Easter ½lb pepper. And sold as within   It balances.

Works from the customs of free men From the issue of the customs [*consu'*] of free men[26] at the time of the sowing of wheat, two plough works with food from the lord sufficient for one meal per half day.
And expended at the same season of ploughing on the lord's land.   It balances.

Ploughings From the issue of the customars[27] at the sowing of wheat this year, one plough work per half day with the lord's food sufficient for one meal.
And expended on the lord's land ploughed in the said sowing.   It balances.

Winter and summer works From the issue of customary works between the Feast of St Michael and Lammas Day, 80 works by the half day, price per work ½d.[28]
From which, in making drainage furrows for the wheat by William Woodbite, 4 works.
In harrowing at the sowing of barley by the same, 5 works.
In thatching [*illeg.*] by the same for thatching the large barn, 7 works.
In weeding the lord's corn by the same, 7 works.
Item in the lord's corn weeded by John Woodbite, 10 works.
In dung spread by John de Angerhale, 2 works.
Item in various works by John Woodbite, recently the reeve [*illeg.*], 45 works.
                    It balances.

[*Torn, but* **Harvest boonworks**] of free and customary men between the Feast of St Peter Advincular and the Feast of St Michael,[29] 130 works for the whole day for which each receives [*torn*] … from mixed grains sufficient for one meal of pottage with legumes and two herrings. And for their supper, of which each receives bread from mixed grains, [*baked*] at 20 loaves to the bus., and two herrings, price per work 1d.
Of which, [*torn*] … upon Gilbert Helpe the reeve, 8 works. Item in 58 acres 38 perches of various grains, as above, sown, reaped, bound [*torn*], 63 boonworks this year.   It balances.

---

26 Labour services were usually characteristic of unfree tenure, but it was not uncommon for free tenants to owe some light seasonal labour services.
27 Customary tenants, i.e. the tenants of land also known as unfree, native, bond or villein land.
28 The labour services owed by the customary tenants between 29 September and 1 August each year: the 'work' was for a half day, and the set charge for commuting it (i.e. rendering cash in lieu of performing the work) was a halfpenny.
29 August to 29 September.

Document 4: Account of Walsham High Hall manor,
28 September 1373 to 28 September 1374

SA/B HA504/3/1c

Walsham

Account of Stephen le Wrighte,[30] bailiff of John Brinkelee,[31] of his manor there from the eve of St Michael in the 47th year of Edward III until the eve of the same feast next coming in the 48th year of the same King Edward.

Arrears [*blank*]

Rents of assize The same answers for 10s. 11d. for rents of assize for the term of St Michael.
And for 7¼d. and 4 parts of a ¼d for the same for the term of All Saints.
And for 10s. for the same for the term of St Edmund the King.
And for 4d. for the same for the term of St Katherine.
And for 2s. 8½d. for the same for the term of Christmas.
And for 22½d. for the same for the term of the Purification of the Blessed Virgin Mary.
And for 9s. 6½d. for the same for the term of Easter.
And for 20¼d. for the same for the term of Pentecost.
And for 3d. received p.a. from Simon Pyttok for castle ward for the terms of Michaelmas, Christmas, Easter and the Nativity of St John the Baptist equally.
And for 2d. received from Adam Pitlake for the same for the same terms.
Sum 38s. 1d. and 4 parts of ¼d.

Farm of land with lease of pasture[32] And for 2s. 2d. for the farm of one pightle containing 3 roods, parcel of the tenement of Nicholas Kembald leased to Robert Cooper for a term for which the aforesaid pays at the terms of Michaelmas and Easter.
And for 7s. for the tenement Paynes and half an acre of land of the tenement Angerhale leased to Elias Tiptot for a term of 6 years, this year is the 2nd.
And for 5s. for 2½ acres of land in a certain croft called Allwood Close leased to Walter de Aldewode for a term of 6 years, this year is the 2nd, paying at the same terms.
And for 18d. for 2 acres 1 rood of land of the tenement Angerhale leased to Richard Sewell senior for a term of 6 years, this year is the 2nd, paying at the same terms.
And for 8s. for the tenement Goches leased to Richard Sewell junior to hold for a term of 6 years, this year is the 2nd, paying at the same terms.
And for 2s. for the farm of Angerhale messuage, 3 roods of land and ½ acre of wood leased to John Church paying at the same terms.

---

[30] Stephen Wright, the bailiff, was not a local man, and was probably a professional administrator supervising several manors.
[31] John Brinkley was lord of High Hall manor from 1365, when he held his first court there. He was the abbot of Bury St Edmunds from 1362 to 1378. *VCH II*, p. 72.
[32] This section deals with leases of customary land and demesne land: the conversion of customary land held on the old service tenancy, which included liability for labour services and the payment of rent in kind, such as hens and eggs, to leasehold was a common feature after the Black Death, as lords encountered difficulties finding tenants for the former. Most of these leases were for land located in the east of the parish around the site of High Hall manor itself.

And for 2s. 4d. for the farm of the tenement recently of John Chapman leased to William Blunt and Agnes his wife and the legitimate heirs of the same William.

And for 7s. 2d. for pasture called Nether Haugh and Burchards Way leased to William Swift and Adam Pitlake this year.

And for 6s. 8d. for pasture around the manor and two pightles of pasture near there leased to Robert Payne.

And for untilled land in the preceding year leased to the same, nothing because it was fallow for which received this year 3s. 10d.

And for 8d. from High Hall 2 acres of land leased to William Grocer.

And for 4d. from High Hall 1 acre of land leased to the same William.

And for 8d. from High Hall 2 acres of land in two pieces leased to the same William.

From High Hall 3 roods of land, nothing here because it is [*accounted for*] elsewhere.

From High Hall 1 acre of land leased in the preceding year for 4d., nothing for want of a tenant.

From High Hall 9 acres of land leased in the preceding year for 2s. 3d., nothing because it was sown with oats to the benefit of the lord.

From High Hall 5 acres of land and two pightles leased in the preceding year for 4s. 2d., nothing here because it is now granted by the lord for services and customs, and so the responsibility of the hayward.[33]

From High Hall one croft leased in the preceding year for 12d., nothing because it is for [*grazing*] the animals of the manor.

And for 3s. for 15 acres of land leased to Walter Rampley.

And for 15s. 6d. for three foals, 6 bullocks and [*blank*] sheep of the cullet[34] [*collect'*] grazing in summer.

And for 2s. for the herbage in the Great Meadow sold this year to Robert Margery.

And for 10d. from High Hall 1 acre of land called Stony Acre with one piece of herbage near there leased to Thomas Fuller this year.

And 15d. for a certain pig pasture at Turf Pits leased to Robert Man.

Sum 66s. 1d.

Sale of underwood And for 18d. from 60 faggots sold.

Sum 18d.

Perquisites of court And for 18s. 1d. from a court held on Thursday next before the Feast of St Michael.

Sum 18s. 1d.

Sale of corn And for 5s. 4d. from 1 qr of wheat sold.

And for 6s. 8d. from 2 qrs 4 bus. of wheat chaff sold, price per qr 2s. 8d.

And for 23s. 10d. from 8 qrs 7½ bus. of peas sold, price per qr 2s. 8d.

And for 23s. 11d. from 10 qrs 2 bus. of oats sold, price per qr 2s. 4d.

And for 15s. 8½d. from 3 qrs 5 bus. of barley malt sold, price per qr 4s. 4d.

Sum 75s. 5½d.

---

[33] This villein land had been converted to a leasehold for a while, but had just been re-granted to a new tenant on the old terms, i.e. a service tenancy for labour services.

[34] The pasturing of sheep on the open fields of Walsham was organised through a system known as the foldcourse, in which all sheep were required to graze in designated folds. Villagers who did not possess the right to have their own fold were required to place their sheep in a collective fold, also known as cullet. M. Bailey, 'Sand into gold. The foldcourse system in west Suffolk, 1200–1600', *Agricultural History Review* 38 (1990), pp. 40–57; Belcher, *The foldcourse.*

Sale of stock [*blank*]

Chickens with the dovecote And for 2s. 6d. from 15 hens sold from rent, price per head 2d.
And for 3¾d. from 73½ eggs from rent sold, price per 20 eggs, 1d.
And for 5s. from 180 pigeons sold, price per 3 pigeons 1d.
Sum 7s. 9¾d.

Profits of the manor And for 2s. 6d. from one hedge-row [*heggerow*] sold to Robert Man.
And for 1d. from a certain portion of a thorn bush sold to William Taylor.
And for 4d. from branches of trees sold to Roger Prede.
And for 6d. from branches of one poplar [*ebell*] sold to John Hawes.[35]
And for 3s. from hay sold to Walter Rampley.
And from 20d. from the farm of one cow in calf thus leased to Agnes Woodbite, coming from a heriot after the Purification and before calving.[36]
And for 12d. from hay sold to Nicholas Patel.
Sum 9s. 10d.

Foreign receipts [*blank*]

Sales at the audit And for 7s. 9¾d. from various items sold at the audit.
Sum 7s. 9¾d.

Sum total of receipts £11 4s. 8d. and a fourth part of ¼d.
Excesses In excesses of the preceding account acquitted, 10s. 7¼d. and a fourth part of a ¼d.
Sum 10s. 7¼d. and a fourth part of ¼d.

Rent resolute with decays The same accountant paid to the manor of Ashfield for castle ward 17d. etc. Item there 4d. for rent.
Item from the hall of Walsham, 4d. from rent p.a. for land of Osbern in the lord's hands.
Item the manor formerly of Alexander de Walsham[37] in Walsham, 8d. p.a. for the land of Allwood.
Item in decay upon various tenements in the lord's hands being both from ancient time and from later time until now <13s. 11d.> \15s. 7¾d., and no more because the tenement of Walter Woodbite is in the lord's hands/.
Item for rent from various tenements in Westhorpe and Cotton, sold by Nicholas de Walsham then lord of this manor, 2s. 6½d.
Item upon 3 acres of land of the tenement Angerhale free by charter as shown elsewhere for the term of the life of John Packard senior, 4¾d.

---

[35] Branches or fronds of trees that had been pollarded were sold as animal feed.
[36] Agnes Woodbite's husband John died in 1374, surrendering a messuage, 12 acres of land and a piece of pasture. The heriot was a cow after calving, which was to be paid at the Feast of the Purification: SA/B HA504/1/7.18. Clearly, Agnes retained the use of the cow, but now had to pay to lease it from the lord.
[37] Alexander de Walsham was lord of High Hall manor from 1316 to 1324 and was succeeded by Nicholas de Walsham.

18

Item upon 1 acre of land of the tenement Woodbite, free by the same, 7½d.
Sum 21s. 10¾d.

Cost of ploughs In hiring a smith for shoeing the lord's mare and forging one plough together with the shoeing of 4 stots and mending a clout on the plough <15s. 1d.> 14s. by one tally against the said smith.
In 4 halters bought, 4d.
In 6 ploughs repaired [*assid'*] from the lord's timber, 12d.
In one carpenter for one day shaping felled timber and making the timber into ploughs, 4d.
Sum 15s. 8d.

Cost of carts In one cart body repaired from the lord's timber, 6d. altogether [*in grosso*].[38]
Item in one new tumbrel made from the lord's timber, 8d. altogether.
In 8 clouts bought for the carts, 16d.
In one axle made and fixed [*impend'*], 2d.
In grease for the same, 2d.
Sum 2s. 10d.

Threshing and winnowing In 4 qrs of wheat threshed by task, 20d. per qr 5d.
Item in 8 qrs of barley threshed by task, 2s., per qr 3d.
Item in 11 qrs of oats threshed by task, <2s. 3½d.> 22½d., per qr 2½d.
Item in 65 qrs 5 bus. 1 peck of various corn winnowed by task, 3s. 7¾d., per qr 4 bus. 1d.[39]
Sum 9s. 1¾d.

Stipends and bonuses In the stipend of Gilbert Helpe, the plough-driver for the whole year, 6s. 8d.
Item of one shepherd for the same time, 5s. 6d.
In a bonus to a servant at the days of Christmas and Easter, 1d.
Item to one manorial ploughman and one shepherd on the same days, 2d.
In wax bought for candles for the manorial servants on the day of the Purification, 1d.
Sum 12s. 6d.

Corn bought In 3 bus. 1 peck of maslin [*mixtur'*] bought for harvest expenses, 16¼d.
Sum 16¼d.

Stock bought nil.

Cost of the buildings In one thatcher with his servant for 10 days thatching upon the hall and barn 5s., per day jointly 6d.
In one hired man for one day for repairing the dais [*les Deys*] in the hall with daub, 4d.

---

[38] The manorial supplies of timber were plentiful in High Hall wood, hence the decision to use local sources rather than purchase timber from an outside source.

[39] The cost per qr of threshing wheat had almost doubled since 1327, reflecting the general shortages of workers in the post-plague era.

Item in one lock with a key bought for the barn door, <6d.> 5d. old price.
Sum 5s. 9d.

Minute costs In two sawyers hired for 2½ days for sawing 21 boards [*bord*] for making a new gate, 2s. 6d., per day jointly 12d.
Item in two carpenters for 5 days making one new pair of gates from the said board 3s. 4d., per day jointly 8d.
In two clasps bought for the said gate, 6d.
In 100 nails bought for the same, 8d.
Item in two gudgeons, two plates and two ferules bought for the said gate, 6d.
In one iron bolt bought for the same, 2d.
In two padlocks with keys [*cerur' cum clav' pend'*] bought for the same, 4d.
Item in one carpenter for 7 days making one other pair of new gates for the manor next to [*illeg.*], 2s. 4d., per day 4d.
In two iron clasps bought for the same, 6d.
In two gudgeons, two plates and two ferules bought for the same, 6d.
Item in nails bought for the same, 6d.
Item in 5 qrs of malt <bought> made 2s. 6d., per qr 6d.
In one hired man for 36 days at the same with food from the said manorial servants threshing in the grange, 4s. 6d., per day 1½d.
Item in one hired man for 12 days sowing the strips at the time of sowing peas and oats <18d.>, per day 1½d.
Item in one hired man for 10 days for the same at the time of sowing barley, 15d., per day 1½d.
In one hired man for one day making one new trough, 4d.
In two carpenters for two days making a new fence next to the said gate, 8d.
In one hired man for one day for repairing certain walls with clay <3d.>
In nails bought for the said fence <2d.>
In parchment bought for making the final account, <4d.> in the preceding year and omitted.[40]
Item in parchment bought for a court roll and this account <5d.> 2d.
Sum 21s. 3d.

Cost of the fold In 42 hurdles made for the fold, <21d.> 14d.[41]
Item in 2½ gallons of bitumen bought for treating sheep, 20d.[42]
In grease bought for the same, 8d.
Sum 2s. 4d.

Mowing of the meadows In 3 acres ½ rood mowed in the Great Meadow and 1 acre 3½ roods in Harts Haugh, 2s. 10d. altogether.[43]

---

[40] The auditor had cancelled this claim for parchment on the grounds that sufficient parchment had been bought in the previous year.
[41] Sheep in their various folds were penned onto parcels of arable land at night, hence the requirement for portable hurdles woven from willow and hazel.
[42] Although knowledge of diseases was rudimentary, attempts were made to protect the sheep against skin diseases through the use of bitumen and tar washes.
[43] Most of Walsham's meadow was in the Great or Mickle Meadow, but land around the stream near Harts Haugh is low lying and yielded additional hay.

In herbage of the same [*torn*] apportioned, <12d.> 4d. paid for the help of the manorial servants.

Sum 3s. 2d.

Wages with expenses of the steward In the wages of Stephen the bailiff for the whole year, except 4 weeks in the harvest when the lord provided food, 48s., per week 12d.
In expenses of the steward for one court held there, 4d. without a bill.

Sum 48s. 4d.

Foreign expenses nil.

Costs of the harvest In the purchase of 183 herrings bought for harvest expenses [*illeg.*] for the customary works of the manor, for a full day for food at noon and to each tenant 4 herrings equally, 3s. 0½d., at 20d. per 100.
Item in the expenses of six reapers from the customary services of the manor and of 61 hired workers by the day; with expenses of the bailiff and one household servant for four weeks in the harvest; bread made from [*illeg.*] <1 qr 2 bus.> \5 bus. 11 pecks/ of wheat price <6s. 8d.> \6s. 10d./; 1 qr 2 bus. of malt, price 5s. 5d.; in meat, fish, milk, butter and cheese; in total 10s. 10d., and thus per head for each day per work all accounted for, 1¾d.[44]
Item in the stipend of eleven reapers hired for one day for reaping, tying and gathering up 53½ acres of various corn of the lord, 12s. 3d., to each of them per day 3d. with food provided by the lord.
In salt bought for the harvest, 2d.
Item in candles bought, 3d.[45]
In two pairs of gloves bought, 4d.[46]

Sum 29s. 10½d.

Sum total of expenses £9 4s. 8½d. three ... [*torn*]
And thus owed to the lord, 39s. 11¼d. From which allowed to the same from [*torn*] and sold at the audit both within and without, 22½d. And thus owed to the lord [*torn*] 38s. 0¾d., after which 2s. was charged back for one tawed horse hide and various ... [*torn*]. Thus owed to the lord in total, 40s. 0¾d.
From which, allowed to the same for various sums [*torn*] allowed by the special favour of the lord, namely from Agnes Woodbite 40d.,[47] from a certain fine of John

---

[44] A rather dense paragraph detailing the purchase of food for the harvest workers, whether they were performing labour services or hired for cash by the day.

[45] The harvesting would have continued until dusk or dark, hence the need for candles to light the hall or barn while they ate.

[46] The provision of suitable protective clothing to workers was already a feature of the employer's responsibilities.

[47] In a court held in 1374, SA/B HA504/1/17.18, Agnes Woodbite paid an entry fine of 40d. to enter a messuage and 12 acres of customary land following the death of her husband, but the custom of the manor was to waive entry fines from heirs if a heriot had been paid on the death of the tenant. The account has already detailed how the payment of a heriot of a cow was delayed until the Feast of the Purification, i.e. 2 February, at which point the entry fine was no longer to be rendered.

21

Church 3s. 6d., Elias Tiptot <4s. 4d.> 5s., John Cook shepherd of Robert Ashfield, 4s. 6d.[48]

And thus owed to the lord clear, 23s. 8¾d.

[*Reverse*]

Walsham account of corn and livestock there, year as within.

Wheat The same answers for 12 qrs 4 bus. of wheat from the issue of the grange, including 2 qrs 4 bus. are chaff by one tally against Gilbert Helpe servant of the manor, of which threshed by the manorial servants 8 qrs 4 bus. and by task 4 qrs. And for 2 qrs of wheat received from the bailiff of Elmswell without tally.[49]

Sum 14 qrs 4 bus.

From which, in seed upon 20 acres at Thirty Acres and 5 acres at Doucedeux, thus in total 25 acres, 6 qrs 2 bus. by one tally against Gilbert Helpe the sower, at 2 bus. per acre.

In the livery of the manorial servants as shown below, 3 qrs 2½ bus.

Item in bread baked for the expenses of 113 reapers this year at the harvest by the day, 6½ bus.

In sales as within, 3 qrs 4 bus. of wheat, of which 2 qrs 4 bus. are chaff.

In sales at the audit, 5 bus. for 3s. 6d.[50]

Sum as above.   It balances.

Rye [*blank*]

Barley The same answers for 18 qrs of barley from the issues of the grange, of which 1 qr is chaff, by one tally against the said sower of the manorial servants, of which threshed by the manorial servants, 10 qrs and by task, 8 qrs.[51]

Sum 18 qrs.

From which, in seed upon 20 acres at Holner and 5 acres at Doucedeux thus in total, 25 acres, 9 qrs 3 bus., at 3 bus. per acre.

Item livery of the manorial servants as below, 2 qrs 5 bus.

Item in malt as below, 5 qrs barley.

Item allowed to peas below for bread and 1 qr of barley chaff.

It balances.   Sum as above.

Peas 10 qrs of old peas remain in the grange. And for 9 qrs of peas from the issue of the grange by one tally against the said sower of the manor household, threshed by the manorial servants. And for 1 qr of barley chaff received above for bread.[52]

Sum 20 qrs.

From which, in seed upon 20 acres above the wood, 4 qrs 6 bus., at 2 bus. per acre 2 bus. minus in total 2 bus.

---

[48] These are all fines or amercements imposed by the manor court this year which the auditor has chosen to waive for some undisclosed reasons.

[49] A marginal note states: 'R. 5 bus. less the following year and ½'.

[50] Marginal note.

[51] Marginal note: 'R' the following year in equal parts.'

[52] Marginal note: 'R' the following year in equal parts.'

In the livery of the manorial servants as below, 3 qrs 2½ bus.
Item allowed for bullimong below for sowing, 4 bus. peas.
Item in bread baked for stots, for which 2 qrs.
Item in expenses upon the dovecote in winter, 4 bus.
In sales as within, 8 qrs 7½ bus.

It balances.

Sum as above.

Bullimong The same answers for 1 qr of bullimong from the issues of the grange by one tally against the said sower of the manor household, threshed by the manorial servants. And for 4 bus. of peas above and 4 bus. of oats below received for bullimong seed, which were sown upon 8 acres at Nether Haugh.[53]

Sum 1 qr

It balances.

Oats 2 qrs of old oats remain in the grange. And for 25 qrs 1 bus. 1 peck of oats from the issues of the grange by one tally against the said sower of the manor household, of which threshed by the manorial servants 14 qrs 1 bus. 1 peck and by task, 11 qrs. From the issues as sheaves by estimation below, 6½ bus., of which 8 sheaves make 1 bus.[54]

Sum 27 qrs 7 bus. 3 pecks.

From which, in seed upon 9 acres at Howes Haugh, 15 acres at Angrave and 9 acres at Market Path, thus in total 33 acres, 9 qrs 2 bus., at 3 bus. of oats per acre, in total 3 qrs.
Item in meals made as pottage for the manorial servants, <4 bus.> \2 bus./
Item allowed for bullimong above for sowing, 4 bus.
Item in fodder for 3 stots, 5 qrs 2 bus.
Item in fodder for 4 bullocks by estimation in 52 sheaves, 6½ bus. as charged above.
Item in remuneration for supervising the stots after November, at the time of sowing and in the fallow, 2 bus. 1 peck.
Item in meal made into pottage at harvest, <2 bus.> \1 bus./
Item destroyed by rats and mice in the granary, <7 bus.> <7 bus.> [sic].
In sales as within, 10 qrs 2 bus.
In sales at the audit, 1 qr 2 bus.[55]

Sum as above.

It balances.

Malted barley For making 5 qrs malted barley this year.
From increment of the same, nothing because it was malted by measure and delivered in malt by the good heaped measure according to the aforesaid use.

Sum 5 qrs.

From which brewed for harvest, 1 qr 2 bus.
Item in remuneration of one thatcher thatching various buildings, <1 bus..> because it was agreed.
In sales as within, 3 qrs 5 bus.
In sales at the audit, 1 bus.[56]

Sum as above.

It balances.

---

53 Marginal note: 'R' from 2 bus. last year.'
54 Marginal note: 'Equals 3 qrs 2 bus. 1 peck'.
55 Marginal note: 'for 2s. 11d.'
56 Marginal note: 'for 6½d.'

23

Mixture for the manorial servants And for 3 qrs 2½ bus. of wheat, 2 qrs 5 bus. of barley and 3 qrs 2½ bus. of peas received as above for the livery of the manorial servants. And bought, as within, for the harvest, 3 bus. 1 peck.

Sum 9 qrs <2> \5/ bus. 1 peck.

From which, for the livery of one servant for a whole year, less 4 weeks in the harvest with food provided by the lord, 4 qrs taking one qr every 12 weeks.

Item of one shepherd for the whole year, 5 qrs 2 bus. taking one qr every 10 weeks.

Item in bread baked for expenses of 65 workers from custom this year [*illeg.*] not threshed, 3 bus. 1 peck.

It balances.

Land sown Sown this year with the seed of various grains, 111 acres, which were reaped by customary works as below and for money as within.

Stots 4 stots remain.   Sum 4.   And 4 stots remain.

Bullocks 2 bullocks remain.

Sum 2.   And 2 bullocks remain.

Cows From a heriot after the death of John Woodbite, 1 cow.

And 1 cow remains in the hands of Agnes Woodbite.

Sum 1.

Undressed hides [*blank*]

Bleached and tanned hides [*blank*]

Hens For rent at Christmas, 39 hens and four parts of one.

Sum 39 and four parts of one.

From which, in decay upon various tenements in the lord's hands both from ancient times and from the time of the pestilence[57] up to now, <24>\23/ and half a quarter of one.

Item upon 3 acres of land of the tenement Angerhale, free by charter of lord Edmund de Welle lord of this manor, from John Packard senior, ½ hen.

Item upon 1 acre of land of the tenement Woodbite free by the same charter, 2 quarters of half of one hen.

In sales as within, 15.

Sum as above.   It balances.

Egg For rent at Easter, 111 eggs.

Sum 111.

From which, in decay upon various tenements in the lord's hands as above, 36 eggs.

Item upon 3 acres of land of the tenement Angerhale free by charter of the aforesaid lord. And now as above, 5 eggs.

Item upon 1 acre of land of the tenement Woodbite free by the same, now 1½ eggs.

In sales as within, 73½ eggs.

Sum 116.   And thus excess, 5 eggs.

---

57 The Black Death of 1349.

Pepper For rent at Christmas, ½lb of pepper received p.a. from the heirs of a certain Peter Pinfold.

Sum ½lb

And reckoned in the lord's hands   It balances.

Account of works

Ploughing by services of free men For the issue of free men ploughing 2 acres, with food provided by the lord sufficient for one meal for half a day.

Sum 2 acres.

From which, in decay upon the tenement of William Cranmer, 1.
In the land of the lord ploughed at the time of sowing peas, 1.

Sum as above.   It balances.

Ploughing by customary tenants For the issue of the works of customary tenants this year, 2 ploughings, with food provided by the lord for one meal.

Sum 2.

And expended in ploughing the lord's land in the aforesaid season.   It balances.

Summer and winter works by half days For the issue of the customary tenants, including the Feasts of St Michael and Lammas, 80 works for a half day, price per work ½d.

Sum 80.   It balances.

From which, in decay upon various tenements in the lord's hands[58] as above, 40 works.
Item upon the tenement Angerhale free by charter as above for the total rent in money, 14 works, of which 4 are for 1 acre of the land of Woodbite.
In harrowing at the time of sowing wheat and peas, 20½ works.
In sales at the audit, 10½.

Sum 85.   Thus excess, 5 works.

Weeding For the issues of customary tenants p.a., 8 weeding works for a half day, price per work ½d.

Sum 8.

From which, in decay upon various tenements in the lord's hands as above, 4 works.
Item upon 3 acres of land of the tenement Angerhale free as above, one.
Item upon 1 acre of land of the tenement Wodebite free by the same, now ½.
In weeding the lord's corn, 2.
In sales at the audit, ½.

Sum as above.   It balances.

Harvest works for whole days For the services of free men and customary tenants from the Feast of St Peter Advincula to the Feast of St Michael, 124. Of which, for

---

[58] A rather complex accounting procedure, in which the decay relates to the labour services rather than to the land. The 'decay' in the number of services available to the lord is partly due to an undisclosed proportion of these holdings lying unoccupied 'in the lord's hands' for want of tenants, but also and partly due to the land having been converted from the old customary service tenure, which owed labour services, to leases, which did not. See M. Bailey, 'The transformation of customary tenures in southern England, *c.*1350 to *c.*1500', *Agricultural History Review* 62 (2014), pp. 210–30.

a full day, for which each man shall have from the lord at noon [*ad horam nonam*] bread of mixed grains, sufficient pottage, water, legumes and 2 herrings. And to each of the same tenants 1 loaf of bread, of which 20 loaves to the bus., and two herrings, price per work 1d.

Sum 124.

From which, in decay upon various tenements in the lord's hands as above, 55.
Item upon 3 acres of land of the tenement Angerhale free by charter as above, 4 works.
Item upon 1 acre of land of the tenement Woodbite free as above, 5½ works.
In 52 acres of the lord's corn, reaped, tied and stacked, 65½ works.
In sales [*blank*].

Sum 130. Thus excess, 6 works.

Harvest works and boonworks For the issues of customary tenants p.a., 16 works and they work as above and shall take as above.

Sum 16.

From which, in decay upon various tenements in the lord's hands as above, 10.
In sales at the audit, 6.[59]

It balances.

Harvest boonworks For the issue of free and customary this year, with food provided by the lord 6.

Sum 6.

And expended on 5½ acres of various grains of the lord by reaping and tying.

Sum 6.

It balances.

Faggots For faggots this year, 60.

Sum 60. And sold as within.

Timber Remaining, 12 boards. From felling this year, 22.

Sum 34.

From which, in expenses of two new pairs of gates made, 20 boards.
Item in shutters made and repaired, 2 boards.

Sum 22. 12 boards remain.

---

[59] Marginal note: '6d.'

Section Three

Accounts of Walsham manor with High Hall, 1390–1407
Documents 5 to 8[1]

Document 5: Walsham account, 28 September 1390 to 28 September 1391

SA/B HA504/3/3

Walsham

Account of Nicholas Fuller, sergeant[2] there, from the eve of St Michael the Archangel in the 14th year of Richard II until the eve of the same Feast of St Michael next coming in the 15th year of the same Richard for one whole year.[3]

Arrears [*He answers*] for arrears of his last account in the preceding year, 42s. 5d. two quarters of half ¼d. and two parts of ¼d.
        Sum 42s. 5d. two quarters of half ¼d. and two parts of ¼d.

Rents of assize

For rents of assize for the term of Michaelmas, 76s. 6½d.
For rents of assize for the term of Christmas, 60s.
For rents of assize for the term of Easter, 68s. 9¾d.
For rent of increment from Walter Tiptot, 2s.
For rent of increment from Richard Patel, 1¼d.
For rent of increment from a certain forge recently leased to Simon Smith, 6d.
For rent of increment from Peter Hawes, ½d.
From John Lester and Rose his mother for *Taylloerswong*, 3s.
From George Brockley for land at Taylors Wong, 12d.
For rent of increment from Robert Osbern of Rickinghall, ¼d.
From Henry Breton for 2 acres of land recently of Henry Osbern, 1d.
For various increments for the term of Michaelmas, 10¼d.
From William Hawes and Robert his brother, 1d.
From William Pye for a certain portion of one messuage formerly of Gilbert Helpe, 1d.

---

[1]   See Introduction, pp. xxix–xxx.
[2]   In the court held in September 1389 Nicholas Fuller had been elected to the office of reeve for the year 1389–90. See Lock, *Walsham II*, p. 167, and 1390–1 account in this volume. John Frost was elected but, according to this account, paid a fine not to serve in the office. Fuller is described in this account as the sergeant of Westhorpe, so he was evidently overseeing the management of at least two manors on the estate.
[3]   The lordship of the manor changed during the course of this financial year: see the Introduction, p. xix. The only hint of the change in lordship within this account is the payment of expenses to Sir John Wingfield, one of the new co-feoffees of the manor, attending the first manorial court of the new lordship on the Thursday in Easter week.

For rent of increment from Matthew Gilbert, ¼d.

For new rent from John Lester for 4 acres 33 perches of land from the lord's demesne lying on the east side of Taylors Wong towards the south, 4s. 3d.

For new rent from Robert Rampley, the smith, for 2 acres 6 perches of land from the lord's demesne of Taylors Wong, 2s.[4]

For rent of increment received annually from Bartholomew, the parson of the church of Langham, for 6 acres of land of mollond of the lord's bondage that Robert Warde neif [*nativus*] of the lord recently purchased by charter, 1d.[5]

For new rent received annually from John Baxter for one piece of land called *Ayleld-estuft* granted to him and his heirs by court roll, 10s.

For new rent received annually from John, son of John Margery for one piece of land containing 2 acres lying on the west side of *Howestuft* granted to him and his heirs by court roll, 18d.

For new rent received annually from the tenants of the land and tenement recently of Robert Hawes of 6s. 8d., nothing here this year nor from the other because it was found by the evidence of the same lord that he was unjustly charged and therefore he is exonerated.

For new rent from John Baxter of one acre from the lord's demesne at fee farm lying opposite the cemetery of the church granted to him and his heirs by the rod by the court roll, 16d.

From John Coggeshall for 1 acre of land at fee farm from the demesne there granted to him and his heirs by the court roll p.a.,[6] 16d.

Sum £11 13s. 7¾d.   Approved.

Rents of assize from High Hall with ward For rents of assize there p.a., 28s 0¼d. For castle ward there p.a., 2d.

Sum 28s. 2¼d.   Approved.

Castle ward For castle ward received from the manor of Wyken [*Wykes*] at the terms of St Michael, Christmas, Easter and St John the Baptist, 11s. 2d. For castle ward received from the manor of Ixworth, 2s. 10d.

Sum 14s.   Approved.

Capitage[7] of neifs Nil.

---

4   At a court in 1385 Robert Rampley, the smith, was granted a forge in Church Street for the term of his life for 2s. p.a., SA/B HA504/1/8.10. He was to maintain the forge, in exchange for which the lord was to supply him with sufficient timber and straw.

5   Mollond was a form of free tenure. Serfs by blood were not permitted to acquire free land without seigniorial permission, which, as this example shows, was usually granted in return for a notional fee.

6   The two new rents, one each for Baxter and Coggeshall, were created by granting slivers of the arable demesne on hereditary fee farms for an annual cash rent. The original grants in the court rolls for 1389 are both explicit that the land is held on condition that the tenants build thereon. See Lock, *Walsham II*, pp. 164–5. The new rent from John Baxter was for 1½ acres of land opposite the churchyard, which is now occupied by the Six Bells public house. Ten years later it was surrendered by Joan, his widow, to Nicholas Fuller and others, and became known as Fullers tenement, SA/B HA504/1/9.20. The grant to John Coggeshall was later known as Dages.

7   Capitage, or *capitagium*, is usually a payment from neifs/serfs by blood who live on the manor but do not hold land. It is sometimes used to mean chevage, a payment by a serf to live away from the manor. Chevage was not often levied on Walsham serfs, although absent serfs are occasionally recorded. For an analysis of the Walsham migrants, see M. Bailey, 'Servile and gender migration in late medieval England: the evidence of manorial court rolls', *Past and Present* 261 (2023), pp. 63–4.

Farm [*firma*] **of land and pasture**[8] For the farm of various land and tenements in the lord's hands leased to various men as shown by one bill attached to this roll from the responsibility [*de onere*] of the hayward, 39s. 4½d.[9]

For pasture at *Pynchonnes Weye* recently leased for 2s., nothing because it was grazed by the lord's sheep.

For pasture at *Fyshpondfeld* recently leased to John Hawes for 2s. 4d., nothing because as aforesaid.

From Robert Man for pasture in *Hallecroft* at the south head, 4d.

From the same Robert for pasture on the east side of Hall Croft, 6d.

From allowances to the hayward.[10] From Adam Blayer[11] for the farm of one piece of land at *Mycklemedwe* and for land at *Westmell* from the responsibility of the hayward, 4s.

From Adam Ebell for 2 acres of land called *Nunneslond* and 3 roods of land in three pieces of the same tenement from the responsibility of the hayward, 18d.

From Adam Blayer for farm of one pightle of pasture called *Cawlpictel* for a term of 5 years, this year is the last, 3s.

From the same Adam for one acre of land at Fishpond Field for a term of 5 years, this year is the last, 6d.

For pasture in *le Newepictel* recently leased for 4s. 4d. nothing this year partly because it was grazed by the lord's sheep and partly charged in rent above.

For a headland of pasture in the *Launde*[12] at *Ladyeswod* and for pasture land in the same grazed by three colts in summer, 18d., and no more because the residue was grazed by the lord's lambs after separation and by three of the lord's foals.

From John Margery for a headland of pasture towards the north side of the meadow, 2d.

For 17½ acres of land recently leased to the lord by William Sparschoy and afterwards to Robert Lester for 5s. 10d. p.a., nothing this year because it was grazed by the lord's sheep.

For one close at the sheepfold next to *Alwodegrene* recently leased to Peter Robwood for 4s. p.a., nothing this year because it was grazed by the lord's lambs.

For 12 acres of land called *Blunteslond* leased in the preceding year to John Syre for 4s., nothing because it was grazed by the lord's sheep.[13]

---

8 The 'farm' or leasing of land is explained in the Introduction, p. xxiv. The swing to leasing parts of the demesne and also some of the unfree land (rather than it being held on the traditional service tenancy) is a feature of many manors towards the end of the fourteenth century. As leases were renegotiated on expiry, the fluctuation of leasehold values per acre over time provides a good indicator of the changing demand for land locally: for some analysis of the demesne values at Walsham see Bailey, *Decline of serfdom*, graph 6.1.

9 Throughout these accounts, dues are often broken down into the responsibility of either the reeve or the hayward: part of the accounting procedure to specify with whom a particular charge lay.

10 Marginal note.

11 Adam Blayer was the sergeant or bailiff of Westhorpe manor, part of the same estate as Walsham. He had inherited two messuages and 12 acres of land in Walsham on the death of his father in 1391 (see Lock, *Walsham II*, p. 177), then increased his holdings during the early part of the fifteenth century through the acquisition of several small parcels of unfree land, in addition to the land leased here.

12 Launde usually means a clearing in a deer park. As Walsham had no park, in this case it means a small open space in the wood.

13 The reasons for the lapse of a number of leases and the switch to grazing the land with the lord's sheep instead are unclear: either the sheep were being given precedence or lessees for the land could not be found. It was probably the former, because in this year extreme weather conditions were recorded throughout England: see footnote 17 below. Whatever the reason, these entries are indicative of former arable land now reverting to pasture.

From Robert Levy for 5 acres of land on the east side of Fishpond Field between the land of Robert Sare, 20d.

From Robert Syre for the farm of *Burchardesclos* newly purchased by the lord,[14] this year is the 2nd, 15s. 4d. this year and in the following year leased to him at a term of 9 years for 12s. p.a.

From the same Robert for one curtilage and 4 acres of land in three pieces called *Sparshoos* purchased by the lord, this year is the 2nd, 4s.

From Thomas Bonde for 4 acres of land by estimate of the tenement Burchards on the west side of Burchards Croft, 12d.

From the same Thomas for one piece of land of the said tenement lying towards *Rekynghale Wylwes* [Rickinghall Willows] next to the land of Adam Pitlake, 8d.

Sum 73s. 6½d., of which on the hayward 44s. 10½d.

Farm of land and meadow at High Hall For the farm of land and tenement, meadow and pasture there leased as shown by one bill attached to this roll, £4 15s. 3d., of which within the bounds [*bundas*] of Westhorpe 40s. 8d.[15]

Sum £4 15s. 3d.   Approved.

Sales of hay and herbage of the meadow belonging to the manor and from perquisites For hay produced from 4½ acres of meadow called *Brodole* sold this year to William Sparshoo chaplain \16s. 6d./ and Almary Grym \one mark/, 29s. 10d.

From John Margery for the herbage of 3 roods of meadow in Mickle Meadow purchased by the lord from John Rampolye, chaplain, this year the 2nd, 5s.

From John Wells for the herbage of 1 acre of meadow there, recently of the said Master John this year, 5s.

Sum 39s. 10d.   Approved.

Perquisites of the court For one court held there on Thursday in the Feast of the Apostles Peter and Paul, 32s. 3d.

From John Frost as a fine for [*declining*] the office of reeve this year, 40s.[16]

Sum 72s. 3d.   Approved.

Sales of corn For 2 bus. of wheat sold for expenses around the Ploughale as [*recorded*] elsewhere, 2s. 6d.

For 1 bus. of wheat sold for expenses of washing and shearing the lord's sheep, 15d.

For 1 bus. of wheat sold for winnowing, 2s. 6d.

For 6 bus. of wheat sold to Thomas Hereward and his wife for threshing and winnowing, 7s. 6d., price per bus. 15d.

---

[14] The small manor of Burchards, which had recently been acquired and absorbed within the main manor of Walsham. See Introduction, p. xxxiii.

[15] Some land pertaining to High Hall manor evidently lay within the neighbouring vill of Westhorpe. The lands of one manor in a given vill were often dispersed across the boundaries of other vill(s) in East Anglia.

[16] Liability to perform the office of reeve as a villein tenant was unavoidable, but a tenant could pay to evade the duty when their turn came. The 40s. fine was a set rate on this manor: large enough to discourage tenants from routinely declining, but affordable enough for those determined to avoid the office.

For 1 qr of wheat sold to John Pye for threshing, 10s.[17]
For 1 qr of wheat sold for the expenses of the harvest, 8s.
For 1½ bus. of rye sold for the expenses of the harvest, 12d.
For 2 qrs 5 bus. of barley sold as elsewhere, 15s. 9d., price per bus. 9d.
For 2 bus. of barley sold to John Pye at the time of sowing barley 2s.
For 4 bus. of barley sold to John winnowed for the lady 4s. at the time of [*sowing*] barley.[18]
For 3 qrs 5 bus. of peas sold to various men whose names were shown at the view of the account, 24s. 2d., price per qr 6s. 8d.
For 21 qrs 1 bus. 3 pecks half a quarter of 1 peck, a third part of half a bus. and two parts of 1 peck of oats from rent and from profits of the grange sold, price per qr 4s. minus in total 7½d., £4 4s. 5¾d.

Sum £8 3s. 1¾d. Approved.

Sale of stock For 2 crone wethers and one ewe sold elsewhere for the expenses of the harvest, price of pelts, 2s.[19]
For 2 lambs from the residue [*de refus'*][20] sold to John Man, 8d.
For 38 lambs from the residue similarly sold to Richard Gardener, 9s.

Sum 11s. 8d. Approved.

Farm of the dovecotes For the farm of one dovecote at the manor and one dovecote at High Hall this year, nothing because the young doves were delivered for the lord's hospitality, as shown elsewhere.[21]

Sum nil.

Works and customary services sold For 16¼ hens from rent sold elsewhere, of which from the responsibility of the hayward 8¾ hens, 2s. 0¼d. and half a ¼d., price for each 1½d.
For 113 eggs from rent sold as elsewhere, 4¾d., at 1d. per 24 eggs.
For ½lb of cumin from rent sold as elsewhere, 3d.
For ½lb of pepper from rent sold elsewhere from the responsibility of the reeve, 12d.

---

17 The price of grain was very high this year. The summers of 1390 and 1391 were unusually hot and dry in south-east England, and harvest failures caused food shortages in places; there was also an outbreak of plague. See K. Pribyl, *Farming, famine and plague. The impact of climate in late medieval England* (Cham, 2017), pp. 104–5, 201, 207–8.
18 This entry, as with others so far in this section, was not a sale as such in the open market, but a monetary valuation of grain from the manor given as expenses and supplements to various local people performing tasks on the manor.
19 Three sheep were killed to feed harvest workers and the pelts of the dead sheep are accounted for separately.
20 Lambs of residue refers to older lambs, i.e. those born in the previous year but not yet one year old, as opposed to lambs of issue born in the most recent lambing season.
21 Audrey McLaughlin consistently translated the Latin phrase *ad hosp'domini* as 'the lord's guesthouse', which she located at the lord's primary residence in Westhorpe. Here, we consistently translate it as 'for the lord's hospitality', meaning that produce was sent to the lord's residence for consumption and entertainment of guests. The routine abbreviation of the original word means we cannot be certain whether it referred to a specific guest house (*hospitium, domus hospitum*) or to general consumption and hospitality (*hospitalitas, ad hospicium domini*). The latter has been preferred because it does not preclude the existence of a guest house at Westhorpe.

For 130¾ and two parts of whole[22] customary winter works sold, 5s. 5½d. and half a ¼d., price per work ½d.[23]

For 6 customary carrying works sold elsewhere, 6d.

For a quarter and half a quarter of one carrying and two parts of one carrying and two parts of half a carrying of manure sold as elsewhere, 3d., \price per carriage 2d./

For 160½ customary weeding works sold elsewhere, 6s. 8¼d., price per work ½d.

For 42 customary mowing works sold elsewhere, 5s. 3d., per work 1½d.

For 77¼ and half a quarter of one customary harvest works of this manor sold as elsewhere, 6s. 5¼d. and a half, price per work 1d.

For 15 customary harvest works from High Hall sold, 3s. 9d., price per work 3d. because they were summoned.[24]

For 19 customary harvest boonworks sold elsewhere, 6s. 4d., price per boonwork 4d. because they were summoned.

Sum 38s. 4¼d. and half a ¼d.   Approved.

Farm of cows and hens For the farm of the lactage and calves of 19 cows leased to Roger Daye at full farm, at 6s. per head,[25] 114s.[26]

For the farm of a cow aged one year [*vacc' anular'*] this year and received at half farm, 3s.

For the farm of 12 hens this year, per head 6d., 6s.

Sum £6 3s.   Approved.

Issues of the garden with pasture in Lady's Wood [*Le Ladyeswode*] For the fruit in the gardens of the lord at Walsham Hall and High Hall, nothing this year because it was delivered for the lord's hospitality at Westhorpe, valued at 12d.

For pasture in Lady's Wood, nothing here because it was charged above within farms and pasture.

Sum nil.

Sale of wool and pelts For 252 ewe skins weighing 34 stone of wool, a stone of 10lbs sold to Simon Hauker, 56s. 8d. \not paid/, price per stone 20d.

For 394 lamb-skins weighing 16½ stone, a stone of 10lb, sold to the same Simon, 22s., price per stone 16d. \the lady has received the money/.

---

22 Meaning a full day for the completion of the work.

23 The lord did not use all of the labour services due as part of the rent package of customary holdings, so commuted those not used for cash at a set rate.

24 The standard rate for commuting these works was 2d. and the higher rate here of 3d. is explained by the statement that the workers had been summoned: the implication is that the lord wished the works to be performed and was not amenable to commuting them for cash. When the workers did not perform, the lord increased the rate charged per work as a means of building in an extra charge for their refusal.

25 Dairy farming was relatively labour intensive, requiring daily rather than seasonal supervision, so many manors leased out their herd of cows to local people rather than carry the onerous burden of daily supervision of the milking and of making cheese and butter. Here the lessee received both the milk and any births of calves during the year, a full lease, whereas some leases stipulated that any calves born during the year were to be transferred to the demesne.

26 The rate per cow, 6s., was relatively high by national standards, and around the norm for Suffolk: which reflects that in the century after the Black Death intensive dairying was rapidly emerging as a specialism of the central, boulder clay, areas of East Anglia. See Bailey, *Medieval Suffolk*, pp. 81–6.

For 51 wether, hogget and ewe pelts in murrain[27] sold to Thomas Haylok, in total 5s. 2d.

For 2 wether pelts, 2 ram pelts and 13 ewe pelts similarly sold to Peter Hirde,[28] 3s. 1d.

For 22 damaged hogget pelts sold to him in total, 2s.

For 11 wether pelts received from Wattisfield, of which 4 were poor quality [*debil'*], sold to him, 2s.

For 11 pelts in murrain sold, 10d.

For 11 lamb pelts in murrain sold, 4d.

For 9 \poor quality/ pelts and 2 lamb pelts in murrain sold, 3d.

Sum £4 12s. 4d.   Approved.

Sale of wood[29] From William Man for 2 quarters of faggots sold to him in *Northagh*, 20d.

From Thomas Baldere for 1 quarter of faggots sold to him, 10d.

From Olive living in the house of William Margery for 1 quarter of faggots sold to her, 10d.

From Roger Prede for willow fronds [*frondic'*] at the sheepfold, 6d.

From Thomas Haylok for fronds of trees in Katherines Croft sold to him, 6d.

From Robert Cooper for fronds of trees in *le Oxepasture* at High Hall, 12d.

From John Lester for elm fronds at *Cherchegate*, 16d.

From the same John for 1½ acres of underwood in North Haugh sold to him, 12s.

From John Spilman for 1 acre 1 rood of underwood in Lady's Wood sold to him, 10s.[30]

From John Warde for 1 rood of underwood there, 2s.

From John Freeburn for thorn bushes and underwood growing in le Launde at Lady's Wood, 2s.

From John Hereward for thorn bushes and underwood there, 20d.

From John Bradmere for thorn bushes and underwood there, 2s.

From Robert Poye for 1 rood of underwood there, 12d.

From William Margery for ½ rood of underwood there, 12d.

From John Bygge for 1 rood there, 2s.

From a certain shearman [*cissor'*] for 1 rood of underwood there, 2s.

From Robert Margery for 1 acre 1 rood there, 10s.

From lord William Langham for 1 acre 1 rood there, 10s.

From John Bradmere for oak fronds next to Lady's Wood on the west side, 2s.

From John Cooper for ½ acre of underwood there, 4s.

From Robert Lester for ½ acre of underwood in North Haugh, 4s.

From William Lakenham for 1 rood there, 2s.

From William Trusse for 1 rood there, 2s.

---

27 The sheared skins of sheep that had died through some unspecified disease.

28 None of the men listed here who had bought sheepskins from the manor were Walsham residents.

29 The details of the sale of wood – usually underwood, *subboscum* – are a distinctive and significant aspect of the Walsham material, because they identify the buyers and the prices paid. Underwood was purchased by local craftworkers to construct hurdles and fencing, but also by various local people as a major source of fuel. See D.L. Farmer, 'Marketing the produce of the countryside 1200 to 1500', in E. Miller, ed., *The agrarian history of England and Wales, volume III, 1348–1500* (Cambridge, 1991), pp. 411–14.

30 John Spilman's tenement, on the site of the Old Vicarage in Palmer Street, comprised 18 acres of land, 4 acres of meadow and 1 acre of wood: SA/B HA504/1/6.7.

From John Green for 1 rood 16 perches of underwood there, 2s. 11d.
From Peter Poye for 1½ roods of underwood there, 3s.
From John Baxter for 1 rood there, 2s.[31]
From William Pye for ½ acre there, 4s.
From William Frances for 1 rood at High Hall, 2s.
From John Pye for 1 rood there, 2s.
From William Grocer for 1 quarter of faggots sold to him, 10d.
From Roger Banham for 1 quarter of faggots, 10d.
From William Pye for 3 quarters of faggots in North Haugh sold to him, 2s. 3d.
From Henry Warde for 1 rood in the Launde, 2s.
From Robert Margery for oak fronds in North Haugh, 16d.

Sum 100s. 6d.   Approved.

Issues of the manor For straw sold to John Bradmere in the present year, 8d.
For straw sold to William Swift in the present year, 6d.
For one old pair of cart wheels with old broken iron-work upon the same sold to John Lester, 5s.
For the grazing of sheep, nothing this year.
For litter [*stramen*] sold, nothing this year.
For one white poplar tree trunk lying in the manor garden sold to William Man, 4d.
For the share-beam of a plough [*chyppis*] sold to Roger Daye at the end of the year, 10d.

Sum 7s. 4d.   Approved.

Foreign receipts from a hayward Received from Walter Frances, hayward of Wattisfield, as shown in an allowance of money there, 17s. 11½d. from his responsibility.

Sum 17s. 11½d.   Approved.

Sales at the audit For things sold at the audit as shown elsewhere, 11s. 8d.

Sum 11s. 8d.   Approved.

Total sum of receipts with arrears £58 5s. 0½d. half a ¼d. and half a quarter of a ¼d. and two parts.

Rent resolute with decays The same accounts for rent resolute for the hall of Thelnetham of 2s. p.a., nothing because the fee is outside the lord's hands.[32]
Item for the hall of Rickinghall p.a., 3s. 1½d.
Paid for castle ward of Norwich p.a., 16s. <8d.> because it is not in the preceding account.[33]
Item paid to John Margery, 1½d.
In rent allowed for the tenement of John Frost, reeve this year, 2s. 7d. and a quarter of a ¼d.

---

[31] John Baxter was routinely amerced for baking bread against the assize between 1383 and 1391 (SA/B HA504/1/8.8 to HA504/1/9.6), so perhaps this wood was destined to fuel his oven.

[32] The manor had once possessed land in Thelnetham, for which it paid 2s. rent to another lord, but either it has been sold or leased to a third party.

[33] The draft account has 16s. 8d., but the 8d. was crossed out at the audit because the previous account had 16s., not 16s. 8d.

Item for the tenement of John Frances, hayward this year, 21¼d.

In rent allowed for Champeneys p.a. 12d.

Item in rent allowed for various villein tenements in the lord's hands, 29s. 0d. three quarters of a ¼d., half a quarter of a ¼d. and a third part of a ¼d.

In allowance for a forge [*fabric'*] formerly of Walter Smith because it is charged within rents of assize above, 6d.

Item for the tenement Outlawes, 6¼d.

In rent allowed for 1 acre of land formerly of Master John of Walsham, 2½d.

Item for 1 acre 1 rood recently of Edmund Pakenham, 2¼d.

Item for a smithy [*domo fabric'*] in Palmer Street because it is empty and lying in the highway p.a., 8d.

In rent released to Robert Osbern by the deed of Lady Roesia of Pakenham, ¼d.

Item in rent allowed from High Hall in the lord's hands namely purchased in perpetuity, 4d.

Item for sheriff's aid [*Shirrivesselver*] for the same, 2½d.

In allowance for sheriff's aid of Burchards and Sparschoys p.a., 1d.

Paid to the hall of Ashfield [*Aisshfeld*] for castle ward of Norwich for High Hall p.a., 17d.

Paid to the castle of Eye for castle ward for High Hall this year once, 9d.

In rent allowed for various tenements in the lord's hands pertaining to High Hall, 15s. 9¾d.

Paid to the hall of Ashfield for rent p.a., 2d.

Item paid for release from suit to the hundred[34] for Burchards this year, 16d.

Item paid to Helimot[35] for hidage and ward of Burchards p.a. <this year>, 9d.

In rent resolute payable to Master Sir William Bardwell[36] for 1 acre of meadow at Turf Pits [*Turvepetts*] purchased by the lord from Master John Rampley p.a., 4d.

    Sum 76s. 11d. half a quarter of a ¼d. and a third part of a ¼d.

Cost of ploughs In hiring a smith for providing and forging ironwork on two ploughs with shoeing stots p.a., plus 4 bus. of wheat as elsewhere, 28s.

Item in one iron chain bought for binding the broken shaft of one plough, ½d.

In the stipend of Nicholas Patel for 5 days' work, of which 3 days were in winter shaping [*scapul'*] wood for a plough and fixing and making a new plough and shaping three axles for a cart and shaping wood for sleds,[37] 17d.

In 6 canvas [*canab'*] halters bought for the stots, 3d.

    Sum 29s. 8½d.   Approved.

Cost of carts In one pair of body traces and one pair of chain traces bought, 14d.

In the stipend of Simon Sadler for 2 days' work in the present year mending a cart harness, 8d.

Item in one canvas halter bought for a carthorse, 1d.

Item in 4 canvas reins bought for the same, 3d.

---

[34] The requirement for the lord of the small manor of Burchard – now the lord of Walsham following the recent purchase – to attend the hundred court.

[35] Helimot was a small manor in Wattisfield, an adjoining parish.

[36] Sir William Bardwell held Wyken manor and also 1 acre of meadow in Walsham.

[37] A path called Sled Way leading from Upstrete (now Crownland Road) to Clay Street near to East Mill suggests it was used for pulling sacks of grain up to the mill: SA/B HA504/1/15.19.

In the stipend of one man from Thelnetham for 4 days' work making and mending harnesses for the harvest and making 3 new collars, 16d.
In 3½ ells of canvas bought for the same, 7d.
Item in thread bought for the same, 2d.
In one tanned hide bought for the same, 15d.
In one tanned calfskin bought, 2½d.
In grease bought for lubricating the carts this year, 6d.
In 4 clouts bought for the cart axle with nails, 6d.
In making one pair of new wheels from the lord's timber with spokes bought for the same, 4s.

Sum 10s. 8½d. Approved.

Cost of the buildings In the stipend of John Cooper, carpenter, and of Thomas Cooper, carpenter, for 1 day's work in winter underpinning a wall between the dovecote and the lord's stable, 6d.
In the stipend of Adam Frances for 11 days' work covering the kitchen from new by binding [*circuit'*] and putting wattle on [*watlant'*] the said building, 2s. 9d., per day 3d. And supplemented by winter works.
In the stipend of the same Adam for 18 days' work covering over the walls next to the barn, upon the sheepcote at East End, upon the sheepcote at the hall, upon the sheepcote at High Hall, upon two walls next to the chapel and the new kitchen, upon the chapel and knight's chamber, 4s. 6d., per day 3d. And supplemented by customary works, as [*recorded*] elsewhere.
In 100 lath nails bought for the kitchen, 4d.
In mending one lock for the door of the barn at High Hall, 1d.
Item in mending one lock for the door of the wheat barn, 1d.
Item in buying one lock with a key for the door of the stots' stable, 3d.
Item in mending one lock and one key for the door of the knight's chamber, ½d.
Item in nails bought for the kitchen and for the wall next to the kitchen, 4½d.
In the stipend of John Cooper for 5 days' \20d./ work, Thomas Cooper for 7 days' \2s. 4d./ work, John Manser for 9 days' \3s./ and Robert his son for 4½ days' \13½d./ making and mending a cowshed by carpentry at the end of the year, 8s. 1½d.

Sum 17s. 0½d. Approved.

Cost of the mill In the stipend of John Manser and his sons for 1¼ days making corbles[38] [*les Curbles*] and laying them in the mill and for making one key for binding the head of the axle of the mill 9d., taken between them per day, 7d.
In nails bought for the wall-plates of one house at the mill, ½d.

Sum 9½d. Approved.

Cost of the sheepfold In one barrel of tar bought for treating sheep, 4s. 3d.
Item in grease bought to mix with the same for sheep and lambs of this manor and wethers from Wattisfield,[39] 5s. 1d.
In expenses of various men helping to grease hoggets on various occasions during the year, 10d.

---

[38] Wood surrounding the stones to hold them together.
[39] Wethers were often kept in separate flocks from ewes and lambs, which appears to be the case here in Wattisfield, the neighbouring parish to the north of Walsham where the lord also held the small manor of Helimot.

Item in 282 sheep and 394 lambs from this manor and wethers from Wattisfield, washing and shearing this year 10s., with cost of one bushel of wheat sold as above, 15d.[40]

In red ochre[41] bought for marking sheep on two occasions, 2d.

Sum 20s. 7d.   Approved.

Stipend of the household servants [*famuli*] In the stipend of four ploughmen p.a. 28s., to each of them p.a. 7s.

In the stipend of John Dennis, shepherd of the ewes p.a., 6s.

In the stipend of Roger, shepherd of the hoggets for the first half of this year, 2s. 8d. by agreement.

Item in stipend of John Man, shepherd of the hoggets for the last half of the said year, 3s.

Sum 39s. 8d.   Approved.

Threshing and winnowing In 52 qrs 2 bus. of wheat and rye threshed by task, 17s. 5d., per qr 4d.

In 118 qrs ½ bus. of barley, peas, bullimong and oats threshed by task, 19s. 8d., per qr 2d.

In 170 qrs 2½ bus. of various corn winnowed by task, 9s. 5½d., per 3 qrs 2d.

Sum 46s. 6½d. Approved.

Corn bought None this year.

Stock bought In one cow bought from John Lester before calving, 8s. 1d.

Item in one cow bought from Roger Prede before calving, 7s. 7½d.

In 6 calves bought from the [*lessee of the*] dairy by agreement as shown elsewhere,[42] 6s.

Item in 12 chickens bought for making capons, 12d.

Sum 22s. 8½d.   Approved.

Minute expenses In bonuses to 4 ploughmen, 2 shepherds and one dairyherd, and one shepherd at Wattisfield, at Christmas and Easter, 16d. In a bonus to the same at the Purification of St Mary, 4d.

In expenses of 28 men with 14 ploughs all coming to the Ploughale from the lord's custom for one day, with expenses of the household servants of the manor and others all counted, of which in the price of 2 bushels of wheat from sales, 2s. 6d. <9s. 5d.> \7s./

In 480[43] faggots made by task, 2s. 4d., per 120 7d.

In tawing one stot hide remaining in the hands of the tawer, 11d.

In forging one dung fork, 1d.

In castrating the lord's lambs this year, 4d.

---

[40] The wheat was presumably for bread for the shearers.
[41] Red ochre was used for marking the sheep, perhaps to identify the lord's sheep or for marking rams before mating.
[42] The six calves appear in the stock account, below.
[43] Most numerals in these accounts are given using the small hundred (five score), but the faggots are enumerated using the large hundred (six score). The former is usually signalled by the presence of a superscript *Cmi* above the numerals, the latter by a superscript *Cma*. So, in this case, CCCC \Cma/ = 4 x 120 = 480.

In tithes given for 18 faggots \from tithes/ not out of stock cash in lieu, 6d.
In 4 fetlocks with two nails bought for a stot, 7d.
Given to the household ploughmen of the manor at the time of sowing all of the seed, in order that they work better this year [*ut melior' labore*], <6s. 8d.> 5s.[44]
In 4 acres of pasture hired [*loc'*] from Walter Frances to enable the lord's sheep to be driven to pasture, 16d.[45]
In parchment bought for writing this account, 6d.

Sum 20s. 3d.

Approved.

Weeding and mowing In weeding the lord's corn, nothing this year because by works as elsewhere.
In mowing the great meadow and the little meadow this year altogether, 10s. 2d.
In spreading and turning the herbage and likewise collecting the hay, nothing this year because by customary works as elsewhere.
In mowing one piece of pasture at Harts Haugh [*Horteshagh*] pertaining to High Hall, 13d.
In spreading herbage and turning and likewise collecting hay, 8d.

Sum 11s. 11d.

Approved.

Customary harvest works In expenses of the sergeant, hayward, two carters, one overseer of the harvest, one cook and stacker and one loader for 5 weeks at harvest with the expenses of 81 harvest boonworks from this manor and 6 boonworks and harvest works from High Hall, likewise with the expenses of 2 ploughmen, three shepherds, one dairyherd, one smith, one miller and others at the Reapale.
In bread bought as in the price of wheat above and rye, 9s. In ale bought, 14s. In meat bought, 8s. 7d., of which the price of 2 wethers and one ewe as sold above, price of pelts, 2s. In 5 geese bought, 15d. Item in fish and herrings bought, 2s. 1d.
In milk, cheese, eggs and butter bought, 2s. 10d. In pepper and saffron bought, 4d.
In garlic bought, 1d. In salt bought, 2d. In oat meal, 6d. And so per head [*for the harvest workers*] in food and pottage 1¾d., minus 6½d.[46]
In candles bought, 3d.
In 4 pairs of gloves bought, 8d.
In a bonus to the hayward at the day of the boonworks by order of the lord, 14d.
Item in payment to Goodal, overseer of the harvest, as the cost of his stipend, 12d.
In the stipend of John Cook, cook and stacker at the harvest, 4s.
In the stipend of John Frances, loader at the harvest, 4s.
In 456½ customary harvest works from this manor and 3 works from High Hall, expenses of each of them ¼d. 9s. 6¾d. and half a ¼d. of which for the reeve ¾d.
Item in 81 customary boonworks from this manor and 3 boonworks from High Hall, expenses of each of them ¾d., 10½d., of which for the reeve ¼d. and ½.
Given to the reapers at Doucedeux by the hayward by the order of the lord, 4d.

Sum 60s. 8¼d. and half a ¼d.

Approved.

---

[44] The ploughmen were *famuli*, employees of the manor, whose 5s. bonus was paid for helping the customary tenants at the Ploughale.

[45] An exceptional arrangement, which indicates shortages of pasture and, again, hints at extreme weather conditions.

[46] Marginal note.

38

Wages In the wages of Nicholas Fuller sergeant there for the year, less 5 weeks during the harvest because he was at the lord's table, 47s., taken per week 12d.

Sum 47s.   Approved.

Steward's expenses In the expenses of the steward at the court held there on Thursday in the Feast of the Apostles Peter and Paul, 3s. 5d., the price of one ewe and 3 capons from stock elsewhere.

In parchment bought for two courts, 6d.

In expenses of the lord's supervisor at the branding of the lambs, 5d.

Sum 4s. 4d.   Approved.

Lady's expenses In the expenses of lady and lord Sir John Wingfield and others being there on Thursday in Easter week for one court held and for necessaries taken in this manor. In cheese, 6d., and no more from expenses here because all charged through the lord's hospitality.

Sum 6d.   Approved.

Foreign expenses with pardons In the expenses of a carter from this manor going up to Bury seeking salt fish for the lord's hospitality, 1d.

In pardons made by the lady to William Hawes for certain amercements in the court 5s., from the responsibility of the hayward. Item in allowances, [*blank*].

Sum 5s. 1d.   Approved.

Cash delivered Delivered to the lady by the hand of Nicholas Fuller on two occasions from issues of the manor by one tally, 40s.

Item delivered to the same lady by the hand of the same at the end of the year by <one> \the said/ tally, 56s.

Item delivered to the same lady by the hand of Vincent for 4 bushels of barley, sold to the same above for the lady, nothing because the bailiff accounts for it.

Item delivered to the lady by the hand of Simon Hauker for lambs' wool sold to him this year, 22s.

Item delivered to the same lady by the hand of Roger Daye for the lease of the dairy by one tally, 117s.

Item delivered to the same lady by the hand of Walter Frances the hayward for rents and farms by one tally, £9 14s.

Item delivered to the same lady by the hand of the same Walter at other times at the end of the year by one tally, 50s.

Item delivered to Alexander Bron <to the lady at other times> from the responsibility of the same Walter <by the hand of Alexander Bron> when the lady was absent in London, 13s. 4d.

Item delivered to the same lady by the hand of the said Walter on the lady's return [*recess'*] from London by one tally, 30s.

Item delivered to Nicholas Tiptot, sergeant of Westhorpe, for rents and farms of High Hall by the hands of tenants of the lord of High Hall in Westhorpe without tally, as shown in foreign receipts, 48s. 3d.

Item delivered to the lady for the arrears of Walter Frances in the preceding year without tally, 12s. 2d.

Item delivered to the same lady by the hand of Simon Hauker for wool sold to him last year, so from arrears, 25s.

Sum £30 7s. 9d.   Approved.

39

Sum of all expenses and deliveries £51 0s. 23d. quarter of half a ¼d., half a ¼d. and a third part of ¼d. And owed, £7 3s. 1¼d. and a third part of ¼d.

From which, allowed to him 14s. 4d. for various payments, charges, disallowances and sales at the audit.

And thus owed £6 8s. 9¼d. and a third part of ¼d. Of which, upon [*i.e. owed by*] John Brangwayn recently the shepherd 6s. 8d.; upon Nicholas Swon recently shepherd 17s. 1d.; upon Julian Osbern and his sister 13s. 4d.; upon Robert Osbern 40d.; upon the tenants of the land recently of Robert Hawes 6s. 8d.; upon Walter Frances, hayward this year, 16s. 8¼d. [*torn*] half a quarter of ¼d. and a third part of ¼d.; upon Simon Hauker for skins of the ewes sold to him above, 6s. 8d.

And thus upon the said Nicholas Fuller by himself 8s. 4¼d. half a ¼d. and half a quarter of ¼d.

[*Reverse*]

Walsham

Issues of the grange there [*illeg.*] and allowances of various grains and other stock during the 14th and 15th years of Richard II.

Wheat

7 qrs remain. From the total issues of the grange there by 2 tallies against John Page the lord's granger sworn, 40 qrs 6 bus. of wheat threshed by task. From the issues of a new grange for harvest expenses without tally, 5½ bus. of wheat threshed and winnowed at harvest by the manorial servants. Received from [*illeg.*] for harvest expenses, 2 bus. of wheat.[47]

Sum 42 qrs 4 bus.

From which, in seed upon 64 acres of land in various pieces of land, of which in Hall Croft 16 acres; in one piece below North Haugh 10 acres; item at *Childerwell* 6 acres, except another 6 acres there [*which are sown*] with barley, as below; item at High Hall below Burchards Close 18 acres; item there in Hall Croft 9 acres; item in *Walpoles Croft* 5 acres, [*total seed*] 16 qrs 1 bus. by one tally against the hayward, sown at 2 bus. an acre plus in total 1 bus.

In the contract [*convenc'*] of the granger, 1 bus.

Delivered to Westhorpe for provisioning the lord's hospitality by 1 tally with beans below against Thomas Baker the lord's baker, 7 qrs 4 bus.

Item delivered to Westhorpe to sell at Ipswich in the present year by 1 tally against the steward of the lord's hospitality and for the lady, 2 qrs of wheat.

In the contract of a smith for forging iron for two ploughs p.a., cost stated within, 4 bus.

In livery of the manorial servants as shown below and for bread above, 11 qrs 5 bus. of which for bread at harvest, cost within 3 qrs 6 bus.

Given to Adam Blayer, sergeant, of Bowthorpe [*Bouthorp*][48] p.a. in remuneration for his services, 2 bus.

Item delivered to Wattisfield for livery of Ralph the shepherd there without tally, 1 qr.

---

[47] Marginal note: 'R Received 1 bus. more allowed to him and ½.'
[48] Possibly of Burthorpe, a hamlet in Barrow, west of Bury St Edmunds.

In sales within 3 qrs 3 bus., of which for harvest expenses 1 qr and for the Ploughale 2 bus.

And for expenses around the washing and shearing of sheep, 1 bus.

Sum as above.   It balances.

Rye

From the total issues of the grange there this year by 1 tally against the lord's granger, 11 qrs 4 bus. and threshed by task. From the issues of the new grange without tally for the livery of the manorial servants and expenses of the harvest, 1½ bus. of rye threshed and winnowed by the manorial servants at the harvest.[49]

Sum 11 qrs 5½ bus.

From which, in seed sown upon \11/ acres of land in *le Conynger Wong*, 2 qrs 2 bus. of rye by 1 tally against the said hayward, at 2 bus. per acre, less in total this year, 4 qrs.

In the contract of the granger, 1 bus.

In livery of the manorial servants as shown below, 8 qrs 2 bus. of which for the present year 3 qrs.

Item delivered to Wattisfield for the livery of the shepherd there without tally, 7 bus.

In sales within for harvest expenses, 1½ bus. of rye.

Sum as below.   It balances.

Barley

Remaining from the preceding account for harvest bread, 2½ bus. \approved/. From the total issues of the grange there this year by 2 tallies against the said granger, 58 quarters 6½ bus. of barley threshed by task, of which at High Hall, 19 qrs 2 bus.[50]

Sum 59 qrs 1 bus.   Approved.

From which, in seed upon 61 acres of land in various parcels, by estimate 23 qrs of barley by 1 tally against the said hayward, sown at 4 bus. per acre plus in total 1 bus.

In the contract of the granger, 1 bus.

In livery of the manorial servants shown below and for harvest bread, 7 qrs 6 bus., of which for harvest bread 2½ bus.

Delivered to Wattisfield for the livery of the shepherd there without tally, 1 qr.

Item delivered to Westhorpe to make malt, by 1 tally against Thomas Baker the lord's baker with oats below, 23 qrs 7 bus.

In sales within, 3 qrs 3 bus. of barley of which to John Vincent 4 bus.

Sum as above.   It balances.   Approved.

Beans and Peas

And remaining in the grange, 2½ bus. of peas. From the issues of the grange there this year by 2 tallies against the said granger, 17 qrs 1 bus. threshed by task. From the same issues by estimate in straw for feeding stots, ewes, wethers and hoggets of the lord in winter, 5 qrs of peas.[51]

Sum 22 qrs 3½ bus.   Approved.

---

[49] Marginal note: 'R' 1 bus. more 6 bus. of grain and ½.'
[50] Marginal note: 'R' 3 qrs 6½ bus. more allowed to him.'
[51] Marginal note: 'R' 2 qrs 5 bus. more allowed to him.'

41

From which, in seed upon 36 acres of land in various parcels by estimate, 9 qrs 2 bus. by 1 tally against the said hayward, at 2 bus. per acre plus in total 2 bus. because equally [*quia pars*] beans.

In the contract of the granger, 1 bus.

In the livery of the manorial servants as shown below, 2 qrs 3½ bus. of which for the harvest bread and for bread for stots from custom, 7½ bus.

Delivered to Thomas Baker the lord's baker for bread for the lord's horses for the lord's hospitality by 1 tally with wheat above, 1 qr of beans.

In feeding pigeons in winter, 2 bus.

In fattening 12 piglets for the lord's hospitality from here in winter, 2 bus.

In bread baked for stots this year, 4 bus.

In sales within, 3 qrs 5 bus. of peas.

In feeding the lord's ewes, wethers, gimmers and stots in winter by estimate in straw above, 5 qrs.

Sum as above.   It balances.   Approved.

Bullemong[52]

From the issues of the grange there this year by 1 tally with oats below against the said granger, 1 qr threshed by works, and no more because the residue was expended as feed for the lord's hoggets in winter. [*The quantity is*] not entered, because was partly expended as straw and the quantity unknown.[53]

Sum 1 qr. And delivered to oats below.   It balances.   Approved.

Oats

From the issues of the grange there this year by 2 tallies of which 1 tally with bullemong above against the said granger, 41 qrs 1 bus. threshed by task. From the same issues by estimate in 160 sheaves of oats for fodder for calves of issue and ewes and lambs, of which 15 sheaves to the bushel, 1 qr 2 bus. 3 pecks of oats. Received from bullemong above for feed, 1 qr And from rent at the Feast of St Edmund King and Martyr p.a., 20 qrs 2 bus. of oats.[54]

Sum 63 qrs 5 bus. 3 pecks.   Approved.

From which, in seed upon 65 acres of land in various pieces by estimate, 20 qrs 2 bus. by 1 tally against the said hayward, at 2½ bus. per acre less in total ½ bus.

In allowance for the tenement of John Frost, reeve this year, 2 bus. ½ peck and a third part of a peck.

Item in allowance for the tenement of John Frances, hayward this year, 3 pecks.

Item in allowance for various tenements in the lord's hands, both longstanding and new [*tam de veteri quam de novo*], as shown by 1 bill, 3 qrs 1 bus. a quarter and ½ a quarter of 1 pk. and 2 parts of ½ a bus. of oats.

In meal made for pottage for 4 ploughmen, 2 shepherds and one dairyherd p.a. 1 qr 6 bus.

In the contract of the granger, 1 bus.

Delivered to Wattisfield for the livery of the shepherd there, 2 bus. of oats.

Item delivered to Westhorpe for fodder for the horses of the lord and visitors [*superven'*] by 1 tally with barley above, 2 qrs 6 bus.

---

[52] Bullemong is an equal mix of oats and peas seed.

[53] Marginal note. This entry indicates that the bullemong was not threshed after harvest, but left tied up in sheaves and the sheaves were then given to the livestock as fodder.

[54] Marginal note: 'R' 1 bus. 3 pks. more allowed to him ½.'

In fodder for the carthorses and stots this year, 11 qrs 11 bus.
In fodder for 3 carthorses going by cart to Norwich with other horses to fetch from there a certain millstone for the mill at Westhorpe, 3 bus.
In fodder for the horses of lady and lord Sir John Wingfield and others visiting the manor on Thursday in Easter week, 3½ bus.
In fodder for the steward's horse and others for a court held there in the Feast of the Apostles Peter and Paul, 2 bus. of oats.
In feed for ewes at the time of lambing, for calves of issue[55] and lambs of issue, by estimation in sheaves above 1 qr 2 bus. 3 pecks of oats.
In sales within 21 qrs 1 bus. 3 pecks half a quarter of 1 peck and a third of ½ bus. and 2 parts of 1 peck of oats, of which 1 bus. was for harvest expenses.
Sum as above.   It balances.   Approved.

Multure at the mill
Remaining in the hands of the miller for harvest bread, 1 qr 7 bus. \Approved./
From the farm of one windmill leased this year to Thomas Hauker, 12 qrs of multure at the mill.
Sum 13 qrs 7 bus. Approved.
From which, in the livery of the manorial servants and for harvest bread and customary ploughteams as shown below, 9 qrs 4½ bus.
In bread baked for carthorses and stots this year 1 qr 2 bus. 3 pecks.
In expenses of the carthorses drawing carts to Bury to fetch salt fish for the lord's hospitality, ½ bus.
Delivered to Wattisfield for the livery of the shepherd there, 1 qr ½ bus. of multure.
Sum 12 qrs.   Approved.
And remaining in the hands of the miller, 1 qr 6 bus. 3 pecks of multure at the mill for harvest bread.

Livery of the manorial servants
From wheat as above, 11 qrs 5 bus. From rye as above, 8 qrs 2 bus. From barley as above to the same, 7 qrs 6 bus. From peas as above to the same, 2 qrs 3½ bus. From multure at the mill as above to the same, 9 qrs 4½ bus.
Sum 39 qrs 5 bus.
From which, in issues after the account was discharged, 17 qrs 2 bus. 3 pecks of multure of which for the manorial servants 4 qrs 4 bus.; and for customary tenants for their harvest bread in arrears for 2 years, 2 qrs 6 bus. 3 pecks.
In the livery of 4 ploughmen, 1 shepherd and 1 dairyherd for the year, less 4 weeks in the harvest because 2 manorial servants were fed at the lord's table, 25 qrs 2 bus. Each taking each one quarter per 12 weeks, of which the 4th part is wheat.
In the livery of Roger the shepherd looking after the lord's hoggets for the first half of the year this year, 2 qrs 1 bus. taken by the quarter as above.
Item in the livery of John Man shepherd of hoggets and lambs for the last half-year, this year, 2 qrs 1 bus. 1 peck taking one quarter as above.
Item in the livery of Nicholas Shepherd looking after the sheep of the cullet for 7½ weeks in the present year, 5 bus. taking one quarter as above, of which 3 bus. were wheat.

[55] Calves and lambs born in this season.

In bread baked for expenses of customary tenants making 41 plough services, as shown below, of which each customary tenant takes for each plough work 6 loaves, of which 20 are baked from each bushel, 1 qr 4 bus. 1 peck.

In bread baked for 456½ harvest works from this manor below expenses and 3 works from High Hall made this year, that is for each work 2 loaves, of which 20 are baked from each bushel. And for 81 boonworks from this manor and 3 boonworks from High Hall, that is for each work 1 loaf, of which 20 are baked from each bushel as above, 6 qrs 2 bus. ½ peck.

Sum 55 qrs 2 bus. 1½ pecks.　　　　　　Approved.

And so exceeded by 15 qrs 5 bus. 1½ pks., of which owed to the manorial servants 2 qrs 6½ bus. and arrears for harvest bread of customary tenants for 2 years, 12 qrs 6 bus. 3½ pecks altogether.

Acres sown this year issues of all kinds of corn, 237 acres.　　　Approved.
And reaped by customary works.　　　　　　　　　　　　　　It balances.

Carthorses

4 carthorses remain.　　　Sum 4.
From which in murrain in the winter, one old [*cron'*] \testified [*ti*] by the supervisor/[56]
Sum 1.　　　3 cart horses remain.　　　Approved.

Stots

4 remain. Received from the lord's stable by the hand of Coggeshall, 1.
Sum 5.
From which in murrain in summer, 1 weak stot. \testified/
And in murrain at the end of the year, 1 weak stot. \testified/
Sum 2.　　　3 stots remain.　　　Approved.

Colts

From Nicholas Tiptot sergeant of Westhorpe in the present year 3 \approved/ colts beyond issues.
Sum 3.　3 colts aged 1½ years remain.　　　Approved.

Oxen

4 oxen remain. Added from castrated bull below 1
Sum 5.　　　　　　　Approved.
From which delivered for the use of the lord's hospitality at Westhorpe in the present year by 1 tally with cows below, 1 old ox.
Sum 1.　　　4 oxen remain for stock.

Bulls

One remains from the preceding account 1
Sum 1.
And castrated and added to total oxen above.　　　　　　It balances.

---

[56] The sign *ti* appears above a number of livestock items in this account, and was clearly added at the audit. It appears when those presenting the account claimed that an animal had died, so the auditors must have sought additional verification and noted 'testified', *testifico*, when they were satisfied.

Cows

20 cows remain, of which 2 are old. From purchases within before calving, 2 cows.
Sum 22.
From which, delivered to Westhorpe for the lord's larder in the present year by 1 tally with oxen above, 2 cows. Stolen from the pasture at the end of the year on the eve of St Matthew the Apostle <one cow> \disallowed because not testified by the homage of the court/. In sales at the audit, 1 stolen cow.[57]
Sum 3.   19 cows remain of which 4 are old.   Approved.

Steers and heifers

Added from un-castrated bullocks below 1.
Sum 1.   1 un-castrated bullock remains for stock.   Approved.

Bullocks and heifers

One un-castrated bullock remains. Added from calves below, 6. From a heriot after the death of Simon Puttock in winter as shown by the court roll, 1 heifer first calving.
Sum 8.   Approved.
From which added to bullocks above, 1 un-castrated
Delivered to Richard Bass, leader of the ploughs at Rickinghall, and to the deputy [*loco*] sergeant there by 1 tally in winter 5, of which 1 is first calving. And 1 heifer from a heriot above.
Sum 7.   1 un-castrated bullock remains.

Calves

6 remain
From purchases from the farmer of cows by agreement as shown within, 6 calves.
Sum 12.   Approved.
From which added to bullocks and heifers above, 6. In murrain at the end of the year, 1\testified/.
Sum 7.   5 calves remain over and above issues.   Approved.

Hides

From murrain of a carthorse above, 1. From murrain of stots above, 2. From murrain of a calf above, 1.
Sum 4 hides.   Approved.
From which, added to dressed hides below, 1 stot hide.
Item added to tanned hides below, 1 calf hide Approved.
Sum 2.   2 horse hides remain unfinished [*crud'*].

Dressed hides

1 dressed stot hide remains in the hands of the bleacher. Received from dressed stot hides above, 1.
Sum 2 hides.   Approved.
From which, used for repairs, 1 horse hide.
Sum 1.   1 dressed stot hide remains in the hands of John Combes.

---

[57] The claim of the relevant official that the cow had been stolen had to be verified by the homage of the manorial court, and the failure to do so – whether because the official was lying or because the procedure had simply not been followed – resulted in the claim for loss being charged as a notional 'sale' at the audit of the account against the official.

Tanned hides
From a tanned calf-skin added above 1.
  Sum 1. 1 tanned calf-skin remains in the hands of John Barker.   Approved.

Rams
5 rams remain in the custody of John Dennis.
                              Sum 5.   Approved.
From which in murrain in the present year, 2 rams.
Delivered to Wattisfield before shearing to the fold of Ralph the shepherd there
without tally, 3 rams.
                    Sum as above.   It balances.

Wethers
4 remain in the custody of Dennis. Received from Wattisfield after shearing for
harvest expenses, 2 wethers. From a heriot after the death of William son of the late
Elias Tiptot, 1 as shown by the court roll.
                              Sum 7.   Approved.
From which, in murrain in the present year, 1 \testified/. Delivered to Wattisfield
before shearing without tally, 3 wethers. And after shearing, 1 from a heriot. In sales
within for harvest expenses, the cost of the pelts of 2 wethers.
                    Sum as above.   It balances.   Approved.

Ewes
274 ewes remain in the custody of Dennis, of which 20 are crones, for the lord's
larder in the coming year. Added from gimmers below in the custody of Dennis, 40.
From Nicholas Tiptot, sergeant of Westhorpe, before lambing and shearing, 6 ewes.
                            Sum 320.   Approved.
From which delivered to the lord's larder in the present year by 1 tally, 20 crone
ewes. In murrain before lambing and shearing, 13 \testified/. Delivered to Nicholas Tiptot, sergeant of Westhorpe, to the fold of the shepherd of the ewes there
after lambing and before shearing without tally, 5 ewes. Killed by the dogs of John
Hawes in the little meadow before lambing and shearing <1 ewe>. In murrain after
shearing, 2 \testified/. Item to the butchers for the expenses of lord Sir John Wingfield and others being there for one court held in the Feast of Apostles Peter and
Paul, after shearing, 1. In sales within for harvest expenses, price of a pelt of 1 ewe.
In sales at the audit, 1 ewe devoured before lambing and shearing as above, 12d.[58]
    Sum 43. 277 ewes remain, of which 52 are crones and of which 1 is in the
custody of Peter Robwood.   Approved.

Hoggets and Gimmers
40 gimmers remain in the custody of Dennis. And added from lambs below 469
hoggets and gimmers, of which 449 are in the custody of Brangwayn and 20 older
lambs [de refus'] are in the custody of Dennis. Received from Nicholas Tiptot
sergeant of Westhorpe at the Feast of the Purification of St Mary before shearing, 2
hoggets supplied from Willisham [Wylasham].[59]
                              Sum 511.

---

[58] Marginal note: not an actual sale, but a debit against the official because the story about John Hawes'
    dogs having eaten the sheep was not accepted.
[59] Willisham, located 18 miles south-east of Walsham, was another manor in this estate. An account
    for Willisham from 1385–6 is incorrectly described in the SA/B catalogue as being for Walsham,
    HA504/3/2, see Introduction, p. xxix.

From which added to ewes above, 40 gimmers. In murrain in winter before shearing, 63, of which 41 are from the responsibility of Roger the shepherd and 22 are from the responsibility of John Man the shepherd. Delivered to Nicholas Typtot sergeant of Westhorpe at the fold of Wroo [*ad faldam Wroo*] before shearing, 407 hoggets and gimmers, of which in the present year 220 of the best and 187 [*delivered*] on the day of shearing, 187.

Sum 510. And remaining 1 gimmer in the custody of Dennis.   Approved.

Lambs
469 lambs remain, of which in the custody of Brangwayn 449 and in the custody of Dennis 20 older lambs. And from the issues of ewes above, 264 lambs, of which from the responsibility of Dennis 259 and from the responsibility of John Man 5 lambs. And no more because 22 ewes are sterile this year. From Richard Bas, deputy sergeant of Rickinghall, at the Feast of St Barnabas the Apostle before shearing by 1 tally, 165 lambs. Approved.
From Nicholas Tiptot, sergeant of Westhorpe, at the same feast by 1 tally, 48 lambs.
Approved.
Sum 946.   Approved.
From which, added to hoggets and gimmers above, 469. In murrain before tithes, 11. In tithes given, 25. Given to the shepherd, one called the *Markinglamb*. In expenses of lady and lord John Wingfield and others being there for one court held in Easter week, 1 lamb before shearing.
Delivered to Westhorpe for provisioning the lord's hospitality without tally, 2 *cokerell* [*sic*], of which one was from the pasture before shearing. In murrain before shearing, 2 lambs \testified/. Item in murrain after shearing, 9 \testified/. Killed by dogs after shearing, <1 lamb>. In sales within before shearing, 40 older lambs. Approved. In sales at the audit after shearing, 1 lamb priced 6d.[60]
Sum 561.   Approved.
385 lambs remain, of which one is in the custody of Peter Robwood.

Fleeces
From sheep above sheared from the responsibility of Dennis, 282 wool fleeces.
Sum 282 fleeces.   Approved.
From which in tithes given, 28 wool fleeces. In sales within, 252 fleeces weighing in total 34 stone of wool, a stone of 10lbs. In sales at the audit, 2 poor quality fleeces upon Peter Robhood, 5d.[61]
Sum as above.   It balances.   Approved.

Lamb fleeces
From lambs above sheared 394 skins, and no more because one lamb was not sheared because of weakness.
Sum 394.   And sales within.   It balances.   Approved.

---

[60] Marginal note. The claim that dogs had killed one of the lambs was rejected, and the lamb charged as a sale instead against the official.
[61] Marginal note.

Sheep skins[62]
From sheep above in murrain 79 skins, of which 63 are hogget skins. Received from Wattisfield, of which sold on the day of shearing, 22 skins.

Sum 101. And sales within. It balances. Approved.

Pelts[63]
From sheep above in murrain, 2. From ewes butchered above, 4. From Wattisfield, 5 pelts.

Sum 11. From sales within. It balances. Approved.

Lamb skins
From lambs above in murrain 22, of which 9 were weak and after shearing.

Sum 22. And sales within. It balances. Approved.

Capons
12 remain. And rent p.a. 8. From moving up from poultry below, this year 12.

Sum 32.

From which, in allowance for *tenementa* in the hands of the lord as shown by the said bill, 4. Delivered to Westhorpe for provisioning the lord's hospitality by 1 tally, 8. In expenses of lady and lord Sir John Wingfield and others being there at one court held in Easter week and for supervising in this manor, 2 capons. In expenses of said lord Sir John Wingfield and the steward and others for one court held in the Feast of the Apostles Peter and Paul, 3 capons. In murrain, 3 capons \testified/, price 9d.[64] In sales at the audit, 3 capons.

Sum 20. 12 capons remain for stock. Approved.

Hens and cockerels
1 cockerel, 12 hens remain. From rent p.a. at Christmas, 123½ hens. From rent of High Hall p.a., 21.

Sum 157½ chickens. Approved.

From which, in allowance for the *tenementum* of John Frost, reeve this year, 3. Item for the *tenementum* of John Franceys, hayward this year, 1. Item in allowance for various tenements in the lord's hands as shown by the said bill, 9¾ hens. Item from various tenements pertaining to High Hall in the lord's hands, 11½ hens. Delivered to Nicholas Tiptot, sergeant of Westhorpe, by the hands of tenants of High Hall in Westhorpe, 2 hens. Item allowed for provisions of the lord's hospitality by 2 tallies against the steward of the lord's hospitality, 89 hens. In murrain in winter from stock, 12 hens \testified/. In sales within 16¼ hens, of which from the responsibility of the hayward 8¾ hens and from the responsibility of the reeve 7½ hens.

Sum 144½. And remain 1 cockerel 12 hens for stock. Approved.

Eggs
From the issues of hens above, nothing because the hens were leased at farm for money within. From rent at Easter, 720[65] eggs. From rent at High Hall for the same term, 105 eggs.

Sum 825 eggs. Approved.

---

[62] The skins of sheep which had died before shearing.
[63] The skins of sheep which had died after shearing, and so there was less wool on a pelt than on a skin.
[64] Marginal note.
[65] Using the long hundred of 120.

From which, in allowance for the reeve's tenement this year, 21. Item for the hayward's tenement, 10 eggs. Item in allowance for tenements in the lord's hands as shown by the said bill, 102 eggs. Item for various tenements in the lord's hands pertaining to High Hall, 39 eggs. Delivered for provisioning the lord's hospitality at Westhorpe by 1 tally against the steward of the lord's hospitality, 540 eggs. In sales within, 113 eggs of which from the responsibility of the reeve, 66 and from the responsibility of the hayward, 47 eggs.

Sum as above.   It balances.   Approved.

Poultry
From the issues of hens, nothing because aforesaid. And purchased within, 12.

Sum 12.   And reckoned in capons made above.   It balances.

Dovecote
From the issues of one dovecote at the manor and one dovecote at High Hall this year, 543 pigeons, tithes excepted.

Sum 543.

And delivered for provisioning the lord's hospitality by 1 tally against the steward of the lord's guests. It balances.

Cumin
From rent from the Prior of Bricett[66] p.a., ½lb cumin.

Sum ½lb cumin.   And sales within. It balances.

Pepper
From rent received from Walter Frances for the tenement recently of John Pinfold pertaining to High Hall, ½lb pepper.

Sum ½lb pepper.   And sales within. It balances.

Ploughing services
From the issues of 9 greater customary *tenementa* this year who provide 5½ plough-teams this year, 27½ ploughing services taken at the seasons of winter and Lent. That is, from each whole ploughteam five ploughings services, and they shall receive from the lord for each ploughteam, 6 loaves of mixed grain, of which 20 made per bushel, plus an allowance of 2 winter works.

From the issues of 9 other customary tenants who provide 4½ plough-teams this year, 13½ ploughing services. Of which, each ploughteam shall do 3 ploughing services and receive from the lord for each plough, 6 loaves made from the said grains at the said weight, but without any allowance of works.

From the issues of customary tenants of High Hall this year, nothing.

Sum 41 ploughings.

And expended in ploughing the lord's land at the aforesaid seasons.   It balances.

---

[66] In 1291 Bricett priory was assessed for rent worth 11s. from the land it held in Walsham: *Taxatio Ecclesiastica Angliae et Walliae Auctoritate P. Nicholai IV Circa A.D.1291* (London, 1802), p. 131. For the priory itself see E. Martin, *Great Bricett manor and priory* (Suffolk Institute of Archaeology and History, 2021).

Boonwork called Ploughale

From the issues of the lord's customary tenants who provide this year 14 boonworks.
Sum 14. And expended in sowing the lord's wheat.

It balances.

Winter works

From customary services for a half day, 963 winter and summer works, price per work ½d. From customary services from High Hall, 10 works.

Sum 973 works. Approved.

From which, in allowance for the reeve's tenement because as above this year, 29 works. Item for the hayward's tenement this year because as above, 8½ works. In allowance for various tenements in the lord's hands, 176¾ and a third part of 1 work.[67]

In 27½ ploughings expended above 55 works, for each ploughing 2 works. In 4½ tumbrels loaded this year, 4½ works that is for each man carrying manure, 1 winter work.

Item in allowance for the tenement of Robert Wynge pertaining to High Hall in the lord's hands and at farm, 10 works.

In stubble gathered in the present year, 159 works. In weeds [*loll' and darnel*] removed in preparation for sowing wheat, 66. In harrowing rye, 4. In harrowing oats, 9. In sowing furrows of wheat, 31. In sowing furrows of peas, 20. In drainage furrows made at the time of sowing wheat, 26.

In stacking straw to serve one thatcher upon the kitchen and upon another building, 61 works. In daubing clay [*argilland*] and plastering the kitchen, and in one oven made in the dairy, 69 works.

In filling dung carts with dung, 40 works. In spreading dung upon the land in summer, 10. In spreading herbage in *Brodole* and in the little meadow, 10. In loading carts with stubble in the present year, 11.

In laying clay and stamping it for the millcote and in putting clay on the said building, 13. In shredding withies [*virs'*] for making hurdles, 4. In making a hedge at North Haugh and other places, 10. In harrowing barley, 20. In stopping up gaps at Lady's Wood, 4 works.

In sales within, 130¾ and two parts of 1 work.

Sum as above. It balances. Approved.

Carrying services

From the issues of 7 customary carrying services at the will of the lord [*averagium peddat' ad voluntatem domini*][68] from custom, price per work 1d.

Sum 7 carrying services.

---

[67] Thus a total of 176¾ winter works were unavailable for deployment on the lord's demesne in this year, because the villein lands from which they were due were no longer tenanted on the traditional service tenancy. Either the land has been abandoned and is lying uncultivated or it has been leased out for cash instead. Over half of the works are still used, which is an unusually high uptake for demesnes at this date, but reflects the importance of securing a labour force during the critical period of the harvest. Most lords were leasing their demesnes by this late date or winding down their use of labour services, which were generally unpopular among tenants of villein land.

[68] In the 1396–7, 1402–3, 1406–7 and 1426–7 accounts this phrase appears unequivocally as *averagium pedat'*. Audrey McLaughlin translated the entry here as carrying services on foot, from the Latin *pedale*. But the later references are unquestionably *pedat'* and the word probably relates 'to the will of the lord' rather than to the carrying service, in which case *pedacia* (vagabond, wanderer, roamer) suggests itself: these were probably carrying services to any place as directed by the lord.

From which in allowance of various tenements in the lord's hands, 1 carrying service. In sales within, 6 carrying works.

Sum as above.   It balances.

Manure carrying services

From customary services without resumption [*sine resumpt'*], 9 manure carrying services and allowed to the same for each man carrying manure, 1 winter work, price per carrying service 2d.

Sum 9 carrying services.   Approved.

From which, in allowance for the reeve's tenement, ¼ of a work. Item for the hayward's tenement this year, ¼. In allowance for various tenements in the lord's hands, 2¾ carryings, a third part of a carry and a third part of ½ a manure carrying service.

In carrying manure this year, 4½ carrying services. In sales within, ¼ of ½ a ¼ of 1 carry and 2 parts of 1 carry and 2 parts of ½ a manure carrying services.

Sum as above.   It balances.

Weeding works

From customary services 188, price per work ½d. From customary services of High Hall, 3.

Sum 191.

From which in allowance for the reeve's tenement this year, 4¾ works. Item for the hayward's tenement this year, 2¼ works. Item in allowance for various tenements in the lord's hands, 24¾ weeding works.

In weeding the lord's barley this year, nil. In sales within, 157½ works from the responsibility of the hayward and 3 from the responsibility of the reeve.

Sum as above. It balances. Approved.

Mowing works

From customary services by ½ days 49 mowing works, price per work 1½d.

Sum 49 works.   Approved.

From which in allowance for the reeve's tenement, ¾. Item in allowance for the hayward's tenement this year, 3¼. Item in allowance for various tenements in the lord's hands, 6¾ mowing works.

In sales within, 42 mowing works.

Sum as above. It balances. Approved.

Carriage of hay

From services according to custom that have carriage without resumption and without price [*torn*] works, 10 carryings this year.

Sum 10 carryings. And expended fully in carrying hay.

It balances.

Haymaking works

From the issues of customary services as many as the lord indicates, lifting, turning and stacking all the hay without resumption. It balances.

Harvest works

From customary services for a whole day to reap, tie and stack the lord's corn, 643 works, for which each shall receive from the lord at noon and for his supper 2 loaves of mixed grain, of which 20 made per bushel, and 4 herrings, price per work 1d. From the issues of customary tenants from High Hall p.a., 111 works.

Sum 754 works.

From which, in allowance for the reeve's tenement this year, 6¼ works. Item for the hayward's tenement this year, 6¾ works. In allowance for various tenements in the lord's hands, 96¾ works. Item for various tenements in the lord's hands pertaining to High Hall, 77 works. Allowed to the bailiff of Westhorpe by the hands of the tenants of High Hall in Westhorpe, 16 works.

In 195 acres of various grains reaped, tied and similarly collected, 459 works of which from High Hall 3 works, upon each acre 2½ works less in total 28 works this year.

In sales within, 92¾ works, of which from the responsibility of the hayward 77¾ works and 15 from the responsibility of the reeve.

Sum as above.

Harvest boonworks

From customary services this year, 108 boonworks, for which each free man has from the lord for his food at noon and for his supper [cena] 1 wheat loaf, of which 20 made per bus. Each customary tenant shall have for his food at noon as for free tenants and for his supper 1 mixed grain loaf, of which 20 made per bushel, and 1 herring.

From customary services from High Hall, 19.

Sum 127 boonworks.

From which, in allowance for the reeve's tenement this year, 3. Item for the hayward's tenement this year, 1 boonwork. In allowance for various tenements in the lord's hands, 7. Item for various tenements pertaining to High Hall in the lord's hands, 10 [torn]. Allowed to the bailiff of Westhorpe by the hands of the tenants of High Hall in Westhorpe, 3 boonworks.

In reaping and tying 42 acres [torn] 84 boonworks of which from High Hall, 3. In sales within 19 boonworks, 16 from the responsibility of the hayward and 3 from the responsibility of the reeve.

Sum as above.

Document 6: Walsham account, 28 September 1396 to 28 September 1397

SA/B HA504/3/4

Walsham[69]
Account of Nicholas Fuller, sergeant there, from the eve of St Michael the Archangel in the 20th year of Richard II up to eve of the same Feast of St Michael next coming in the 21st year of the same Richard for one whole year.

Arrears [*He answers*] for arrears of the last account in the preceding year, £9 19s. 1½d.

Sum £9 19s. 1½d. and half a ¼d.

Rents of assize
For rents of assize for the term of Michaelmas, 76s. 6½d.

For rents of assize for the term of Christmas, 60s.

For rents of assize for the term of Easter, 68s. 9¾d.

For rent of increment from Walter Tiptot, 2s.

For rent of increment from Richard Patel, 1¼d.

For rent of increment from a certain forge recently leased to Simon Smith, 6d.

For rent of increment from Peter Hawes, ½d.

From John Lester and Rose his mother for Taylors Wong, 3s.

From George Brockley for land at Taylors Wong, 12d.

For rent of increment from Robert Osbern of Rickinghall, ¼d.

From Henry Breton for 2 acres of land recently of Henry Osbern, 1d.

For various increments for the term of Michaelmas, 10¼d.

From William Hawes and Robert his brother, 1d.

From William Pye for a certain portion of one messuage formerly of Gilbert Helpe, 1d.

For rent of increment from Matthew Gilbert, ¼d.

For new rent from John Lester for 4 acres 33 perches of land from the lord's demesne lying on the east side of Taylors Wong towards the south, 4s. 3d.

For new rent from Robert Rampley, the smith, for 2 acres 6 perches of land from the lord's demesne of Taylors Wong, 2s.

For rent of increment received annually from Bartholomew, the parson of the church of Langham, for 6 acres of land of mollond of the lord's bondage that Robert Warde neif of the lord recently purchased by charter, 1d.

For new rent received annually from John Baxter for one piece of land called Ayeldes Toft granted to him and his heirs by court roll, 10s.

For new rent received annually from John, son of John Margery for one piece of land containing 2 acres lying on the west side of Howes Toft granted to him and his heirs by court roll, 18d.

For new rent received annually from the tenants of the land and tenement recently of Robert Hawes of 6s. 8d., nothing here this year nor from the other because it was

---

[69] Damp has damaged between two and four centimetres of the whole of the right-hand side of this account to a varying extent, although the manuscript has been skilfully repaired. Where the lost wording is uncontentious, because it is a standard and formulaic repetition of information either elsewhere in the account or in the 1390–1 account, it has been restored without comment. The word [*damaged*] … appears where the lost wording or figures cannot be recovered.

found by the evidence of the same lord that he was unjustly charged and therefore he is exonerated.

For new rent from John Baxter of one acre from the lord's demesne at fee farm lying opposite the cemetery of the church granted to him and his heirs by the rod by the court roll, 16d.

From John Coggeshall for 1 acre of land at fee farm from the demesne there granted to him and his heirs by the court roll p.a., 16d.

For increased rent received annually from Robert Margery for 3 roods of land of mollond which [*damaged*] ... John Warde purchased by charter, ¼d.

For new rent from Adam Goodal for one piece of land [*damaged*] ...

... and ditches from the lord's demesne parcel of Church Wong granted to him and his heirs by court roll ...

[*damaged*] ... rent from Robert Springald for 1½ roods of meadow formerly purchased from Robert Margery p.a., ¼d.

[*damaged*] ... neif of the lord for 1 rood of land abutting upon the curtilage recently Kembalds purchased from Robert Syre by [*damaged*] ...

Sum £11 18s. 6½d.[70]

Rents of assize from High Hall with ward For rents of assize there p.a. 28s. 0¼d. For castle ward there p.a., 2d.

Sum 28s. 2¼d.

Castle ward For castle ward received from the manor of Wyken for the terms of Michaelmas, Christmas, Easter and St John the Baptist, 11s. 2d.

For castle ward received from the manor of Ixworth, 2s. 10d.

Sum 14s.

Farm of land and pasture For the farm of various land and tenements in the lord's hands variously leased as shown by a bill attached to the roll [*damaged*] ...

For pasture at Pinchons Way recently leased for 12d., nothing this year because it was grazed by the lord's sheep. For pasture at Fishpond Field recently leased to John Hawes for 2s., nothing because aforesaid.

From Robert Man for pasture in [*damaged*] ..., 6d.

From Adam Blayer for pasture on the south side of Hall Croft this year[71] \usually leased for 12d./ 10d. [*damaged*] ... of one piece of land at Mickle Meadow and for land at West Mill from the responsibility of the hayward, 4s. [*damaged*] ... 2 acres of land called Nunns Land and 3 roods of land in three pieces of the same tenement from the responsibility of the hayward.

From Adam Blayer for one pightle of pasture called Chalk Pightle this year, 3s.

From the same Adam for 1 [*damaged*] ... this year, 6d.

For a headland of pasture in the Launde at Lady's Wood and from pasture [*damaged*] ... because the whole was depastured by the lord's ewes and lambs both in winter and summer.

From [*damaged*] ... p.a. 4s.

---

[70] The basic rents of assize are the same as for 1390–1, with the addition of four items which added another 4s. 10¾d. rent, bringing the total to £11 18s. 6½d.

[71] Marginal note: 'from the responsibility of the hayward'.

From John Green for a headland of pasture on the north side of the little meadow this year, 2d.

[*damaged*] ... recently leased to William Sparschoy for 5s. 10d., nothing this year because it was grazed by the lord's ewes.

[*damaged*] ... at the sheepcote next to Allwood green recently leased to Peter Robwood for 4s., nothing because it was grazed [*damaged*] ...

[*damaged*] ... pasture 12 acres of land called Blunts Land[72] recently leased to John Syre for 4s., nothing because it was grazed [*damaged*] ...

[*damaged*] ... Leve for 5 acres of land on the east side of Fishpond Field between the land of Robert Sare, 20d.

From Robert Syre for the lease of Burchards Close purchased by the lord and granted to him for a term of 9 years, this year is the 6th, 12s.

From Robert Syre for a curtilage and 4 acres of land in three pieces called Sparshoys purchased by the lord, this year is the 6th, 4s.

From Thomas Bonde for 4 acres of land by estimate of the tenement Burchards on the west side of Burchards Land this year, 12d.

From Walter Tuddenham for one piece of land of the said tenement lying towards Rickinghall Willows next to the land recently of Adam Pitlake, 8d.

From John Fuller for pasture ... in summer, 12d.

Sum 73s. 8d. of which from the responsibility of [*damaged*] ...

Farm of land and meadow at High Hall For the lease of lands and tenements, meadow and pasture, leased there as shown by one bill attached to this roll ... of which from tenements in Westhorpe, 44s. 10d.

Sum £4 19s. 0¼d.

Farm of East House [*Esthouse*] **in the hands of the lord at lease** For the farm of parcels of land and of the tenements of East House variously leased this year, 30s. 8d., and not more because some land grazed by the lord's lambs.

Sum 30s. 8d.

Sale of hay and herbage of the meadows – For hay produced from 4½ acres of meadow sold in Broad Dole this year 31s. 10d., of which from ... Fanerale 5s., from Andrew Bocher 3s., from Robert Margery 2s. 6d., from William Swift 2s., from [*damaged*] ... Rampley 3s., from John Lepere 8s., from Metewynd 2s. 2d., from John Frances 3s., [*damaged*] ... and no more because one cartload is retained [*intrat'*] in the grange for the lord's livestock.

From Robert Man for herbage of 3 roods of land Mickle meadow, purchased by the lord from John Rampley, 5s. this year.

From John [*damaged*] ... there called Turf Pit Acre, 4s. 6d. this year and \usually leased for/ 5s. 6d.

Sum 41s. 5d.

Perquisites of court For one court held there on Thursday next after the Feast of St Gregory the Pope [*damaged*] ...

---

72 Robert Blunt or Blund held land in Walsham in the Domesday Survey of 1086 and a field bearing this name survived until 1819, when it is shown on the Enclosure Map, SA/B Q/RI 41. See also Martin and Satchell, *Where most enclosures be*, figure 14.

For one other court held there on Monday next after the Feast of Ascension of the Lord [*damaged*] …

For Nicholas Patel for the office of reeve released \from the same/ this year [*damaged*] …

Sum 75s. 2d.

Sales of corn For 2 qrs of wheat sold as elsewhere, threshed and winnowed, price per bus. 11d., 14s. 8d.

For wheat sold elsewhere for <love bedripe> \the Ploughale/, 20d.

For 1 qr 1 bus. of wheat sold as elsewhere for the harvest, as below, 8s. 3d.

For 5 qrs 2 bus. of barley sold to various men at various prices [*damaged*] … 24s. 1¼d., per qr 4s. 8d. less 5d.

For 4 bus. of peas sold to John [*damaged*] … 20d.

For 1 qr 5 bus. of peas sold elsewhere, price per bus. 6d., 6s. 6d.

For 9 qrs [*damaged*] … 1 peck three parts of ½ bus. and two parts of 1 peck of oats sold as elsewhere, 30s. 6d. [*damaged*] … less in total, 2½d.

Sum £4 7s. 4d.

Sale of stock For one female foal [*pullan' femell*] sold as elsewhere, 4s.

For two infirm cows sold for stock as elsewhere, 16s. 8d.[73]

For 38 crone wethers sold in the previous year to John Green [*damaged*] …

For [*damaged*] … three ewes sold as elsewhere for the harvest expenses, price of the pelts 2s.

For 8 lambs of residue [*damaged*] … 16d.

Sum 62s.

Farm of the dovecote For 10 pigeons sold elsewhere for harvest expenses, 3d. And no more from the issues of one dovecote, because 500 pigeons were delivered for the lord's hospitality as elsewhere.

For the farm of one dovecote at High Hall to [*damaged*] Painter and Richard Lester, 2s. 6d.

Sum 2s. 9d.

Works and customary services sold For 15¼ hens from rent sold elsewhere, 22¾d., price per hen, 1½d.

For 66 eggs from rent sold from the responsibility of the bailiff, 2¾d.

For ½lb of cumin from rent sold, [*damaged*] …

For ½lb of pepper from rent sold, 6d.

For 360½ customary winter works sold,[74] price per work ½d., 15s. ½d.

For [*damaged*] … and two parts of a carrying work from custom sold as elsewhere, 6¾d.

For two parts of a carry and two parts half a carrying of manure from custom sold elsewhere, price per carrying, 2d. [*damaged*] …

---

[73] Reeves were generally held responsible to check for weak or barren animals and sell them before they became unprofitable and while it was still possible to get a reasonable price for them. See Oschinsky, *Walter of Henley*, p. 439.

[74] The number of sold winter works has increased from 130 in 1390/1 to 360 and the number of harvest works sold has doubled.

For sales of 130 and one quarter of half of one weeding from custom sold elsewhere, price per work ½d., 5s. 5d.

For 42 mowing works sold as elsewhere, 5s. 3d., price per work, 1½d.

For 144 harvest works and 2 parts of one work sold, price per work 1d. as valued in the extent,[75] because they came when summoned, 12s. 0¾d.

For [damaged] … customary services sold as elsewhere, 5s. 4d.

Sum 46s. 11¾d. and half a ¼d.

Farm of cows, sheep and hens For the farm of lactage and calves, 20 cows leased to Roger Daye at farm per head 6s. with allowances of [damaged] … of which 2s. to the dairy herd for winter milk, and for three cows bought in February before calving, 117s.

For the farm of 12 hens leased to the same Roger, per head 6d., 6s.

For milking ewes this year, nothing because they were not in milk due to weakness.[76]

Sum £6 3s.

Issues of the garden For the fruit of 2 gardens of the lord at the manor and at High Hall sold this year, nothing because the produce was expended on the lord's hospitality at Westhorpe, that is 9 qrs of apples.[77]

Sum nil.

Sale of wool and pelts For 54 hogget skins likewise sold to Thomas Grocer as elsewhere altogether 8s. 5d., and no more because the rest were delivered to the lady as shown elsewhere.

Sum 8s. 5d.

Sale of wood From Geoffrey Berningham for 3 qr of faggot sticks sold to him, 4s.

From John [damaged] … for faggots sold to him from sticks, 10d.

From John Shepherd for 30 faggots [damaged] …

From William Man for 30 faggots sold to him, 8d.

From John Banyard for [damaged] …

From John Green for 1 rood 5 perches of underwood in North Haugh sold to him this year, 2s. 3d.

From [damaged] … for ½ rood of underwood in Lady's Wood, 12d.

From Adam Blakewell for ½ rood of underwood [damaged] …

From Robert Lester for 35 perches of underwood there, 21d.

---

[75] The extent was the record of the rents and customs of the tenants of the manor, which documented the standard charge for commuting these labour services. The accountant felt the need to justify the charging of this standard rate, because the tenants had turned up for the works as requested. Contrast the situation in 1390–1, when a higher rate had been charged to commute the services because the tenants had been summoned but did not perform the works. Reading between the lines, a deal had been struck: the manor would not request as many services to be performed this year (hence the increase in the volume of sales from 1390–1) on condition that the tenants would perform those requested.

[76] Milking sheep was a common practice in west Suffolk in the early fourteenth century, when general shortages of food and of cow's milk in particular following the great bovine pandemic of the late 1310s increased its appeal. It was much less common after the Black Death.

[77] Two manor gardens were leased but 9 qrs of apples were delivered to Westhorpe. 10 qrs of apples would yield one tun of cider. See Oschinsky, *Walter of Henley*, p. 429.

From Adam Ebell for ½ acre [*damaged*] … there, 5s. 10½d.

From Robert Margery and his brother for 1 acre 1 rood 36 perches [*damaged*] … sold, 11s. 9½d.

From Richard Lester for 1 acre 17½ perches of underwood there [*damaged*] …

From William Trusse for thorn bushes and underwood growing in the Launde there, 5s.

From [*damaged*] … growing upon the ditch of the wood called Burchards on the west side, 2s.

From John Wells for straw at Dovehouse Wong, 14d.

From Nicholas Fuller for fronds of one white poplar [*damaged*] … 12d.

From John Jay for fronds of willow at Broad Dole, 2s. 5d.

From Robert [*damaged*] … around the sheepcote of the Prior of Ixworth, 14d.

From John Manser for fronds of willow at [*damaged*] …

From Thomas Hereward for fronds of willow next to the stream at the sheepcote of the wethers, 10d.

Sum 53s. 1½d.

Issues of the manor For stubble sold this year in Burchards Croft and at Fishpond Field by [*damaged*] … namely as appears at the view of account, 10s. 11d.

From John Hawes for wheat straw sold to him, 16d.

From John Pye for barley straw there, 8s.

From John Cooper for [*damaged*] …

From William Man for pea straw there, 5d.

From John Pye for oat straw at [*damaged*] …

From John Frances for two carts of the lord leased to him for one day, 16d.

From [*damaged*] … carts of the lord leased to him for one day, 16d.

From John Pye for one cart [*damaged*] … 8d.

Sum 17s. 4d.

Sales at the audit From things sold at the audit as elsewhere 5s. 10d., of which upon the shepherd [*damaged*] …

Sum 5s. 10d.

Total sum of receipts with arrears £60 6s. 7d. half a quarter of a ¼d.

Rent resolute

The same accounts for rent resolute for the hall of Thelnetham of 2s. p.a., nothing because the fee is outside the lord's hands.

Item for the hall of Rickinghall p.a., 3s. 1½d.

Paid for castle ward of Norwich p.a., 16s. 8d. \by the bailiff/

Item paid to John Margery, 1½d.

In rent allowed for the tenement of Nicholas Patel reeve this year, 16d.

Item for the tenement of John Cook [*damaged*] …

In rent allowed for Champeneys p.a. 12d.

Item in rent allowed for various villein tenements in the lord's hands 29s. 0d. three quarters of a ¼d., half a quarter of a ¼d. and a third part of a ¼d.

Item for a messuage, 3 acres 1 rood of land … in the lord's hands, 13¼d. and a third part of a ¼d.

In allowance for a forge formerly of Walter Smith because it is charged within rents of assize above, 6d.

Item for the tenement Outlawes, 6¼d.

In rent allowed for 1 acre of land formerly of Master John of Walsham, 2½d.

Item for 1 acre 1 rood recently of Edmund Pakenham, 2¼d.

Item for a smithy in Palmer Street because it is empty and lying in the highway p.a., 8d.

In rent released to Robert Osbern by the deed of Lady Roesia of Pakenham, ¼d.

Item in rent allowed from High Hall in the lord's hands namely purchased in perpetuity, 4d.

Item for sheriff's aid for the same, 2½d.

Item in allowance for sheriff's aid of Burchards and Sparschoys p.a., 1d.

Paid to the hall of Ashfield for castle ward of Norwich for High Hall p.a., 17d.

Paid to the castle of Eye for castle ward for High Hall this year, 9d.

In rent allowed for various tenements in the lord's hands pertaining to High Hall, 15s. 9¾d.

Paid to the hall of Ashfield for rent p.a., 2d.

Item paid for release from suit to the hundred for Burchards this year, 16d. \bailiff/

Item paid to Helimot for hidage and ward of Burchards p.a., 9d. \bailiff/

In rent resolute payable to Master Sir William Bardwell for 1 acre of meadow at Turf Pits [*Turvepetts*] purchased by the lord from Master John Rampley, chaplain ...

Sum £4 6s. 5½d. three quarters of half ...

Cost of ploughs and carts In contracting Robert Smith, blacksmith, for providing and forging iron-work on two ploughs, including the cost of 4 bushels of wheat as elsewhere, 28s., of which the hayward paid 10s.

Item in 3 ploughs fixed from [*damaged*] ...

Item [*damaged*] ... 7 halters of canvas bought for stots, 3½d.

In two reins bought for carthorses, 2d.

Item [*damaged*] ... on two occasions, an axle made from the lord's timber, 4d.

Item in one tawed horse hide bought for a collar and [*damaged*] ...

Item in one tanned horse hide and one pair of girths [*wombes*] likewise bought for the same, 2s. 5d.

Item [*damaged*] ... bought, 9d.

Item in thread bought, 2d.

Item in 5 ells of canvas bought for the same [*damaged*] ...

Item [*damaged*] ... men for 4 days' work making 4 new collars and mending 7 old collars [*damaged*] ... cart 2s., 1d. taking between them per day 6d., each of them 1d.

Item in 14 clouts bought [*damaged*] ...

Item in two metal plates bought, 2d.

Item in 2 new ploughs made from the lord's timber, 8 [*damaged*] ...

Item [*damaged*] ... and John his son for one day shaping timber for one cart body, 8d.

Item in 8 [*damaged*] ... year, 5d.

Item in one pair of wheels bought from Robert Cooper ?half price [*p't' meditull'*] and in one [*damaged*] ... shaped from the lord's timber as above, 7s.

In one cart saddle bought without a saddle-pad [*damaged*] ...

Sum 48s. 5d.

Cost of the buildings In the stipend of one carpenter for one day's work mending the door of the barn of the peas at the manor, 4d.

Item [*damaged*] ... bought for the same, 2½d.

Item in iron nails bought for the same, ½d.

Item in the stipend of one thatcher [*damaged*] … thatching upon the barn and dove-cote at High Hall, 20d., taken per day 4d.

Item [*damaged*] … 2½ days' work thatching upon the knight's chamber and upon the hay barn, 10d. And [*damaged*] …

Sum 3s. 1d.

Cost of the mill Nothing

Cost of the fold In tar bought, nothing because it was from stock in the preceding year.

In grease bought to mix with the same [*damaged*] …

Item for washing and shearing the lord's sheep, with all expenses, 8s. 6d.

Item in 382 lambs washed and sheared [*damaged*] …

In 6lb of red ochre bought for marking sheep and lambs, 6d.

Item in 8 dozen hurdles made for the fold as elsewhere, 2s. 8d.

Sum 17s. 9d.

Stipend of the manorial servants In the stipend of 4 ploughmen p.a. 28s, to each of them 7s.

Item in remuneration made to John [*damaged*] … over and above his stipend 3s.

Item in stipend of John Dennis shepherd of the ewes p.a. 6s. and of [*damaged*] … shepherd of the wethers p.a. 8s.

Item in stipend of the shepherd of the lambs p.a. 8s.

In [*damaged*] …

Sum 53s.

Threshing and winnowing In 61 qrs 6 bus. of wheat and rye threshed by task, per qr 4d., 20s. 7d.

Item 146 quarters of barley, peas and oats threshed by task, per qr 2d., 24s. 4d.

In winnowing the grain by task in total 217 qrs 4 bus. of various grains, per 3 qrs 2d., 12s. 1d.

Sum 57s.

Corn and stock bought In corn bought [*blank*].

Item in 2 cows bought in February before calving, 16s. 8d.

Item in [*damaged*] …, 6s.

In 12 hoggets bought in May before shearing, 14s. 6d.

Item 12 chickens [*damaged*] …

Sum 38s. 2d.

Minute expenses In a bonus to 4 ploughmen, 3 shepherds and one dairyherd at Christmas and Easter, 16d.

Item in [*damaged*] … at the Purification of the Blessed Mary, 4d.

Item paid to the chaplain of the parish of Walsham for tithes of apples [*damaged*] … as above not tithed on the order of the lady, 6d.[78]

---

[78] This clearly refers to the unusual transfer of a large amount of apples from the manorial garden at Walsham Hall to Westhorpe.

Item in expenses of 30 men with 14 carts [*damaged*] … from the lord's custom for one day with expenses of the servants of the manor and all other things reckoned, 8s.
Item [*damaged*] … carpenter mending a gate at High Hall for ½ day, 2d.
Item in 2 locks with [*damaged*] …
Item in 540 faggot \sticks/ made in the lord's wood by task as elsewhere, 2s. 7½d., at 7d. per 120.
Item given to the ploughmen of the lord in sowing all the seed this year in order that they work better, 6s. 8d.
Item in parchment for court rolls and accounts, 6d.
In iron for one shovel, 2d.

Sum 21s. 3½d.

Lease of East House Paid to the Prior of Ixworth for lands and tenements called East House, which he had leased for the term of 10 years, this year [*damaged*] …

Sum 40s.

Weeding and mowing In weeding the lord's corn this year, nothing here because by customary works elsewhere.
In a great [*damaged*] … this year altogether, 10s.
Item in the herbage, spreading, turning and lifting the hay, nothing here because by customary works as elsewhere.

Sum 10s.

Customary harvest works In expenses of one bailiff, one hayward, one cook and stacker and 2 carters from the servants of the manor [*damaged*] … expenses of 79 harvest boonworks of this manor, 2 ploughmen, 3 shepherds, one dairyherd, one smith [*damaged*] … reapale at noon and with expenses of 3 harvest boonworks and 6 harvest works from [*damaged*] … for one day:[79]
In bread in the price of 1 qr 1 bus. of wheat as sold above, 8s. 3d. Item in [*damaged*] … In meat bought, 6s. 10d. Item in the price of 3 ewes as sold above [*damaged*] … fish and herrings bought, 20d. In milk, cheese, eggs and butter bought, 16d. Item in [*damaged*] … Item in salt bought, 2d. Item in oat meal, 5d. In candles bought, 1½d. In herrings bought, 1d.
In 2 pairs of gloves bought for the manorial servants, 4d.
In the stipend of one cook and stacker at harvest, [*damaged*] …
… reaped by the lord at the Reapale, 12d.
In the custom of 394 works [*damaged*] … each of them ¼d., 8s. 2½d.
In the customary harvest boonworks 79, from which [*damaged*] … ¾d., 9¾d. half

Sum 45s. 5¾d.

Wages In the wages of Nicholas Fuller, sergeant there, for the year, minus 4 weeks during the harvest because at the table of the lord, at 12d. per week.

Sum 48s.

---

[79] Marginal note: 'And in total per head in food and maintenance for a whole day 2d., minus in total 13d.'

61

Expenses of steward In the expenses of the steward of the lord at the first court held there, as testified by the supervisor of the lord, 2s. And for expenses at the second court held there, 16½d.

Sum 4s. 1½d.

Expenses of the lord nil.

Foreign expenses with allowances In shoeing one horse of John Lester travelling in the lord's cart to London with the lord's food at parliament[80] after Christmas, 1d. Item paid to Robert Bray for 10 days going with the lord's cart up to London by order of the lord, 3s. 4d.

Sum 3s. 5d.

Cash delivered Delivered to the lady by the hand of Walter Frances the hayward for his arrears of the preceding year as shown at the foot of the said account [damaged] …

To the same lady by the hand of Roger Daye for his arrears of the preceding year as shown at the foot of the said account [damaged] …

To the same lady by the hand of the same Roger Daye for the lease of the dairy this year by one tally [damaged] …

To the same lady by the hand of the same Roger for the lease of the dairy at the end of the year by one bill [damaged] …

To the same lady by the hand of John Cook the hayward this year for rents and leases by one tally [damaged] …

To the same lady by the hand of the same John for rents and services this year at the end of the year by one tally [damaged] …

To the same lady by the hand of the same for a certain fine from Katherine Frances in the court for licence to marry [damaged] …

To the same lady from the responsibility of the same John by the hand of John Man for a fine from his wife in the court [damaged] …

To the same lady from the responsibility of the same John by the hand of Edmund Patel from the office of reeve this year [damaged] …

To the same lady by the hand of Nicholas Fuller bailiff from the profits of the manor at the end of the year by one bill [damaged] …

Item delivered to Adam Blayer, sergeant of Westhorpe, \7s. 7d./ from rent and farm of High Hall \44s. 10d./ by the hand of [damaged] … for lands and tenements of the lord of High Hall in Westhorpe, as appears in foreign receipts there.

Item delivered to the lady by the hand of Edmund Patel in full payment for the office of reeve for his father [damaged] …

Sum £29 6s. 9¼d. half and half

Sum of all expenses and deliveries £53 3s. 0¼d.

And they owe [damaged] … 6¾d. half a quarter of ¼d. and a third part of a ¼d.

Of which, on John Brangwayne, recently the shepherd there, for sheep for his default 6s. 8d.[81]

---

[80] Sir William Elmham was an MP for Suffolk in 1397.

[81] A number of manorial officials have been charged for 'default', meaning that the explanations they have given for the loss of animals in their care were not accepted by the auditors, so the cost of the relevant stock has been charged to them.

Upon [*damaged*] … Swon, recently the swineherd, for 20 hoggets and one lamb recently upon his default, 17s. 1d.

Upon [*damaged*] … Osbern and his sister from an amercement in the court in the 8th year preceding, 13s. 4d.[82]

Upon [*damaged*] … Hawker for wool sold to him in the 6th year preceding, 56s. 8d.

Upon [*damaged*] … an amercement in the court in the 5th year preceding, 16s. 4d.

Upon Roger Prede for an amercement in the court, 6s. 8d.

Upon Robert Osbern, recently swineherd at Westhorpe, [*damaged*] … in the court, 3s. 4d.

And so upon Nicholas Fuller, the accountant now, 20s. [*damaged*] … three quarters of a ¼d. and a third part of a ¼d.

Upon Ralph the shepherd for two wethers for his default [*damaged*] …

And upon John Dennis for one sheep for his default as elsewhere, 12d.

[*Reverse*][83]

Grange and stock account there by measure and various grains in the 20th and 21st year of Richard II.

Wheat

Issues of the grange there from this year by one tally against John Pye granger of the lord there sworn, 57 qrs 6 bus., of which 3 qrs 4 bus. are *curl'*, and threshed by task.

Sum 57 qrs 6 bus.   Approved.

From which, in seed upon 56 acres of land in various parcels 13 qrs 5 bus. by one tally against the hayward, sown at 2 bus. per acre less in total this year 3 bus.

Item the contract of the granger for keeping the keys of the grange one bus.

Item given as livery to the manorial servants as shown below 12 qrs 4 bus., of which 3 qrs 4 bus. *curl'* for the bread of the harvest workers by custom.

In the contract of Robert Smith, blacksmith, for making iron for two ploughs p.a., just as in money as within, 4 bus.

Item given to William Brook by the lady, 2 bus.

Item delivered to Thomas Baker, baker of the lord at Westhorpe, for the hospitality of the lord by one tally, 24 qrs 7 bus.

Item delivered to Edmund Knight with his lease at Wyverstone by order of the lady, 2 qrs 4 bus. of wheat by tally.

In sales within, 3 qrs 3 bus., of which for expenses of the harvest 1 qr 1 bus. and for the ploughale 2 bus.

Sum as above.   It balances.

Rye

Issues of the grange there this year by one tally against the same John, 4 qrs threshed by task.

Received from Westhorpe out of the hospitality of the lord by one tally against Thomas Baker, baker of the lord, 2 qrs of rye \approved/.[84]

---

[82] Likewise, a number of people are being pursued for fines levied in the manorial court but still unpaid.

[83] The damage to the reverse of the document is down the left-hand side, so that most of the missing parchment was originally given over to the margin: hence less text is lost from this stock account than from the revenue side of the account.

[84] An unusual transfer – grain was normally sent *to* the seigniorial kitchen at Westhorpe, not received from it – and so the auditors added the superscript 'approved' to validate the transaction.

Item received from Roger Littlehall, sergeant of Frenze, for the livery of the manorial servants by one tally 2 qrs \approved/.

Sum 8 qrs.   Approved.

Of which, in seed upon 7 acres of land at Cocksdirt, 1 qr 6 bus. by one tally against the same sergeant, sown at 2 bus. an acre.

In the contract of the granger, 1 bus.

In livery of the manorial servants shown below, 6 qrs 1 bus.

Sum as above.   It balances.

Barley

Issues of the grange there this year by one tally against the same John, 66 qrs 3½ bus. and threshed by task.

Sum 66 qrs 3½ bus.   Approved.

Of which, in seed upon 64 acres of land in various parcels 24 qrs by one tally against the same hayward, sown at 3 bus. per acre.

In the contract of the granger, 1 bus.

In livery of the manorial servants as shown below, 8 qrs 4½ bus.

Delivered to Thomas Baker, baker of the lord, at Westhorpe to make malt by one tally, 23 qrs.

Item delivered to Edmund Knight with his lease at Wyverstone by order of the lady, 5 qrs of barley

In a bonus to Alice [*damaged*] ... by the order of the lady, 4 bus.

In sales within, 5 qrs 2 bus. of barley.

Sum as above.   It balances.

Beans and peas

Issues of the grange there this year by one tally against the same John 17 qrs 5½ bus., of which 9 qrs 6 bus. were threshed by services and 7 qrs 7½ bus. by task.

From the same issues by estimate in straw, 6 qrs.

Sum 23 qrs 5½ bus. Approved.

Of which, in seed upon 36 acres of land in various pieces, 9 qrs of peas by one tally against the said hayward, sown at 2 bus. an acre.

In the contract of the granger, 1 bus.

In livery of the manorial servants as shown below for harvest expenses, 3 qrs 1½ bus.

In feed for the pigeons in the winter, 3 bus.

In feed for the cart horses, ewes, wethers and hoggets of the lord in winter by estimate in straw above, 6 qrs.

Item for expending in the hospitality of the lord by one tally with oats as below against Thomas Baker, 3 bus. of peas.

Item given to Edmund Knight with his lease at Wyverstone by the order of the lady by one tally, 2 qrs 4 bus. peas.

In sales within, 2 qr 1 bus.

Sum as above.   It balances.

Oats

Issues of the grange there this year by one tally against the same John, 71 qrs 5 bus. of oats threshed by task.

From issues by estimate in 80 sheaves of oats for feed for oxen, stots, calves and lambs of residue, 1 qr.

From rent paid at the Feast of St Edmund King and Martyr, 20 qrs 2 bus. of oats.
Sum 92 qrs 7 bus.   Approved.

Of which, in seed upon 60 acres of land in various parcels, 20 qrs 4 bus. by one tally against the same hayward, sown at 2½ bus. per acre by heaped measure plus in total this year, 1 qr 6 bus.

In the contract of the granger, 1 bus.

In meal made for pottage for eight manorial servants p.a., 2 qrs.

In feed for the lord's carthorses and stots this year when there was a great need for their work, 10 qrs 4 bus.

In allowance for the tenement of Nicholas Patel, reeve this year, 3 bus. ½ peck and 3 parts of a peck of oats from rent.

Item for the tenement of \John Cook/ hayward this year [*damaged*] … peck of oats

Item for various tenements in the lord's hands both from old and new, 3 qrs 2 bus. [*damaged*] … half of one peck and two parts of ½ bus. of oats.

In the loss of rent on one messuage and 3 acres 1 rood of land, recently of Walter Dennis, abandoned in the lord's hands by Robert Osbern, this year is the 6th, ½ bus.

Delivered to Westhorpe for feeding the horses of the lord and visitors by one tally with peas above against Thomas Baker, baker of the lord, 19 qrs 6 bus. of oats.

Item delivered to Edmund Knight with his lease as above by one tally, 5 qrs.

In feed for calves and new-born lambs as elsewhere by estimate in sheaves above, 1 qr.

Item in feed for horses in eight carts fetching barley at Santon [*Downham*] coming from Frenge for seed at Westhorpe by the order of the lady, 1 qr.

In sales within, 9 qrs 1 bus. 1½ pecks and half a quarter of one peck threshed by task and two parts of one peck of oats.
Sum as above.   It balances.

Multure

There remains 1 qr 2 bus. in the hands of the miller.

Item, for the farm of one windmill leased to John the miller for the term of [*damaged*] …, this year the 2nd, 11 qrs 4 bus.
Sum 12 qrs 6 bus.   Approved.

From which, in bread baked for stots this year, 2 bus.

In livery of the manorial servants shown below and for bread for the harvest, 11 qrs 2½ bus.
Sum 11 qrs 4½ bus.

And remaining, 1 qr 1½ bus. of multure for harvest bread for customary tenants. Approved.

Livery of manorial servants

Received from wheat as above, 12 qrs 4 bus.

From rye above to the same, 6 qrs 1 bus.

From barley above to the same, 4 qrs 4½ bus.

From peas above to the same, 3 qrs 1½ bus.

From multure from the miller above, 11 qrs 2½ bus.
Sum 41 qrs 5½ bus.

From which, in quittance of the excess of the last account, 8 qrs 1 bus., of which for the harvest bread in the preceding year 5 qrs 4 bus. and 2 qrs 5 bus. for [*damaged*] …

65

In livery of four ploughmen, three shepherds and one dairyherd p.a., less four weeks \in the harvest/ when two manorial servants were provided with food by the lord, 33 qrs 7 bus., taking one qr every twelve weeks.

In bread baked for customary tenants making forty ploughings shown below of which each customary tenant takes for each ploughing six loaves, at 20 to the bus., 1 qr 4 bus.

Item in bread baked for 394 harvest works for this manor below, that is for each work 2 loaves, at 20 to the bus.

And for 79 harvest boonworks from this manor viz: for each work one loaf, 20 to the bus. above, 5 qrs 3 bus. 1½ pecks.

In livery of one groom working with the shepherd of the ewes at the time of lambing this year, 2 bus.

Sum 49 qrs 1 bus. 1½ pecks. And thus exceeds, 7 qrs 3 bus. 3½ pecks of which owed viz: costs of harvest 5 qrs 3 bus. 1½ pecks and to the manorial servants, 2 qrs ½ bus. Approved.

Total land seeded with various grains 223 acres \approved/. And reaped by customary works within. It balances.

Carthorses
And 6 remain. Sum 6. And 6 cart horses remain.

Stots
And 4 remain. Sum 4. And 4 stots remain.

Colts
And received from Rickinghall in the present year, 1 female and also of one year and a half.

Sum shown. And sold within. It balances.

Oxen
And in the preceding account 5 remain, of which 1 is old.

Of which, delivered to the lord's larder in the present year by 1 tally with cows below, 1 old ox.

Sum shown. And 4 oxen remain for stock.

Cows
20 cows, of which 4 are old [*cron'*].

From Rickinghall in the present year by 1 tally 4, of which 2 are sterile.

And purchased in February before calving, 2 cows,

Sum 26.

From which, delivered to the lord's larder in the present year by 1 tally with oxen above, 4 old cows.

In sales at Lammas, 2 infirm [*inhabil'*] and sterile.

Sum 6. And remaining, 20 cows.

Bullocks and heifers
From Rickinghall in the present year by 1 tally with cows above, one bullock uncastrated.

Sum shown. And 1 uncastrated bullock remains. Approved.

Added from calves below, 6.   Sum 6. And delivered to Rickinghall in winter by 1 tally.   It balances.

Calves
6 remain.
And purchased from the farmer of the cows by agreement shown below, 6 calves.
Sum 12.
From which, added to bullocks and heifers above, 6.
And 6 calves remain over and above issues.

Hides
And 1 tanned bullock hide remains.   Approved.
Sum shown.
And 1 tanned bullock hide remains in the hands of John Barker.

Wethers
And 242 wethers remain of which 39 are crones.
And added from hoggets below, 36.
Sum 278.
Of which, in murrain before shearing 33 \testified/, of which one is a crone.
Item in murrain after shearing 3 and the pelts are valued but not the skins.
Item in murrain after shearing 8 \testified/ and the pelts were damaged.
Delivered to Rickinghall in the previous year without tally, 1 wether.
Item delivered to Adam Blayer, sergeant of Westhorpe, after shearing 12 wethers from the responsibility of Dennis.
Item delivered for the lord's hospitality at the end of the year by 1 tally with gimmers, 1 decrepit [desed'] wether.
In sales as within in the previous year, 38 crone wethers.
In sales at the audit, 2 defective wethers upon Ralph the shepherd before shearing, for [blank].[85]
Sum 98.   And 180 wethers remain, of which 50 are old.

Ewes
And 197 ewes remain.
Added from gimmers below, 109. Received from Adam Blayer, sergeant of Westhorpe, before lambing and shearing from the fold of Thomas the shepherd there without tally, 12 ewes.
Sum 318 ewes.   Approved.
From which, in murrain before lambing and shearing, 12 ewes \testified/.
Item in murrain after shearing, 5 \testified/.
Delivered for the lord's hospitality at the end of the year by 1 written tally [de tractibus], 29 ewes.
In sales as within for expenses of the harvest, excluding the price of the pelts, [damaged] …
Item in sales at the audit, 1 defective ewe upon Dennis before \lambing and/ shearing.
Sum 50.   And 268 ewes and gimmers remain.

---

[85] The proceeds of the sale at the audit would have been recorded in the margin, which of course is lost due to the damp damage to the roll.

Hoggets and gimmers
145 remain, of which 36 are hoggets and 109 are gimmers.
Added from lambs below 282 in custody of John Man.
And purchased as within in May before shearing, 12 hoggets.

Sum 439.   Approved.

From which, added to wethers above, 36.
And with all gimmers above, 109.
In murrain before shearing 73 \testified/ and the pelts were damaged [*as verified*]
by the lord's supervisor.
Item in murrain after shearing 9 \testified/, of which 3 pelts are valued.
Delivered for expending on the lord's hospitality at the end of the year by 1 tally
with wethers as above, 1 decrepit [*desed'*] gimmer.
Delivered to Richard Bas, sergeant of Rickinghall, after shearing by 1 tally, 40
gimmers.
Item delivered to Adam Blayer, sergeant of Westhorpe, after shearing by 1 tally, 50
hoggets.
Item killed by dogs before shearing, as testified through the rolls of the court, 13.[86]

Sum 331.

And 118 hoggets and gimmers remain, of which 53 are hoggets and 65 are gimmers.

Lambs
282 remain in the custody of John Man the shepherd.
Item from the issues of the said ewes, 244 lambs and no more because 11 sheep
were sterile this year.
Received \approved/ from Rickinghall by 1 tally before shearing, 204 lambs.

Sum 730.

From which added to hoggets and gimmers above, 282.
In murrain before tithes, 44 \testified/.
In tithes, 20.
Delivered for expending on the lord's hospitality at Westhorpe around the Feast of
St John by 1 tally, 2 lambs.
Item in murrain after shearing, 11 \testified/.
In sales within, 8 lambs of residue.

Sum 367.

And 363 lambs remain, of which 1 is in the custody of Dennis and was recently in
the custody of Cobbe.

Fleeces
From sheep above sheared, 717.

Sum 717.   Approved.

Of which, in tithes 70 fleeces, and no more because 12 hoggets were purchased as
above in May and their fleeces tithed elsewhere.
Delivered to the lady at Westhorpe to the wool house there by 1 tally, 647.

Sum as above.   It balances.

---

[86] One of the methods of verifying losses of demesne livestock was for the jurors of the manorial court
to confirm on oath the reasons for the loss.

Lamb fleeces
From lambs as above sheared 382 fleeces, and no more because 2 were suckling and not sheared.
Sum 382 fleeces.
And delivered to the lady, weighing 135lbs.   It balances.

Sheep skins
As above in murrain, 118.
Sum 118. Approved.
From which, delivered to the lady by 1 tally 64 pelts.
In sales within, 54 hogget pelts from [*damaged*] …
Sum as above.   It balances.

Pelts
As above in murrain 22.
And from sheep slaughtered as above for the harvest expenses, 3.
Sum 25.
And sold at the audit for [*blank*]   It balances.

Lamb skins
From deaths through murrain before shearing, 44.
From lambs in murrain after shearing, 11.
Sum 55.   Approved.
From which, delivered to the lady by 1 tally, 41.
In sales at the audit, 14 from residue for [*blank*] \approved/.
Sum as above.   It balances.

Capons
And 19 remain. From rent p.a. 8. And made this year from poultry below, 12.
Sum 39. Approved.
Of which, in allowance for tenements in the lord's hands, 4. Delivered for expending in the lord's hospitality by 1 tally, 17. In expenses of one court held there, 1. In sales at the audit, because there was a deficiency [*quia defic'*], 5.
Sum 27.   12 remain.

Hens and cockerels
1 cockerel 12 hens remain.
From rent p.a. at Christmas, 123½ hens.
From rent from High Hall, 21.
Sum 157½ hens.   Approved.
From which, in allowance for the tenement of Nicholas Patel reeve this year, 3.
Item for the tenement of John Cook hayward this year, 5.
Item for various tenements in the lord's hands, 9¾ hens.
Item in the loss of rent on one messuage, 3 acres 1 rood of land, recently of Walter Dennis, abandoned in the lord's hands by Robert Osbern this year, a sixth part of 1 hen.
Item in allowance for various tenements pertaining to High Hall in the lord's hands, 11½ hens.

69

Item in allowance made to Gilbert Moundmill and Katherine his wife and their legitimate heirs by a deed of the lord p.a. for the tenement Helpes in Westhorpe pertaining to High Hall, 1.

Delivered to the steward of the lord's hospitality at Westhorpe by 1 tally, 97.

In sales as above 15¼ hens, of which 7 from the responsibility of the hayward and 7¾ from the responsibility of the bailiff.

Delivered to Adam Blayer, sergeant at Westhorpe, pertaining to the tenants of High Hall, 1.

Sum 144½ hens.

And 1 cockerel 12 hens remain in the dairy.

Eggs

From the issue of hens above, nil because they were leased at farm for money within.

From rent at Easter, 720 eggs. From rent from High Hall at the same time, 105 eggs.

Sum 825 eggs.

In allowance for the reeve's tenement, 30.

Item for the hayward's tenement, 24½ eggs.

Item for various tenements in the lord's hands, 102 eggs.

Item allowed for 3 acres 1 rood of land recently of Walter Dennis in the lord's hands above, 3½ eggs.

Item for various tenements in the lord's hands pertaining to High Hall, 39 eggs.

Delivered for expending on the lord's hospitality by 1 tally, 560.

In sales within from the responsibility of the bailiff, 66 eggs.

Sum as above.   It balances.

Poultry

From the issues of hens above, nothing as they were leased at farm above.

From purchases within, 12.

Sum 12.   It balances.

And reckoned in capons made above.

Dovecote

From the issues of one dovecote at the manor this year, excluding tithes, 510 pigeons. And from one dovecote at High Hall, nothing because it was leased at farm for money within.

Sum 510.   It balances.

From which, delivered for expending on the hospitality of the lord by 1 tally against the steward of hospitality, 500.

In sales within for the harvest, 10.

Sum as above.   It balances.

Cumin From rent from the Prior of Bricett p.a., ½lb cumin.

Sum ½lb cumin. And sold within.   It balances.

Pepper From rent received from Walter Frances for the tenement recently of John Pinfold pertaining to High Hall, ½lb pepper.

Sum ½lb pepper. And sold within.   It balances.

Ploughing services From the issues of 10 customary greater tenures this year, providing 5 ploughteams this year with 25 ploughing services taken at the seasons of winter and Lent, that is from each whole ploughteam 5 ploughing services, and they shall receive from the lord for each ploughteam, 6 loaves of mixed grain, at 20 to the bus., and allowance of 2 winter works.

From the issues of 10 other customary tenants, providing 5 ploughteams this year with 15 ploughing services, so each plough shall do 3 ploughing services and receive from the lord for each plough-team 6 loaves of the said grain and the said weight, no allowance of works.

From the issues of customary tenants of High Hall this year, nothing.

Sum 40 ploughing services.

And expended in ploughing the lord's land at the aforesaid times. It balances.

Boonwork called Ploughale From the issues of the lord's customary tenants this year 14 ploughing services.

And expended in sowing wheat. It balances.

Winter works From customary services for a half day 963 winter and summer works, price per work ½d.

From customary services from High Hall, 10.

Sum 973 works. Approved.

From which, in allowance for the reeve's tenement this year, 2¼ works.

Item for the hayward's tenement this year, 1.

Item for various tenements in the lord's hands, 176¾ works and three parts of 1 work.

Item for the tenement recently of Walter Dennis, 9 works.

In 25 ploughing services expenses above 50 works, for each ploughing service 2 works.

In three Tumbrels made this year, 3.

Item in allowance for the tenement recently of Robert Wenge pertaining to High Hall in the lord's hands, 10 works.

In stubble gathered in the present year, 67 works.

In carrying stubble, 4.

In weeds removed prior to the wheat sowing, 87.

In sowing furrows of wheat and rye, 21.

In sowing furrows of peas, 12.

In harrowing oats, 25.

In harrowing barley, 20.

In making drainage furrows at the time [*of sowing*] wheat, 23.

In stacking straw for thatching a house at East End and at the manor, 20.

In filling dung carts with manure, 21.

In spreading manure on the fields, 19.

In laying gravel at the lord's work at Westhorpe, 3.

In cleaning 2 harrows of manure at High Hall, 14.

In spreading herbage in the meadow, 14.

In stopping up gaps at Lady's Wood, 6.

In mending a gate there, 2.

In breaking clods of ground [*in glebis*] at the time of [*the sowing*] of barley, 3.

In sales within, 360½ works.

Sum as above. It balances.

71

Carrying services From 7 customary carrying services at the will of the lord from custom, price per work 1d

Sum 7.

From which, in allowance for the reeve's tenement, 3 services.
In sales within, 2 and 2 parts.

Sum as above.   It balances.

Manure carrying services From customary works without resumption 9 manure carryings and allowed to the same for each man carrying manure, 1 winter work, price per carry 2d.

Sum 9 carryings.

From which, in allowance for the reeve's tenement this year, ¼.
In allowance for various tenements in the lord's hands, 2¾ carryings, two parts of a carry and two parts of half a carrying of manure.
In carrying manure this year, 3.
In sales within, 2¾ carries, two parts of a carry and two parts of half a manure carrying.

Sum as above.

Weeding works From customary works 188, price per work ½d.
From customary works from High Hall, 3.

Sum 191.

From which, in allowance for the reeve's tenement this year, 6 works.
Item for the hayward's tenement this year, ½.
Item in allowance for various tenements in the lord's hands, 24¾ weeding works.
In weeding the lord's barley this year, 30.
In sales within 130¾ works, of which from the responsibility of the bailiff.

Sum as above.   It balances.

Mowing works From customary works for a half day, 49 mowing works, price per work 1½d.

Sum 49 works.

From which in allowances for reeve's tenement, ¾ of ½.
Item in allowance for various tenements in the lord's hands, 6¾ works.
In sales within, 42 works.

Sum as above.   It balances.

Carriage of hay From services according to custom that have carriage without resumption and without price of works 10 carries this year.

Sum 10 carries. And expended in hay between carriage.   It balances.

Haymaking works From the issues of customary haymaking works as many as the lord requires, lifting, turning and stacking all the hay without resumption. It balances.

Harvest works From customary works for a whole day in the lord's grain, reaping, tying and stacking, 643 works for which each man shall receive from the lord at noon and for his supper 2 loaves of mixed grain, at 20 to the bus., and 1 herring, price per work 1d.
From customary services from High Hall p.a., 111 works.

Sum 754 works.   Approved.

72

From which, in allowance for the reeve's tenement this year, 8 works one quarter and 3 parts of one work.

Item for the hayward's tenement, 8 works.

Item for various tenements in the lord's hands, 96¾ works.

Item for various tenements in the lord's hands pertaining to High Hall, 77 works.

Item for one messuage 3 acres 1 rood of land recently of Walter Dennis in the lord's hands, 3½ works.

Item in allowance of Gilbert Moundmill and Katherine his wife by a deed of the lord p.a. for the tenement Helpes, 16 works.

In 182 acres of various corn reaped, tied and similarly collected in the harvest, 394 works from the responsibility of the hayward and 6 works from the responsibility of the bailiff, upon each acre more in total this year that is in total 36 works, and so many because the corn had less chaff [*minus curter*] this year.

In sales within, 144 and 2 parts of one work, of which from the responsibility of the hayward 132 works and 12 works from the responsibility of the bailiff.

Sum as above.   It balances.

Harvest boonworks From customary services this year 108 boonworks, from which each free man receives from the lord for his food at noon and for his supper 1 wheat loaf, at 20 to the bus.

Each customary tenant shall have for his food at noon as for free tenants and for his supper 1 loaf of mixed grain, at 20 to the bus., and 1 herring.

From customary services from High Hall, 19 boonworks.

Sum 127 boonworks.

From which in allowance for the reeve's tenement this year, 3.

Item for the hayward's tenement this year, 5.

Item for various tenements in the lord's hands, 7.

In allowance of one messuage, 3 acres 1 rood of land recently of Walter Dennis in the lord's hands, 1.

Item in allowance for various tenements in the lord's hands pertaining to High Hall, 10.

Item in allowance made to Gilbert Moundmill and Katherine his wife by a deed of the lord p.a., 2.

Item in allowance of the tenement Chapmans in the lord's hand because it is escheat after the death of William Blunt [*Blounpart*] pertaining to High Hall, 1.

Item in 41 acres of wheat and oats reaped and tied, 82 works, upon an acre 2 works of which from the responsibility of the bailiff 3.

In sales within, 16 of which from the responsibility of the hayward 13 and from the responsibility of the bailiff 3.

Sum as above.   It balances.

Item. And making faggot sticks this year in the lord's wood 540, and no more because the remainder was sold by the acre as shown within.

Sum 540.

From which in tithes, 54 faggots.

In 8 dozen hurdles made at the lord's fold as shown within, 276.

In sales within, 210 faggot sticks

Sum as above.   It balances.

Document 7: Walsham draft account, 28 September 1402 to 28 September 1403

SA/B HA504/3/5a

Walsham[87]

Account of John Magges sergeant there from the eve of St Michael the Archangel in the 3rd year of the reign of Henry IV until the eve of the same Henry IV for one whole year.

Arrears [*He answers*] for arrears of the last account.

Rents of assize For rents of assize there p.a. as appears in detail in the view of the preceding year,[88] £12 22½d.
For rents of assize purchased from William, son of the late William Hore, this year is the 2nd, 6s. 4½d. And in the price of one hen, four harvest works and one ploughing service at the winter sowing, 22d.

Sum £12 10s. 1d.

Rents of assize of High Hall For rents of assize there p.a., 28s. ¼d.
For castle ward there p.a., 2d.

Sum 28s. 2¼d.

Castle ward For castle ward received from the manor of Wyken for the terms of Michaelmas, Christmas and the Nativity of St John the Baptist, 11s. 2d.
For castle ward received from the manor of Ixworth p.a., 2s. 10d.

Sum 14s.

Farm of land and pasture For the farm of the lands and tenements in the lord's hands leased to various people, as shown by a bill attached to this roll[89] from the responsibility of the hayward, 40s. 5½d.
From Peter Poye for pasture of Pinchons Way with pasture of two pieces of land there called Hatchmere this year, 7s.
From John Frances senior for 18 acres of land there called Blunteshawe for a term of 10 years, this year is the 3rd, 4s. 6d.
For pasture at Fishpond Field leased in the preceding year to John Lester for 18d., nothing this year because it was grazed by the lord's sheep.
From Adam Blayer for a headland of pasture in Hall Croft at the south head and on the east side of the same with pasture at the north head of the same this year, 16d.
From 14 acres of fallow land there leased to the same Adam in the preceding year for 2s. 8d., nothing this year because it was sown with the lord's oats.
From Adam Blayer for the farm of one piece of land at Mickle Meadow and for one piece of land at West Mill from the responsibility of the hayward, 4s.

---

[87] Many of the sum totals for the individual sections of this account are left blank, including the sections relating to individual grains. In addition, it does not contain the usual marginal comments, late adjustments (such as 'sales beyond the account'), and the balancing of the charge and discharge section. Hence this was a draft account, sufficiently detailed and complete to be presented for audit, and providing plenty of useful information for the historian, but it is not an audited account.

[88] The rents of assize were not written out in full in this account, but instead calculated as for the preceding year plus two new items bringing the total to £12 10s. 1d.

[89] The attachment has not survived.

From Adam dil Ebell for 2 acres of land called Nunns Land and 3 roods of land in three pieces of the same tenement from the responsibility of the hayward, 18d.

From Adam Blayer for a pightle of pasture called Calk Pightle [*Cawlpictel*], 3s.

From the same Adam for one acre of land at Fishpond Field this year, 6d.

For a headland of pasture in the Launde at Lady's Wood and for pasture land in the same grazed by horses and foals of various men this year in winter as well as in summer, 4s. 6d.

From John Syre for winter and summer pasture in a close at High Hall, 8s. 6d.

For a headland of pasture on the north side of the little meadow 2d., nothing because it was grazed by the cows of the manor.

For a certain portion of pasture of Oldetoft, parcel of Cow Pasture leased in the preceding year to John Backynge, chaplain, for 4d., nothing this year because the land there lies fallow and was grazed by the lord's sheep.

From 17½ acres of land recently leased to William Sparshoo for 4s. 4½d. nothing this year because it was grazed by the lord's sheep.

From William Grocer for winter and summer pasture in a close at the sheepcote next to Allwood Green this year, 5s.

From Robert Fletcher for 5 acres of land on the east side of Fishpond Field between the land of Robert Sare this year, 20d.

From the same Robert for 2 acres of land lying next to Strondes Way this year, 6d.

From Roger Prede for the farm of Burchards Close this year, 12s.

From Robert Syre for a curtilage and 4 acres of land in three pieces called Sparchoo purchased by the lord this year, 4s.

From Thomas Bonde for 4 acres of land by estimate of the tenement Burchards on the west side of Burchards Close, 12d.

From the same Thomas for a piece of land of the said tenement lying at Rickinghall Willows next to the land recently of Adam Pitlake, 8d.

For pasture next to Fishpond Field on the west side, nothing this year because it was grazed by sheep.

For pasture in the outer Launde at North Haugh leased in the preceding year to Robert Smith for 4s. 6d., nothing this year because it was grazed by the lord's sheep.

For the pasture of one piece of land called Brooms Wong, nothing this year because aforesaid.

For 6 acres of land at the north head of Fishpond Field, nothing because it was grazed by sheep.

For 12 acres of land at Summer Way from the land of the Prior,[90] nothing because it was sown with the lord's oats.

From John Fuller junior of East End [*Estende*] for 10 acres of land of the Prior recently leased to Richard Morton and Walter Robwood this year, 3s. 4d.

From Robert Frances for 6 acres of land called Okland from the land of the Prior leased to him with ploughing services, per acre 8d., 4s.

From John Fuller junior for one acre of land of the said Prior there this year, 4d.

From Peter Robwood for 7 acres of land of the said Prior there this year, 21d.

From Robert Frances and John Cooper for 7 acres of land of the same Prior there this year, 2s. 8d.

From the same John for one acre of land of the same Prior there this year, 4d.

---

90 The manor was leasing Easthouse from the prior of Ixworth, and in turn subleasing some of the land to others.

From Peter Robwood for 6 acres of land called Short Land this year, 2s.

For 12 acres of land called Blunts Land and 5½ acres of land on the west side of Blunts Land nothing this year because it was not possible to lease, as per an amercement in the court.[91]

From John Syre for 2 acres of land in one piece at Doucedeux from the land of the Prior, 12d.

From Thomas Daye for 6 acres of land at the north end of a new close[92] this year, per acre 3d., 18d.

For pasture for the bailiff's foal in summer this year, 6d.

Sum [*blank*]

Farm of land and meadows of High Hall For the farm of land, tenements, meadows and pasture there leased as shown by a bill 117s. 9¼d., of which from the tenants in Westhorpe 42s. 5d. and from the responsibility of the sergeant, 75s. 4¼d.

Sum [*blank*]

Farm of land of East House[93] in the lord's hands at farm For the farm of parcels of land and tenement of East House to various lessees for 29s. 8d., that is to Robert Syre 20s., Roger Prede 7s., Richard Rampley 16d., John Cooper 16d.[94] And no more because the residue of the said land is leased elsewhere for herbage.

Sum [*blank*]

Sale of hay and herbage of the meadows For all the hay coming from 4½ acres of meadow in Broad Dole [*Broodole*] sold to various men this year 36s., that is Thomas Bote with carriage 15s., Henry Chapman with carriage 13s., Roger Prede 4s.[95] item from certain men from Bury, with carriage, 4s.

For 3 roods of meadow in Mickle Meadow purchased from John Rampoyle, chaplain this year, 3s. 8d.

From John Cook for the herbage of one acre of meadow called Turf Pit Acre, 3s. 8d.

Sum [*blank*]

Perquisites of court For one court held there on Tuesday next before the Feast of the Conversion of St Paul, 60s. 11d.

For one court held there on Thursday next before the Feast of St Michael, 58s. 7d.

Sum [*blank*]

Sale of corn and stock For 1qr 4 bus. of wheat sold as elsewhere, price per bus. 10d., 10s.

For 6 bus. of wheat sold for harvest expenses as elsewhere, 4s.

For 13 qrs 2 bus. of barley sold as elsewhere at various prices, 54s. 5d.

For 2 qrs 1 bus. of peas sold as elsewhere, 6s. 4d.

---

[91] The suggestion is that the sergeant was somehow at fault for the want of a lessee.

[92] The piecemeal enclosure of strips of open fields with hedges and ditches, usually involving the conversion of arable to pasture, became common in this area of Suffolk in the century and a half after the Black Death. See Bailey, 'Form, function', pp. 25–9.

[93] For East House, or Church House, see Introduction, pp. xxii–xxiii.

[94] As detailed above, p. 75.

[95] Three men bought the surplus hay produced in Broad Dole, two of them paying to use the lord's carts to carry it away. Thomas Bote was from Bury St Edmunds, Roger Prede was from Walsham which explains why he had no need for carriage; Henry Chapman was not a Walsham resident.

For 3 qrs 4 bus. of oats from elsewhere sold as elsewhere, 8s. 11d.
For 2 qrs 5 bus. 3 pecks three quarters of ½ a peck and 3 parts of ½ a bus. of oats \from rent received elsewhere, price per qr 2s. 4d./, 7s. 5¼d.
For 4 bus. of dross barley sold to Olive Prede at High Hall, 8d.
Sum [blank]

Farm of the dovecote For 20 pigeons sold elsewhere for harvest expenses 7d.
Sum [blank]

Works and customary services sold For 7½ hens from rent from H[igh Hall] sold, 15d.
For 7¾ hens from rent from the responsibility of the hayward, 15½d.
For 66 eggs from High Hall sold, 3¼d.
For 31½ eggs from rent from the responsibility of the hayward, 1½d.
For ½lb of cumin from rent sold, 1½d.
For 190¾ and 2 parts of a winter work sold, price per work ½d., 7s. 11¾d.
For 6 and 2 parts of one carrying service, price per work 1d., 6¾d.
For 6 and one quarter carriage of manure sold, price per work 2d., 12½d.
For 3 weeding works from the responsibility of the bailiff, 1½d.
For 99¾ weeding works from the responsibility of the hayward, price per work ½d., 4s. 1½d.
For 39¾ mowings sold, price per work 1½d., 4s. 11½d. and half a ¼d.
For 9 harvest works from the responsibility of the bailiff sold, 18d.
For 145¾ harvest works sold, per work 2d., 24s. 3½d.
For 25 harvest boonworks from the responsibility of the hayward sold, per work 4d., 8s. 4d.
Sum [blank]

Farm of the cows For the farm of the lactage and the calves of 19 cows, leased to Thomas Daye at full lease, per head 6s., 114s.
For the farm of the lactage and the calf of one cow of first calving, he answers for half a cow, 3s.
For the farm of 12 hens leased to Thomas Daye, per head 6d., 6s.
Sum [blank]

Issues of the garden For fruit in the garden of the lord at the manor and at High Hall nothing here because it was delivered for the lady's hospitality as appears elsewhere.
Sum nil.

Sale of wool and pelts For locks and broken wool sold, nothing here because it was delivered to the lady as appears elsewhere.
For 3 pelts of wool in murrain sold to Olive Prede as elsewhere, 12d.
For 2 pelts from slaughter sold to John Knight as elsewhere, 3d.
For one pelt in murrain sold as elsewhere, ½d.
Sum [blank]

Sale of wood From Amice Marler for 39 perches of underwood in Lady's Wood, price per acre 8s., 23½d.
From John Barker for 3 roods 5½ perches of underwood there, 6s. 3d.

From William Lakenham for one rood 2 perches of underwood there, 2s. 1d.
From Robert Lester for ½ rood of underwood there, 12d.
From John Fuller for 17 perches of underwood there, 10d.
From John Coggeshall for 15 perches of underwood there, 9d.
From Simon Wright for ½ acre 5 perches of underwood there, 4s. 3d.
From Alice Pye for one rood 6 perches of underwood there, 2s. 3½d.
From John Pye for 39 perches of underwood there, 23½d.
From Thomas Herring for ½ rood 10 perches of underwood there, 18d.
And timber given by the lady to William Sare, 100 faggots coming from 1 rood.
And to Sarah Codenham by the lady, ½ acre of underwood.
From John Grene for 34 perches of underwood in North Haugh, 20½d.
From Peter Poye for 36 perches of underwood there, 21½d.
From John Margery for 1½ roods 15 perches of underwood there, 3s. 9d.
From John Frances senior for a parcel of a border [*bordur*'] at High Hall Wood, 2s.
From John Wells for a parcel of a border there, 22d.
From Edmund Patel for an elm growing upon a ditch of the manor behind the barn, 8d.
From John Syre for fronds of three ash trees felled at High Hall for the mill, 3d.
From John Vincent for fronds and branches [*escaet*'] of two oaks felled in the same
manor for raising the mill, sold to him, 5s.
For the stakes [*escaet*'] from the old mill sold, that is to John Frances 8d. and Peter
Poye 2s., 2s. 8d.

Sum [blank]

Issues of the manor From John Coggeshall for pea straw at High Hall, 14d.
From John Frances senior for pea straw there, 6d.
From John Syre for pea straw there, 8d.
From John Frances senior for pea straw at Walsham Hall, 8d.
From Roger Prede for pea straw there, 8d.
From John Lester for bracken in the rabbit warren [*conicular*'], 8½d.
For the lord's cart leased to the bailiff for one day carrying faggots from Wattisfield
to Barningham in the summer, 10d.
For the lord's cart leased to the same bailiff on the eve of St Laurence from after-
noon to nightfall to carry three cartloads of peas, 5d.
For the lord's cart leased to William Lakenham for ½ day, 5d.[96]
For two ploughs of the lady leased to Thomas Abraham for 1 day, 16d.
From John Cook for the fronds of one elm felled in the rabbit warren for the body
of a cart, 3d.
For the skin of a calf in murrain sold elsewhere, 1½d.

Sum [blank]

Foreign receipts [*blank*]

Sales at the audit [*blank*]

---

[96] Manor carts were often leased to tenants for cash when they were not being used for the demesne.
Sir William Elmham, lord of the manor, died early in 1403 and was succeeded by Elizabeth, his wife,
which explains why the carts are described as belonging to the lord (leased before his death) and the
plough as belonging to the lady (after his death).

Rent resolute with decays The same accounts for rent resolute for the hall of Thelnetham of 2s. p.a., nothing because the fee is outside the lord's hands.

Item for the hall of Rickinghall p.a. \hayward/, 3s. 1½d.

Item paid for castle ward of Norwich p.a. \bailiff/, 16s.

Item paid to John Margery p.a. \hayward/, 1½d.

Item in allowance for the tenement of Nicholas Tiptot the reeve this year, 3s. 7d. and half a ¼d.

Item for the tenement of Thomas Fuller the hayward this year, 18¾d.

In allowance of rent for Champneys p.a., 12d.

Item in allowance of rent for various villein tenements in the lord's hands, 29s. three quarters of a ¼d. and half a quarter of a ¼d. and three parts of a ¼d.

Item for a messuage, 3 acres 1 rood of villein land recently of Walter Dennis in the lord's hands, 13¼d. and three parts of a ¼d.

Item in allowance of a forge formerly of Walter Smith because it is charged in rents of assize above, 6d.

Item for the tenement Outlaws, 6¼d.

In allowance of rent on one acre of land formerly of Master John of Walsham, 2½d.

Item for one acre one rood of land recently of Edmund of Pakenham, 2¼d.

Item for a smithy [*domo fabrico*] in Palmer Street, because it is vacant and lies on the highway [*iacet alter' via'*] p.a., 8d.

In rent released to Robert Osbern by a deed of the lady Rose of Pakenham, ¼d.

Item in allowance of rent from High Hall in the lord's hands, newly purchased in perpetuity, 4d. Item for sheriff's aid of the same, 2½d.

Item in allowance of sheriff's aid of Burchards and Sparshoos p.a., 1d.

Item to the hall of Ashfield for castle ward of Norwich for High Hall p.a. \bailiff/, 17d.

Item paid to Eye castle for castle ward for High Hall this year once \bailiff/, 9d.

In allowance for various tenements in the lord's hands pertaining to High Hall p.a. \by the bailiff/, 15s. 9¾d.

Item paid to the hall of Ashfield for rent p.a. \by the bailiff/, 2d.

Item paid for hundred suit released for Burchards this year \by the bailiff/, 16d.

Item paid to Helimot from hidage and for ward for Burchardes p.a. \by the bailiff/, 9d.

Item in rent resolute for lord Sir William Bardwell for one acre of meadow at Turf Pits purchased by the lord from John Rampley, chaplain p.a. \by the bailiff/, 4d.

Item in allowance made to Richard Morton for two and a half messuages and certain land granted to him and his heirs by a deed of the lord p.a., 10d. and a quarter of a ¼d.

Sum [*blank*]

Cost of the ploughs and carts In hiring a smith for providing and forging the iron on two ploughs and for shoeing the stots and carthorses p.a., including the cost of 4 bus. of wheat,[97] 28s., of which 10s. paid by the hayward.

In fitting eight ploughs from the lord's timber with a shaft bought for one plough, 19d.

In two new canvas halters bought, 1d.

In four canvas reins bought for carthorses, 2d.

---

[97] Provision of 4 bus. of wheat was part of the contract with the smith, and the payment is covered in the stock account below.

In the stipend of William Sadler and his son from Stanton for five days' work making five new leather collars and three new headstalls; and mending ten old collars and two saddle-pads for a saddle of a cart; and four pairs of chain-traces and traces for a cart and a pair of shafts; and two pairs of tacks for shaft-heads, between them per day 8d., 3s. 4d.

In 5 ells of canvas bought for the same, 15d.

In 12 lb of flock bought for the same, 12d.

In thread bought for the same, 3d.

In a tanned hide and 2 pairs of girths and a calfskin likewise bought for the same from John Barker, 5s. 2d.

In the stipend of John Cooper for one day's piece-work felling and cutting one elm for three pairs of ?medium-sized [*meditull'*] carts and making four felloes for them, 4d.

In 7 lb of grease bought for greasing carts, 8d.

In 6 clouts bought for a cart-axle with nails, 11½d.

Item in ironwork bought for 4 leather halters, 7d.

In iron nails bought for fastening the cart traces, ½d.

Item in 2 metal plates made from old iron of the lord, 2d.

Paid to John Cooper for making a cart body from new from the lord's timber, 20d.[98]

Item in a cord for a cart 16 fathoms long bought for binding a cart, 15d.

In a pair of body traces bought for a cart, 10d.

In half a tawed hide bought for mending a harness, 11d.

In the stipend of William Sadler and his son for 2 days' work mending collars and other cart harness, 16d.

Sum [*blank*]

Cost of the buildings In the stipend of John Miller from Wattisfield, thatcher for 11 days' work thatching upon the east side of the knight's chamber[99] and upon the east side of the dairy, at 4d. per day, 3s. 8d. And supplemented by winter works, as appears elsewhere.

In the stipend of Robert Manser, carpenter for 6 days' work making a new gate next to the granary and a wicket-gate next to there and a bay for calves in the cowshed and for putting in nails in an old external gate, at 4d. per day, 2s.

Item in an iron clout and an iron plate bought for the said new gate next to the granary and for the outer gate, 5d.

Item in one iron bolt and one iron hasp bought for the external gate, 5d.

Sum [*blank*]

Cost of the mill In the expenses of 12 carters with 6 carts from boonworks fetching timber at Haddiscoe [*Norfolk*] for the mill, 16d.[100]

Item in 2 bases carried from the manor up to the mill, 2½d.

Item in fetching a mill post and carrying it from Hinderclay up to the mill, 7d.

---

[98] Cooper's tenement was in the hamlet at East End.

[99] The building costs in the accounts show that the capital messuage of the manor contained a range of domestic and agricultural buildings in close proximity.

[100] The millstone was fetched using the labour services of the unfree tenants rather than hired labour, but they were able to claim reasonable expenses for the trip.

Item in expenses of various men digging the old mill post out of the ground and the ?poles [*les powelyn*], 16d.[101]

Sum [blank]

Cost of the sheepfold In 2 gallons and 3 quarts of tar bought for sheep salve, 22d.
In grease bought to mix with the same, 10d.
In 36 hurdles made from sticks at the lord's fold, 12d.
In washing and shearing 202 sheep of the lady, 2s. 6½d.
Item in 6 hurdles bought from Robert Margery, 5d.
In red ochre bought for marking sheep after shearing, 1d.
In 12 hurdles bought from John Margery for the fold, 10d.

Sum [blank]

Stipend of the manorial servants In the stipend of John Tiptot, ploughman p.a., 8s.
In the stipend of Robert, his brother, ploughman p.a., 8s.
In the stipend of William Man, the plough-holder p.a., 8s. In a reward made to him for his good service this year, 2s.[102]
In the stipend of John Dennis, ploughman p.a., 8s.
In the stipend of John Cook, shepherd p.a., 13s. 4d.
In the stipend of the dairyherd, nothing.

Sum [blank]

Threshing and winnowing In threshing 31 qrs 6 bus. of wheat and rye by task, 4d. per qr, 10s. 7d.
In threshing 122 qrs 1 bus. of barley, peas and oats by task, 2d. per qr, 20s. 4½d.
In winnowing all the abovesaid grain, containing 153 qrs 7 bus. of various grain, for 3 qrs 2d., 8s. 6½d.

Sum [blank]

Purchase of corn and stock In 1 qr of rye bought for alternative [*alternand'*] seed[103] as elsewhere, 8s. 4d.
In one stot bought on the Feast of St Simon and Jude, as elsewhere, 10s. 2d.
In 6 calves bought from the lessee of the cows, by agreement, 6s.
In 12 chickens bought for making into capons as elsewhere, 12d.

Sum [blank]

Minute [*expenses*] In bonus payments to 4 ploughmen, one shepherd and one dairyherd on the days of Christmas and Easter, 12d.
In bonus payments to the same on the day of the Purification, 3d.
In gifts to the ploughmen at the time of sowing wheat, oats, barley and peas, 4s. 7d.

---

[101] A mill was being built or rebuilt with second-hand rather than new timber: the timber from Haddiscoe, about 30 miles away, was probably boards (to make the buck of the mill). The mill post was brought from Hinderclay, about 4 miles away.

[102] William Man was rewarded for his good service as a ploughman. If 'this year' relates to the year of payment rather than the service, then this may well have been a retirement gift: sixteen customary works were used to cover some of his duties due to illness (see below) and in the 1406/7 account his son had taken over as the plough-holder.

[103] Seed was occasionally bought from other manors to rejuvenate the stock.

Item in expenses at the Ploughale, 8s. 1½d., of which in the price of 2 bus. of wheat 20d. and in the price of 12 hens, 2s.

In mending a pair of fetters for horses, 3d.

Item paid for tanning a calf-skin elsewhere, 2d.

In one pair of new harrows made from the lord's timber, 6d.

In 120 faggots made, as elsewhere, in the wood of High Hall to make a hedge around the wood there,[104] 6d.

Item in 2 new sacks bought, which measure 4 bus. of wheat, 20d.

In parchment bought for court rolls and accounts, 8d.

Sum [blank]

Lease of East House Paid to the Prior of Ixworth for the land and tenement called East House leased from him for a term of 10 years, this year is the 8th, for the terms of Easter and Michaelmas, 40s.

Sum [blank]

Weeding and mowing Weeding in the lady's corn this year, nothing here because it was done by customary works as elsewhere.

In mowing the great meadow and the little meadow this year, in total 10s.

In spreading herbage and turning the hay, lifting and likewise collecting, nothing here because it was done by customary works as elsewhere.

In services bought for customary expenses in the carriage of hay this year, 4d.

Sum [blank]

Cost of the harvest In the expenses of the bailiff, hayward, cook and stacker, loader and 2 carters of the lord for 4 works at harvest with the expenses of 69 harvest boonworks from this manor, 2 ploughmen, a dairymaid, a smith, a miller and others at the Reapale at noon with the expenses of 6 harvest boonworks and 9 harvest works from the customary tenants of High Hall for one day, as elsewhere.

In bread, for the price of 6 bushels of wheat, as sold above, 2s. 3d.

In ale bought, 12s. 8d.

In meat bought, 8s. 10d.

And in the price of 2 hoggets above sold, price of pelts, 2s.

In the price of 20 pigeons from stock above sold, 7d.

In fish and herrings bought, 16d.

In milk, cheese, eggs and butter bought, 3s. 5½d.

In oat meal bought, 3d.

In salt bought, 3½d.

In pepper bought, ½d.

In candles bought, 2d.[105]

In the stipend of John Coggeshall, cook and the stacker at the harvest this year, 5s.

In the stipend of John, the servant [famulus] of John Frances, loader at harvest this year, 4s.

In 4 pairs of gloves bought for 2 carters, a loader and a stacker, 8d.

In customary works 367½ harvest works from this manor, the expenses of each one ¼d., 7s. 10¼d.

---

[104] Evidence of dead hedges being made. The faggots were enumerated using the long hundred.

[105] To light the hall or barn during the meal because all the daylight hours were spent in the fields.

In customary works 69 harvest boonworks from this manor, the expenses of each one ¾d., 8½d. and half a ¼d.

Sum [*blank*]

Wages In the wages of John Magges, sergeant there p.a., less 4 weeks at harvest taken at the lord's table, per week 12d., 48s.

Sum [*blank*]

Steward's expenses In the steward's expenses at the first court held there, 23½d.
In ale bought for the steward's expenses for a court held at High Hall, 4d.[106]
In the steward's expenses for a court held on Thursday next before the Feast of St Michael the Archangel, 2s. 3½d.

Sum [*blank*]

Lord's expenses Nil.

Foreign expenses In an allowance made by the lady to William Hawes and Robert Hawes from two fines in court, 4s.
Paid for half a 15th to the lord king[107] in the first year, 2s. 6d.
Item paid for quarter of a 15th to the lord king, 15d.
In the expenses of the bailiff and 9 men with 4 carts fetching barley at Bowthorpe for seed, going and coming back, 4s. 11½d.
Item in expenses of 6 men for 4 weeks looking after the manor after the death of the lord etc. in ale, 5s., in meat and fish, 5s.
Item in expenses of various men for taking game birds [*pro volcribus*] for the lord's hospitality at Christmas,[108] 4d.

Sum [*blank*]

Cash payments Delivered to the lady for the proceeds of one cart of hay, given to Thomas Bote of Bury by the lady, above sold with carriage, 5s.
To the same lady, to cover the cost of 12 pigeons bought by the bailiff for the lord's burial,[109] 4d.
To the same lady from the responsibility of the hayward for food by one tally, £8 10s.
To the same lady by the hand of Nicholas Tiptot as part of a fine for the office of reeve, 23s. 4d.
To the same lady by the hand of the dairyherd at various times by one tally, £4.
Item delivered to Adam Blayer, sergeant of Westhorpe from rent and farm of High Hall \42s. 5d./ by the hand of the tenant of High Hall in Westhorpe as appears in foreign receipts there, 50s.

Sum [*blank*]

[*Reverse*]

---

[106] There was no separate court for High Hall manor at this date, because its business had been subsumed into that of Walsham manor following its acquisition sometime in the 1380s, but clearly the steward maintained the practice of holding the occasional court at the manor of High Hall itself.

[107] The contribution of the lord to the tax payable by the vill of Walsham to the Lay Subsidy this year.

[108] Sir William Elmham died early in 1403, having spent Christmas 1402 at Westhorpe.

[109] For the funeral feast.

Issues of the grange there after the Feast of St Michael the Archangel in the 4th year of Henry IV.

Wheat

From the total issue of the grange there this year by tally against Adam Brook, granger of the lord sworn, 27 qrs 2 bus. threshed by task. Received from Peter Poye by agreement for harvest expenses of harvest, 4 bus. of wheat. From the issue of the new grange, 2 bus. threshed and winnowed by the manorial servants for the harvest.

Sum [*blank*]

From which, in seed upon 47 acres of land in various parcels by estimate by one tally, with rye below against Walter Fraunceys, the hayward, 11 qrs 2 bus., at 2 bus. per acre minus in total 4 bus.

In the livery of the manorial servants shown below and for the harvest bread [*blank*]. Delivered to Thomas Baker, the baker of the lord, for expending in the hospitality of the lord at Westhorpe by one tally, 6 qrs 3 bus.

In the livery of the granger, 1 bus.

In the livery of the smith for iron for ploughs p.a., the cost in money as within, 4 bus.

Item in provisioning various tenants of the lady looking after the manor after the death of the lord with Sir William Bardwell, 3 bus.

In sales within [*blank*], of which for harvest expenses, 6 bus., and for the Ploughale, 2 bus.

Sum [*blank*]

Rye

4 bus. remain in the grange. From the total issue of the grange there this year by tally against the said Adam, 4 qrs 4 bus., threshed by task. From purchases within for alternative seed, 1 qr.

Sum [*blank*]

From which, in seed upon 6 acres of land in one parcel, 1 qr 4 bus. by one tally with wheat above, sown at 2 bus. per acre.

In the livery of the manorial servants, as appears below, and for the harvest bread, [*blank*] … of which for harvest bread, 4 bus.

In the livery of the granger, 1 bus.

Sum [*blank*]

Barley

5 bus. of barley remain from last year, from damage assessed. From the issue of the grange there this year by one tally against the said Adam, 49 qrs 6 bus., threshed by task. Received from the bailiff of Bowthorpe [*Benthorpe*] for seed by one tally, 20 qrs razed measure which makes 16 qrs gross measure. From damages assessed in the lord's barley, as appears by court roll, 1 bus. of barley.

Sum [*blank*]

From which, in seed upon 56 acres of land in various parcels by estimate, 21 qrs by one tally against the said sower, at 3 bus. per acre, in total [*blank*].

In the livery of the manorial servants, as appears below, and for the harvest bread, 8 qrs 5 bus. of which for harvest bread, 2 qrs 3 bus.

Delivered to Thomas Baker, the lord's baker to make malt for expending on the lord's hospitality at Westhorpe by one tally, 23 qrs 4 bus.

In sales within [*blank*].

Sum [*blank*]

And remaining, 1 bushel of barley from damage assessed in the hands of Peter Poye and Thomas Daye.

Peas

1 qr remains in the grange. From the issue of the grange there this year by one tally against the said Adam, 22 qrs 5 bus., threshed by task. From the same issue by estimate in straw for feeding young [*vit'*] stots as elsewhere, and hoggets and gimmers in winter, 4 qrs.

Sum [*blank*]

From which, in seed upon 46 acres of land in various parcels by estimate, 9 qrs 7 bus. by one tally against the said sower, at 2 bus. per acre, plus in total 1 qr 5 bus.
Delivered to Thomas Baker the lord's baker for expending on the lord's hospitality at Westhorpe by one tally, 8 qrs of which 4 bus. of the remaining stock.
In the livery of the manorial servants viz: for harvest bread last year, 1 qr 2 bus.
Item in the livery of the manorial servants viz: for bread for feeding horses, 1 qr.
Item delivered for the lady's hospitality in summer, 1 qr.
Item in bread baked for the horses with 4 carts going to Bowthorpe to fetch barley for seed, 3 bus.
In feed for the stots, new-born calves, and hoggets and gimmers in winter by estimation, in straw above, 4 qrs.
In sales within [*blank*].

Sum [*blank*]

Oats

1 qr 6 bus. remain from damage assessed. From the issue of the grange there this year by one tally against the said Adam, 49 qrs 6 bus., threshed by task. From the same issue by estimate 60 sheaves for feed for calves from elsewhere, 5 bus. From annual rents at the Feast of St Edmund King and Martyr, 20 qrs 2 bus.

Sum [*blank*]

From which, in seed upon 68 acres of land in various parcels by estimate, 21 qrs 5 bus. by one tally against the said sower, at 2½ bus. per acre, plus 3 bus. more in total.
In meal made for pottage for 4 ploughmen, one shepherd and one dairyherd, 1 qr 4 bus.
Delivered to Thomas Baker, the lord's baker for fodder for the lord's horses at Westhorpe by one tally, 25 qrs 5 bus. as elsewhere.
In fodder for cart-horses and stots this year, because of a great need [*quia mag' indig'*], 2 qrs 4 bus.
In allowance for the tenement of Nicholas Tiptot, reeve this year, 3 bus.
Item for the tenement of Thomas Fuller, hayward this year, nothing because it is not due.
Item in allowance for tenements in the lord's hands, 3 qrs 2½ bus. a quarter and half a quarter of 1 pk. and two parts of ½ bus. of oats from rent.
Item in allowance made to Richard Morton for two and a half messuages and certain land granted to him and his heirs by a deed of the lord, this year is the third, 3¾ pk. of oats.
In livery of the granger, 1 bus.
Item delivered to Bury against the burial of the lord, 6 qrs.

Item delivered for hospitality against the coming of the Earl Marshall,[110] 1 qr 4 bus.
Item in fodder for the horses of 4 carts going to Bowthorpe to fetch barley seed, 1 qr 2 bus.
In feed for calves of issue, by estimate in sheaves around 5 bus.
In sales within [blank].

Sum [blank]

And remaining, 1 qr 4 bus. in the hands of John Manser from [illeg.] of the lady and 1 qr from damage assessed in the hands of John Syre.

Multure at the mill [blank]

Livery of the manorial servant [blank]

Acres sown This year with all types of grain, 223 acres.

Sum 223 acres.

Cart horses
6 remain.
From a heriot after the death of Robert Poye as shown by a court roll in the present year, 1.

Sum [blank]

From which in sales to John Markant, 1 weak [cart horse].

Sum shown.

Stots
3 remain.
Item bought as within at the Feast of Simon and Jude, 1.

Sum [blank]

From which, in murrain at the end of the year, 1 of white colour.

Sum shown.

And remaining 3 stots at Michaelmas.

Oxen
4 remain.

Sum 4.

And remaining 4 oxen, of which one is old [cron'].

Bulls
1 remains.

Sum shown.

And remaining 1 bull

Cows
19 remain, of which 3 are old.
Added from heifers below, 1.

---

[110] The Earl Marshall in this year was Ralph Neville, Earl of Westmorland, who had probably fought with William de Elmham in the royal armies of the 1380s and so must have been attending the funeral.

From a heriot after the death of Olivia Cranmer, 1, as appears in the court roll in the present year.

From a purchase of the lady in the present year from the executors of Robert Aysshfeld in the present year, 1 old cow.

Received from Westhorpe in the present year, 2 cows.

Sum [blank]

From which, sold at the fair of Ixworth[111] on the Feast of St Luke before calving, 1 old cow.

Item delivered to Westhorpe for the lord's larder in the present year, 2.

In sales within, 1 old cow in the present year.

Sum 4.

And remaining   20 cows of which 2 are old.   It balances.

Heifers

1 remains.

Sum shown.

And added to cows above.   It balances.

Young bullocks and heifers

3 added from calves below.

Sum 3.

And delivered to John Rampley, sergeant of Rickinghall, on the Feast of St Martin.

It balances.

Calves

3 remain.

Purchased from the farmer of the cows by agreement, 6.

Sum [blank]

From which, added to young bullocks and heifers above, 3.

Item in murrain, 1 calf of issue.

Item delivered to Westhorpe by tally against Adam Blayer, 5 calves.

Sum [blank]

Hides

1 hide from a calf in murrain above.

And a stot in murrain as above, 1

Sum 2.

From which, in sales as within, 1.

Sum shown.

And remaining 1 stot hide in the hands of the bailiff.

Tawed hides

1 tawed stot hide remains.

Sum shown.

From which, in repairing and mending harnesses, 1 tawed stot hide.

Sum as above.   It balances.

---

[111] Where produce was bought or sold is seldom stated in manorial accounts. This rare glimpse reflects the importance of Ixworth's October fair as a venue for livestock purchases, attracting traders from northern England. See N. Amor, 'Riding out recession: Ixworth and Woolpit in the later Middle Ages', *PSIAH* 40 (2002), pp. 134–5.

Tanned hides
2 tanned calfskins remain.
Sum 2 tanned hides.

And remaining 2 tanned hides, of which one is in the hands of the bailiff and one is in the hands of John Barker, the tanner.

Ewes
3 sheep remain.
Sum 3.

And remaining, 3 old sheep.

Hoggets and gimmers
Added from lambs below, 203.
Sum 203.

From which, in murrain in winter before shearing, 3.
Item in murrain after shearing, 1.
Item in sales as within for harvest expenses, excluding the skins, 2 rigs [*reggynges*].[112]
Sum 6.

And remaining 197 hoggets and gimmers, of which 92 are gimmers.

Lambs
203 remain.
From the issue of ewes above, 3.
From the issue of gimmers fawned before the accepted time [*fetanc' ante tempus admittenc'*], 47.
Sum [*blank*]

From which, added to hoggets and gimmers, 203.
In tithes given, 5.
Item delivered to the lady against the burial of the lord, 40 lambs.
Item delivered to John Nawton, steward of lord's hospitality, in the summer for expending in hospitality, 2 suckling [*suckerell'*] lambs.
Sum [*blank*]

And remaining 3 lambs, of which 2 are female.

Fleeces
202 fleeces from sheep at shearing and no more because one sheep lost its fleece.
Sum [*blank*]

From which, in tithes given 20 fleeces.
Delivered to the lady at the wool house [*ad domum lan'*], 182 fleeces.
Sum [*blank*]

Sheepskins
3 from sheep above in murrain.
Sum 3.

From which, in sales as within, 3.
Sum as above.　　　　　　　　　　　It balances.

---

[112] A partially developed or half-castrated ram known, in Suffolk, as a rig.

Skins
1 from sheep as above in murrain.
2 from sheep, as above, slaughtered for the harvest.
Sum 3.
From which, in sales within, 3.
Sum as above.

Lambskins Nil.
Sum nil.

Capons
16 remaining, of which 4 are from rent.
From rent p.a., 8.
Made up from poultry as below this year, 12.
Received from the lady out of the hospitality of the lord's shortly after Christmas to look after them, 24.
Sum [*blank*]
From which, in allowance for tenements in the lord's hands, 4.
Delivered to the lady for provisions against the lord's burial, 35 capons.
In murrain in winter, 5.
In provisions of various men looking after the manor after the lord's death, 1.
Sum [*blank*]
And remaining 15 capons, of which 4 are from rent.

Cockerels and hens
1 cockerel, 12 hens remain in the dairy.
From rent p.a. at Christmas, 123½ hens.
From rent of Heighall p.a., 21.
Sum [*blank*]
From which, in allowance for the reeve's tenement this year, 3.
Item for the tenement of Thomas Fuller the hayward, 2.
Item for various tenements in the lord's hands, 9¾ hens.
Item in rent resolute for a messuage, 3 acres 1 rood of villein land recently of Walter Dennis remaining in the lord's hands by Robert Dennis this year is the 12th, 1.
Item in allowance for various tenements in the lord's hands pertaining to High Hall, 11½ hens.
Item in allowance made to Gilbert Moundemyll and Katherine his wife and their legal heirs granted to them by a deed of the lord p.a. for the tenement Helpes in Westhorpe pertaining to High Hall, 1.
Item in allowance made to Richard Morton for two and a half messuages and certain land granted to him and his heirs by a deed of the lord as appears in the section on oats, 1 hen.
Delivered to Adam Blayer sergeant of Westhorpe by the hand of the tenant of High Hall in Westhorpe, 1.
Item delivered to the steward of hospitality at Westhorpe for hospitality of the lord by 1 tally from the responsibility of the hayward, 95 hens.
In murrain in the dairy, 3.
In sales within 15¼ hens, of which from the responsibility of the bailiff 7½ hens and from the responsibility of the hayward, 7¾ hens.
Sum [*blank*]
And remaining in the dairy, 1 cockerel and 12 hens.

Eggs

From the issue of hens above, nothing because the hens were leased at farm for money as within. From rent from the term of Easter, 720 eggs. From rent from High Hall for the same term, 105 eggs.

Sum 825 eggs.

From which, in allowance for the reeve's tenement this year, 30 eggs.

Item for the hayward's tenement this year, 8.

Item for various tenements in the lord's hands, 102 eggs.

Item for a messuage, 3 acres 1 rood of land recently of Walter Dennis in the lord's hands, 3½ eggs.

Item for various tenements pertaining to High Hall in the lord's hands, 39.

Item delivered for expending in the hospitality of the lord by a tally against the steward there, 540 eggs.

Item allowance made to Richard Morton for two and a half messuages and certain land granted to him and his heirs by a deed of the lord as appears above in the section on oats, 5 eggs.

In sales within 98½ eggs, of which from the responsibility of the bailiff 66 eggs and from the responsibility of the hayward 31½ eggs.

Sum [*blank*]

Poultry

From the issue of hens above, nothing because the hens were granted at farm for money within.

Bought as within, 12.

Sum 12.

And accounted as capons above.   It balances.

Dovecote

From the issue of a dovecote at the manor, except tithes [*blank*].

And from a dovecote at High Hall this year, 2 pigeons.

Sum [*blank*]

From which delivered for the lord's hospitality [*blank*]. In sales as within for the harvest expenses, 20 pigeons.

Sum [*blank*]

Cumin From rent from the Prior of Bricett p.a., ½lb cumin.

Sum ½lb cumin. And sold as within.   It balances.

Pepper

Remaining ½lb pepper. From rent received from Walter Frances for a tenement recently of John Pinfold pertaining to High Hall, ½lb pepper.

Sum 1 lb pepper.

And remaining, 1 lb pepper.

Ploughing services From the issue of 9 greater customary *tenementa* this year that accordingly provide 5½ ploughs this year, 27½ ploughing services taken at the seasons of winter and Lent, that is from each whole plough 5 ploughing services and they receive from the lord for each plough 6 loaves of mixed corn, of which 20 to the bus., and to be allowed 2 winter works.

90

From the issue of 13 other customary *tenementa* that provide annually 21 ploughing services, of which each plough shall make 3 ploughing services and receive from the lord for each plough 6 loaves of the said grain and the said weight, and no allowance of works.

From the issue of customary tenants of High Hall this year, nothing.

Sum [*blank*]   It balances.

And expended in ploughing the lord's land at the aforesaid time.

Ploughale From the issue of customary tenants that provide 14 ploughing services this year.   Sum 14.

And expended in ploughing the lord's land.   It balances.

Winter and summer works From customary services for a half day, 963 winter and summer works, price per work ½d.

From customary services from High Hall, 10 works.

Sum 973 works.

From which for allowance for the reeve's tenement this year, 28.

And for the hayward's tenement this year, 8¾ works.

Item for various tenements in the lord's hands, 176¾ and 3 parts of a work.

Item for the tenement of Walter Dennis, 9½ works.

Item in allowance for the tenement recently of Robert Wynge pertaining to High Hall in the lord's hands, 10.

In allowance made to Richard Morton for two and a half messuages and certain land granted to him and his heirs by a deed of the lord as appears above in the section on oats 7¼ winter works.

Item in 27½ ploughing services expended, 60 works, for each ploughing service 2 works.

Item tumbrels[113] made this year, nothing.

In weeds [*bolles and darnell*] removed from the wheat to prepare for seeding, 23 works.

In making drainage furrows at the time of sowing wheat, 18 works.

In sowing furrows of wheat, 24 works.

In harrowing rye, 5 works.

In sowing furrows of peas, 16 works.

In making drainage furrows at the time of [*sowing*] peas, 7 works.

In harrowing oats, 27 works.

In harrowing barley and in harrowing land before ploughing at the time of sowing barley, 25.

In sowing furrows of oats, 8 works.

In carrying straw from threshing in other buildings to keep for the thatcher, 18 works.

In fetching straw and in supplying one thatcher in Lent, 22 works.

In spreading manure in Hall Croft in the present year, 16 works.

In spreading manure upon Old Toft in summer, 15 works.

In filling dung carts with manure both in the present year and in the summer [*sic*], 39 works.

---

[113] One of the boonworks.

In making hedges at Walsham Hall around the manor garden and in cutting down thorn and underwood there, 51 works.

Item in making hedges at High Hall next to Ox Pasture, 22 works.

Item in making hedges there at the end of The Entry [*dil Entre*], 1 work.

In stopping up gaps at Luchesdell [*Lenerechdel*], 1 work.

Item in stopping up gaps at Lady's Wood, 6 works.

Item in making hedges around the wood of High Hall, 35 works.

In plastering the barn and the granary at the manor with clay, 13 works.

Item in mowing teasels [*cardonibus*] before ploughing the fallow land, 12 works.

Item in repairs at Mickle Meadow opposite the lord's meadow, cleaning and scouring by customary works, 74 works.

In spreading hay on the meadow this year, 10 works.

In driving the lord's plough while William Man was ill, 16 works.

In sales as within, 190¾ and 2 parts of a work.

Sum [blank]

Carrying services From the issue of customary carrying services at the will of the lord from custom, price per work 2d.

Sum 7.

From which, in allowance for the reeve's tenement, a third part.

In sales as within, 6 and 2/3 parts.

Sum as above.   It balances.

Manure carrying services From customary services without resumption, 9 manure-carryings and allowed to the same for each man carrying manure 1 winter work, price per carry 2d.

Sum 9.

From which, in allowance for the reeve's tenement, 8 parts of 1 manure carrying service.

Item for various tenements in the lord's hands, 2¾ and 3 parts of 1 and 3 parts of ½ a manure-carrying work.

In allowance made to Richard Morton for two and a half messuages and certain land granted to him and his heirs by a deed of the lord as appears above in the section on oats a third part of ½ a carrying service.

In carrying manure this year, nothing.

In sales as within, 4 carries quarter of half a carry 2 parts of 1 carry a third part of half a carry and 7 parts of a carry.

Sum [blank]

Weeding works From customary services 188 works, price per work ½d.

From customary services at High Hall, 3.

Sum 191.

From which in allowance for the reeve's tenement this year, 3.

And for the hayward's tenement, 1 weeding.

Item for various tenements in the lord's hands, 24¾ works.

In allowance made to Richard Morton because as above, ¾ of a weeding work.

In weeding the lord's corn and in clearing bracken [*fenger'*] from barley in Conyger Close [*Conynggerclos*][114] and Cocks Dirt, 10 works.
In sales within 102¾ works, of which 3 from the responsibility of the bailiff and from the responsibility of the hayward 99¾ works.
Sum [blank]

Mowing works From customary services per half day, 49 mowing works, price per work 1½d.
Sum 49.
From which, in allowance for the reeve's tenement this year, 3 mowing works.
Item for various tenements in the lord's hands, 6¾ works.
Item in allowance made to Richard Morton, because as above, ¾ of a mowing work.
In sales as within, 39¾ mowing works.
Sum [blank]

Carriage of hay From customary services that have carriage without resumption and without price, 9 works this year.
Sum 9.
From expenses in carriage of hay [*illeg.*]

Haymaking works From the issue of customary works as many as the lord requires for lifting, turning and stacking all the hay without resumption. And equals [*sic*].

Harvest works From customary services for a whole day to reap, tie and stack the lord's grain, 643 works, for which each receives from the lord at noon and for his supper 2 loaves of mixed grains, at 20 to one bus., and 4 herrings, price per work, 1d. From customary services at High Hall p.a., 111 works.
Sum 754 works.
From which, in allowance for the reeve's tenement this year, 15½ works.
And for the hayward's tenement this year, 2¼ works.
And for various tenements in the lord's hands, 96¾ works.
Item for various tenements pertaining to High Hall in the lord's hands, 77 works.
Item for the tenement recently of Walter Dennis in the lord's hands as above 3½ works.
Item in allowance made to Gilbert Moundemyll and Katherine his wife granted by a deed of the lord as above and for the tenement Helpes pertaining to High Hall p.a., 16 works.
In allowance made to Richard Morton, because as above, 2 and a quarter of a half of a harvest work.
Item in [*blank*] acres of barley and [*blank*] acres of various grain reaped, tied and collected, 386½ works, of which from High Hall 9 works and 377½ works from the responsibility of the hayward, of which on [*blank*] acres of barley [*blank*] works and [*blank*] acres of other grains [*blank*] works, in total [*blank*].
In sales as within, 154¾ works, of which 9 from the responsibility of the bailiff and from the responsibility of the hayward, 145¾ works.
Sum [blank]

---

[114] The close of the rabbit warren.

Harvest boonworks From customary services this year, 108 boonworks from which each free man shall receive from the lord for his food at noon and for his supper, 1 loaf of wheat, of which 20 per bus. Each customary tenant shall receive for his food at noon the same as for the free tenants [*sic*] and for his supper a loaf of mixed grain, of which 20 to the bus., and 1 herring.

From customary services at High Hall, 19 boonworks.

Sum 127 boonworks.

From which in allowance for the reeve's tenement this year, 3.

And for the hayward's tenement, 2 boonworks.

And for various tenements in the lord's hands, 7.

Item for the tenement recently of Walter Dennis in the lord's hands as above, 1.

Item in allowance for tenements in the lord's hands pertaining to High Hall, 10.

In allowance made to Gilbert Moundemyll and Katherine his wife and for the tenement Helpes pertaining to High Hall by a deed of the lord p.a., 2.

Item in allowance for the tenement Champneys in the lord's hands by escheat after the death of William Blunt pertaining to High Hall, 1.

Item in allowance to Richard Morton because as above, 1.

In [*blank*] acres of barley reaped, tied and collected this year 75 boonworks, of which from High Hall 6 and 69 from the responsibility of the hayward.

In sales as within, 25 boonworks from the responsibility of the hayward.

Sum [*blank*]

Document 8: Walsham account, 28 September 1406 to 28 September 1407

SA/B HA504/3/5b

Walsham

Account of William Wright sergeant there from the eve of St Michael the Archangel in the 7th year of the reign of Henry IV until the eve of the same St Michael next coming in the 8th year of the same Henry for one whole year.

Arrears [*He answers*] for arrears of the last account of William Hawes, reeve, in the preceding year, £11 11s. 3d. half a quarter of a ¼d. and a third part of a ¼d., of which 40s. in respite[115] of an amercement in the court from Thomas Badwell from the preceding year.

Sum £11 11s. 3d. half a quarter of a ¼d. and a third part of a ¼d.

Rents of assize For rents of assize for the term of Michaelmas, 76s. 6½d.

For rents of assize for the term of Christmas, 60s.

For rents of assize for the term of Easter, 68s. 9¾d.

For increased rent from Walter Tiptot, 2s.

For increased rent from Richard Patel, 1¼d.

For increased rent from a certain forge recently leased to Simon Smith, 6d.

For increased rent from Peter Hawes, ½d.

For John Lester and Rose his mother for Taylors Wong, 3s.

For George Brockley for land of Taylors Wong, 12d.

---

[115] A respite is an official postponement of a payment rather than a permanent write off. Thomas had clearly not paid his amercement from the court, but the auditors were still encouraging the sergeant to try and collect it.

For increased rent from Robert Osbern of Rickinghall, ¼d.

For Henry Breton for 2 acres of land recently of Henry Osbern, 1d.

For various increases for the term of Michaelmas, 10¼d.

For William Hawes and Robert his brother, 1d.

For William Pye for a certain portion of a messuage formerly of Gilbert Helpe, 1d.

For increased rent from Matthew Gilbert, ¼d.

For new rent from John Lester for 4 acres 33 perches of land of demesne land of the lord lying on the east side of Taylors Wong, 4s. 3d.

For new rent from Robert Rampley the smith for 2 acres 6 perches of land from the demesne of the lord in Taylors Wong, 2s.

For increased rent received annually from Bartholomew, the parson of the church of Langham, for 6 acres of mollond land of the lord's bondage that Robert Warde, neif of the lord, recently purchased by charter, 1d.

For new rent received annually from John Baxter for a piece of land called Aylelds Toft granted to him and his heirs by court roll, 10s.

For new rent received annually from John son of John Margery for a piece of land containing 2 acres lying on the west side of Howes Toft granted to him and his heirs by court roll, 18d.

For new rent from John Baxter for 1 acre of land from the lord's demesne lying opposite the cemetery of the church granted to him and his heirs by court roll p.a., 16d.

From John Coggeshall for 1 acre of land from the lord's demesne there granted to him and his heirs by court roll p.a., 16d.

For increased rent received annually from Robert Margery for 3 roods of mollond that William Warde, neif of the lord, father of John Warde purchased by charter, ¼d.

For new rent from Adam Goodale for a piece of land containing 3 acres 3½ roods with hedges and ditches from the lord's demesne at Church Wong granted to him and his heirs by court roll, 4s. 10d.

For increased rent from Robert Springald for 1½ roods of meadow purchased from Robert Margery p.a., ¼d.

For increased rent from Robert Payne, neif of the lord, for 1 rood of land abutting upon a curtilage recently Kembalds purchased from Robert Syre by charter p.a., ¼d.

For new rent received from Richard Morton for half a messuage and two pieces of land containing 1 acre of the tenement formerly of John Frances and for half a messuage and four pieces of land containing 3 acres 3½ roods of land of the tenement formerly Robbes granted to him and his heirs by a deed of the lord p.a., 3s. 4d.

For rent purchased by William son of former William Hore, this year is the 6th, 6s. 4½d.

And in the price of a hen, 4 harvest works and one ploughing service at the winter sowing, 22d.

For new rent received from Adam Blayer for a certain tenement granted to him for money [*arentat'*][116] by a deed [*per scriptum*] of the lady p.a., 3s. 4d.

    Sum £12 13s. 5d., of which from the responsibility of the bailiff, 8s. 2½d.

Rents of assize from High Hall with ward For rents of assize there p.a., 28s. ¼d. For castle ward there p.a., 2d.

    Sum 28s. 2¼d., of which for Westhorpe 7s. 7d.

---

[116] This holding had been converted from the old villein service tenancy, which would have include labour services, renders in kind and liability for other dues, to a straight, fixed, money rent each year.

Castle ward For castle ward received from the manor of Wyken for the terms of Michaelmas, Christmas and the Nativity of St John the Baptist, 11s. 2d.
For castle ward received from the manor of Ixworth p.a., 2s. 10d.

Sum 14s.

Farm of land and pasture For the farm of various land and tenements in the lord's hands by various leases as shown by a bill attached to this roll from the responsibility of the hayward, 38s. 11½d.
For a piece of land containing 22 acres called Hatchmere, nothing this year because it is sown with peas, barley and oats.
From John Lester for a piece of land containing 20 acres in the same piece there this year 12d., and no more because it cannot be leased \usually leased for 5s./
From John Hawes for pasture of Pinchons Way there this year, 10d.
From John Frances senior for 18 acres of land there called Blunts Haugh for a term of 10 years, this year is the 8th, 4s. 6d.
From Margery Lakenham for pasture, 4 acres of land parcel of Fishpond Field this year 12d., and no more from pasture land there because it is grazed by sheep of the cullet.
From Adam Blayer for a \headland/ of pasture, nothing because it is a new close called Hall Croft with a piece of land containing 14 acres in the same at the north end this year, 5s.
From Adam Blayer for the farm of a piece of land at Mickle Meadow and for a piece of land at West Mill from the responsibility of the hayward, 4s.[117]
From Adam Ebell for 2 acres of land called Nunns Land and 3 roods of land in 3 pieces of the same tenement from the responsibility of the said hayward, 18d.
From Adam Blayer for a parcel of pasture called Chalk Pightle, 3s.
From the same Adam for 1 acre of land at Fishpond Field this year, 6d.
For a headland of pasture in the Launde at Ladys Wood and from pasture land in the same grazed by horses and foals this year, 2s. 4d., that is from Robert Frances 2 foals 12d., from John Frances senior 1 foal 6d., from John Fuller 1 foal 4d. for 6 weeks, from the bailiff 1 foal 6d.
From Robert Margery for a headland of pasture on the north side of the Little Meadow, 5d.
From the same for grazing upon fallow land there this year, 3d.
From Peter Poye for grazing upon fallow land at Old Toft this year, 20d.
For 17½ acres of land at Hell Green recently leased to William Sparschoy for 4s. 4½d. nothing this year because it is grazed by the lady's sheep.
From Robert Syre for pasture of a close at the sheepcote next to Allwood Green this year, 5s.
From Robert Fletcher for 5 acres of land on the east side of Fishpond Field next to the land of Robert Sare this year, 20d.
From the same Robert for 2 acres of land lying next to Stronds Way this year, 6d.
From Roger Prede for the farm of Burchards Close, 12s.
From Robert Syre for a curtilage and 4 acres of land in three pieces called Sparschoys purchased by the lord, 4s.

---

[117] This and the next entry are bracketed in the margin with a note stating 'from the responsibility of the hayward'.

From Thomas Bonde for 2 acres of land of the tenement Burchards on the west side of Burchards Land, 12d.

From the same Thomas for a piece of land of the said tenement lying at Rickinghall Willows next to the land of Adam Pitlake and next to the Marketmere, 8d.

From Annis Marler for pasture of the Butts at the south head of Fishpond Field with the pasture of a way there this year, 20d.

For pasture next to Fishpond Field on the west side, nothing this year because it is sown with oats.

For a headland of pasture in the outer Launde at North Haugh, recently to the said Adam Blayer for 10d., nothing this year because it is grazed by the sheep of the cullet.

For land in the same, nothing for the aforesaid reason.

For pasture of one piece of land called Brooms Wong, nothing this year because it is grazed by the lady's sheep.

For 6 acres of land at the north head of Fishpond Field nothing for the aforesaid reason.

For 12 acres of land at Summer Way from the land of the Prior of Ixworth granted in the preceding year for 3s. nothing because it is grazed by the sheep of the cullet.

From Walter Robwood for 3 acres 3 roods of land of the same Prior recently leased to him this year, 11d.

From John Robwood for 3 acres 1 rood of land of the same Prior recently leased to the same Walter, 9¾d.

For 3 acres there recently leased to the same Walter, nothing because it is grazed by sheep.

For 6 acres of land at Okland of the same Prior, nothing for the aforesaid reason.

For 1 acre of land of the same Prior next to Knots Hedge leased in the preceding year to John Cooper for 3d., nothing because it is leased to the same John with other land of High Hall as shown by a bill there.

For 7 acres of land of the same Prior recently leased for 21d., nothing because it is grazed by sheep.

For 8 acres of land of the same Prior recently leased for 2s., nothing for the aforesaid reason.

For 6 acres of land of the same Prior called Short Land, nothing this year because it is sown \with the lady's oats./

For 12 acres of land called Blunts Land, nothing this year because it is grazed by sheep.

From John Syre for 5½ acres of land on the west side of Blunts Land this year, 16d.

From William Vincent for 2 acres of land in one piece at Doucedeux from the land of the Prior for a term of 5 years, this year is the 2nd., 12d.

For 6 acres of land at the end of the new close of Hall Croft recently leased to Thomas Daye for 18d., nothing because it is grazed by sheep.

For 9 acres of land on the west side of Old Toft recently leased for 2s. 3d., nothing because it is fallow for wheat in the next year.

From Katherine Robwood for 2 acres of land of the same Prior lying next to West Hall Brook this year, 6d.

Sum £4 16s. ¼d., of which from the responsibility of the hayward 44s. 5½d.

Farm of lands, meadows and tenements of High Hall For the farm of land and tenements, meadows and pasture there leased as shown by a bill, £6 6s. 5½d., of which from the tenants in Westhorpe 43s. 5d. and from the responsibility of the bailiff, £4 3s. 0½d.

Sum £6 6s. 5½d.

Farm of land of East House in the lord's hands at farm For the farm of parcels of land and tenements of East House to various leases, 29s. 8d., that is to William Vincent 20s., Roger Prede 7s., Richard Rampley 16d. and John Cooper 16d., and no more because the rest of the said land is leased elsewhere for herbage.

Sum 29s. 8d.

Sale of hay and herbage of the meadows For all the hay coming from 4½ acres of meadow in Broad Dole sold to various men this year, 25s. 4d.

For hay sold in the little meadow, nothing this year.

From Robert Margery for the herbage of 3 roods of meadow in Mickle Meadow, for the herbage of 1 acre of meadow called Turf Pit Acre recently purchased from John Rampley, chaplain, this year, 8s.

Sum 33s. 4d.

Perquisites of court For one court held there on Thursday in Easter week, 33s. 3d.

From William Swift as a fine for declining the office of reeve this year, 40s.

Sum 73s. 3d.

Sale of corn and stock For 21 qrs 5½ bus. of wheat, of which 2 bus. are for the Ploughale and 1 qr 1 bus. are for the harvest expenses sold as elsewhere, price per qr 6s., £6 10s. 1½d.

For 8 qrs 4 bus. of barley sold as elsewhere, price per qr 2s. 8d., 22s. 8d.

For 4 qrs 4 bus. of peas sold as elsewhere, price per qr 2s. 8d., 12s.

For 10 qrs of oats sold as elsewhere, at Bury, price per qr 2s. 2d., 21s. 8d.

For 22 qrs 4 bus. and quarter of ½ a peck and a third part of ½ bus. of oats sold as elsewhere, price per qr 2s., 45s. 0¾d.

Sum £11 11s. 6¼d.

Farm of the dovecote For the farm of a dovecote at the manor nothing here because the pigeons were delivered to the lady for hospitality, as elsewhere.

For the farm of a dovecote \at High Hall/, nothing here because there were none in stock.

Sum nil.

Works and customary services sold[118] For 2¼ hens from rent from the responsibility of the hayward sold elsewhere, 4½d.

For ½lb cumin from rent sold as elsewhere, 1½d.

For ½lb pepper from rent sold as elsewhere, 6d.

For 37½ and half a quarter and 2 parts of a winter work from custom sold as elsewhere, price per work ½d., 19d.

---

[118] More of the customary labour services were utilised this year than in 1402–3: compare the 37 winter works sold here with the 190 works in 1402–3, and the 50 harvest works here with 145 in 1402–3. The commutation price for the harvest services is 3d. per work this year, although it had been 2d. in 1402–3. It would seem that, as in 1390–1, the higher rate reflects the lord's preference to utilise the works, but the refusal of the tenants to do so … hence the higher rate to commute.

For 7 carrying services from custom sold as elsewhere, price per work 1d., 7d.

For 4½ and half a quarter and 2 parts of 1 carrying service and a third part of half a manure-carrying service from custom sold as elsewhere, price per carrying service 2d., 11d.

For 86 and half a quarter of a weeding work from custom sold as elsewhere, price per work ½d., 3s. 7¾d.

For 41 mowing works from custom sold as elsewhere, price per work 1½d., 5s. 1½d.

For 50¼ harvest works from custom sold as elsewhere, from the responsibility of the hayward, per work 3d., 12s. 6¾d.

For 7½ hens from rent from the responsibility of the bailiff sold as elsewhere, 15d.

For 49½ eggs \from rent from the responsibility/ of the said bailiff sold as elsewhere, 2½d.

For 3 weeding works from custom sold as elsewhere, 1½d.

For 4 harvest works from custom \from the responsibility of the same man/ sold as elsewhere, 12d.

For 4 harvest boonworks from custom sold as elsewhere, 16d.

  Sum 29s. 3d. and half a ¼d., of which from the responsibility of the bailiff 3s. 11d., and from the responsibility of the hayward, 25s. 4d. and half a ¼d.

Farm of cows and hens For the farm of lactage and calves, 17 cows leased to Ralph Daye at farm, per head 6s., allowed to him 2s. for winter lactage; 2 cows bought at Christmas before calving as shown elsewhere, total 100s.

For the farm of the lactage of 1 cow of first calving, he answers for half a cow, 3s.

For the farm of 12 hens p.a. 6d. per head, 6s.

  Sum 109s.

Produce of the garden From James the shepherd for fruit in the lady's garden at H[*igh Hall*] sold to him, 2s.

For fruit in the garden at the manor sold this year, nothing because it was delivered to the lady at Westhorpe for the provision of hospitality.

  Sum 2s.

Sale of wool and pelts For wool sold, nothing this year. For 222 sheepskins in murrain sold elsewhere, 43s. 8d.

  Sum 43s. 8d.

Sale of wood From Robert Syre, part payment of £25 for all the wood and underwood sold to him in Ladys Wood by an indenture, for this term of Michaelmas, £8 6s. 8d.[119]

From John Vincent for one old ash tree, 8d.

From Peter Poye for a thorn hedge at Old Toft and a border of thorn hedge at Ladys Wood and for a felled white poplar sold, 3s.

From John Cooper for 3 white poplars at High Hall sold to him, 3s.

---

[119] A change in the demesne's approach to underwood, which was usually sold in small batches to multiple people, but here the output of the main wood on the Walsham demesne is effectively being sublet to Robert Syre, who is from a local family. He paid this year's instalment in full, so the reference to an indenture for a grand total of £25 indicates this was an agreement lasting for three years.

From John Frances junior for 2 small white poplars [*abell'*] and one black poplar [*popular*][120] there, 16d.

From John Wells for 1 thorn hedge on the east side of Katherines Croft at High Hall, 3s.

From Nicholas Tiptot for 1 white poplar, 8d.

From Walter Frances for a border on the south side of Katherines Croft, 12d.

From John Margery for 37½ perches of underwood in North Haugh sold to him, 22½d.

From Robert Margery[121] for 1 rood 14 perches of underwood there sold to him, 2s. 8d.

From John Lester for 1 rood 8 perches of underwood there, 2s. 5d.

From Olive Margery for 14 perches of underwood there, 8d.

Sum £9 6s. 11½d.

Issues of the manor From John Frances senior for 1 acre of stubble at Hatchmere sold to him, 4d.

From John Man for a portion of pea straw at High Hall, 6d.

From John Vincent for a portion of pea straw at the manor, 3d.

Sum 13d.

Foreign receipts Nil

Sales at the audit For items sold at the audit as shown elsewhere, 3s. 10d.

Sum 3s. 10d.

Total sum of receipts with arrears £74 12s. 11d. half a ¼d. half a quarter of a ¼d. and a third part of a ¼d.[122]

Rent resolute with decays The same accounts for rent resolute for the hall of Thelnetham of 2s. p.a., nothing because the fee is outside the lord's hands.

Item for the hall of Rickinghall p.a. \hayward/, 3s. 1½d.

Item paid for castle ward of Norwich p.a. \bailiff/, 16s.

Item paid to John Margery p.a.\hayward/, 1½d.

Item in allowance for the tenement of William Swift, reeve this year, 23¾d.

Item for the tenement of Adam Ebell, hayward this year, 4s. 0¼d.

Item in allowance of rent for Champneys p.a., 12d.

Item in allowance of rent for various villein tenements in the lady's hands, 29s. three quarters of a ¼d., half a quarter of a ¼d. and a third part of a ¼d.

Item for a messuage, 3 acres 1 rood of villein land recently of Walter Dennis in the lady's hands, 13¼d. and a third part of ¼d.

Item in allowance for a forge formerly of Walter Smith because it is over charged in rents of assize above, 6d.

Item for the tenement Outlaws, 6¼d.

Item in allowance of rent on 1 acre of land formerly of Master John of Walsham, 2½d.

---

[120] 'The word *popel* or *popular* is systematically distinguished from aspen (*aspe*) and white poplar (*abel*) and must denote black poplar.' O. Rackham, *The history of the countryside* (London, 1986), p. 207.

[121] See below in this account, in 'costs of the fold', for Margery's contract to make wooden hurdles, presumably from coppiced ash and hazel, for the manor's sheepfold.

[122] Total receipts for 1406 were the highest of all the accounts. Apart from the extra profit from underwood sold to Robert Syre, far more grain and peas were sold than in other years.

Item for 1 acre 1 rood of land recently of Edmund of Pakenham, 2¼d.

Item for a smith's shop in Palmer Street because it is vacant and encroaching upon the highway p.a., 8d.

In rent released to Robert Osbern by a deed of lady Rose of Pakenham, ¼d.

Item in allowance of rent from High Hall in the lady's hands namely purchased in perpetuity, 4d.

Item for sheriff's aid for the same, 2½d.

Item in allowance of sheriff's aid of Burchards and Sparschoys p.a., 1d.

Item paid to the hall of Ashfield for castle ward of Norwich for High Hall p.a. \bailiff/, 17d.

Item paid to Eye castle for castle ward for High Hall this year once \bailiff/, 9d.

Item in allowance for various tenements in the lady's hands pertaining to High Hall p.a.\bailiff/, 15s. 9¾d.

Item paid to the hall of Ashfield from rent p.a. \bailiff/, 2d.

Item paid for hundred suit released this year for Burchards p.a. \bailiff/, 16d.

Item paid to Helimot from hidage and from ward for Burchards p.a. \bailiff/, 9d.

Item in rent resolute for Sir William Bardwell for 1 acre of meadow at Turf Pits purchased by the lord from John Rampley p.a. \bailiff/, 4d.

Item in allowance made to Richard Morton for two and a half messuages and certain land granted to him and his heirs by a deed of the lord p.a. \hayward/, 10¼d.

Item in allowance of rent for certain land and tenements of Adam Blayer rented free by him and his heirs by a deed of the lord as shown above p.a., 23¾d.

> Sum £4 2s. 5¼d. half a ¼d. and half a quarter of a ¼d. and 2 parts of a ¼d., of which from the responsibility of the hayward 45s. 10½d. half a ¼d., half a quarter of a ¼d. and 2 parts of ¼d., and from the responsibility of the bailiff 36s. 6¾d.

Cost of the ploughs and carts In hiring a smith for finding and forging the iron work on 2 ploughs and for shoeing the stots and carthorses p.a. the price of 4 bushels of wheat as elsewhere, 28s.

In the stipend of Thomas Warde for 3 days' work making 3 new ploughs and shaping the timber for the ploughs, 12d.

In 7 ploughs fitted from the lord's timber, 14d.

In grease bought for greasing carts, 2d.

In the stipend of Thomas Warde for 1 day's work felling trees for timber for ploughs and handles thus made, 3d.

In the stipend of William Saddler and his son for 6½ days' work making and mending collars and other head harness, between them per day 8d., 4s. 4d.

In half a tawed horse hide bought for the same, 12d.

In thread bought for the same, 2d.

In 9 ells of canvas bought for the same, 22½d.

In 10 lbs of flock bought for the same, 10d.

In a pair of body traces and a pair of chain traces also bought, 19d.

In 3 tanned calf skins bought for the said harness, 15d.

In the stipend of Thomas Warde for 1 day's work cutting handles and 3 shafts for ploughs, 3d.

In 5 clouts bought for the cart axles with nails, 11d.

Item in 2 metal plates bought for the cart, 4d.

Item paid for mending the body of the cart at harvest, 6d.

In a pair of wheels for a tumbrel made [*anuland*] from the lady's timber and in a new tumbrel cover also made with the said tumbrel axle from the lord's timber, 2s. 2d.
In one other new tumbrel cover made, 6d.
In 16 canvas halters bought, 11d.

Sum 47s. 9½d.

Cost of the buildings Paid to John Manser in the final payment for making a new barn at High Hall, 12d.
In 100 iron nails bought for mending the dovecote and sheepcote at High Hall, 4d.
In the stipend of John Manser and Robert his son for 4 days' work mending and making a dovecote there, 16d.
In the stipend of John Miller thatcher for 16 days' work thatching upon the cowshed, dovecote and barn at High Hall, per day 4d., 5s. 4d. And supplemented by winter works as elsewhere.
In ramming around the said dovecote there by work, 16d.
In a lock with a key bought for the dovecote at High Hall, 3d.
In one iron bar bought for the same, 1d.
In the stipend of John Manser and Robert his son, [*and of*] John Cooper and Thomas his brother, hired for 70½ days' work making and mending two gates [*ij port'*] at the manor, and making the bars and for fitting laths at the cowshed at High Hall, each taken per day 4d., 23s. 6d.[123]
Item in pikes, ferrules and plates similarly bought for the said gates, 19d.
In iron nails bought for fastening the said gates and the wall plates at the manor, and for fitting laths and bars at High Hall, 21d.
In the stipend of Adam Frances and John Miller for 19½ days' work thatching a building in the manor, taken between them per day 4d., 6s. 6d. And supplemented by winter works as elsewhere.
In putting clay on partitions in a cowshed at High Hall by works, 7s.
Item in making a floor with clay at the barn and the granary by works there, 20d.
In the stipend of Robert Manser for 5 days' work fitting laths and plastering the garret and plastering the stable and making a wall there and mending other defects, 20d.
In the stipend of John Miller, thatcher for 4 days' work thatching the lodge upon the lower gate and the oat barn, per day 4d., 16d.
In the stipend of John Pye, John Pepper and Ralph Daye for 14 days' work putting clay on a wall next to the bailiff's room and the garret and defects in other places, taken each per day 3d., 3s. 6d.
In 100 nails called wall-plate nails bought, 5d.
Item in eaves-board nails bought, 1d.
In a lock with a key and a bar bought for a door of the barn at High Hall, 7d.
In iron nails bought for mending the said door, 1d.
In 2 iron pins bought for the said door, 4d.

Sum 59s. 8d.[124]

---

[123] The gates were sizeable structures judging by the high cost of the labour to repair them. This section also mentions plastering 'the Garret', and the grant of the site of the manor in 1453 also refers to this separate building: SA/B HA504/1/13.18. The garret signifies some kind of defensive structure, perhaps a high gatehouse providing entry to the secure manorial enclosure. This might explain why these two gates appear to have been so mighty.

[124] The expenditure on building work this year is the highest outlay in all the extant accounts. The entries reveal that the manorial complex at High Hall was being maintained as a working unit, with

Cost of the mill In a circular band bought for tying a millstone with the fitting of the same upon the same millstone, 3d.

Sum 3d.

Cost of the fold Paid to Robert Margery for making 60 hurdles by contracted work from wood provided by the lady, 20d.

Sum 20d.

Stipends of the manorial servants In the stipend of John Tiptot, plough-driver p.a., 10s.

In the stipend of William Man junior, plough-holder p.a., 10s.

In the stipend of John Sad, plough-holder p.a., 10s.

In the stipend of Thomas Joye, plough-driver p.a., 10s.

In the stipend of John Dennis, shepherd of the ewes p.a., 10s.

In the stipend of James the shepherd, nothing here because he takes a stipend for the sheep of the cullet.

In the stipend of the dairyherd, nothing.

Sum 50s.

Threshing and winnowing In threshing 58 qrs 4½ bus. of wheat and rye by task, per qr 4d., 19s. 6¼d.

In threshing 124 qrs 2 bus. of barley, peas and oats by task, per qr 2d., 20s. 8½d.

In winnowing all the abovesaid corn, containing in total 182 qrs 6½ bus. of various corn, per 3 qrs 2d., 10s. 1¾d.

Sum 50s. 4½d.

Corn and stock bought In 2 cows bought before calving from Peter Poye for the dairy at Christmas, 17s.

In 2 qrs 4 bus. of rye bought for livery of the manorial servants, 10s.

In 12 chickens bought for making into capons above, 12d.

In 6 calves bought from the farmer of cows by agreement from the responsibility of the dairyherd, 6s.

In a cow bought at the end of the year, 7s. 6d.

In 1 bus. of multure bought for livery of the manorial servants, 6d.

Sum 42s.

Minute expenses In bonus payments to 4 ploughmen, a shepherd and a dairyherd p.a. at Christmas and Easter, 12d.

In bonus payments to the same on the day of the Purification, 3d.

In one dung fork 4d. and one rye shovel bought, 3d.

In mending the iron of the said shovel, 1d.

In one osier winnowing fan bought, 12d.

In a gift to the ploughmen at the time of sowing in order that they work better, 5s. 11d.

In one cow hide and one tanned bullock hide elsewhere, 18d.

In one tawed horse hide, 12d.

---

a dovecote, sheepcote, grange and cowshed. Likewise, the manorial site for Walsham. The decision to spend more on repairs this year might explain why sales of wood and grain were also high: the latter generating the cash to spend on the upkeep.

103

In the expenses of 25 men coming with 12 ploughs to sow wheat at the Ploughale with the expenses of the bailiff, hayward, miller and manorial servants on the same day at the ninth hour, 7s. 11d.

In 7 ells of canvas bought for making 2 sacks, 18d.

In thread bought for the same, ½d.

Item in sewing the said sacks, 1d.

In one pair of double harrows made from the lord's timber, 6d.

Paid to Robert Margery for making a gate from sticks and strips of hide next to the \pig/ <cow> house, 2d.

In 240 faggots made by the same Robert by task, 12d.

Item paid for faggots at High Hall for making hedges there, 2s. 6d.

Paid for 3 qrs 6 bus. of weeds sifted from 19 qrs 6 bus. of barley for sowing, 11d.

In 3 iron chains bought for tying a shaft of a tumbrel, 3d.

In parchment bought for court rolls and accounts, 7d.

In making one wall, 36 perches long, next to the garret, 3s. 2d.

In making 93½ perches of ditch at High Hall by John Man and Ralph Daye with a hedge made upon it, per perch 2d., 15s. 7d.

In making 85¼ perches of ditch there with a hedge made upon it and with underwood cut there, per perch 2¼d., 15s. 11¾d.

Item in 3 locks with keys and 3 iron fetters bought for stots, 3s. 3d.

Paid to Robert Margery for making a gate from sticks for a new close at High Hall, 3d.

In sticks cut for making hurdles and for ?springs [*sprengelys*] and thatching pegs [*sweyes*], 3d.

Sum 64s. 11¼d.

Lease of East House Paid to the Prior of Ixworth for land and tenement called East House leased from him for a term of 10 years, this year is the 2nd, for the terms of Easter and Michaelmas p.a., 40s.[125]

Sum 40s.

Weeding and mowing In weeding the lady's corn and in digging up bracken out of the barley this year, nothing here because it was done by customary works elsewhere.

In mowing the great meadow and the little meadow this year, in total 10s.

In spreading herbage and turning, raising and also collecting the hay this year, nothing here because it was done by customary works elsewhere.

Sum 10s.

Costs of the harvest In expenses of the sergeant, hayward, two carters, a cook and stacker and a loader at harvest for 4 weeks with the expenses of 92 harvest boon-works from this manor and 14 works from High Hall as shown elsewhere, with food provided by the lady at the ninth hour:

In bread in the price of 1 qr 1 bus. of wheat above sold, 6s. 10d.

In ale bought, 10s. 6d.

---

[125] The previous lease for ten years had expired at Michaelmas 1405 and now has been renewed for a further ten for the same sum. Note how the lord of Walsham has recouped nearly 30s. of the lease through subletting, and the rest of the land has been deployed to supplement the running of the demesne.

In meat bought, 12s. 1d.

In saffron <saffs> \crocs/, 1d.

In fish and herrings bought, 18d.

In milk, cheese, eggs and butter bought, 3s. 1d.

In the stipend of a cook and stacker at harvest this year, 6s.

In stipend of a loader at harvest, 5s.

In 4 pairs of gloves bought for the manorial servants, 8d.

In candles bought, 2d.

In salt bought, 2d.

In oat meal, 3d.

In customary works, 463 harvest works from this manor, expenses of each of them ¼d., 9s. 7¾d.

In customary works, 72 harvest boonworks from this manor, viz: expenses of each of them ¾d., 11½d.

In herrings bought, 1d.

Sum 57s. 0¼d., of which on the hayward 10s. 7¼d.

Wages In the wages of William Wright sergeant there p.a., less 4 weeks at the harvest when food provided by the lady, taking per week 12d., 48s.

Sum 48s.

Steward's expenses In expenses of the steward for one court held, 18d.

Sum 18d.

Foreign expenses with pardons Paid for a 15th to the lord king at the Feast of the Purification, 5s.

Item in ale bought for the lady being here in summer [*exist' hic in estat'*],[126] 23d.

Item in meat bought for the same, 12d.

In 12 chickens bought for the same, 12d.

In salt bought, 1d.

In butter bought, 1d.

Item in the stipend of John Man and John Pye for 3 days' work laying gravel [*iaccant' zabula'*] for <the lady> at Westhorpe, taking per day 4d., 2s. for mending the house within the moat.

In a pardon made to William Pye by the lady for an amercement [*charged on him*] in the [*manorial*] court, 6d.

Sum 11s. 7d.

Cash payments Delivered to the lady for the agistment of 4 cows \5s./ from the shepherd, 8 oxen aged 2 years \5s. 4d./, and 21 bullocks grazing in a new close \10s. 6d./ from the Feast of the Finding of the Holy Cross until Lammas Day, 20s. 10d.

To the same lady by the hand of William Swift as a fine for declining the office of reeve, 40s.

---

[126] The implication from this reference is that Elizabeth de Elmham was resident at Walsham for a while during the summer of 1407. This seems unlikely, given the proximity of the main residence at Westhorpe Hall and given the probable unsuitability of the residence at Walsham, which had not been an active residence for years. It might be that she stayed at Walsham briefly while some remedial works at Westhorpe were being carried out, perhaps as suggested by the reference to the gravel works there in the later part of this section.

To the same lady from rent and farm by the hand of Walter Frances, hayward, by one tally with money of Wattisfield, £10.

To the same lady by the hand of James the shepherd for fruit from the garden at High Hall sold to him by her, 2s.

To the same lady by the hand of Robert Syre for sales of wood above for the term of Michaelmas, £8 6s. 8d.

To the same lady by the hand of Ralph Daye for the farm of cows above by one tally, 60s.

To the same lady by the hand of the same Ralph for the cost of 12 geese, 2s.

Delivered to Adam Blayer, sergeant of Westhorpe, for rents and farms of High Hall by the hand of the tenants of High Hall in Westhorpe as appears in foreign receipts there, of which 7s. 7d. from rents and 43s. 5d. from farms, 51s.

To the same lady by the hand of Thomas Abraham for his arrears above, 57s. 8d.

To the same lady by the hand of Walter Frances, hayward, for his arrears above, 35s. 6¼d. half a quarter of a ¼d. and a third part of a ¼d.

To the same lady by the hand of William Hawes, reeve for the preceding year, for his arrears above, £4 18s. 0¾d.

Sum £36 13s. 9d. half a quarter of a ¼d. and a third part of a ¼d. Approved.

Total sum of expenses and deliveries £65 0s. 12d. and three quarters of a ¼d. And owed, £9 11s. 10¾d. three quarters of half a ¼d. and a third part of a ¼d.

From which, a respite of 40s. for the amercement of Thomas Badwell in the 2nd court of the preceding year, [*authorised*] by the lady until etc.[127]

And therefore finally owed to the lady, £7 11s. 10¾d. three quarters of half a ¼d. and a third part of a ¼d.

Of which, on Ralph the farmer of the cows this year, 41s. On Walter Frances, hayward this year, £4 15s. 1d. three quarters of half a ¼d. and a third part of ¼d. On William Wright, bailiff, now accounted by him and verified, 15s. 9¾d.

Walsham Issues of the grange there by heaped bushel measure in the 7th year of Henry IV.

Wheat

And there remain 7 bushels of wheat, of which 4 bushels are from damages charged to the hayward.

From the issue of the old granary in the preceding year remaining in the stack at one threshing by one tally with wheat from the issue this year \against John Wells, granger of the lady sworn/, 32 qrs 5 bus. threshed by task. From the whole issue of the grange there this year by one tally against John Wells, granger of the lady sworn, 17 qrs 7½ bushels and threshed as above.

R' 7½ bus. more seed.[128]

Sum 51 qrs 3½ bushels.

From which, in seed upon 52 acres of land in various pieces by estimate, 13 qrs 1 bus., sown per acre 2 bushels, plus in total 1 bus.

---

[127] The amercement, referred to above, has now been formally allowed, i.e. written off, rather than simply postponed.

[128] Marginal calculation indicating received or answered.

In the livery of the manorial servants as shown below 11 qrs 3 bus., of which for harvest bread 3 qrs 4 bus.
In the contract of the smith for iron for ploughs p.a., the sum in money within, 4 bus.
Delivered to John Goche, sergeant of Wyverstone,[129] 3 qrs 3 bus.
In the livery of the granger, 1 bus.
In baking bread for the lady being there in summer, 3 bus.
In sales as within, 21 qrs 5½ bus.
In the merchant's profit [*avantagium mercatoris*],[130] 3 bus.
In sales at the audit 4 bushels from damage assessed from the responsibility of the hayward for [*blank*].[131]

Sum as above.   It balances.

Rye and maslin
From the whole issue of the grange there this year by one tally with barley below against the said John, 8 qrs threshed as above. From the issue of the new grange there for harvest bread for the customary tenants, 1 qr threshed by the manorial servants. From purchases within for livery of the manorial servants, 2 qrs 4 bus.
R' 4½ bus. more, a third of rye and half with 1 qr 6 bus. of the same charged to the reeve.[132]

Sum 11 qrs 4 bus.

From which, in seed upon 8½ acres of land in one piece, 2 qrs 1 bus., at 2 bus. per acre.
In livery of the granger, 1 bus.
In livery of the manorial servants as appears below 9 qrs 2 bus., of which for harvest bread 1 qr.

Sum as above.   It balances.

Barley
2½ bushels of barley remain in the hands of Peter Poye from damages assessed against the responsibility of the hayward. From the whole issue of the grange there this year by 2 tallies with rye above and peas below against the said John, 42 qrs 2 bus. of barley, threshed as above, of which 3 qrs 6 bus. are contaminated with weeds [*de lolles et darnel combrac' seminat'*]. From receipts at the audit, 1 bus.
Deducted, 3½ bus. of seed.[133]

Sum 42 qrs 5½ bus.

From which, in seed upon 53 acres of land in various pieces by estimate, 19 qrs 6 bus., at 3 bus. per acre minus in total 1 bus.
In the livery of the granger, 1 bus.
Delivered to Thomas Baker, housekeeper of the lady, to make malt for provisioning the lady's hospitality at Westhorpe by 1 tally, 3 qrs 4 bus.

---

[129] A manor in Wyverstone, just south of Westhorpe, was also part of the de Elmham estate.
[130] Essentially, a customary tip paid by the vendor in transactions involving bulk sales of grain, which was above and beyond the agreed quantity covered in the sale contract to the merchant. See R.H. Britnell, '*Advantagium mercatoris*: a custom in medieval English trade', *Nottingham Medieval Studies* 27 (1983), pp. 37–50.
[131] Marginal note: '3s.'
[132] Marginal calculation.
[133] Marginal calculation.

Item delivered to the same Thomas for provisions there for *hennepyk*,[134] 3 qrs 6 bus. of contaminated barley.

In the livery of the manorial servants as appears below, 6 qrs 6 bus.

In sales within, 8 qrs 4 bus.

Item in sales at the audit, 2½ bus. from the responsibility of the hayward [*blank*].[135]

Sum as above.   It balances.

Peas

From the issue of the grange there this year by 2 tallies against the said John, 24 qrs threshed as above. From the same issue by estimate in sheaves[136] for feed for stots and newly-born calves, 2 qrs 4 bus. *R'* 7½ bus. more allowed to him.[137]

Sum 26 qrs 4 bus.

From which, in seed upon 34 acres of land in various pieces by estimate, 8 qrs 4 bus., at 2 bus. an acre.

In the livery of the granger, 1 bus.

Delivered to John Goche, sergeant of Wyverstone, by 1 tally, 4 qrs 7 bus.

Delivered to Thomas Baker, housekeeper of the lady, for provisions for the lady's hospitality at Westhorpe by 1 tally, 6 qrs.

In feed for stots and calves from issue by estimate in sheaves as above, 2 qrs 4 bus.

In sales within, 4 qrs 4 bus.

Sum as above.   It balances.

Oats

2 bushels of oats remain in the hands of Thomas Daye from damages assessed. From the issue of the grange there this year by 1 tally against the said John, 58 qrs threshed as above. From the same issue by estimate in the granary for feed for newly-born calves and bullocks this year, 3 qrs. From rent at the Feast of St Edmund King and Martyr p.a., 20 qrs 2 bus. Deducted 4½ qrs of oats from his allowance.[138]

Sum 81 qrs 4 bus.

From which, in seed upon 90 acres of land in various pieces by estimate, 34 qrs 6 bus., at 2½ bus. per acre plus, in total 6 qrs 5 bus.

In meal made as pottage for 4 ploughmen, a shepherd and a dairyherd p.a. \and a shepherd for the last half year this year/, 1 qr 5 bus.

Delivered to Thomas Baker the lady's housekeeper for fodder for the lady's horse at Westhorpe by 1 tally, 5 qrs.

In feed for calves and bullocks from issue by estimate in sheaves above, 3 qrs.

In the livery of the granger, 1 bus.

In fodder for the horses of the lady, Richard Burgh esq. and others being there in summer, 1 bus.

---

[134] Presumably used to fatten the hens ready for the lady's kitchen: an obvious use for barley accidentally mixed with the seeds of weeds such as darnel.

[135] Marginal note: '*R'*10d.'

[136] The reaped peas are left unthreshed as tied sheaves with the intention of using them as fodder for the livestock, hence an estimate of their volume rather than an exact measure.

[137] Marginal note.

[138] Marginal note.

108

Item in fodder for all the horses in 3 carts at boonwork going towards Santon[139] to fetch bricks [*waltyl*] from there and carrying to Westhorpe for the use of the lady there, 2 bus.

In allowance for the tenement of William Swift, reeve this year, 1½ pecks.

Item in allowance for the tenement of Adam Ebell hayward this year, 4 bus.

Item in allowance for various tenements in the lady's hands, 3 qrs 2½ bus. quarter of half a peck and 2 parts of ½ a bus. of oats.

Item in allowance made to Richard Morton for two half messuages and certain land granted to him and his heirs by a deed of the lord, 3¾ pecks.

Item in allowance made to Adam Blayer for a certain tenement granted to him and his heirs in money rent by a deed of the lady p.a., ½ bus.

In sales as within, both for rent received and from oats from issue, 32 qrs 4 bus. quarter of half a peck and 3 parts of ½ bus. of oats.

Sum as above. It balances.

Multure at the mill 2 bushels of multure remain in the hands of the miller. For the farm of a windmill leased to John the miller this year, 11 qrs 4 bus.

And bought as below for livery of the manorial servants, 1 bus.

Sum 11 qrs 7 bus.

From which, in the livery of the manorial servants as appears below, 11 qrs 4 bus. Of which, 1 qr 4 bus. for baking bread to feed the horses 1 qr 4 bus., 2 qrs for bread at the harvest, and 8 qrs for the livery of the manorial servants.

Sum 11 qrs 4 bus.

3 bushels of multure remain in the hands of the miller.

Livery of the manorial servants

For wheat as above to the same, 11 qrs 3 bus.

For rye as above to the same, 9 qrs 2 bus.

For barley as above to the same, 6 qrs 6 bus.

For multure at the mill as above to the same, 11 qrs 4 bus.

For receipts at the audit to satisfy the manorial servants for the same livery in arrears from the preceding years, 7 bus. 3 pecks.

Sum 39 qrs 6 bus. 3 pecks.

From which, in quittance of the excess expended in the last account, 5 qrs 1½ bus., of which 1 qr ½ bus. is wheat.

In the livery of 4 ploughmen, a shepherd and a dairyherd p.a., less 4 weeks in the harvest when 2 servants were at the lady's table each of whom takes a quarter every 12 weeks, of which 4 pecks of wheat, 25 qrs 2 bus.

Item in the livery of James the shepherd for the last half of this year, 2 qrs 1 bus., 1 peck taken as wheat as above.

Item in the livery of Ralph Daye, keeper of the lady's oxen in winter, this year 2 bus. of wheat.

In bread baked for the provisions of customary tenants doing 46½ ploughing services as appears below of which each one takes for each ploughing service 6 loaves, baked at 20 to the bushel, 1 qr 6 bus.

---

[139] Santon Downham, near Thetford, was on a navigable stretch of the River Ouse, where bulky goods were often brought by boat then unloaded and taken by carts to various places in west Suffolk. See M. Bailey, *A marginal economy? East Anglian Breckland in the later Middle Ages* (Cambridge, 1989), p. 150; and Bailey, *Medieval Suffolk*, p. 164.

Item in bread baked for the expenses of 463 harvest works on this manor, that is for each work 2 loaves of bread, at 20 to the bus.
And for the expenses of 92 harvest boonworks on this manor below, that is for each work 1 loaf, at 20 to the bus., 6 qrs 3 bus.

Sum 40 qrs 7 bus. 3 pks.

And so exceeded by 1 qr 1 bus. of multure, which is owed to the manorial servants to be paid in the following year.

Acres sown Expended this year on all kinds of corn on 237½ acres of land.

Sum 237½ acres of land.

Of which, 47 acres reaped by harvest boonworks below and 190½ acres of land by harvest works.

Cart horses
6 remain.

Sum 6.   And 6 horses remain.

Stots
4 remain.

Sum 4.   And 4 stots remain.

Oxen
3 remain.
1 added from bullocks below.
Received from John Rampley, sergeant of Rickinghall, at the Feast of St Nicholas to keep one ox previously a bullock in winter.
Received from a castrated bull below, 1.

Sum 6.

From which delivered to John Rampley sergeant of Rickinghall at the Feast of the Finding of the Holy Cross, 1 ox previously a bullock.
Item delivered to John Link, steward of hospitality, for the lady's larder at the end of the year by 1 tally with cows below.

Sum 2.   And 4 bullocks remain.

Bulls
1 bull remains.
Received from John Goche sergeant of Wyverstone in the Feast of the Finding of the Holy Cross, 1 bull.

Sum 2.

From which delivered and castrated in the section of oxen above, 1.

Sum shown.   And 1 bull remains.

Cows
19 remain, of which from a heriot 1, in the hands of John Rampley, and 1 *brosty*.
From the foresight of the lady [*de previdenc' domine*], that is on the eve of Michaelmas to the end of the year, 26 cows.[140]

---

[140] This must relate to the livestock disease this year (pp. 111–13). It seems the lady ordered the isolation of these cows while the epizootic was raging elsewhere.

From purchases within, 3 by a bill, of which 2 before calving at Christmas and 1 at the end of the year.

Sum 48.

From which, in a pardon made by the lady to John Rampley in the present year 1 cow from a heriot.

Item delivered to John Link steward of the lady's hospitality at the end of the year by 1 tally with bullocks above and calves below, 3 old cows.

Delivered to the lady's larder last year, 1 old cow.

Item delivered to John Goche, sergeant of Wyverstone, at the Feast of the Finding of the Holy Cross, 1 sterile cow.

Item in murrain at the Feast of St Bartholomew after calving, 1.

Sum 7.

And remain 41 cows, of which at High Hall 24 cows and at the manor 17 cows.

Bullocks and steers

1 bullock remains for the plough.

Received from John Rampley, sergeant of Rickinghall, at the Feast of St Nicholas, 6 uncastrated bullocks newly added.

Sum 7.

From which, in murrain in winter, 1 uncastrated bullock newly added.

Item delivered to John Rampley sergeant of Rickinghall at the Feast of the Finding of the Holy Cross to look after 5 uncastrated bullocks newly added.

Added to bullocks above, 1.

Sum as above.   It balances.

Bullocks and heifers

6 added from calves below.

Sum 6.

From which, in murrain in the previous year, 1, and not skinned because it was rotten.

Delivered to John Rampley sergeant of Rickinghall at the Feast of the Finding of the Holy Cross, 5 bullocks and steers newly added.

Sum as above.

Calves

6 remain.

And bought from the cow farmer by custom as shown within 6 calves for which received from the lady 6s.

Sum 12.

From which, added to bullocks and steers above, 6.

In murrain at the end of the year, 1 calf and no skins because the carcasses were rotten and fetid [*quia putredo et fetu*].[141]

Delivered to Adam Blayer sergeant of Westhorpe at the end of the year by 1 tally, 5 calves.

Sum as above.   It balances.

---

[141] Accounts seldom provide an indication of what type of disease delivered the mortal blow to livestock, preferring to use the generic word *morina* instead, but in this case the inability to obtain a hide from the dead animals is indicative of a bacterial infection causing gangrenous skin.

Hides

From cows above in murrain, 1 hide.

From bullocks above in murrain, 1 hide.

Sum 2.

And delivered to the tanner below. It balances.

Tanned hides

3 hides remain, of which 1 tanned cow hide is in the hands of the bailiff and 2 hides in the hands of the tanner at Ixworth.

From tanned hides received above, 2.

Sum 5.

From which, in making 7 new collars and in repairing 7 other collars, 3 hides.

Sum 3.

1 cow hide and 1 bullock hide remain in the hands of the tanner at Ixworth.

Tawed hides

1 tawed stot hide remains in the hands of John Skinner.

Sum shown. It balances.

And expended in repairing harness.

Ewes

5 ewes remain in the custody of John Dennis.

56 added from gimmers below in the custody of the same John.

Sum 61.

From which, in murrain before lambing and shearing, 60.

Sum 60.

And 1 sterile ewe remains this year in the custody of Dennis.

Hoggets and gimmers

56 gimmers remain. Added from lambs below 164, of which 11 are in the custody of Dennis and 153 in the custody of James the shepherd.

Sum 220.

From which added to ewes above, 56. Item in murrain before shearing, 162.

Sum 218.

And 2 gimmers remain in the custody of Dennis.

Lambs

164 remain.

From the offspring of ewes above, nothing this year because 1 ewe was sterile this year.

Sum 164. It balances.

And added to hoggets and gimmers above.

Fleeces

From the issue of sheep above, 3.

Sum 3. It balances.

And delivered to the lady.

Sheepskins
From sheep above in murrain, 222 pelts.[142]

Sum 222 pelts. It balances.

And sold within.

Boars 1 boar remains.

Sum shown. It balances.

And delivered to the lady's larder in the present year.

Capons
8 remain.
From rent p.a., 8. Added this year from chickens below, 12.

Sum 28.

From which, in allowance for the tenements in the lady's hands, 4. Item delivered for the lady's hospitality in the summer, 8. In expenses of the steward at one court, 1. In murrain, 3.

Sum 12.

And 12 capons remain. <of which from rent 4>

Cockerels and hens
1 cockerel, 11 hens remain in the dairy. From rent p.a. at Christmas, 123½ hens. From rent from High Hall p.a., 21.

Sum 156½ hens.

From which, in allowance for the tenement of William Swift reeve this year, 3 hens. Item for the tenement of Adam Ebell hayward this year, 3½ hens.
Item for various tenements in the lady's hands, 9¾ hens.
Item for rent resolute on 1 messuage 3 acres 1 rood of villein land recently of Walter Dennis remaining in the lady's hands by Robert Dennis, this year is the 16th, 1 hen.
Item in allowance for various tenements in the lady's hands pertaining to High Hall, 11½ hens.
Item in allowance made to Gilbert Moundmill and Katherine his wife and their legal heirs purchased by a deed of the lord p.a. for the tenement Helpes in Westhorpe pertaining to High Hall, 1 hen.
In allowance made to Richard Morton for two and a half messuages and certain land granted to him and his heirs by a deed of the lord as appears in the section on oats, 1 hen.
In allowance made to Adam Blayer for a certain tenement as above p.a., 1 hen.
Delivered to Adam Blayer, sergeant of Westhorpe, by the hand of Richard Sewell tenant of High Hall in Westhorpe, 1 hen.
Delivered to John Link, steward of the lady's hospitality at Westhorpe, for provisions for hospitality there by 1 tally, 101 hens.
In sales within, 9¾ hens, of which from the responsibility of the hayward, 2¼ hens, and from the responsibility of the bailiff, 7½ hens.

Sum 143½ hens.

And 1 cockerel, 12 hens remain in the dairy.

---

[142] A devastating epidemic among some of the sheep this year, with a 98 per cent mortality rate among the ewes and 99 per cent among the year-old sheep: but, curiously, no deaths among the lambs. Clearly, the lambs were folded separately from the ewes and yearlings, which prevented the infection spreading, perhaps explaining those additional hurdles made by Robert Margery this year.

Eggs
From the issues of the hens above, nothing because the hens were leased out for money within.
From rent at Easter, 720 eggs.
From rent of High Hall for the same term, 105 eggs.
Sum 825 eggs.

From which in allowance for the reeve's tenement this year, 30 eggs.
Item for the hayward's tenement this year, 22 eggs.
Item for various tenements in the lady's hands, 102 eggs.
Item for a messuage, 3 acres 1 rood of land recently of Walter Dennis now in the lord's hands, 3½ eggs.
Item for various tenements pertaining to High Hall in the lady's hands, 39.
Item delivered to John Link steward of the lady's guests for provisions of the lady's guesthouse at Westhorpe by 1 tally against the said steward, 560 eggs.
Item in allowance made to Richard Morton for two and a half messuages and certain land granted to him and his heirs by a deed of the lord as appears in the oats section, 5 eggs.
In allowance made to Adam Blayer for a certain tenement as above p.a., 14 eggs.
In sales within 49½ eggs, from the responsibility of the bailiff.
Sum as above.   It balances.

Poultry
From the issue of the hens above nothing because they were leased at farm for money within.
From purchased within, 12.
Sum 12.   It balances.

And reckoned in capons made above

Dovecote
From the issue of a dovecote at the manor, except tithes, 360 pigeons.
From the issue of a dovecote at High Hall, nothing this year because there are no pigeons in stock.
Sum 360 pigeons.   It balances.

And delivered to the lady for the lady's hospitality by 1 tally.

Cumin From rent from the Prior of Bricett p.a. ½lb cumin.
Sum ½lb cumin.   It balances.

And sold within.

Pepper From rent received from Walter Frances for the tenement recently of John Pinfold pertaining to High Hall, ½lb pepper.
Sum ½lb pepper.   And sold within.

Ploughing services From the issue of 10 customary greater tenures this year that provide 6 ploughs this year, 30 ploughings taken at the seasons of winter and Lent. That is, for each whole plough, 5 ploughings, and they receive from the lady for each plough 6 loaves of mixed grain, of which 20 loaves per bus., and allowed 2 winter works.

From the issue of 9 other customary tenants that provide 10 ploughs this year, 16 ploughings, of which each plough shall make 3 ploughings and receive from the lady 6 loaves for each plough of the said grain and the said weight, no works allowed.

From the issues on customary tenants of High Hall this year, nothing.

Sum 46½ ploughing services.

And expended in ploughing the lady's land at the aforesaid time.

Ploughale From the issue of the customary tenants that provide 12½ ploughings this year.

Sum 12½ ploughings.

And expended in ploughing the lady's land at the aforesaid time.

Winter works From customary half-day services, 963 winter and summer works, price per work ½d.

From customary services from High Hall, 10 works.

Sum 973 works.

From which, in allowance for the reeve's tenement this year, 33 works and ¼ of ½ a work.

In allowance for the hayward's tenement this year, 22½ works.

Item for various tenements in the lady's hands, 176¾ and three parts of a work.

Item for the tenement of Walter Dennis, 9½ works.

Item in allowance for the tenement recently of Robert Wing pertaining to High Hall in the lord's hands, 10.

In allowance made to Richard Morton for two and a half messuages and certain land granted to him and his heirs by a deed of the lord as appears above in the section on oats, 7¼ works.

Item in allowance made to Adam Blayer for a certain tenement above p.a., 5 winter works.

Item in 30 ploughing services expended above 60 works, for each ploughing service, 2 works.

In tumbrels carried out this year, nothing.

In making drainage furrows at the time of sowing wheat, 30 works.

In making drainage furrows at the time of sowing peas and barley, 14 works.

In sowing furrows of wheat, 20 works.

In harrowing rye, 3 works.

In sowing furrows of peas, 15 works.

In sowing furrows of oats and in harrowing oats, 27 works.

Item in re-ploughing land, harrowing before ploughing and in harrowing barley, 24 works.

In carrying straw before threshing in winter and making one stack from it at High Hall and in making a hedge by circling the said stack, 10 works.

In cutting thorn bushes and making a new ditch at High Hall around a new close, 190 works.

Item in making a certain parcel of the said ditch next to Burchards Way by works and in making a hedge upon the same, 22 works.

Item in making a hedge around High Hall Wood and the Entry there, 20 works.

Item in making a hedge at the manor upon the ditch of a new close there and the Conyger, 12 works.

In filling dung carts with manure in winter, 16 works.

Item in spreading the said manure at the same time, 25 works.

115

Item in spreading manure in summer upon Old Toft, 25 works.

In stacking straw and in a thatcher employed at High Hall, 49 works.

Item in stacking straw for a thatcher employed at the manor, 45 works.

Item in carrying straw for threshing and in making a hedge for encircling the same straw in a stack at High Hall, 8 works.

In repairing two gates at the manor, 19 works.

Item in mowing teasles before ploughing upon the land at High Hall in summer, 18 works.

Item in stacking hay in the barn, 4 works.

In spreading herbage in the meadows this year, 14 works.

In sales within, 37½ works and half a quarter and 2 parts of 1 work from the responsibility of the hayward.

Sum as above.   It balances.

Carrying services From the issue of 7 customary carrying services at the will of the lord from custom, price per work 1d.

Sum 7. It balances. And sold within.

Manure carrying services From customary services without resumption, 9 manure carrying services and allowed to the same for each man carrying manure 1 winter work, price per carry 2d.

Sum 9.

From which, in allowance for the reeve's tenement this year, ¼ of a carrying service.

Item for the hayward's tenement this year, ½ a carrying service.

Item for various tenements in the lord's hands, 2 carrying services half a quarter of a carry a third part of a carry and a third part of half a carry of manure.

Item in allowance made to Richard Morton for two and a half messuages and certain land granted to him and his heirs by a deed of the lord as appears above in the oats section, 3 parts of ½ a carry.

In carrying manure this year, nothing.

In sales within, 4½ and half a quarter of a carry 2 parts of a carry and a third part of half a carry of manure.

Sum as above.   It balances.

Weeding works From customary services 188 works, price per work ½d.

From customary services at High Hall, 3 works.

Sum 191 works.

From which, in allowance for the reeve's tenement this year, 2 weeding works.

Item for the hayward's tenement this year, 9 weeding works.

Item for various tenements in the lord's hands, 24¾ works.

In allowance made to Richard Morton as above, ¾ of a weeding work.

In allowance made to Adam Blayer for a certain tenement as above p.a., 2 weeding works.

Item in weeding teasels and in clearing bracken from the oats and barley, 64 weeding works.

In sales within, 89¾ works, of which 3 from the responsibility of the bailiff, and 86¾ works from the responsibility of the hayward.

Sum as above.

Mowing works From customary services for ½ days, 49 mowing works, price per work 1½d.

Sum 49 works.

From which, in allowance for the reeve's tenement this year, ¼ of a mowing work.
Item for the tenement of the hayward this year, 1½ mowing works.
Item for various tenements in the lord's hands, 6¾ works.
In allowance made to Richard Morton as above, ¾, of a work.
In sales within, 41 mowing works.

Sum as above.   It balances.

Carriage of hay From customary tenants that have carriage without resumption and without price, works this year, 8 carrying services.

Sum 8.   It balances.

And expenses in hay including carriage.

Haymaking works From customary services as many as the lord requires for lifting, turning and stacking all the hay without resumption. It balances.

Harvest works From customary tenants for a whole day to reap, tie and stack the lord's grain, 643 works, for which each receives from the lord at the ninth hour and for his supper 2 loaves of mixed corn, of which 20 to the bushel, and 4 herrings, price per work 1d.
From customary services at High Hall p.a., 111 works

Sum 754 works.

From which, in allowance for the reeve's tenement this year, 11¾ works.
Item for the hayward's tenement this year, 12 works.
Item for various tenements in the lady's hands, 96¾ works.
Item for various tenements pertaining to High Hall in the lady's hands, 77 works.
Item for the tenement of Walter Dennis in the lord's hands as above, 3½ works.
In allowance made to Gilbert Moundmill and Katherine his wife by a deed of the lord as above for Helpes tenement pertaining to High Hall p.a., 16 works.[143]
In allowance made to Richard Morton as above, 2 works and quarter of half a harvest work.
In allowance made to Adam Blayer for a certain tenement as above p.a., 4 works.
Item in 190½ acres of various grains reaping, tying and gathering in total, 477 works, of which 14 works are from High Hall and 463 works from the responsibility of the hayward. There are 2 works on each acre, plus in total 96 works.[144]
In sales within, 54¼ works, of which from the responsibility of the hayward, 50¼ works and 4 works from the responsibility of the bailiff, 4 works.

Sum as above.   It balances.

Harvest boonworks From customary services this year, 108 boonworks, from which each free man shall receive from the lord for his food at noon and for his

---

[143] The implication is that the terms on which this land is held have been changed from the traditional villein service tenancy, which included labour services, to a straight cash rent without any services: hence the allowance.

[144] Hence each of these harvest works comprise a full day of work, and the officials have allocated two works to each sown acre of demesne grain (190.5 x 2 = 381 works), plus another 96 works makes the total of 477.

117

supper one wheat loaf, of which 20 to the bushel. Each customary tenant shall have for his food at noon as for free tenants, and for his supper one loaf of mixed grain, of which 20 to the bushel, and 1 herring.

From customary services from High Hall, 19 boonworks.

Sum 127 boonworks.

From which, in allowance for the reeve's tenement, 3.

Item for the hayward's tenement, 3 boonworks.

Item for various tenements in the lady's hands, 7.

Item for the tenement recently of Walter Dennis in the lord's hands as above, 1.

Item in allowance for tenements in the lord's hands pertaining to High Hall, 10.

Item in allowance made to Gilbert Moundmill and Katherine his wife for Helpes tenement pertaining to High Hall by a deed of the lord p.a., 2.

Item in allowance for the tenement Chapmans in the lord's hands by escheat after the death of William Blunt pertaining to High Hall, 1.

Item in allowance made to Richard Morton as above, 1.

Item in allowance made to Adam Blayer for certain land and tenement as above, 1.

In 47 acres of various corn reaped, tied and gathered together this year, 94 works, of which 2 from High Hall and 92 boonworks from the responsibility of the hayward.

In sales within, from the responsibility of the bailiff, 4 boonworks.

Sum as above.

Section Four

Accounts of Walsham manor with High Hall, 1426–1559
Documents 9 to 23[1]

Document 9: Walsham account, 28 September 1426 to 28 September 1427

SA/B HA504/3/15 m.1

Walsham
Account of John Fuller reeve and hayward[2] there from the eve of St Michael the Archangel in the 5th year of Henry VI until the eve of the same St Michael next coming in the 6th year of the same Henry VI for one whole year.

Arrears [*He answers*] for arrears from the last account of the preceding year, nothing.

Sum nil.

Rents of assize For rents of assize there from both free and customary tenants for this manor and for H[*igh Hall*] not including [*deduct'*] rent in Westhorpe with ward of High Hall there for the terms of St Michael, Christmas, Easter and the Nativity of St John the Baptist, £13 11s. 9½d. half a ¼d. and two parts of a ¼d.
For new rent received from Edmund Hovell of Badwell for a messuage formerly of Roger Griggs in Badwell Street 1d.

Sum £13 11s. 10½d. half a ¼d. and two parts of a ¼d.

Castle ward For castle ward received from the manor of Wyken for the terms of St Michael, Christmas, Easter and the Nativity of St John the Baptist, 11s. 2d.
For castle ward received from the manor of <Wyken> Ixworth, 2s. 10d.

Sum 14s.

Farm of land, meadow and pasture And for £9 from Peter Poye[3] for the lease of land and meadow shown as a parcel by an indenture with the liberty of a fold of up to 300 sheep and no more because the same Peter is allowed 60s. for all the wood retained in the hands of the lord and sold by parcels within.
For \John Brabon/ a dairy house [*domo dayer'*] in the manor, nothing this year because it was not leased \this year 20d./

---

1 See Introduction, pp. xxx–xxxiv.
2 John Fuller was first elected hayward in 1409, bailiff in 1410 and also acted as affeerer at several courts.
3 Contemporary court rolls attest to the breadth and scale of Peter Poye's pastoral pursuits. A 1393–4 cellarer's account for Ixworth priory names him as the bailiff of Church House manor in Walsham, SA/B 553/112.

And for 14s. 7d. from Adam Blayer for a close called New Close[4] containing by estimation 35 acres with the liberty of a fold of up to 40 sheep, per acre 5d.

And for 20s. 6d. from Robert Vincent for the farm of a close \9s./ called Katherine's Croft with hedges and ditches there, one piece of land and pasture containing by estimation 6 acres \3s./ with leafy willows there, two pieces of land \12d./ containing 4½ acres lying at Trendle Wood [*Trendywode*], one piece of land \12d./ containing 5 roods called Stony Land, one piece of land \10d./ containing 5 roods lying in South Field, 4 acres of land \12d./ called Knots Hedge [*Knotesheg*] and one close called Sheepcote Close with the liberty of a fold of up to 40 sheep.

And for 10s. 6d. from Robert Hawes for one piece of land containing 42 acres called Hatchmere and 1½ acres of land lying in the Bottom [*Botme*] formerly of Walter Terwald with the liberty of a fold of up to 80 sheep.

And for 12s. from William Hawes for a piece of land containing 42 acres called Fishpond Field with the liberty of a fold of up to 80 sheep.[5]

And for 24s. \usually leased for 26s. 8d./ from a piece of meadow called Broad Dole containing 4½ acres \per acre 6s./ sold to various men this year \and no more because ½ acre of the same meadow was reserved for the use of the lord/

And for 5s. 6d. from Adam Ebell for a piece of land at Mickle Meadow and a piece of land at West Mill and 2 acres of land called Nunns Land.[6]

And for 3s. from Matilda Bonde for 4 acres 1 rood of land abutting upon Howes Haugh [*Howeshawe*] formerly of Nicholas Dennis, 1½ acres of land called the Butts of the tenement Osbern near Rickinghall Willows, 2 acres of land of the tenement Cranmer next to the land formerly of Nicholas Tiptot at Rickinghall Willows next to the land of John Man and the Market Mere, 2 acres of land of the tenement Burchards on the west side of Burchards Land, one piece of land of the said tenement at Rickinghall Willows.

And for <4s.> \3s. 9d./ for 3 roods of meadow lying in Mickle Meadow sold this year.

And for 10s. 2d. from John Cooper[7] for two pieces of land containing 22 acres called Doucedeux, 6 acres of land called Walpoles Croft, a pightle called Jacks Yard and ½ acre of land abutting upon the land of the Prior of Ixworth with the liberty of a fold of up to 40 sheep.

And for 4s. 10d. from William Syre for a close next to his dwelling house granted to him and his heirs by court roll for Sheepcote Yard, 1½ acres of land at Clay Hill, two pieces of land near there of the tenement Paynes, 1½ roods of land of the tenement Dennis abutting upon the Brook.

And for 6s. 8d. from Peter Poye for the Launde in Ladys Wood.

And for 5s. 9d. from John Swift for 1½ acres of land of the tenement Paynes next to Market Way, 5 acres of land of the tenement Paynes with 1½ roods of land at

---

4   The lease of this large parcel of arable land, together with a succession of similar leases below, relates to the demesne lands of the manor and of High Hall. Likewise, the reverse of the account no longer includes details about the sowing of the demesne and the subsequent disposal of crops: most of the labour services are sold, because the lord has no demesne to deploy them on and the lessees of the demesne parcels would have no use for them. Hence the lord has ceased direct exploitation of the demesne.

5   Hawes' tenement was one of the largest in Walsham, and its site is now occupied by the Rookery on Wattisfield Road.

6   These lands are at the west end of the parish. Ebell tenement was where West Cottage now stands in West Street.

7   Cooper's tenement was almost opposite High Hall manor, so these parcels of land were close to John's residence.

Burchards Wood, 1 acre of land of the tenement Robbys abutting upon Howes Haugh, ½ acre of land at Frances Row of the tenement Robbys, 2 acres of land at Brook Pits, 6 acres of land and pasture called Home Stall, of which 2s. 8d. is fee farm.[8]

And for 4s. 8d. from Robert Margery senior for one piece of land and pasture containing 7 acres called Howes Toft per acre 8d. and granted for a term of 10 years, this year is the 7th.

And for 14s. 8d. from John Fuller of East End for a close called Ox Pasture with hedges and ditches there, one piece of land containing 6 acres called Godelards Land, 10 acres of land parcel of Guspers Field, herbage of the meadow in Small Brook, a curtilage formerly Robeteles with ½ acre of land formerly of William Payne, 2 acres of land of the tenement formerly of Robert Fornham, near Gode-lards Land next to the land formerly of Robert Payne and 1 rood of land at Willow Mere formerly of Adam Pitlake, 2 acres 2½ roods of land recently of Walter Dennis remaining in the lord's hands abutting upon Hundred Mere with the liberty of a fold of up to 12 ewes and 12 lambs granted to him for a term of 10 years, this year is the 7th.

For 12 acres of land at Allwood Green recently granted to Robert Payne for 2s. 6d. nothing this year because it was grazed by the lord's sheep.

And for 3s. 3d. from Robert Robwood for 1½ acres of land of the tenement Paynes, one curtilage, 3 roods of land formerly of William Payne, 2 roods of land of the tenement of William Payne with the third part of a way called the Outgong towards Westhorpe, 1 acre of land in two pieces abutting upon the Hundred Mere[9] granted to him this year.

And for 5s. 11d. from William Grocer for 4 acres of land next to the close of the said William lying there on the east side of the land formerly of Thomas Hereward, 2 roods of land called Stony Land and 2 acres of land abutting upon Helpes Wood from the land of High Hall and for 16 acres 1 rood of land in one piece parcel of Guspers Field recently in farm to Hugh Littlehall.

And for 15d. from John Tiptot senior for 5 acres of land parcel of Guspers Field.

And for 7s. 11d. from Richard Rampley for 7 acres of land parcel of Guspers Field of which one head abuts upon Howes Haugh, two pieces of land containing 4 acres in the field of Angrave of the tenement formerly of Agnes de Angerhale and for herbage of a piece of meadow at Howes Haugh with pasture at the head of the same granted to him for a term of 10 years, this year is the 7th.

And for 2s. from John Ringbell for one close lying at Hall Gate on the north side of his messuage granted to him for the said term.

And for 10s. for 7 roods of meadow lying in Mickle Meadow in various pieces of meadow sold this year.

---

8 From the later fourteenth century some lords began to grant parcels of villein land on 'fee farm' [*feoda firma*], which was essentially a hereditary tenure for a fixed annual cash rent, plus an entry fine, heriot and suit of court. The absence of liability for any labour services or payments in kind made it more attractive to tenants than the traditional villein service tenure, and the phrase 'fee farm' also conveyed a superior form of tenure. See Bailey, *Decline of serfdom*, pp. 34, 47, 200, 222, 232–4, 248–50.

9 The Hundred Mere is the boundary between Walsham and Westhorpe, which also served as the boundary between Blackbourn and Hartismere Hundreds and also East and West Suffolk.

And for 5s. 10d. from William Syre for a cotland with a curtilage called Walpoles Croft, 1 acre of land near the sheepfold of the Prior of Ixworth and 1 acre of land next to Gurrys Croft granted to him and his heirs by court roll.

And for 16d. from John Fletcher for Godfreys Yard with 1½ acres of land of the same tenement.

And for 9d. from Henry Dinglove for 1 acre of land of the tenement Cranmer at Hulkes Bridge [*granted*] to him and his heirs and 3 roods of land of the tenement Kebbils recently leased to John Cook.

And for 8s. from John Page for the farm of land and a tenement formerly Coppelowes granted to him and his heirs by court roll.

And for 5s. 10d. from William Sare for 3½ acres of land in various pieces of the tenement Kebbils at Blunts Hall and for 18 acres of land called Blunts Hall.

And for 3s. 4d. from John Man for 8 acres of land by estimate of the same tenement in Long Wheat in one piece and for 4 acres of land of the said tenement lying at the end of the croft formerly of John Bonde.

And for 3d. from Adam Frances for 1 acre of land of the tenement Robbys on the south side of Trendle Wood.

And for 4½d. from Alice Morton for 1½ roods of land of the tenement Paynes at the head of the croft of the said Alice and 1 rood of land at the north head of the same.

And for 4d. from John Robwood junior for 1 acre 3 roods of land at Willow Mere of the tenement Paynes \usually leased for 8d./ recently in farm to the same Alice.

And for 2d. from John Ermitt for ½ acre of land next to the Green Way formerly of John son of William Clevehog of the tenement Man.

And for 10d. from John Spilman for ½ acre of land recently leased to Thomas Bonde of the tenement Gosling, 1 acre of land abutting upon Wood Way of the same tenement at Pedders Path and ½ acre of land of the tenement Ratches lying at Dales.

And for 6d. from Robert Syre for 3 roods of land in the croft of Godfreys of the tenement of William Payne.

And for 3d. from Thomas Wells for 1 acre of land of the tenement Clevehog above the Brook.

And for 12d. from John Fletcher for a messuage \usually leased for 18d./, 2½ roods of land lying in the croft recently of Walter Dennis remaining in the lord's hands by Robert Osbern.

And for 2s. 2d. from Robert Fletcher for 5 acres of land on the east side of Fishpond Field next to the land of William Sare, 2 acres of land lying next to Strondes Way.

And for 18d. from Thomas Wells for 3 acres of land of the tenement Paynes and 6 acres of land formerly of Nicholas Dennis at New Haugh.

And for 5s. for herbage of 1 acre of meadow called Turfpit Acre.

And for 1½d. from John Margery senior for 1½ roods of land in four parcels in the field of Langham.

And for 5s. 10d. from John Tiptot junior for two headlands containing 1 rood of pasture of the tenement of Peter Painter at Howes Haugh pasture of Painters Yard, 1 acre 3 roods of land in two pieces of the tenement Painters recently leased to Robert Bray, 5 acres 3 roods in six pieces of the same tenement of which 3 acres in three pieces lie in the field of Ashfield and 2 acres 3 roods of land in three pieces at the Brook recently leased to John Brook, 1 acre 1 rood of land abutting upon the Brook towards the east of the same tenement recently leased to Robert Man, 3 roods of land in two pieces of the same tenement next to Ashfield Way recently leased to John Ermitt, ½ acre of land at Brook Bridge of the same tenement recently leased to Robert Man, 2 acres of land of the tenement Pudding lying at Procession Way abutting upon Hundred Mere, 1 rood of land of the said tenement next to Stubbing Way next to the land formerly of Richard Qwalm, 3 acres of land of the same tenement near East Mill in three pieces recently leased to Walter Frances granted to him and his heirs by court roll.

From Robert Vincent for one piece of land called the Holner, 12 acres of land next to Nether Haugh, 18 acres of land in Burchards Croft and a piece of land in High Hall Croft and a piece of land this year 30s.

From the same Robert for summer pasture of High Hall Close this year 16s. From winter pasture of the same, nothing this year because it was grazed by the lord's sheep.

From John Swift for summer pasture of Burchards Close this year 8s. For winter pasture of the same, nothing this year because it was grazed by the same sheep.

For one piece of pasture called Nether Haugh, one piece of land called Seventeen Acres, 18 acres of land called Blunts Land, nothing because it was grazed by the same sheep.

For two messuages \John Robwood/ formerly of Nicholas Dennis, one tenement called Sparschoys recently granted for <4s. 8d., nothing because it was not granted> this year, 2s. 4d. \usually leased for 4s. 8d./

From John Bertram for a close recently of Robert Cokerell lying next to Ladys Wood purchased from Peter Poye this year 6s. 8d., nothing in this account.

Sum [blank] £22 12s. 4d.[10]

Perquisites of the courts From perquisites of two courts held there this year, 114s. 7d.

[11]Sum [blank]

Farm of the mill with sale of stock And for 33s. 4d. from a certain miller for farm of a windmill leased this year.

Sum 33s. 4d.

Sale of works and services For 16 qrs 4 bus. of oats from rent sold elsewhere, price 2s. 8d. per qr, 44s.

For 4 capons from rent sold elsewhere, 10d.

For 100½ hens from rent sold elsewhere, price 1½d. each, 14s. 5¼d.

For 661½ eggs from services sold elsewhere, price per 120 4d., 22d.

For ½lb of cumin sold elsewhere, 1½d.

For ½lb of pepper sold elsewhere, 9d.

For 28 customary ploughing services sold elsewhere, price per ploughing service 6d., 14s. 3d.

For 9 customary Ploughales sold elsewhere, price 4s. 6d.

For 753½ winter works sold elsewhere, price per work ½d., 31s. 4¾d.

For 7 customary carrying services sold elsewhere, price 7d.

For 6 customary manure carrying services sold elsewhere, price per carry 2d., 12d.

For 149 customary weeding works sold elsewhere, price per work ½d., 6s. 2½d.

For 36 mowing works sold elsewhere, price per work 1½d., 4s. 6d.

For 555 customary harvest works sold elsewhere, price per work 2d., £4 12s. 6d.

---

[10] Marginal note.
[11] Marginal note, 'in expenses 6s. 11d.'

123

For 116 customary harvest boonworks sold elsewhere, price per work 2d., 19s. 4d.
Sum [*blank*] £11 16s. 3d.[12]

Sale of underwood And for 78s. 7½d. from John Lines for 32 perches of under-
wood at Ladys Wood, 16d.
From John Pollard for 32 perches there, 16d.
From Walter Stroppe for 32 perches there, 16d.
From John Bene for 32 perches there, 16d.
From William Lakenham for 1 rood there, 20d.
From Margery Wyke for one [*sic*] underwood there, 20d.
From John Fuller junior for ½ acre there, 3s. 4d.
From Margaret Painter for 1 rood there, 20d.
From John Margery junior for ½ acre there, 3s. 4d.
From Richard Rampley for ½ acre there, 3s. 4d.
From Robert Lester for 1 rood there, 20d.
From William Newman for 1½ acres there, 10s. 0½d.
From John Smith for 1½ acres there, 10s.
From John Tiptot junior for ½ acre there, 3s. 4d.
From Robert Margery senior for 1 rood, 20d.
From John Brabon for 1 rood, 20d.
From Marion Pollard for 1 rood, 20d.
From John Pepper for 1 rood 8 perches, 2s.
From John Margery senior for 3 roods, 5s.
From John Margery senior for 1½ roods 4 perches, 2s. 8d.
From John Page for underwood in the Launde sold to him, altogether 10s.
From John Finte for a thorn hedge, 12d.
From William Man for underwood sold to him, 4d.
From John Ringbell for leafy oaks in North Haugh, 12d.
From John Fuller of East End for 1 rood of underwood in Luchesdell 15d.
From Henry Corsour for 1 rood there, 15d.
From John Manser for 1 portion of underwood there, 12d.
From Thomas Wells for 1 rood of underwood in High Hall Wood, 15d.
From Peter Rollesby for one white poplar, 18d.
Sum [*blank*]

Foreign Receipts nil.

Sales at the audit From sales at the audit, nothing this year. Sum nil.

Sum total of receipts with arrears [*blank*] £60 0s. 12d. half a ¼d. and two parts
of ¼d.[13]

Rent resolute with allowances and decays From which in allowances of rent,
works and services reckoned in money for the tenement of Richard Rampoyl in the
office of reeve and from a fine of 2 marks for not carrying out the said office [*de
dicto officio non portand'*], 9s. 6¾d. and a quarter of a ¼d.

---

[12] Marginal note.
[13] Marginal note.

And in allowances of rent, works and services likewise reckoned in money for the tenement [*sic*], 4s. 0¾d. and from a fine of 13s. 4d. for not carrying out the said office. The same accounts for rent resolute for the hall of Thelnetham of 2s., nothing because it is outside the lord's hands.
Item for the hall of Rickinghall p.a., 3s. 1½d.
Item paid for castle ward service of Norwich p.a., 16s.
Item paid to John Margery p.a., 1½d.
Item in allowance of rent for various tenements in the lord's hands both for this manor and for High Hall, 52s. 5¼d. half a quarter of a ¼d. and two parts of a ¼d. of which for High Hall, 15s. 11¾d.
Item paid for the hall of Ashfield for castle ward of Norwich for High Hall p.a. this year, 17d.
Item paid to the same hall for rent p.a., 3s. 2d.
Item paid to Eye castle this year once, 9d.
Item paid for hundred suit released p.a. for Burchards, 16d.
Item paid to Helimot and from ward for Burchards p.a., 9d.
Item in rent resolute for Sir William Bardwell for 1 acre of meadow at Turf Pits purchased by the lord from John Rampley, chaplain, 4d.
Item in allowed rent on 4 acres of land remaining in the lord's hands by John Syre, 18d. three quarters of a ¼d. and a third part of a ¼d.
Item in allowed works and services reckoned in money for the tenement formerly of John Spilman[14] granted to John Bertram[15] freely by a charter [*per scriptum*] of the lord.
Sum £4 11s. 7d. half a quarter of a ¼d., two parts of a ¼d. and a third part of a ¼d.

Cost of the buildings with pardons and allowances   In the cost of buildings, nothing. In pardons made, nothing.
Sum [blank]

Cost of the mill   In mending the sails and cogs and staves [*baclands*] by the carpenter, 8d.
Sum 8d.

Minute expenses   In the stipend of William Syre for 10 days' work making hedges around the wood of High Hall, per day 4d., 3s. 4d.
In parchment bought for writing the court rolls and accounts, 4d.
In stipend of Robert Margery for 3 days' work making hedges at Ladys Wood and North Hawe, 12d.
Item paid to John Man for scouring a ditch at High Hall and for mending a hedge upon the said ditch, 5s. <4>   Sum [*blank*] <4s.> 9s. 8d.[16]

Weeding and mowing   In weeding the corn, nothing.
In mowing the lord's meadow, nothing.
Price paid for ½ acre of meadow mowed and hay made, 4d.

---

[14] The tenement of John Spilman was on the site of the house in Palmer Street now known as the Old Vicarage.
[15] John Bertram was one of seven men who, as lords or feoffees of the manor, held their first court on 23 May 1426: SA/B HA504/1/12.3.
[16] Marginal note.

In 40 hurdles made from the lord's sticks for the lord's fold, 3s. 1½d.
Sum [blank] 3s. 5½d.[17]

Steward's expenses In expenses of the steward and others being here for two courts held this year, 6s. 11d.
Sum [blank] 6s. 11d.[18]

Wages and stipends In the wages of the bailiff reckoned this year with his clothing, 33s. 4d.
And in the fees of the clerk of the account and courts this year, 20s.
And for the clothing of Peter Poye, farmer, as in the preceding account by agreement, 6s. 8d.
Sum 60s.

Cash delivered Delivered to John Bertram from rent and farm this year by one tally, £24 16s. 8d.
£24 16s. 8d.
Received Bertram[19]

Sum of all expenses and allowances £33 8s. 11½d. half a quarter of a ¼d., two parts of a ¼d. and a third part of a ¼d. And owed £26 12s. 0½d. half a ¼d. and half a quarter of a ¼d., of which paid to the farmer of the Prior of Ixworth for pasture of the lord's sheep received by John Bertram, 13s. 4d.
Item paid to Robert Vincent for carrying underwood to make hedges at High Hall, 5s.
And thus owed, £25 13s. 8½d. half a ¼d. and half a quarter of a ¼d.
Which was delivered to John Bertram [different hand] It balances.
<£33 8s. 11½d. half a quarter of a ¼d., 2 parts of a ¼d. and a third part of a ¼d. And owed £26 12s. 0½d. half a ¼d. and half a quarter of a ¼d. of which paid to the farmer of the Prior of Ixworth for pasture for the lord's sheep received by John Bertram.>[20]

[Reverse]
Walsham Account of John Fuller bailiff there.

Walsham Account of works and services there in the 5th year of Henry VI.

Multure of the mill For the farm of one windmill leased this year to certain men from Bury, who pay in cash for 10 qrs of mixed grain.[21]
Sum nil.
Stots For heriots this year, nothing.
Sum nil.

---

[17] Marginal note.
[18] Marginal note.
[19] Marginal note in different hand.
[20] Marginal note, crossed out.
[21] That is, they opted to pay in cash rather than render the lease in kind.

126

Oats For rent from the lord's tenants at the Feast of St Edmund King and Martyr, 20 qrs two parts of ½ a bus. and half a ¼ of a peck of oats.
      Sum 20 qrs two parts of ½ a bus. and half a ¼ of a peck of oats.
From which, in allowances for various tenements in the lord's hands both for this manor and for High Hall this year, 3 qrs 4 bus. and two parts of ½ a bus. and half a ¼ of a peck of oats. In sales within, 16 qrs 4 bus. of oats.
      Sum as above.   It balances.

Capons For rent from the lord's tenants at Easter, 8 capons.
      Sum 8.
From which in allowances for various tenements in the lord's hands, 4. In sales within, 4.
      Sum as above.   It balances.

Hens and cockerels For rent from the lord's tenants at Christmas, 141¾ hens and cockerels of which two are cockerels.
      Sum 141¾ hens and cockerels of which two are cockerels.
From which, in allowances for various tenements in the lord's hands both for this manor and for High Hall, 25¼ hens.
Allowed to Thomas Smith, sergeant of Westhorpe, by the hand of Robert Sewell tenant of High Hall in Westhorpe. In sales within, 115½ hens.
      Sum as above.

Eggs For rent from the lord's tenants at Easter, 825 eggs.
      Sum 825 eggs.
From which in allowances for various tenements in the lord's hands both for this manor and for High Hall, 163½ eggs. In sales within, 661½ eggs.
      Sum as above.   It balances.

Dovecote For the issues of one dovecote this year, nothing here because it was granted to Peter Poye with other lands as within.
      Sum nil.

Cumin For rent from the Prior of Bricett p.a. ½lb cumin.
      Sum shown and sales within.   It balances.

Pepper For pepper rent from Adam Frances for the tenement recently of John Pinfold pertaining to High Hall, ½lb pepper.
      Sum as shown and sales within.

Ploughing services For the issue of 5 customary greater tenures this year providing 3½ ploughteams this year for 15½ ploughing services taken at the seasons of winter and Lent, that is for each whole ploughteam providing 5 ploughing services and receiving from the lord for each ploughteam 6 loaves of mixed grain, at 20 to the bushel, and to be allowed two winter works.
For the issues of 4 other customary tenants providing 4 ploughteams this year, 12 ploughing services, for which each plough shall do 3 ploughing services and receive from the lord 6 loaves of the said grain at the said weight, with no allowance of works.
For the issues of customary tenants of High Hall, nothing because none here.

For a customary perquisite from William Hore pertaining to the tenement Patches for the winter season, 1 ploughing service.

Sum 28½ ploughing services. And sold within. It balances.

Ploughales For customary tenants providing 9 ploughing services this year.

Sum 9 ploughing services. And sales within.

Winter and summer works For customary services for half days, 962 winter works and a third part of a winter work.

Sum 962 and a third part of a winter work.

From which in allowances for various tenements in the lord's hands both for this manor and for High Hall, 208½ and a third part of a winter work.

In sales within, 753½, price per work ½d.

Sum as above. It balances.

Carrying services For customary issues of carrying services at the will of the lord from custom, price per work 1d.

Sum 7 carrying services. And sold within. It balances.

Manure carrying services For customary services without resumption, 9 manure carryings and allowed to them for each man carrying manure, one winter work priced 2d. per carry.

Sum 9 carrying services.

From which, in allowance for various tenements in the hands of the lord, 3 carryings. In sales within, 6 carryings.

Sum as above. It balances.

Weeding works For customary services, 175 and ¾ of ½ a work, price per work ½d.

Sum 175 weeding works.

From which, in allowance for various tenements in the lord's hands both for this manor and for High Hall, 26 and ¾ of ½ a weeding work.

In sales within, 149 works of which 3 from the responsibility of the bailiff.

Sum as above. It balances.

Mowing works For customary services by ½ days, 42¼ mowing works, price per work ½d.

Sum 42½ mowing works.

From which, in allowances for various tenements in the lord's hands 6¼ mowing works.

In sales within 36 mowing works.

Sum as above. It balances.

Carriage of hay For customary services that they have carriage without resumption and without price of a work, nothing this year because they were released by the lady Elmham.

Sum nil.

Haymaking works For customary services as many works as the lord indicates for lifting, turning and stacking all the hay without resumption, nothing this year because aforesaid.

Sum nil.

Harvest works For customary services for the whole day to reap, tie and stack the lord's grain, 754 works of which each receives from the lord at noon and for his supper 2 loaves of mixed grains, at 20 to the bushel, and 4 herrings, price per work 2d.

Sum 754 works.

From which, in allowances for various tenements in the lord's hands both for this manor and for High Hall, 199 works. In sales within, 555.

Sum as above.   It balances.

Harvest boonworks For customary services this year, 139 harvest boonworks for which each free man shall receive from the lord for his food at noon and for his supper one wheat loaf, of which 20 to the bushel, and each customary tenant shall have for his food at noon as for the free tenants and for his supper a loaf of mixed grains, of which 20 to the bushel, and one herring, price per work 2d.

Sum 139 boonworks.

From which, in allowances for various tenements in the lord's hands both for this manor and for High Hall, 23 boonworks.

In sales within, 116 boonworks.

Sum as above. It balances.

Document 10: Walsham account, 28 September 1427 to 28 September 1428

SA/B HA504/3/15 m.2

Walsham

Account of John Fuller, reeve and hayward there, from the eve of St Michael the Archangel in the 6th year of Henry VI until the eve of the same St Michael next coming in the 7th year of the same Henry for one whole year.

Arrears [*He answers*] for arrears of the last account of the preceding year, nothing.

Sum nil.

Rents of assize For rents of assize both from free and villein tenants both for this manor and for High Hall not including rent in Westhorpe with ward of High Hall there for the terms of St Michael, Christmas, Easter and the Nativity of St John the Baptist, £13 11s. 9½d. half a ¼d. and two parts of a ¼d.

For new rent received from Edmund Hovell of Badwell for the messuage formerly of Roger Griggs in Badwell Street, 1d.

For new rent received from John Robwood for a piece of land lying next to Ulveswell purchased by John Bertram[22] and granted by the said John to the profit of the manor, 5d.

For new rent received from John Margery for a piece of land next to Gorommes Way granted in the same way, 6d.

For new rent received from Robert Robwood for a garden of Goslings tenement granted in the same way, 1d.

---

[22] John Bertram, one of several lords or feoffees of the manor, had purchased land within Walsham and added it to the lands of the manor, the income from which increased fixed rents by 1s. 9d. per annum.

129

For new rent received from Nicholas Brond of Gislingham[23] for a piece of land lying in the aforesaid vill between the land of William Goddard on the north part and the land of the Templars on the south part granted to him in the same way, 3d.

For new rent received from Robert Carpenter of Langham for a piece of land lying next to the land of the parson of Langham granted to him in the same way, 2d.

From new rent received from Henry Dinglove for a piece of land lying in Mill Field granted to him in the same way, 2d.

From new rent received from Robert Warde for a piece of land lying next to Chalk Pightle granted the same way, 2d.

£13 13s. 7½d. half a ¼d. and two parts of ¼d.

Castle ward For castle ward received from the manor of Wyken for the terms of St Michael, Christmas, Easter and the Nativity of St John the Baptist, 11s. 2d.

For castle ward received from the manor of Ixworth, 2s. 10d.

Sum 14s.

Farm of land, meadow and pasture And for <£9> \£7 6s. 8d. and no more because 13s. 4d. for the dovecote because no stock and 20s. allowed to him for the meadow because it could not be completely mown/[24] received from John Fuller for the lease of land and meadow as a parcel shown by an indenture, with the liberty of a fold of up to 300 sheep, and no more because the same John is allowed 60s. as the wood was retained in the lord's hands and sold in parcels as below.

For one dairy house in the manor, nothing this year because it is no longer leased.

And for 14s. 7d. from Adam Blayer for a close called New Close containing by estimate 35 acres with the liberty of a fold of up to 40 sheep, per acre 5d.

And for 20s. 6d. from Robert Vincent for farm of a close \9s./ called Katherines Croft with hedges and ditches there, one piece of land and pasture containing by estimate 6 acres \3s./ with leafy willows there, two pieces of land containing 4½ acres \12d./ lying at Trendle Wood, one piece of land containing 5 roods \12d./ called Stony Land, one piece of land containing 5 roods \10d./ lying in South Field, 4 acres of land \12d./ called Knots Hedge and a close called Sheephouse Close \5s./ with the liberty of a fold of up to 40 sheep.

And for 10s. 6d. from Robert Hawes for a piece of land containing 42 acres called Hatch Mere and 1½ acres of land lying in the Bottom formerly of Walter Terwald with the liberty of a fold of up to 80 sheep.

And for 12s. from William Hawes for a piece of land containing 42 acres called Fishpond Field with the liberty of a fold of up to 80 sheep.

For a piece of meadow called Broad Dole containing 4½ acres recently leased for 26s. 8d., nothing because it is no longer leased on account of great flooding [*flumr'*].[25]

And for 5s. 6d. from Adam Ebell for a piece of land at Mickle Meadow and a piece of land at West Mill and 2 acres of land called Nunns Land.

---

[23] Although the parish and manor were almost conterminous, a few acres of land in the parish belonged to other manors and Walsham held some land in other parishes. Gislingham is a neighbouring parish.

[24] Both these unusual events are suggestive of inclement weather.

[25] 1428 was an exceptionally wet and cold year across Europe and in Norfolk the harvest began later than in any other recorded medieval year. Manorial accounts elsewhere in southern England also mention flooded meadows. See Pribyl, *Farming, famine and plague*, pp. 117, 184.

And for 3s. from Matilda Bonde for 4 acres 1 rood of land abutting upon Harts Hall formerly of Nicholas Dennis, 1½ acres of land called the Butts of the tenement Osbern near Rickinghall Willows, 2 acres of land of the tenement Cranmer next to the land formerly of Nicholas Tiptot at Rickinghall Willows next to the land of John Man and the Market Mere, 2 acres of land of the tenement Burchards on the west side of Burchards Land, a piece of land of the said tenement at Rickinghall Willows and 3 roods of meadow lying in Mickle Meadow recently granted for 4s., nothing because it is no longer leased because of flooding [*cretineme' aque*].

And for 10s. 2d. from John Cooper for two pieces of land containing 22 acres called Doucedeux, 6 acres of land called Walpoles Croft, a pightle called Jacks Yard and ½ acre of land abutting upon the land of the Prior of Ixworth with the liberty of a fold of up to 40 sheep.

And for 4s. 10d. from William Syre for a close next to his dwelling house granted to him and his heirs by court roll for Sheepcote Yard, 1½ acres of land at Clay Hill, two pieces of land near there of the tenement Paynes and 1½ roods of the tenement Dennis abutting upon the Brook.

And for 6s. 8d. from Peter Poye for the Launde in Lady's Wood.

And for 5s. 9d. from John Swift for 1½ acres of land of the tenement Paynes next to Market Way, 5 acres of land of Paynes tenement with 1½ roods of land at Burchards Wood, 1 acre of land of the tenement Robbys abutting upon Harts Haugh, ½ acre of land at Frances Row of the tenement Robbys, 2 acres of land at Brook Pits and 6 acres of land and pasture called Home Stall of which 2s. 8d. is from fee farm.

And for 4s. 8d. from Robert Margery senior for a piece of land and pasture containing 7 acres called Howes Toft, per acre 8d., granted to him for a term of 10 years, this is the 8th.

And for 14s. 8d. from John Fuller of East End for a close called Ox Pasture with hedges and ditches there, a piece of land containing 6 acres called Godelards Land, 10 acres of land parcel of Guspers Field, herbage of the meadow in Small Brook, a curtilage formerly Robeteles with ½ acre of land formerly of William Payne, 2 acres of land of the tenement formerly of Robert Fornham near Godelards Land next to the land formerly of Robert Payne and 1 rood of land at Willow Mere formerly of Adam Pitlake, 2 acres 2½ roods of land recently of Walter Dennis remaining in the lord's hands abutting upon Hundred Mere with the liberty of a fold of up to 12 ewes and 12 lambs granted to him for a term of 10 years this is the 8th.

And for 3s. 3d. from Robert Robhood for 1½ acres of land of the tenement Paynes, a curtilage, 3 roods of land formerly of William Payne, 2 roods of land of the tenement of William Payne with the third part of a way called Outgoing towards Westhorpe, 1 acre of land in two pieces abutting upon Hundred Mere granted to him this year.

And for 5s. 11d. from William Grocer for 4 acres of land next to the close of the said William lying there on the east side and the land formerly of Thomas Hereward, 2 roods of land called Stony Land and 2 acres of land abutting upon Helpes Wood from the land of High Hall and for 16 acres 1 rood of land in one piece parcel of Guspers Field recently in farm to Hugh Littlehall.

And for 15d. from John Tiptot senior for 5 acres of land parcel of Guspers Field

And for 7s. 11d. from Richard Rampley for 7 acres of land parcel of Guspers Field of which one head abuts upon Harts Haugh, two pieces of land containing 4 acres in the field of Angrave of the tenement formerly of Agnes de Angerhale and the herbage of a piece of meadow at Harts Haugh with pasture at the head of the same granted to him for a term of 10 years, this year is the 8th.

131

And for 2s. from John Ringbell for a close lying at Hall Gate on the north side of his messuage granted to him for the said term.

And 10s. for 7 roods of meadow lying in Mickle Meadow in various pieces of meadow, nothing this year because it could not be leased.

And for 5s. 10d. from William Syre for a cotland with a curtilage called Walpoles Croft, 1 acre of land near the sheepcote of the Prior of Ixworth and 1 acre of land next to Gurrys Croft granted to him and his heirs by court roll.

And for 16d. from John Fletcher for Godfreys Yard with 1½ acres of land of the same tenement.

And for 9d. from Henry Dinglove for 1 acre of land of the tenement Cranmer at Hulkes Bridge granted to him and his heirs and 3 roods of land of the tenement Kebbils recently granted to John Cook.

And for 7s. 6d. from John Page for the farm of land and a tenement formerly Coppelowes granted to him and his heirs by court roll.

And for 5s. 10d. from William Sare for 3½ acres of land in various pieces of the tenement Kebbils at Blunts Hall and for 18 acres of land called Blunts Hall.

And for 3s. 4d. from John Man for 8 acres of land by estimate of the same tenement in Long Wheat in one piece and for 4 acres of land from the said tenement lying at the end of the croft formerly of John Bonde.

And for 3d. from Adam Frances for 1 acre of land of the tenement Robbys on the south side of Trendle Wood.

And for 4½d. from Alice Morton for 1½ roods of land of the tenement Paynes at the head of the croft of the said Alice, 1 rood of land at the north head of the same.

And for 4d. from John Robhood junior for 1 acre 3 roods of land at Willow Mere of the tenement Paynes formerly at farm to the said Alice \usually leased for 8d. nothing because it cannot be leased/.

And for 2d. from John Ermitt for ½ acre of land next to the Green Way formerly of John son of William Clevehog of the tenement Man.

And for <10d.> 7d. from John Bertram <for ½ acre of land recently leased to Thomas Bonde of the tenement Goslings>, \nothing here henceforth because it was granted to John Bertram by charter/ 1 acre of land abutting upon Wood Way of the same tenement at Pedders Path and ½ acre of land of the tenement Ratches lying at Dales.

And for 6d. from Robert Syre for 3 roods of land in the croft of Godfreys of the tenement of William Payne.

And for 3d. from Thomas Wells for 1 acre of land of the tenement Clevehog above the Brook.

And for 12d. from John Fletcher for one messuage, 2½ roods of land lying in a croft recently of Walter Dennis remaining in the lord's hands by Robert Osbern.

And for 2s. 2d. from Robert Fletcher for 5 acres of land on the east side of Fishpond Field next to the land of William Sare, 2 acres of land lying next to Strondes Way.

And for 18d. from Thomas Wells for 3 acres of land of the tenement Paynes and 6 acres of land formerly of Nicholas Denys at New Haugh.

And the herbage of 1 acre of meadow called Turfpit Acre recently leased for 5s., nothing because it cannot be leased.

And for 1½d. from John Margery senior for 1½ roods of land in four parcels in the field of Langham.

And for 5s. 10d. from John Tiptot junior for two headlands containing 1 rood of pasture of the tenement of Peter Painter at Harts Haugh pasture of Painters Yard, 1 acre 3 roods of land in two pieces of the tenement Painters recently leased to Robert

Bray, 5 acres 3 roods of land in six pieces of the same tenement of which 3 acres in three pieces lie in the field of Ashfield and 2 acres 3 roods of land in three pieces at the Brook recently leased to John Brook, 1 acre 1 rood of land abutting upon the Brook towards the east of the same tenement recently leased to Robert Man, 3 roods of land in two pieces of the same tenement next to Ashfield Way recently leased to John Ermitt, ½ acre of land at Brook Bridge of the same tenement recently leased to Robert Man, 2 acres of land of the tenement Pudding lying at Procession Way abutting upon Hundred Mere, 1 rood of the said tenement next to Stubbing Way next to the land formerly of Richard Qwalm, 3 acres of land of the same tenement near East Mill in three pieces recently of the said Walter Frances granted to him and his heirs by court roll.

From Robert Vincent[26] for a piece of land called le Holner, 12 acres of land next to Nether Haugh, a close called Burchards Close, 18 acres of land lying in Burchards Croft, a piece of land in High Hall Croft, a close called High Hall Close, a piece of pasture called Nether Haugh, a piece of land called Seventeen Acres, 18 acres of land called Blunts Land and 12 acres of land at Allwood Green recently leased to Robert Payne with the liberty of a fold there, 76s. 10d. \and no more because 3 acres 1 rood were granted and leased to John Ringbell for 21d./

From John Robwood for a tenement called Sparchoys tenement and two messuages formerly of Nicholas Dennis granted to him and his heirs this year, 2s. 4d.

From Robert Lester for herbage of a meadow sold to him, 16d.

From Robert Vincent for a tenement formerly of John Syre at East End this year, 16s.

From John Bertram for a close recently of Robert Cokerell lying next to Lady's Wood purchased from Peter Poye, 6s. 8d.

Sum <£21 0s. 7d.> £21 0s. 1d.[27]

Perquisites of court For perquisites of two courts held there this year, 64s. 6½d.

Sum 64s. 6½d.

Farm of the mill with sale of stock And for 33s. 4d. from a certain miller for farm of a windmill leased this year.

Sum 33s. 4d.

Works and services sold For 15 qrs 1 bus. 1 peck and two quarters of ½ a peck of oats from rent sold elsewhere, price per qr 2s. 8d., 40s. 5½d. and half a ¼d.

For 4 capons from rent sold elsewhere, 10d.

For 111½ hens from rent sold elsewhere, price per head 1½d., 13s. 11¼d.

For 621½ eggs from services sold elsewhere, price per 120 4d., 20¾d.

For ½lb of cumin sold elsewhere, 1½d.

For ½lb pepper sold elsewhere, 8d. <nil this year because it was allowed for the office of the reeve>

For 28 ploughing services sold elsewhere, price per ploughing 6d., 14s.

For 8 Ploughales from services sold elsewhere, 4s. 3d.

---

[26] Robert Vincent and his wife Isabel lived in Upstrete; the Vincent tenement comprised a messuage and 30 acres which he surrendered to John Holm in 1437: SA/Bury HA504/1/12.18. He also held a messuage and 5 roods of land in Church Way which his widow surrendered in 1456: SA/B HA504/1/13.23.

[27] Marginal note.

For 723¾ winter works from services sold elsewhere, price per work ½d., 30s. 1¾d. half ¼d.

For 7 carrying services sold elsewhere, 7d.

For 5½ manure carrying services sold elsewhere, price per carry 2d., 11d.

For 138 weeding works sold elsewhere, price per work ½d., 5s. 9d.

For 35¼ mowing works sold elsewhere, price per work 1½d., 4s. 4¾d. and half ¼d.

For 528¼ harvest works sold elsewhere, price per work 2d., £4 8s. 0½d.

For 113 harvest boonworks sold elsewhere, price per work 2d., 18s. 10d.

Sum £11 4s. 8¼d. and half a ¼d.

Sales of underwood And for 48s. 4d. for 7 acres 1 rood of underwood sold to various men in Lady's Wood this year, per acre 6s. 8d.

And for 8d. from John Smith for underwood sold to him in North Haugh.

And for 6d. from John Robwood for underwood sold in Burchards Wood.

And for 6d. from John Grocer for leafy oaks at High Hall Wood.

And for 8d. from John Cooper for leafy oaks there.

Sum 50s. 8d.

Foreign receipts Nil.

Sales at the audit From sales at the audit, nothing.

Sum nil.

Sum total of receipts From receipts £54 0s. 11½d. and two parts of a ¼d.[28]

Rent resolute with decays and allowances From which in allowed rent, works and services reckoned in money for the tenement of Adam Frances in the office of reeve and from a fine of 2 marks for the said office not carried out, 7s. 6¾d. with ½lb of pepper priced 8d. <½d.>

And in allowed rent, works and services similarly reckoned in money for the tenement of John Bene in the office of hayward and from a fine of 13s. 4d. from the said office not carried out, 20¾d.

The same accounts for rent resolute for the hall of Thelnetham of 2s., nothing because it is outside the lord's hands.

Item for the hall of Rickinghall p.a., 3s. 1½d.

Item paid for castle ward of Norwich p.a., 16s.

Item paid to John Margery p.a., 1½d.

Item in allowed rent for various tenements in the lord's hands for this manor and for High Hall, 52s. 5¼d. half a quarter of a ¼d. and two parts of a ¼d., of which for High Hall 15s. 11¾d.

Item paid for the hall of Ashfield for castle ward for High Hall p.a., 17d.

Item paid to the same hall for rent p.a., 2d.

Item paid to the castle of Eye this year twice, 18d.

Item paid for Hundred suit released p.a. for Burchards, 16d.

Item paid to Helimot and from ward for Burchards p.a., 9d.

Item in rent resolute for Sir William Bardwell for 1 acre of meadow at Turf Pits purchased by the lord from John Rampley chaplain, 4d.

---

[28] Marginal note.

Item in allowed rent on 4 acres of land remaining in the lord's hands by John Syre, 18d. three quarters of ¼d. and a third part of a ¼d.

Item allowed on one tenement formerly of John Spilman granted to John Bertram freely by charter 10s. 7¼d. and half a quarter of a ¼d.

Item allowed on ½ acre of land of the tenement Coppelowes granted to him in the same way, 6d.

Item allowed on 1½ acres of land of the tenement formerly of John Page granted to him, 6½d.

Item allowed on a piece of land of the tenement of John Fuller granted to him in the same way, 7d.

Item allowed on ½ acre of land recently leased to Thomas Bonde from the tenement Gosling from the lord's demesne granted to him in the same way, 3d.

Item allowed on the tenement Gorys and for a parcel of the tenement Master Johns granted to him in the same way, 3¾d.

Item allowed on a tenement formerly of John Syre at East End because the lord has all the profits on the same tenement at farm as above, 5½d. and the price of a hen sold above.

Sum 100s. 16d. two parts of ¼d. and three parts of ¼d. <¾d. one and a half quarters of ¼d.>[29]

Cost of the buildings with pardons and allowances In the stipend of William Leper, thatcher, and his boy for 4 days piece-work thatching upon the knight's chamber at the manor and upon the mill-house, taken between them 7d. per day, 2s. 4d.

Item in straw bought from John Robhood for thatching the said mill-house, 8d.

Item barley and rye straw sufficient for two working days [*diet'*] bought for the said chamber, 12d.

Item in iron nails bought for nailing the door of the barn, ½d.

Item in 8 acres of straw bought from Robert Vincent in Katherine's Croft, per acre 7d., 4s. 8d.

Item in gathering the said 7 acres [*sic*] of straw, 4s. 8d., per acre 7d. for thatching a building at High Hall.

Item paid for carriage of the said straw up to the manor, 20d.

Sum 15s. 0½d.[30]

Cost of the mill – In the stipend of Peter Rollesby, carpenter for 3 days piecework felling [*evell*] timber for mending a sailyard [*virga*] and the openings of the mill sail [*les thrushotys*] and making the clamp [*le clampe*] for the said sailyard and the said openings [*thoronshotys*] taken per day 4d., 12d.

Item in three iron chains bought for tying the said sailyard, 14d.

Item in spikes [*les spykynges*] and iron nails bought for the same, 4d.

In iron nails bought for nailing the mill boards, 1d.

Sum 2s. 7d.[31]

---

[29] Marginal note.
[30] Marginal note.
[31] Marginal note.

Minute expenses In the stipend of one man for 20 days' work cutting under-wood for making hedges at Little Meadow[32] and making the hedge around the said meadow, taken per day 4d., 6s. 8d.

In the stipend of William Syre for 3 days' work making hedges around Burchards Wood, per day 4d., 12d.

In the stipend of one man for 5 days' work mending hedges at Lady's Wood and North Haugh, per day 4d., 20d.

In parchment bought for writing court rolls and accounts, 4d.

2s. 7d.[33]

Sum 9s. 8d.

Weeding and mowing In weeding corn and mowing the meadow, nothing this year.

Sum nil.

Expenses of the steward with foreign expenses Item paid for 1 quarter of one knight's fee to the lord king for High Hall, 20d.

In expenses of the steward and others being there for two courts held this year, 9s.

Sum 10s. 8d.

Wages and stipends In the wages of the bailiff reckoned this year with his clothing, 33s. 4d.

And in the fees to the clerk of the account and courts p.a., <20s.> nothing this year because it was paid by John Bertram the receiver.

And in the clothing of John Fuller, farmer, as in the preceding account by custom, 6s. 8d.

Sum 40s.

Cash delivered Delivered to John Bertram from rents and farms this year by one tally, £20 0s. 21d.[34]

Sum £20 0s. 21d.

Sum total of expenses and allowances £28 19s. 23½d. and two parts of a ¼d. and a third part of a ¼d.

And he owes £25, of which 20s. allowed to the same John for pasture for the lord's sheep in the lord's meadow in winter called Little Meadow, nothing from profit in summer, because no more was mowed.

And thus he owes £24, which he paid and thus is acquitted here.

[*Reverse*]

Walsham account of works and services there in the 6th year of Henry VI.

Multure at the mill For the farm of a windmill leased this year to certain men from Bury for money as within.

Sum nil.

---

[32] Little Meadow, part of the demesne, was hedged and ditched to preserve the lord's hay from straying animals. It required regular attention along with the hedges around the woods.

[33] Marginal note.

[34] The rent of leased land and pasture amounted to £21 0s. 1d., but the cash delivered to John Bertram for rent was £20 and 21d.

Stots For heriots this year, nothing.
Sum nil.

Oats For rent from the lord's tenants at the Feast of St Edmund King and Martyr, 20 qrs 2 parts of ½ a bus. and half a quarter of 1 peck of oats.

Sum 20 qrs 2 parts of ½ a bus. and half a quarter of 1 peck of oats.
From which, in allowance for various tenements in the lord's hands both for this manor and for High Hall this year, 3 qrs 3 bus. two parts of ½ bus. and half a quarter of 1 peck of oats.
Item allowed for one tenement, formerly of John Spilman, now granted to John Bertram freely by charter, 1 qr 2½ bus. and a quarter of half of 1 peck of oats.
In sales within, 15 qrs 1 bus. 1 peck and two quarters of ½ a peck of oats.
Sum as above.   It balances.

Capons For rent from the lord's tenants at Easter, 8 capons.
Sum 8.
From which in allowance for various tenements in the lord's hands 4. In sales within 4.
Sum as above.   It balances.

Hens and cockerels For rent from the lord's tenants at Christmas, 141¾ hens and cockerels of which 2 are cockerels.
Sum 141¾ hens and cockerels, of which 2 are cockerels.
From which, allowed for various tenements in the lord's hands both for this manor and for High Hall, 25¼ hens.
Allowed to the bailiff of Westhorpe by the hand of Richard Sewell tenant of High Hall in Westhorpe, 1.
Allowed for one tenement formerly of John Spilman granted as above, 3.
Item for the tenement Sybbes granted to him free by charter, 1.
In sales within, 111½ hens.
Sum as above. It balances.

Eggs From rent of the lord's tenants at Easter, 825 eggs.
Sum 825 eggs.
From which, allowed for various tenements in the lord's hands both for this manor and for High Hall 163½ eggs.
Item allowed for one tenement formerly of John Spilman granted to John Bertram as above, 40 eggs.
In sales within, 621½ eggs.
Sum as above.   It balances.

Dovecote For issues of a dovecote this year, nothing here because it was granted to John Fuller with other land as within.
Sum nil.

Cumin For rent from the Prior of Bricett p.a. ½lb cumin.
Sum shown. It balances.

Pepper For pepper rent from John Frances son of Adam Frances for the tenement recently of John Pinfold pertaining to High Hall ½lb pepper.
Sum shown. And sold within.   It balances.

137

Ploughing services For the issues of 8 customary greater tenures this year providing 4½ ploughteams this year 19 ploughing services taken at the seasons of winter and Lent, that is for each whole ploughteam 5 ploughing services, and received from the lord for each ploughteam 6 loaves of mixed grain, at 20 to the bushel, and allowed 2 winter works.

For the issues of 6 other customary tenants providing 3 ploughteams this year, 8 ploughing services, of which each ploughteam shall do 3 ploughings and receive from the lord 6 loaves of the said grain and the said weight, no works allowed.

For the issues of customary tenants of High Hall, nothing because none here.

For services purchased from William Hore received from the tenement Patches at the season of winter, 1 ploughing service.

Sum [blank] ploughing services. And sold within.   It balances.

Ploughale For customary services providing 8½ ploughing services this year.

Sum 8½ ploughing services. And sold within.   It balances.

Winter and summer works For customary services for a half day, 962 and a third part of a winter work.

Sum 962 and a third part of a winter work.

From which, allowed for various tenements in the lord's hands both for this manor and for High Hall, 208½ and a third part of a winter work.

Allowed on one tenement formerly of John Spilman granted as above, 29¾ winter works.

In sales within, 723¾ winter works.

Sum as above.   It balances.

Carrying works For issues of carrying services at the will of the lord from custom, price per work 1d.

Sum 7. And sales within.   It balances.

Carrying of manure For customary services without resumption, 9 manure carrying services and allowed to them for each man carrying manure 1 winter work, price per carry 2d.

Sum 9 carryings.

From which, allowed on various tenements in the lord's hands 3 carrying services.

Item allowed on one tenement formerly of John Spilman granted as above ½ a carry.

In sales within 5½ carrying services.

Sum as above.   It balances.

Weeding works For customary services 175 and ¾ of ½ a weeding work, price per work ½d.

Sum 175 and ¾ of ½ of one weeding works.

From which, in allowance for various tenements in the lord's hands both for this manor and for High Hall, 26 works and ¾ of ½ a weeding work.

Item allowed on one tenement formerly of John Spilman granted as above, 11 weeding works.

In sales within, 138 works.

Sum as above.   It balances.

Mowing works For customary services for ½ days, 42¼ mowing works.

Sum 42¼.

From which allowed for various tenements in the lord's hands, 6¼ mowing works.
Item allowed on one tenement formerly of John Spilman granted as above ¾ of a
mowing work.
In sales within, 35¼ mowing works.

Sum as above.   It balances.

Carriage of hay For services according to custom that have carriage without
resumption and without the price of a work none this year because they were
released by the lady Elmham.

Sum nil.

Haymaking works For customary services as many works as the lord indicates,
lifting, turning and stacking all the hay without resumption, none this year because
as aforesaid.

Sum nil.

Harvest works For customary services for the whole day in the lord's grain
reaping, tying and stacking 754 works, of which each receives from the lord at
noon and for his supper 2 loaves of mixed grain, at 20 to the bus., and 4 herrings,
price per work 2d.

Sum 754 works.

From which allowed for various tenements in the lord's hands both for this manor
and for High Hall, 199 works.
Item allowed on one tenement formerly of John Spilman granted to John Bertram,
26¼ works and a sixth part of a harvest work.
In sales within, 528¼ works.

Sum as above. It balances.

Harvest boonworks For customary services this year 139 harvest boonworks, for
which each free man shall receive from the lord for his food at noon and for his
supper one wheat loaf, at 20 to the bus., and each customary tenant shall have for
his food at noon as for the free tenants and for his supper one loaf of mixed grain,
at 20 to the bus., and one herring, price per work 2d.

Sum 139 boonworks.

From which, allowed for various tenements in the lord's hands both for this manor
and for High Hall, 23 boonworks.
Item allowed on one tenement formerly of John Spilman granted as above, 2 boonworks.
Item in allowance of a tenement called Sybbes granted as above, 1 boonwork.
In sales within, 113 boonworks.

Sum as above.   It balances.

Receipts and expenditure from seven Walsham manorial accounts, 1428 to 1435

SA/B HA504/3/6 to 10, and HA504/3/15 mm.3 and 4.

[*The next seven accounts are very similar in content to the 1427–8 account, with
much repetition among the entries, so rather than translate each account at length
the key information is presented in tabular form.*]

Table 1. Receipts from seven Walsham manorial accounts from 1428 to 1435

Year	Arrears	Rents of assize	Castle ward	Leases	Court	Mill	Sale of works	Sale of wood	Total
1428–9	0	£13 13s. 6½d.	14s.	£21 19s. 8d.	75s. 1d.	33s. 4d.	£11 2s. 4½d.	13s. 8d.	£53 11s. 8d.
1429–30	0	£14 13s. 8½d.	14s.	£20 16s. 1d.	99s.	30s.	£11 2s. 9½d.	21s. 11d.	£54 7s. 6d.
1430–1	0	£14 13s. 8½d.	14s.	£18 17s. 1d.	57s. 6d.	26s. 8d.	£11 3s. 9¼d.	21s. 11d.	£50 14s. 8d.
1431–2	0	£14 13s. 8½d.	14s.	£18 16s. 4d.	62s. 1d.	26s. 8d.	blank	blank	£50 11s. 9d.
1432–3	0	£14 13s. 8½d.	14s.	£18 17s. 2½d.	122s. 8d.	26s. 8d.	£11 4s. 8¼d.	7s. 4d.	£53 10s. 2d.
1433–4	0	£14 13s. 8½d.	14s.	£19 1s. ½d.	98s. 1d.	26s. 8d.	£11 2s. 7d.	15s. 4½d.	£52 11s. 6d.
1434–5	£14 14s. 6½d.	£14 13s. 8½d.	14s.	£20 0s. 2½d.	98s.	26s. 8d.	£11 0s. ¼d.	19s. 5d.	blank

Table 2. Expenditure from seven Walsham manorial accounts from 1428 to 1435

Year	Decays of rent	Costs of buildings	Costs of mill	Minute expenses	Steward's expenses	Wages	Cash paid	Total expenditure	Sum owed*
1428–9	£6 17s. 5¾d.	24s. 5d.	6s. 1d.	8s. 11d.	9s. 4d.	40s.	£19	£30 5s. 1¼d.	£23 6s. ¼d.
1429–30	£5 18s. 5¼d.	11s. ½d.	20s. 9d.	2s. 4d.	0	40s.	£24	£34 0s. ¾d.	£20 5s. 5d.
1430–1	£5 15s. 4¾d.	0	18d.	6s.	6s. 11½d.	40s.	£24 9s. 6¼d.	blank	£34 5s. 1¾d.
1431–2	£6 8s. 10¾d.	0	11d.	8d.	9s. 8d.	40s.	£26	blank	blank
1432–3	£5 15s. 5½d.	0	7s.	8s. 5d.	10s. 8½d.	40s.	£42	51 1s. 7¼d.	46s. 3¾d.
1433–4	£6 0s. 10d.	18d.	5s. 5½d.	10d.	8s. 4d.	40s.	£29	torn	£14 14s. 6½d.
1434–5	£7 14s. ½d.	12s. 4d.	3d.	12s. 7d.	14s. 8d.	40s.	£31	£47 11s. ½d.	£14 14s.

* The sum owed at the account was paid at the view of account in every year except 1433–4 and 1434–5, when the accountant failed to pay and so the sum was carried forward as arrears.

Document 11: *Walsham account, 28 September 1436 to 28 September 1437*

SA/B HA504/3/15 m.5

Walsham
Account of William Fuller, reeve and hayward there, from the eve of St Michael the Archangel in the 15th year of Henry VI up to the eve of St Michael next coming in the 16th year of the same Henry for one whole year.

Arrears [*He answers*] for the arrears of the last account of the preceding year, £29 8s. 6¼d.

Sum £29 8s. 6¼d.

Rents of assize For rents of assize there from both free and villein tenants both for this manor and for High Hall, not including rent of Westhorpe, with ward of High Hall for the terms of St Michael, Christmas, Easter and the Nativity of St John the Baptist, £13 11s. 5d. half a ½d. and two parts of a ¼d.
For new rent[35] received from John Robwood for a piece of land lying next to Ulveswell purchased by John Bertram and granted by the said John Bertram to the profit of the manor, 5d.
For new rent received from John Margery for a piece of land next to Gorommes Way granted in the same way, 6d.
For new rent received from Robert Margery for a garden of Goslings tenement granted in the same way, 1d.
For new rent received from Nicholas Brond of Gislingham for a piece of land lying in the aforesaid town between the land of William Goddard on the north side and the land of the Templars of Gislingham on the south side granted in the same way, 3d.
For new rent received from Robert Carpenter of Langham for a piece of land lying next to the land of the parson of Langham granted in the same way, 2d.
For new rent received from Henry Dinglove for a piece of land in Mill Field granted in the same way, 2d.
For new rent received from Robert Warde for a piece of land lying next to Chalk Pightle granted in the same way, 2d.
For new rent received from John Page for land and a tenement formerly Coppelowes granted to him and his heirs, 7s. 6d.
For new rent received from John Robwood for a tenement called Sparschoys tenement and two messuages formerly of Nicholas Dennis granted to him and his heirs by the court roll, 2s. 4d.
For new rent received from John Ringbell for 3 acres 1 rood of pasture parcel of Nether Haugh Pasture granted to him and his heirs, 20d.
For new rent received from William Syre for a cotland with a curtilage called Walpoles Croft, 1 acre of land near the sheepcote of the Prior of Ixworth and 1 acre of land next to Gurrys Croft granted to him and his heirs by court roll, 5s. 10d.
For new rent received from the same William for a close next to his dwelling house granted to him and his heirs by court roll, 2s. 10d.

Sum £14 13s. 4d. and half a ¼d. and two parts of a ¼d.

---

35 This spate of new rents do not signify a sudden growth in population or grants of land newly colonised from the waste since the last extant account. Instead, they relate to a relatively new form of tenure, i.e. grants enrolled in the manorial court and described as 'fee farms'. As permanent heritable grants for cash, whose title is recorded in the court roll, they are very different from the fixed-term leases in the section on 'farms and pastures' below. In effect, they are prototype copyholds.

Castle ward For castle ward received from the manor of Wyken for the terms of St Michael, Easter, Christmas and the Nativity of St John the Baptist, 11s. 2d.
For castle ward received from the manor of Ixworth, 2s. 10d.

Sum 14s.

Farm of land and pasture And for 66s. 8d. received from John Ringbell for the farm of a meadow called Little Meadow with Dampond Close, Ox Pightle and Church Brook granted to him this year.
From the same John for 14 acres of land called Dovehouse Wong, per acre 8d., 9s. 4d.
From the same John for pasture called Cocks Dirt, 6s. 8d.
From the same John for 18 acres of land in two pieces called Cocks Dirt, per acre 4d., 6s.
From John Bene and Richard Taylor for 9 acres of land parcel of Old Toft, per acre 6d., 4s. 6d.
From the same John Bene for 7 acres of land parcel of Old Toft, per acre 6d., 3s. 6d.
From John Ringbell for a close called North Haugh this year, 6s. 8d.
From the same John for all the pasture pertaining to the lord's sheep upon Walsham Hall, 10s.
For a building called the knights' chamber leased in the preceding year to John King for 2s., nothing this year because it is no longer leased.
From William Sparke for a close \6s. 8d./ within the manor and 14 acres \4s. 4d./ of land called Hall Croft, 11s.
From Peter Poye for the farm of 20 acres of land, part of Old Toft, per acre 5d., 8s. 4d.
From the same Peter for the farm of Chalk Pightle with pasture below his messuage this year, 6s. 8d.
For a house in the dairy, nothing this year because it was not leased.
From Nicholas Smith for 33½ acres of land and pasture lying in a close called New Close with leafy trees there, granted to him for a term of 10 years, this year is the 7th, 16s. 5d.
From William Potenger, chaplain, for 1½ acres of land parcel of New Close towards his close granted to him and his heirs by court roll, 9d.
From Robert Hawes for a piece of land containing 42 acres called Hatch Mere and 1½ acres of land lying in the Bottom formerly of Walter Terwald granted to him this year, 7s.
From William Hawes for a piece of land containing 42 acres called Fishpond Field with the liberty of a fold of up to 80 sheep this year, 8s.
From the bailiff for a piece of meadow called Broad Dole containing 4½ acres sold to various men this year, 26s. 8d. \23s. 4d./
From Robert Lester for a piece of land at Mickle Meadow and a piece of land at West Mill and 2 acres of land called Nunns Land this year, 5s. 6d.
From Thomas Bonde for 4 acres 1 rood of land abutting upon Harts Haugh formerly of Nicholas Dennis, 1½ acres of land called the Butts of the tenement Osbern at Rickinghall Willows, 2 acres of land of the tenement Cranmer next to the land formerly of Nicholas Tiptot at Rickinghall Willows next to the land formerly of John Man and Market Mere and 2 acres of land of the tenement Burchards on the west side of Burchards Wood this year, 12d. \usually leased for [*illeg.*]/
From John Cooper for two pieces of land containing 22 acres called Doucedeux, 6 acres of land called Walpoles Croft, a pightle called Jacks Yard and ½ acre of land

abutting upon the land of the Prior of Ixworth granted to him and his heirs by court roll, 8s.

From John Robwood for Sheepcote Yard, 1½ acres of land at Clay Hill, two pieces of land near there of the tenement Paynes, 1½ roods of land of the tenement Dennis abutting upon the Brook, 1 acre 3 roods at Willow Mere of the tenement Paynes recently leased to Alice Morton, this year 2s. \18d./

From Robert Lester for the Launde in Lady's Wood this year, 5s.

From John Swift for 1½ acres of land of the tenement Paynes next to Market Way,[36] 5 acres of land of the tenement Paynes, 1 acre of land of the tenement Robbys abutting upon Harts Haugh, ½ acre of land at Frances Row of the tenement Robbys, 2 acres of land at Brook Pits granted to him and his heirs by court roll, 2s. 6d.

From John Robwood senior for 6 acres \2s. 6d./ of land and pasture called Home Stall and 1½ roods of land at Burchards Wood this year, 2s. 8d.

From John Margery junior for a piece of land and pasture containing 7 acres called Howes Toft, per acre 8d., 4s. 8d.

From John Robwood senior for 1½ acres of land of the tenement Paynes, a curtilage, 3 roods of land formerly of William Payne, 2 roods of land of the tenement of William Payne with a third part of a way called Outgoing towards Westhorpe, 1 acre of land in two pieces abutting upon Hundred Mere granted to him this year, 18d.

From William Grocer for 4 acres of land next to the close of the said William lying there on the east of the land formerly of Thomas Hereward, 2 roods of land called Stony Land and 2 acres of land abutting upon Helpes Wood from the land of High Hall granted this year, 2s. 7d.

From John Robwood senior for 16 acres 1 rood of land parcel of Guspers Field this year, 2s. 4d.

From John Tiptot senior for 5 acres of land parcel of Guspers Field this year, 15d.

From John Rampley for 7 acres of land parcel of Guspers Field of which one head abuts upon Harts Haugh, two pieces of land containing 4 acres in the field of Angrave of the tenement formerly of Agnes de Angerhale and for the herbage of a piece of meadow at Harts Haugh with pasture at the head of the same this year, 7s. 11d.

From John Ringbell for a close lying at Hall Gate on the north side of his messuage, this year 2s.

From the bailiff for 7 roods of meadow lying in Mickle Meadow in various pieces of meadow this year, 10s. \8s./

From Henry Corsour for Godfreys Yard with 1½ acres of land of the same tenement, this year 10d.

From the heirs of Henry Dinglove for 1 acre of land of the tenement Cranmer at Hulkes Bridge and 3 roods of land of the tenement Kebbils recently leased to John Cook, granted to him and his heirs this year, 9d.

From John Fletcher for 3½ acres of land in various pieces from the tenement Kebbils this year, 12d.

From Robert Hawes for 18 acres of land called Blunts Hall this year, 2s.

From John Swift for 8 acres of land by estimate in Long Wheat in one piece and for 4 acres of land of the said tenement lying at the end of the croft of Thomas Bonde granted to him and his heirs by court roll, 3s. 4d.

---

[36] No formal grant of the right to hold a weekly market exists for Walsham, but this place name is suggestive that an informal (weekly) market was once held there. See Lock, *Walsham II*, pp. 34–5.

From John Fletcher for 1 acre of land of the tenement Robbys on the south side of Trendle Wood this year, 3d.

From John Robwood senior for 1 acre 1 rood of land of the tenement Paynes at the head of the croft of the said John and 1 rood of land at the north head of the same, recently in farm to Alice Morton this year, 4½d.

From John Ermitt for ½ acre of land next to the Green Way formerly of John son of William Clevehog of the tenement Man this year, 2d.

From William Fuller for 1 acre of land abutting upon Wood Way from the same tenement at Pedders Path and ½ acre of land of the tenement Ratches lying at Dales recently leased for 7d. this year, 2d.

From John Robwood senior for 3 acres of land in the croft of Godfreys of the tenement of William Payne this year, 6d.

From Thomas Welles for 1 acre of land of the tenement Clevehog upon the Brook this year, 3d.

From John Fletcher \Robwood senior/ for a messuage and 2½ roods of land lying in the croft recently of Walter Dennis remaining in the lord's hands by Robert Osbern this year, 12d.

From Thomas Fletcher for 5 acres of land on the east side of Fishpond Field next to the land of Robert Sare and 2 acres of land lying next to Trendle Way this year, 2s.

From Thomas Wells for 3 acres of land of the tenement Paynes and 6 acres of land formerly of Nicholas Dennis at New Hall this year, 18d.

From Robert Carpenter for 1½ roods of land in four parcels in the field of Langham recently leased to John Margery this year, 2d.

From John Tiptot junior for two headlands containing 1 rood of pasture of the tenement of Peter Painter at Harts Haugh, pasture from Painters Yard, 1 acre 3 roods of land in two pieces of the tenement of Peter Painter recently leased to Robert Bray, 5 acres 3 roods of land in six pieces of the same tenement of which 3 acres is in three pieces in the field of Ashfield and 2 acres 3 roods is in three pieces at the Brook recently leased to John Brook, 1 acre 1 rood of land abutting upon the Brook towards the east of the same tenement recently leased to Robert Man, 3 roods of land in two pieces from the same tenement next to Ashfield Way recently leased to John Ermitt, ½ acre of land at Brook Bridge of the same tenement recently leased to Robert Man, 2 acres of land of the tenement Pudding lying at Procession Way abutting upon Hundred Mere, 1 rood of land of the said tenement next to Stubbing Way next to the land formerly of Richard Qwalm, 3 acres of land of the same tenement near the East Mill in three pieces recently leased to Walter Frances, granted to him and his heirs by court roll this year, 5s. 10d.

From Robert Lester for a close recently of Robert Cokerell lying next to Lady's Wood this year, 5s.

From John Robwood senior for lease of a close called Katherines Croft with hedges and ditches there, a piece of land and pasture containing by estimate 6 acres with leafy willows there called Gurrys Croft, two pieces of land containing 4½ acres lying at Trendle Wood, a piece of land containing 5 acres called Stony Land, a piece of land containing 5 roods lying in South Field, 4 acres of land called Knots Hedge, a close called Sheephouse Close \usually leased for 20s. 6d./, 3 roods of meadow lying in the Mickle Meadow \4s./, a close called the Ox Pasture with hedges and ditches there, a piece of land called Godelards Land, 10 acres of land parcel of Guspers Field, the herbage of a meadow in the Small Brook, a curtilage formerly Robetels with ½ acre of land formerly of William Payne, 2 acres of land from the tenement formerly of Robert Fornham near Godelards Land next to the land formerly of William Payne and 1 rood of land at Willow Mere formerly of Adam Pitlake, 2 acres 2½ roods of land recently of Walter Dennis remaining in the lord's hands abutting upon Hundred Mere with herbage of a piece of meadow called Turfpit Acre, a piece of land called the Hulver, 12 acres of land next to Nether Haugh, a close called Burchards Close, 18 acres of land lying in Burchards Croft, a piece of land in High Hall Croft, a close called High Hall Close, a piece of land called Nether Haugh, a piece of land called Seventeen Acres, 18 acres of land called Blunts Land, 12 acres of land at Allwood Green recently leased to Robert Payne and for the farm of a tenement formerly of John Syre at East End with the liberty of a fold by indenture leased to him for a term of 10 years, this year is the 7th, 103s. 4d.

From the same John for Paynes tenement lying in the East End of the lord's bondage granted to him by court roll, 13s. 6d.

From William Sparke for 1 rood of meadow recently of John Ermitt lying in the Mickle Meadow, this year, 18d.

For the farm of a vacant dairy house recently leased to John Wiltoft for 2s., nothing because it was not leased.

Sum £19 14s. 2½d.[37]

Perquisites of court For perquisites of two courts held there this year £4 4s. 2d.
Sum £4 4s. 2d.

Farm of a mill with the sale of stock From Gilbert Miller for the farm of a windmill leased this year to the aforesaid Gilbert 23s. 4d.
Sum 23s. 4d.

Works and services sold For 15 qrs 1 bus. 1¾ peck of oats from rent sold elsewhere, price per qr 2s. 8d., 40s. 5½d.

For 4 capons from rent sold as elsewhere, 10d.

For 112½ hens from rent sold as elsewhere, price per head 1½d., 14s. 0¾d.

For 661½ eggs from rent sold as elsewhere, price per 120 4d., 20¾d.

For ½lb of cumin sold as elsewhere, 1½d.

For ½lb of pepper sold as elsewhere, 7d.

For 31 ploughing services from works sold as elsewhere, price per ploughing service 6d., 15s. 9d.

For 7 Ploughales \½d./ from works sold as elsewhere, 3s. 9d.

For 723¾ winter works sold as elsewhere, price per work ½d., 30s. 1½d.

For 7 carrying services from works sold as elsewhere, 7d.

For 5½ manure carrying services from works sold as elsewhere, price per carrying service 2d., 11d.

For 138 weeding works sold as elsewhere, price per work ½d., 5s. 9d.

For 35½ mowing works sold as elsewhere, price per work 1½d., 4s. 4½d.

For 528¼ harvest works from services sold as elsewhere, price per work 2d., £4 8s. 0½d.

For 113 harvest boonworks from services sold as elsewhere, price per work 2d., 18s. 10d.

Sum £12 6s. 11¾d. and half a ¼d.[38]

---

[37] Marginal note.
[38] Marginal note.

Sale of underwood From John Bene for 1 rood of underwood sold in Lady's Wood this year, 18d.

From Richard Taylor for 1 rood of underwood sold there, 18d.

From John Wyltoft for 1 rood of underwood sold there, 18d.

From John Margery for 1 rood of underwood sold there, 18d.

From Robert Lester for 1 rood of underwood sold there, 18d.

From Robert Cutting for 1 rood of underwood sold there, 18d.

From Walter Bloom for 1 rood of underwood sold there, 18d.

From John Femmete for 1½ roods of underwood sold there, 2s. 4d.

From Stephen Daye for 1 rood of underwood there, 18d.

From Robert Baron for ½ rood of underwood there, 9d.

From William Potenger, chaplain for two cart-loads of thorn bushes sold to him at Lady's Wood, 6d.

Sum 5s. 6d.[39]

Foreign Receipts Nil.

Sum nil.

Sales at the audit From sales at the audit, nothing this year.

Sum nil.

Sum of total receipts with arrears £40 39s. 0¾d. and half a ¼d.[40]

Rent resolute with decays and allowances From which in allowed rent, works and services reckoned in money for the tenement of Robert Robwood in the office of reeve from two marks for the said office not carried out, 6s. 4d.

Item in allowed rent, works and services likewise reckoned in money for the tenement of John Fletcher in the office of hayward this year and for a fine of 13s. 4d. for the said office not carried out, 2s. 5¾d.

Item reckoned in rent resolute for the hall of Thelnetham of 2s., nothing because it is outside the lord's hands.

Item the hall of Rickinghall p.a., 3s. 1½d.

Item paid for castle ward of Norwich p.a., 16s.

Item paid to John Margery p.a. 1½d.

Item in allowance of rent for various tenements in the lord's hands both for this manor and for High Hall 52s. 5¼d. and half a quarter of ¼d. and two parts of ¼d., of which for High Hall 15s. 11¾d.

Item paid to the hall of Ashfield for castle ward for High Hall p.a., 17d.

Item paid to the same hall for rent p.a., 2d.

Item paid to the castle of Eye twice this year, 18d.

Item for hundred suit released p.a. for Burchards, 16d.

Item paid to Helimot and for ward for Burchards p.a., 9d.

Item in rent resolute for Sir William Bardwell for 1 acre of meadow at Turf Pits purchased by the lord from John Rampley, chaplain, 4d.

Item in allowance of rent on 4 acres of land remaining in the lord's hands by John Syre, 18d. and three quarters of ¼d. and a third part of ¼d.

---

[39] Marginal note.
[40] Marginal note.

Item in allowance of the tenement formerly of John Spilman granted to John Bertram free by charter, 10s. 7¼d. and half a quarter of ¼d.

Item in allowance on ½ acre of land of the tenement Coppelowes granted to him in the same way, 6d.

Item in allowance on 1½ acres of land formerly of John Page granted to him, 6½d.

Item in allowance on a piece of land of the tenement of John Fuller granted to him in the same way, 7d.

Item in allowance on ½ acre of land recently leased to Thomas Bonde of the tenement Goslings from the lord's demesne granted to him in the same way, 3d.

Item in allowance on the tenement Gorys and for a parcel of the tenement Master Johns granted to him in the same way, 3¾d.

Item in allowance of a tenement formerly of John Syre because the lord has all the profits of the same tenement at farm as above, 5½d. with the price of a hen sold above.

In allowed rent of the tenement Paynes taken into the lord's hands and at farm as above, 15s. 4d. and a quarter of a ¼d.

Sum 115s. 3½d. three quarters of a ¼d., two parts of a ¼d. and a third part of a ¼d.[41]

Cost of the buildings with pardons and allowances In the stipend of John Frances for 1½ days piecework cutting down timber, that is oak for a gate at the manor and for mending the end of the barn by carpentry, 6d.

In the stipend of Robert Manser and his son for 6½ days piece-work mending the said gate and the said end of the barn by carpentry and making the jambs [*les leggys*] of the lower gate by carpentry, taken between them per day 8d., 4s. 2d.

Item in 60 sheaves of reeds bought for thatching [*arundinat'*] the said end of the barn, with carriage, 14d.

Item in staples, spikenails [*pykes*] and ferrules and iron plates and iron nails made from old iron of the lord and iron bought for the same, 10½d.

Item paid for carriage of the said timber by Robert Lester, 3d.

Item paid for ramming the said gate, 6d.

Item in straw bought for thatching the said barn, 5s.

Item paid for carriage of the said straw, 8d.

Item in the stipend of John Frances and his boy for 6 days piecework thatching upon the said end of the barn, taken between them per day 7d., 3s. 6d.

Item in the stipend of Thomas Bonde and his servant for 5 days piecework thatching upon a room and upon the garret at the manor, taken between them per day 7½d., 3s. 2d.

Item in the stipend of Thomas Bonde and his boy for 5 days piecework thatching upon the knights chamber, taken between them per day 8d., 3s. 4d.

Item paid for mending the plaster of the kitchen by carpentry and clay and for making a shutter and for mending a bin [*benile*] in the cow-shed for 7 days piecework, 2s. 4d.

Item in straw bought for thatching the chamber, 4s.

Sum 29s. 5½d.[42]

---

[41] Marginal note.
[42] Marginal note.

Cost of the mill Item paid to William Hare, carpenter, for making a new mill sail with his servant, 4s. 10d.

Sum 4s. 10d.

Minute expenses with stock bought In the stipend of John Frances for 2 days piecework making a hedge at the manor, 8d.

Item paid to Thomas Murrell and Thomas Hill for one day's work cutting down underwood for making the said hedge, 8d.

Item paid for the carriage of the said underwood from Lady's Wood to the manor, 5d.

In parchment bought for writing the court rolls and account, 8d.

Item in the stipend of Thomas Murrell for 5 days at task mending hedges and underwood upon the ditch at Lady's Wood and other places, 20d.

Item in 90 ewes bought for the stock of the manor of Westhorpe at the Feast of St Peter ad Vincula, £4 10s.

Item in 34 hoggets bought for stock there at the same time, 10s. 5d. received by John Bertram.

Sum 104s. 6d.[43]

Weeding and mowing In weeding corn and mowing meadows, nothing this year.

Sum nil

Expenses of the steward and foreign expenses In the expenses of John Bertram, the steward and other supervisors being here for holding two courts, 10s. 3d.

Item in a quarter of a 15th to the lord king this year, 2s. 6d.

Sum 12s. 9d.

Wages and stipends In wages of the bailiff making the account this year with his crops, 40s.

Sum 40s.

Cash delivered Delivered to Thomas Christmas clerk, receiver of the lord, on various occasions by one tally, £23.

[*Reverse*]
Walsham
Account of works and services there in the 15th year of Henry VI.

Multure at the mill For the farm of one windmill leased this year to certain millers within and usually leased for 1 qr of multure from the mill.

Sum nil.

Stots For heriots, nothing this year.

Sum nil.

Oats For rent from the lord's tenants at the Feast of St Edmund King and Martyr, 20 qrs 2 parts of ½ bus. and half a ¼ of a peck of oats.

Sum 20 qrs 2 parts of ½ bus. and half a ¼ of a peck of oats

---

[43] Marginal note.

148

From which, in allowance for various tenements in the lord's hands both for this manor and for High Hall this year, 4 qrs 5½ and two parts of ½ bus. and two quarters of a peck of oats.
In sales within, 15 qrs 1 bus. 1 and two quarters of ½ a peck of oats.

Sum as above   It balances.

Capons For rent from the lord's tenants there at Easter, 8 capons.
Sum 8.
From which in allowance for various tenements in the lord's hands, 4 capons.
In sales within, 4.

Sum as above.   It balances.

Hens and cockerels For rent of the lord's tenants at Christmas, 141¾ hens and cockerels.
Sum 141¾ hens and cockerels
From which, in allowance for various tenements in the lord's hands both for this manor and for High Hall, 28¼ hens.
Delivered to the bailiff of Westhorpe by the hand of Richard Sewell tenant of High Hall in Westhorpe, 1.
In sales within, 112½ hens.
R[44]   Sum as above.   It balances.

Eggs For rent of the lord's tenants there at Easter, 825 eggs.
Sum 825 eggs.
From which, in allowance for various tenements in the lord's hands both for this manor and for High Hall, 163½.
In sales within, 661½ eggs.

Sum as above.   It balances.

Dovecote For the issues on one dovecote, nothing this year because there was no stock and no sales.
Sum nil.

Cumin For rent from the Prior of Bricett p.a. ½lb of cumin.
Sum shown. And sales within.   It balances.

Pepper For pepper rent from John Frances for the tenement formerly of John Pinfold pertaining to High Hall, ½lb of pepper.
Sum shown. And sales within.   It balances.

Ploughing services For the issues of 5 customary greater tenures this year, providing 4 ploughteams this year for 20 ploughing services taken at the seasons of winter and Lent, from each whole ploughteam doing 5 ploughing services receiving for each ploughteam 6 loaves of mixed grain, at 20 to the bushel, and allowed from 2 winter works.

---

[44] Marginal note.

149

For the issues of 3 other customary tenants providing 3 ploughteams this year, 10½ ploughing services, of which each plough shall do 3 ploughings and receive from the lord 6 loaves of the same grains and said weight, with no allowance of works. For the issues of customary tenants of High Hall, nothing because none here. From services purchased from William Hore received from the tenement Patches at the winter season, 1 ploughing service.

Sum 31½ ploughing services. And sales as below.   It balances.

Ploughales For the services of customary tenants providing this year 7½ ploughing services.

Sum 7½ ploughing services. And sales within.   It balances.

Winter and summer works For the services of customary tenants for half days, 962 and 3 parts of a winter work.

Sum 962 and 3 parts of a winter work.

From which, in allowance for various tenements in the lord's hands both for this manor and for High Hall, 238¼ winter works. In sales within, 723¾ winter works.

Sum as above.   It balances.

Carrying works For the issues of customary tenants of 7 carrying works at the will of the lord by custom, price per work 1d.

Sum 7 carrying works. And sales within.   It balances.

Carrying of manure For the services of customary tenants without resumption, 9 manure carrying works and allowed to them for each man carrying manure, 1 winter work, price per carrying work 2d.

Sum 9 carrying works.

From which, in allowance for various tenements in the lord's hands, 3½ carrying works. In sales within, 5½ carrying works.

Sum as above.   It balances.

Weeding works For the services of customary tenants, 175 and three quarters of half a weeding work, price per work ½d.

Sum 175 and three quarters of half a weeding work.

From which, in allowance for various tenements in the lord's hands both for this manor and for High Hall, 37 and three quarters of half a weeding work. In sales within, 138 works.

Sum as above.   It balances.

Mowing works For the services of customary tenants by half days, 42½ mowing works.

Sum 42½ mowing works.

From which, in allowance for various tenements in the lord's hands, 7 mowing works. In sales within, 35¼ mowing works.

Sum as above.   It balances.

Carriage of hay For the services of customary tenants that have carts without resumption and without meadow works, nothing this year because they were released.

Sum nil.

Haymaking works For the services of customary tenants as many works as the lord requires for lifting, turning and stacking all the hay without resumption, nothing this year.

Sum nil.

Harvest works For the services of customary tenants for the whole day, cutting, tying and stacking, 754 works, from which each shall receive from the lord at noon and for his supper two loaves of mixed grains, at 20 to the bushel, and 4 herrings, price per work 2d.

Sum 754 works.

From which in allowance for various tenements in the lord's hands both for this manor and for High Hall, 225¼ works. In sales within, 128¼ harvest works.

Sum as above.   It balances.

Harvest boonworks For the services of customary tenants this year 139 harvest boonworks, of which each free man shall have for his food at noon and for his supper 1 wheat loaf, at 20 to the bushel.
And each customary tenant shall have for his food at noon the same as for the free men, and for his supper 1 loaf of mixed grain, at 20 to the bushel and 1 herring, price per work 2d.

Sum 139 boonworks.

From which in allowance for various tenements in the lord's hands both for this manor and for High Hall, 26 boonworks. In sales within, 113 boonworks.

Sum as above.   It balances.

Document 12: Walsham account, 28 September 1437 to 28 September 1438

SA/B HA504/3/15 m.6

Walsham
Account of William Fuller,[45] reeve and hayward there, from the eve of St Michael the Archangel in the 16th year of Henry VI until the eve of St Michael next coming in the 17th year of the same Henry for one whole year.

Arrears [*He answers*] for arrears of the last account of the preceding year, £7 3s. 7¾d.

Sum £7 3s. 7¾d.

Rents of assize For rents of assize there for both free and villein tenants for both this and for High Hall not including rent of Westhorpe with ward of High Hall for the terms of St Michael, Christmas, Easter and the Nativity of St John the Baptist, £13 11s. 5d. half ¼d. and two parts of ¼d.
For new rent received from John Robwood for a piece of land lying next to Ulveswell purchased by John Bertram and granted by the said John Bertram to the profit of the manor, 5d.
For new rent received from John Margery for a piece of land next to Gorommes Way granted in the same way, 1d.

---

[45] William Fuller is the reeve for the second year running. He leased the manor site with all the buildings and the demesne land of Walsham manor for a term of seven years, see p. 152.

For new rent received from Robert Margery for a garden of Goslings tenement granted in the same way, 1d.

For new rent received from Nicholas Brond of Gislingham for a piece of land lying in the aforesaid town between the land of William Goddard on the north side and the land of the Templars of Gislingham on the south side granted in the same way, 3d.

For new rent received from Robert Carpenter of Langham for a piece of land lying next to the land of the parson of Langham granted in the same way, 2d.

For new rent received from Henry Dinglove for a piece of land in Mill Field granted in the same way, 2d.

For new rent received from Robert Warde for a piece of land lying next to Chalk Pightle granted in the same way, 2d.

For new rent received from John Page for land and a tenement formerly Coppelowes granted to him and his heirs, 7s. 6d.

For new rent received from John Robwood for a tenement called Sparschoys tenement and two messuages formerly of Nicholas Dennis granted to him and his heirs by court roll, 2s. 4d.

For new rent received from John Ringbell for 3 acres 1 rood of pasture parcel of Nether Haugh Pasture granted to him and his heirs, 20d.

For new rent received from William Syre for a cotland with a curtilage called Walpoles Croft, 1 acre of land near the sheepcote of the Prior of Ixworth and 1 acre of land next to Gurrys Croft granted to him and his heirs by court roll, 5s. 10d.

For new rent received from the same William for a close next to his dwelling house granted to him and his heirs by court roll, 2s. 10d.

Sum £14 13s. 4d. half ¼d. and two parts of ¼d.

Castle ward For castle ward received from the manor of Wyken for the terms of St Michael, Easter, Christmas and the Nativity of St John the Baptist, 11s. 2d.

For castle ward received from the manor of Ixworth, 2s. 10d.

Sum 14s.

Farm of land and pasture From William Fuller for farm of our manor called Walsham Manor with all the buildings situated in the said manor with a certain close called Parkyard within the said manor, a sheepfold next to Conyger Close, a piece of land containing 42 acres called Old Tuft, a close called Little Meadow containing 17 acres of meadow and all the pasture called Cow Pasture pertaining to the aforesaid manor with a small laund on the north side of North Haugh Wood with leafy willows growing in the said pasture there, a close called Conyger Close containing 12 acres and another close called the Conyger next to the aforesaid sheepfold, a piece of land called Dovehouse Wong containing by estimate 16 acres, a piece of land called Cocks Dirt containing 18 acres, a piece of land called Brooms Wong containing 20 acres, a piece of land lying in the Hall Croft containing 16 acres, a piece of land near there called the Eleven Acres, a piece at Childerwell containing 14 acres, a close called the Launde containing 14 acres on the north side of North Haugh Wood, a piece of land upon the New Close containing 10 acres, a piece of land next to Summer Way containing 11 acres, a piece of land next to Hall Green containing 18 acres, a piece of land on the west side of Fishpond Field containing 16 acres, a close called the Chalk Pightle with 1 acre of land at Fishpond Field recently leased to Adam Blayer with liberty of a fold of up to 300 sheep granted to him for a term of 7 years, this year is the first, £6 6s. 8d.

From Nicholas Smith for 33½ acres of land and pasture lying in a close called New Close with leafy trees there, granted to him for a term of 10 years, this year is the 8th, 16s. 5d.

From William Potenger chaplain for 1½ acres of land, parcel of New Close towards his close granted to him and his heirs by court roll, 9d.

From the heirs of Robert Hawes for a piece of land containing 42 acres called Hatchmere and 1½ acres of land lying in the Bottom formerly of Walter Terwald granted to them this year, 7s.

From William Hawes for a piece of land containing 42 acres called Fishpond Field with the liberty of a fold of up to 80 sheep this year, 8s.

From the bailiff for a piece of meadow called Broad Dole containing 4½ acres sold to various men this year, 26s. 8d. \23s. 6d./.

From Robert Lester for a piece of land at Mickle Meadow and a piece of land at West Mill and 2 acres of land called Nunns Land this year, 5s. 6d.

From Thomas Bonde for 4 acres 1 rood of land abutting upon Harts Haugh formerly of Nicholas Dennis, 1½ acres of land called the Butts of the tenement Osbern at Rickinghall Willows, 2 acres of land of the tenement Cranmer next to the land formerly of Nicholas Tiptot at Rickinghall Willows next to the land formerly of John Man and the Market Mere and 2 acres of land of the tenement Burchards on the west side of Burchards Wood this year, 12d.

From John Cooper for two pieces of land containing 22 acres called Doucedeux, 6 acres of land called Walpoles Croft, a pightle called Jacks Yard and ½ acre of land abutting upon the land of the Prior of Ixworth granted to him and his heirs by court roll, 8s.

From John Robwood for Sheepcote Yard, 1½ acres of land at Clay hill, two pieces of land near there of the tenement Paynes, 1½ roods of land of the tenement Dennis abutting upon the Brook, 1 acre 3 roods at Willow Mere of the tenement Paynes, recently leased to Alice Morton, this year, 18d.

From Robert Lester for the Launde in Ladys Wood this year, 5s.

From John Swift for 1½ acres of land of the tenement Paynes next to Market way, 5 acres of land of the tenement Paynes, 1 acre of land of the tenement Robbys abutting upon Harts Haugh, ½ acre of land at Frances Row of the tenement Robbys and 2 acres of land at Brook Pits granted to him and his heirs by court roll, 2s. 6d.

From John Robwood senior for 6 acres of land and pasture called Home Stall and 1½ roods of land at Burchards Wood, this year, 2s. 8d.

From Walter [sic] Beacon for a piece of land and pasture containing 7 acres called Howes Toft, per acre 8d., 4s. 8d.

From John Robwood senior for 1½ acres of land of the tenement Paynes, a curtilage, 3 roods of land formerly of William Payne, 2 roods of land of the tenement of William Payne with the third part of a way called Outgoing towards Westhorpe, 1 acre of land in two pieces abutting upon Hundred Mere granted to him this year, 18d.

From William Grocer for 4 acres of land next to the close of the said William lying next there on the east side and the land formerly of Thomas Hereward, 2 roods of land called Stony Land and 2 acres of land abutting upon Helpes Wood of the land of High Hall thus leased to him this year, 2s. 7d.

From John Robwood senior for 16 acres 1 rood of land, parcel of Guspers Field, this year, 2s. 4d.

From John Tiptot \senior/ <junior> for 5 acres of land, parcel of Guspers Field, this year, 15d.

From John Rampley for 7 acres of land, parcel of Guspers Field of which one head abuts upon Harts Haugh, two pieces of land containing 4 acres in the field of Angrave of the tenement formerly of Agnes de Angerhale and for the herbage of a piece of meadow at Harts Haugh with pasture at the head of the same this year, 7s. 11d.

From John Ringbell for a close lying at Hall Gate on the north side of his messuage this year, 2s.

From Henry Corsour for Godfreys Yard with 1½ acres of land of the same tenement this year, 10d.

From the bailiff for 7 roods of meadow lying in Mickle Meadow in various pieces of meadow this year, 9s. \usually leased for 10s./

From the heirs of Henry Dinglove for 1 acre of land of the tenement Cranmer at Hulkes Bridge and 3 roods of land of the tenement Kebbils recently leased to John Cook, granted to him and his heirs this year, 9d.

From John Fletcher for 3½ acres of land in various pieces of the tenement Kebbils this year, 12d.

From the heirs of Robert Hawes for 18 acres of land called Blunts Hall this year, 2s.

From John Swift for 8 acres of land in Long Wheat in one piece and for 4 acres of land of the said tenement lying at the end of the croft of Thomas Bonde granted to him and his heirs by court roll, 3s. 4d.

From John Fletcher for 1 acre of land of the tenement Robbys on the south side of Trendle Wood this year, 3d.

From John Robwood senior for 1 acre of land of the tenement Paynes at the head of the croft of the said John and 1 rood of land at the north head of the same, recently in farm to Alice Morton this year, 4½d.

From John Ermitt for ½ acre of land next to Green Way formerly of John son of William Clevehog of the tenement Man this year, 2d.

From William Fuller for 1 acre of land abutting upon Wood Way of the same tenement at Pedders Path and ½ acre of land of the tenement Ratches lying at Dales recently leased for 7d. this year, 2d.

From John Robwood senior for 3 acres of land in the croft of Godfreys of the tenement of William Payne, this year 6d.

From Thomas Wells for 1 acre of land of the tenement Clevehog upon the Brook this year, 3d.

From John Fletcher for a messuage and 2½ roods of land lying in the croft recently of Walter Dennis remaining in the lord's hands by Robert Osbern this year, 12d.

From Thomas Fletcher for 5 acres of land on the east side of Fishpond Field next to the land of Robert Sare and 2 acres of land lying next to Trendle Wood Way this year, 2s.

From Thomas Wells for 3 acres of land of the tenement Paynes and 6 acres of land formerly of Nicholas Dennis at New Hall this year, 18d.

From Robert Carpenter for 1½ roods of land in four parcels in the field of Langham recently leased to John Margery this year, 2d.

From John Tiptot junior for two headlands containing 1 rood of pasture of the tenement of Peter Painter at Harts Haugh, pasture of Painters Yard, 1 acre 3 roods of land in two pieces of the tenement of Peter Painter recently leased to Robert Bray, 5 acres 3 roods of land in six pieces of the same tenement of which 3 acres is in three pieces in the field of Ashfield and 2 acres 3 roods is in three pieces at the Brook recently leased to John Brook, 1 acre 1 rood of land abutting upon the Brook towards the east of the same tenement recently leased to Robert Man, 3 roods of land in one piece of the same tenement next to Ashfield Way recently leased to John Ermitt, ½ acre of land at Brook Bridge of the same tenement recently leased to Robert Man, 2 acres of land of the tenement Pudding lying at Procession Way abutting upon Hundred Mere, 1 rood of land of the said tenement next to Stubbing Way next to the land formerly of Richard Qwalm, 3 acres of land of the same tenement near East Mill in three pieces recently leased to Walter Frances, granted to him and his heirs by court roll this year, 5s. 10d.

From Robert Lester for a close recently of Robert Cokerell lying next to Lady's Wood this year, 5s.

From John Robwood senior for the farm of a close called Katherines Croft with hedges and ditches there, a piece of land and pasture containing by estimate 6 acres with leafy willows there called Gurrys Croft, two pieces of land containing 4½ acres lying at Trendle Wood, a piece of land containing 5 acres called Stony Land, a piece of land containing 5 roods lying in South Field, 4 acres of land called Knots Hedge, a close called Sheephouse Close, 3 roods of meadow lying in Mickle Meadow, a close called Ox Pasture with hedges and ditches there, a piece of land containing 6 acres called Godelards Land, 10 acres of land, parcel of Guspers Field, the herbage of a meadow in Small Brook, a curtilage formerly Robetels with ½ acre of land formerly of William Payne, 2 acres of land of the tenement formerly of Robert Fornham near Godelards Land next to the land formerly of William Payne and 1 rood of land at Willow Mere formerly of Adam Pitlake, 2 acres 2½ roods of land recently of Walter Dennis remaining in the lord's hands abutting upon Hundred Mere, the herbage of a piece of meadow called Turf Pit Acre \5s./, a piece of land called the Hulver, 12 acres of land next to Nether Haugh, a close called Burchards Close, 18 acres of land lying in Burchards Croft, a piece of land in High Hall Croft, a close called High Hall Close, a piece of land called Nether Haugh, a piece of land called Seventeen Acres, 18 acres of land called Blunts Land, 12 acres of land at Allwood Green recently leased to Robert Payne and for the farm of a tenement formerly of John Syre at East End with the liberty of a fold by an indenture leased to him for a term of 10 years, this year is the 8th, 103s. 4d.

From the same John for Paynes tenement lying in the East End of the lord's bondage granted to him by court roll, 13s. 6d.

From Robert Robwood for 1 rood of meadow recently of John Ermitt lying in Mickle Meadow this year, 15d.

From Alice Bron for a messuage, once with a house, formerly of Alice Rampley this year, 6d.

Sum – £19 2s. 11½d.[46]

Perquisites of court For perquisites of two courts held there this year, £4 17s. 7d.
Sum £4 17s. 7d.

Farm of a mill with sale of stock From Gilbert Miller for the farm of a windmill leased this year to the same Gilbert, 23s. 4d.
Sum 23s. 4d.

Works and services sold For 15 qrs 1 bus. 1¾ pks. of oats sold from rent as elsewhere, price per qr 2s. 8d., 40s. 5½d.

For 4 capons sold from rent as elsewhere, 10d.

---

[46] Marginal note, '£19 2s. 5½d.'

For 112½ hens sold from rent as elsewhere, price per head 1½d., 14s. 0¾d.

For 661½ eggs sold from rent as elsewhere, price per 120 4d., 20¾d.

For ½lb of cumin sold as elsewhere, 1½d.

For ½lb of pepper sold as elsewhere, 7d.

For 28 ploughing services from services sold as elsewhere, price per ploughing service 6d., 14s. <3d.>

For 7 Ploughales sold from services as elsewhere, 3s. 6d.

For 723¾ winter works sold as elsewhere, price per work ½d., 30s. 1¾d. and half a ¼d.

For 7 carrying services sold from services as elsewhere, 7d.

For 5½ manure carrying services sold from services as elsewhere, price per carrying service 2d., 11d.

For 138 weeding works sold as elsewhere, price per work ½d., 5s. 9d.

For 35¼ mowing works sold as elsewhere, price per work 1½d., 4s. 3¾d. and half ¼d.

For 528¼ harvest works sold from services as elsewhere, price per work 2d., £4 8s. 0½d.

For 113 harvest boonworks sold from services elsewhere, price per work 2d., 18s. 10d.

Sum £11 4s. 1¾d. and half ¼d.[47]

Sale of underwood From John Robhood senior for 3 roods of underwood sold in Lady's Wood this year, 4s. 6d.

From Robert Rokell for 1 rood of underwood there, 18d.

From John Pepper for 1 rood of underwood there, 18d.

From Stephen Baxter and John his son for 1 rood of underwood there, 18d.

From Thomas Page for 1 rood of underwood there, 18d.

From John Shepherd for ½ rood of underwood there, 9d.

From John Wells and John Lines for ½ rood of underwood there, 9d.

From Robert Cutting for 1 rood of underwood there, 18d.

From Robert Lister for a thorn hedge there, 3s. 4d.

From William Syre for ½ rood of underwood in High Hall Wood, 7½d.

From Nicholas Smith for a small oak at North Haugh, 6d.

From John Margery for lifting [*relev'*] a thorn at Little Meadow beyond the hedge made there, 3s. 4d.

From William Margery for an ash sold to him there, 20d.

From a black poplar and a white poplar sold at Hall Gate, 6s. 8d.

Sum 29s. 7½d.[48]

Foreign receipts Nil.

Sum nil.

Sales at the audit For sales at the audit, nothing this year.

Sum nil.

Sum total of receipts with arrears £60 8s. 7¾d. and two parts of ¼d.[49]

---

[47] Marginal note, '£11 4s. 1¾d. and half ¼d.'

[48] Marginal note, '29s. 2½d.'

[49] Marginal note, '£60 21s. 11¾d. and two parts of a ¼d.'

156

Rent resolute with decays From which in allowed rent, works and services reckoned in money for the tenement of John Frances in the office of reeve of 2 marks for the said office not carried out, 7s. 8¼d.

Item in allowed rent, works and services reckoned in money for the tenement of Henry Corsour in the office of hayward this year of a fine of 13s. 4d. for the said office not carried out, 4s. 10d.

Item reckoned in rent resolute for the hall of Thelnetham of 2s., nothing because it is outside the lord's hands.

Item the hall of Rickinghall p.a., 3s. 1½d.

Item paid for castle ward of Norwich p.a., 16s.

Item paid to John Margery p.a. 1½d.

Item in allowance of rent for various tenements in the lord's hands both for this manor and for High Hall 52s. 5¼d. and half a quarter of ¼d. and two parts of ¼d., of which for High Hall 15s. 11¾d.

Item paid to the hall of Ashfield for castle ward for High Hall p.a., 17d.

Item paid to the same hall for rent p.a., 2d.

Item paid to the castle of Eye twice this year, 18d.

Item for hundred suit released p.a. for Burchards, 16d.

Item paid to Helimot and for ward for Burchards p.a., 9d.

Item in rent resolute for Sir William Bardwell for 1 acre of meadow at Turf Pits purchased by the lord from John Rampley, chaplain, 4d.

Item in allowance of rent on 4 acres of land remaining in the lord's hands by John Syre, 18d. and three quarters of ¼d. and a third part of ¼d.

Item in allowance of the tenement formerly of John Spilman granted to John Bertram free by charter, 10s. 7¼d. and half a quarter of ¼d.

Item in allowance on ½ acre of land of the tenement Coppelowes granted to him in the same way, 6d.

Item in allowance on 1½ acres of land formerly of John Page granted to him, 6½d.

Item in allowance on a piece of land of the tenement of John Fuller granted to him in the same way, 7d.

Item in allowance on ½ acre of land recently leased to Thomas Bonde of the tenement Goslings from the lord's demesne granted to him in the same way, 3d.

Item in allowance on the tenement Gorys and for a parcel of the tenement Master Johns granted to him in the same way, 3¾d.

Item in allowance of a tenement formerly of John Syre because the lord has all the profits of the same tenement at farm as above, 5½d. with the price of a hen sold above.

In allowed rent of the tenement Paynes taken into the lord's hands and at farm as above, 15s. 4d. and a quarter of a ¼d.

Item in allowed rent on the tenement formerly of Robert Smith viz: a forge taken into the lord's hands, 2s.

Item claim [*pet'*] allowed on a messuage formerly built in Church Street formerly of Alice Rampley taken into the lord's hands, 13d.

Sum £6 2s. 10¾d. and quarter of a ¼d. and two parts of a ¼d. and a third part of a ¼d.

Cost of the buildings with pardons and allowances In the stipend of John Manser, carpenter for 4 days' work making a bench in the knights chamber and a shutter there and mending the bins [*les bynnes*] in the cow shed, taken per day 4d., 16d.

In a contract made with John Wells and John Lines to throw [*jaciand'*] clay for ramming a barn and for ramming the said barn, altogether 20d.

Item in the stipend of John Frances, thatcher and John Mills his servant for 4 days at table, thatching upon the garret and upon the stots stable and ?fitting with rings [*ringanc'*] the said building at the manor, taken between them per day 8d., 2s. 8d.

Item in two cartloads of straw bought for thatching the same buildings, 20d.

In a contract made with John Wells and John Lines mending and making [*illeg.*] barn and ramming a part of the said barn, fitting laths and plastering with clay the same barn, altogether 5s. 3d.

Item in iron nails bought for the same, 2d.

In the stipend of John Miller for 4 days' work throwing clay for the same task, 16d.

In the stipend of John Frances, thatcher and John Bonde his servant for 4 days' work thatching upon the cow shed and putting clay upon the said thatch, and thatching upon the barn at the manor and mending a gutter [*goter*] upon the knight's chamber, taken between them 8d. per day, 2s. 8d.

Item in two cartloads of straw bought for the same, 2s.

Item in the stipend to the same John, thatcher and his servant, for two days' work thatching upon the tenement formerly of John Syre at East End, 16d.

Item paid for carriage of the clay, 10d.

Sum 20s. 11d.

Cost of the mill Item paid to the miller for cogs and staves [*battis*] and laths for mending the mill this year, 13d.

Sum 13d.

Minute expenses In the stipend of John Frances for 4½ days' work stopping up and mending hedges at Lady's Wood this year, 18d.

In the stipend of the same John for 3½ days' work stopping up and making hedges at Burchards Wood, High Hall and Luchesdell, 14d.

Item paid to John Wells and John Lines for 80 perches cut and a hedge made on the south side of Little Meadow, taken for each perch 1½d., 10s.

Item paid to the same for 32 perches of hedge made there on the east side of the same meadow, taken for each perch 1d., 2s. 8d.

Item paid to the same for 47 perches of hedge made at Ox Pightle and the Conyger, taken for each perch 1d., 3s. 11d.

In parchment bought for writing court rolls and accounts, 8d.

Item paid to Richard Fuller for a certain well filled at the manor 6d., received from John Bertram.

Sum 20s. 5d.

Weeding and mowing In weeding corn and mowing the meadow, nothing this year.
Sum nil.

Foreign expenses with the steward's expenses In the expenses of William Morle, John Bertram and the steward and other supervisors being here for two courts held, 10s. 10d.

Item paid for three quarters of a 15th and 10th to the lord king this year, 7s. 6d.
Sum 18s. 4d.

Wages and stipends In the wages of the bailiff making the account this year with his clothing, 40s.
Sum 40s.

158

Cash delivered Delivered to John Bertram and William Morle for arrears, of which above by one tally £7 3s. 7¾d.
To the same John from rents and farms this year by a tally, £33 10s.
Sum £40 13s. 7¾d.

Sum total of expenses and allowances £51 17s. 3¾d.[50]
And owes £8 11s. 3d., of which granted to John Robhood by the lady for certain fines in court, 8s. 4d.
Item to the same allowed for a tenement [*illeg.*] in Church Street [*illeg.*], 2s.
And thus owed, £8 12d.

[*Reverse*]
Walsham account of works and services in the 16th year of Henry VI.

Multure at the mill For the farm of a windmill leased this year to Gilbert Miller within for money and usually leased for 10 qrs of multure from the mill.
Sum nil.

Stots For a heriot, 1.
Sum shown. And sold within the court.[51]

Oats For rent from the lord's tenants at the Feast of Edmund King and Martyr, 20 qrs two parts of ½ bus. and half a ¼ peck of oats.
Sum 20 qrs two parts of ½ bus. and half a ¼ peck of oats.
From which, in allowance for various tenements in the lord's hands for this manor and for High Hall, this year 4 qrs 5½ bus. two parts of ½ bus. and two quarters of a peck.
In sales within, 15 qrs 1 bus. 1 peck and two quarters of ½ peck of oats.
Sum as above.

Capons For rent from the lord's tenants there at Easter, 8 capons.
Sum 8.
From which in allowances for various tenements in the lord's hands, 4 capons.
In sales within, 4.
Sum as above.

Hens and cockerels For rent from the lord's tenants there at Christmas, 141¾ hens of which 2 are cockerels.
Sum 141¾ of which two are cockerels.
From which, in allowance for various tenements in the lord's hands for this manor and for High Hall, 28¼ hens.
Delivered to the bailiff of Westhorpe by the hand of Richard Sewell tenant of High Hall in Westhorpe, 1.
In sales as within, 112½ hens.
Sum as above.

---

[50] Marginal note, '£51 15s. 11½d. quarter of a ¼d., two parts of a ¼d. and a third part of a ¼d.'
[51] Meaning the animal was not actually added to the demesne stock of horses, but instead either the cash equivalent was paid or someone paid the asking price, and the payment was included as part of the court revenue this year.

Eggs For rent of the lord's tenants there at Easter, 825 eggs.

Sum 825 eggs.

From which, in allowance for various tenements in the lord's hands for this manor and for High Hall, 183½ eggs.

In sales within, 661½ eggs.

Sum as above.

Dovecote For the issues of a dovecote, nothing this year because there was no stock.

Sum nil.

Cumin For rent from the Prior of Bricett p.a. ½lb cumin.

Sum ½lb cumin.   And sold within.

Pepper For rent received from Walter Frances for the tenement recently of John Pinfold pertaining to High Hall, ½lb pepper.

Sum ½lb pepper.

And sold within.

Ploughing services For the issues of 9 customary greater tenures this year, providing [*blank*] ploughteams this year, 15 ploughing services taken at the seasons of winter and Lent, each whole ploughteam doing 5 ploughing services, each ploughteam receiving 6 loaves of mixed grain, at 20 to the bushel, and allowed 2 winter works. For the issues on other customary tenants who provide a ploughteam this year, 10 ploughing services, each ploughteam shall do 3 ploughing services and receive from the lord 6 loaves of the said corn and said weight or allowed works.

For the issues of customary tenants of High Hall, nothing because nothing this year. From services bought from William Hore received from the tenement Patches at the winter season, 1 ploughing.

Sum 28 ploughing services.

And sold within.

Ploughales For the services of customary tenants providing this year 7 ploughing services.

Sum 7 ploughing services.   And sold within.

Winter and summer works For the services of customary tenants by half days, 962 and a third part of a winter work.

Sum 962 and three parts.

From which, in allowance for various tenements in the lord's hands for this manor and for High Hall, 238¼ and a third part of a winter work.

In sales within, 723¾ winter works.

Sum as above.

Carrying services For the issues of 7 customary carrying services at the will of the lord by custom, price per work 1d.

Sum 7.

And sold within.

Carriage of manure For the services of customary tenants without resumption, 9 manure carrying services and allowed to them for each carrying of manure, 1 winter work.

Sum 9 carrying services.

From which, in allowance for various tenements in the lord's hands, 3½ carrying services. In sales within, 5½ carrying services.

Sum as above.

Weeding works For the services of customary tenants, 175 and three quarters of ½ a weeding work, price per work ½d.

Sum 175 etc.

From which in allowance for various tenements in the lord's hands for this manor and for High Hall, 37¾ weeding works. In sales within, 138 works.

Sum as above.

Mowing works For the services of customary tenants for half days, 42¼ mowing works.

Sum 42¼ mowing works.

From which in allowance for various tenements in the lord's hands, 7 mowing works. In sales within, 35¼ mowing works.

Sum as above.

Carriage of hay For the services of customary tenants that have carts without resumption and without meadow works, nothing this year because they were respited.

Sum nil.

Haymaking works For the services of customary tenants as many as the lord requires for lifting, turning and stacking all the hay without resumption.

Harvest works For the services of customary tenants for full days in the lord's corn, reaping, tying and stacking, 754 works, of which each shall receive from the lord at noon and for his supper 2 loaves of mixed grain, at 20 to the bushel and 4 herrings, price per work 2d.

Sum 754 works.

From which, in allowance for various tenements in the lord's hands for this manor and for High Hall, 225¾ harvest works.
In sales within, 528¼ harvest works.

Sum as above.

Harvest boonworks For the services of customary tenants this year, 139 harvest boon-works, for which each free man shall have for his food at noon and for his supper one wheat loaf at 20 to the bushel.
And each customary tenant shall have for his food at noon the same as for the free tenants and for his supper one loaf of mixed grain, at 20 to the bushel, and one herring, price per work 2d.

Sum 139 works.

From which in allowance for various tenements in the lord's hands for this manor and for High Hall, 26 boonworks.
In sales within, 113 boonworks.

Sum as above.

161

Document 13: *Walsham account, 28 September 1439 to 28 September 1440*

SA/B HA504/3/11

Walsham

Account of Robert Lester, reeve and hayward there, from the eve of St Michael the Archangel in the 18th year of Henry VI until the eve of the same St Michael next coming in the 19th year of the same Henry for one whole year.

Arrears [*He answers*] for arrears of the last account at the end of the next preceding year, nil.

Sum nil.

Rents of assize For rents of assize there both for free and villein tenants both for this manor and for High Hall not including rent in Westhorpe with ward of High Hall for the terms of St Michael, Christmas, Easter and the Nativity of St John the Baptist, £13 11s. 5½d. half ¼d. and two parts of ¼d.

For new rent received from John Robwood for a piece of land lying at Ulveswell, 5d.

For new rent received from John Margery for a piece of land called Gorommes Way, 6d.

For new rent received from Robert Margery for a garden of the tenement Goslings, 1d.

For new rent received from Nicholas Brond of Gislingham for a piece of land lying in the aforesaid town between the land of William Goddard on the north and the land of the Templars of Gislingham on the south, 3d.

For new rent received from Robert Carpenter of Langham for a piece of land lying next to the land of the parson of Langham, 2d.

For new rent received from Katherine Dinglove[52] for a piece of land lying in the Mill Field, 2d.

For new rent received from Robert Warde for a piece of land lying next to Chalk Pightle, 2d.

For new rent received from John Page for land and a tenement formerly Coppelowes granted to him and his heirs by court roll, 7s. 6d.

For new rent received from John Robwood for a tenement called East End tenement (*Esthodstenement*)[53] and two messuages formerly of Nicholas Dennis granted to him by court roll, 2s. 4d.

For new rent received from John Ringbell for 3 acres 1 rood of pasture parcel of New Hall Pasture granted to him and his heirs by court roll, 20d.

For new rent received from William Syre for a cottage with a curtilage called Walpoles Croft, 1 acre of land near the sheepcote of the Prior of Ixworth and 1 acre of land next to Gurrys Croft granted to him and his heirs by court roll, 5s. 10d.

For new rent received from the same William for a close next to his dwelling house granted to him and his heirs by court roll, 2s. 10d.

Sum £14 13s. 4d. half a ¼d. and 2 parts of a ¼d.

---

[52] Henry Dinglove died in 1437 and his widow, Katherine, acquired from him a messuage and croft of seven acres: SA/B HA504/1/12.17. The rents of assize now show his widow Katherine holding land in Mill Field. In 1455 she and her new husband surrendered this holding to her son by Henry, who was called John. In return, Katherine and her second husband were to have full use of a room in the messuage with food and clothing for the rest of their lives: SA/B HA504/1/13.22.

[53] The name of Sparschoys tenement has been carelessly copied from the 1437–8 account, which was badly written and has become *Esthodstenement*.

Castle ward For castle ward received from the manor of Wyken for the terms of St Michael, Christmas, Easter and the Nativity of St John the Baptist, 11s. 2d.
For castle ward received from the manor of Ixworth, 2s. 10d.
Sum 14s.

Farm of land and pasture From William Fuller for the farm of the manor called Walsham Hall with all the buildings situated in the said manor with a certain close called Park Yard within the said manor, a sheepcote next to Conyger Close, a piece of land containing 42 acres called Old Toft, a close called Little Meadow containing 17 acres of meadow and all the pasture called Cow Pasture pertaining to the aforesaid manor with a small Launde on the north side of North Haugh Wood with leafy willows growing in the said pasture there, a close called Conyger Close containing 12 acres and another close called the Conyger next to the aforesaid sheepcote, a piece of land called Dovehouse Wong containing by estimate 16 acres, a piece of land called Cocks Dirt containing 18 acres, a piece of land called Brooms Wong containing 20 acres, a piece of land in the Hall Croft containing 16 acres, a piece of land near there called the Eleven Acres, a piece of land at Childerwell containing 14 acres, a close called the Launde containing 14 acres on the north side of North Haugh Wood, a piece of land above the New Close containing 10 acres, a piece of land next to the Summer Way containing 11 acres, a piece of land next to Hall Green containing 18 acres, a piece of land on the west side of Fishpond Field containing 16 acres, a close called the Chalk Pightle with 1 acre of land at Fishpond Field recently leased to Adam Blayer with the liberty of a fold of up to 300 sheep granted to him this year, £6 6s. 8d.
From Nicholas Smith for 33½ acres of land and pasture lying in a close called New Close with leafy trees there granted to him this year, 16s. 5d.
From William Potenger chaplain for 1½ acres of land parcel of New Close towards his close granted to him and his heirs by court roll, 9d.
From George Hawes, chaplain,[54] for a piece of land containing 42 acres called Hatchmere, 1½ acres of land lying in the Bottom formerly of Walter Terwald granted to him this year, 8s.
From William Hawes for a piece of land containing 42 acres called Fishpond Field with liberty of a fold of up to 80 sheep this year, 8s.
From the bailiff for a piece of meadow called Broad Dole containing 4½ acres sold to various men this year, 20s.
From Robert Lester for a piece of land at Mickle Meadow and a piece of land at West Mill and 2 acres of land called Nunns Land granted to him and his heirs by court roll, 6s.
From Thomas Bonde for 4 acres 1 rood of land abutting upon Harts Haugh formerly of Nicholas Dennis, 1½ acres of land called the Butts of the tenement Osbern at Rickinghall Willows, 2 acres of land of the tenement Cranmer next to the land formerly of Nicholas Tiptot at Rickinghall Willows next to the land formerly of

---

54 When Robert Hawes died in 1438 his heirs were his sons George, James and Andrew, who inherited two messuages, land, meadow, pasture and wood. George and James were granted seven acres at Guspers Field and other land, which previously Robert had leased, at fee farm for 7s. 11d. p.a. at a court held in 1438 (SA/B HA504/1/12.20), although only George's name appears in the account. The following year they were granted the lease of 42 acres called Hatchmere, 1½ acres in the Bottom and 18 acres called Boynhall (SA/B HA505/1/12.21). In the accounts it is called Blunts Hall, a scribal error, because the real Blunts Hall, also 18 acres, was leased by John Robwood.

John Man and the Market Mere and 2 acres of land of the tenement Burchards on the west side of Burchards Wood this year, 12d.

From John Cooper for two pieces of land containing 22 acres called Doucedeux, 6 acres of land called Walpoles Croft, a pightle called Jacks Yard and ½ acre of land abutting upon the land of the Prior of Ixworth granted to him and his heirs by court roll, 8s.

From John Robwood senior for Sheepcote Yard and 1½ acres of land at the Clay Hill, two pieces of land near there of the tenement Paynes, 1½ roods of land of the tenement Dennis abutting upon the Brook, 1 acre 3 roods of land at Willow Mere of the tenement Paynes recently leased to Alice Morton this year, 18d.

From Robert Lester for the Launde in Lady's Wood this year, 5s.

From John Swift for 1½ acres of land of the tenement Paynes next to Market Way, 5 acres of land of the tenement Paynes, 1 acre of land of the tenement Robbys abutting upon Harts Haugh, ½ acre of land at Frances Row of the tenement Robbys, 2 acres of land at Brook Pits granted to him and his heirs by court roll, this year 2s. 6d.

From John Robwood senior for 6 acres of land and pasture called Home Stall and 1½ roods of land at Burchards Wood, this year, 2s. 8d.

From John Beacon[55] for a piece of land and pasture containing 7 acres called Howes Toft, per acre 8d., 4s. 8d.

From John Robwood senior for 1½ acres of land of the tenement Paynes, a curtilage, 3 roods of land formerly of William Payne, 2 roods of land of the tenement of William Payne with three parts of a way called Outgoing towards Westhorpe, 1 acre of land in two pieces abutting upon Hundred Mere granted to him, this year, 18d.

From William Grocer for 4 acres of land next to the close of the said William \now of John Robwood/ lying next to there on the east side and the land formerly of Thomas Hereward, 2 roods of land called Stony Land \now in the tenure of John Robwood/, 2 acres of land abutting upon Helpes Wood of the land of High Hall thus leased to him this year \now in the tenure of John Robwood/, 2s. 7d.

From John Robwood senior for 16 acres 1 rood of land parcel of Guspers Field this year, 2s. 4d.

From John Tiptot senior for 5 acres of land parcel of Guspser Field this year, 15d.

From George Hawes chaplain for 7 acres of land parcel of Guspers Field, of which one head abuts upon Harts Haugh, two pieces of land containing 4 acres in the field of Angrave of the tenement formerly of Agnes de Angerhale and for the herbage of a piece of meadow at Harts Haugh with pasture at the head of the same this year granted by court roll, 7s. 11d.

From John Ringbell for a close lying at Hall Gate on the north side of his messuage this year, 2s.

From John Deye for Godfreys Yard with 1½ acres of land of the same tenement, this year, 10d.

From the bailiff for 7 roods of meadow lying in Mickle Meadow in various pieces of meadow this year, 9s.

From Katherine Dinglove for 1 acre of land of the tenement Cranmer at Hulkes Bridge and 3 roods of land of the tenement Kebbils recently leased to John Cook granted to her and her heirs by court roll this year, 9d.

From John Fletcher for 3½ acres of land in various pieces of the tenement Kebbils this year, 12d.

---

[55] Entered as Walter Beacon in the last account, John's name has now been corrected.

From George Hawes chaplain for 18 acres of land called Blunts Hall this year, 2s.

From John Swift for 8 acres of land in Long Wheat in one piece, 4 acres of land of the said tenement lying at the end of the croft of Thomas Bonde granted to him and his heirs by court roll, 3s. 4d.

From John Fletcher for 1 acre of land of the tenement Robbys on the south side of Trendle Wood recently leased to him for 3d., nothing this year because it is no longer leased.

From John Robwood senior for 1½ roods of land of the tenement Paynes at the head of the croft of the said John recently Mortons Croft and 1 rood of land at the north head of the same recently leased to Alice Morton this year, 4½d.

From John Ermitt for ½ acre of land next to the Green Way formerly of John son of William Clevehog of the tenement Man this year, 2d.

From William Fuller for 1 acre of land abutting upon Wood Way of the same tenement at Pedders Path, ½ acre of land of the tenement Ratches lying at Dales recently granted for 7d. this year, 2d.

From John Robwood senior for 3 roods of land in the croft of Godfreys of the tenement of William Payne this year, 6d.

From Thomas Wells for 1 acre of land of the tenement Clevehog upon the Brook this year, 3d.

From John Fletcher for a messuage and 2½ roods of land lying in the croft recently of Walter Dennis remaining in the lord's hands by Robert Osbern this year \granted to him and his heirs by court roll/, 12d.

From Thomas Fletcher for 5 acres of land on the east side of Fishpond Field next to the land of Robert Sare and 2 acres of land lying next to Trendle Wood, this year, 2s.

From Thomas Wells for 3 acres of land of the tenement Paynes and 6 acres of land formerly of Nicholas Dennis at New Hall this year, 18d.

From Robert Carpenter for 1½ roods of land in three parcels in the field of Langham recently leased to John Margery, this year, 2d.

From John Tiptot junior for two headlands containing 1 rood of pasture of the tenement of Peter Painter at Harts Haugh Pasture of Painters Yard, 1 acre 3 roods of land in two pieces of the tenement of Peter Painter recently leased to Robert Bray, 5 acres 3 roods of land in six pieces of the same tenement of which 3 acres in three pieces lie in the field of Ashfield and 2 acres 3 roods of land in three pieces at the Brook recently leased to John Brook, 1 acre 1 rood of land abutting upon the Brook towards the east of the same tenement recently leased to Robert Man, 3 roods of land in one piece of the same tenement next to Ashfield Way recently leased John Ermitt, ½ acre of land at Brook Bridge of the same tenement recently leased Robert Man, 2 acres of land of the tenement Pudding lying at Procession Way abutting upon Hundred Mere, 1 rood of land of the said tenement next to Stubbing Way next to the land formerly of Richard Qwalm, 3 acres of land of the same tenement near the East Mill in three pieces recently leased to Walter Frances granted to him and his heirs by court roll this year, 5s. 10d.

From John Fuller for a close recently of Robert Cokerel lying next to Lady's Wood this year, 3s.

From John Robwood senior for the farm of a close called Katherine's Croft with hedges and ditches there, a piece of land and pasture by estimate 6 acres with leafy willows there called Gurrys Croft, two pieces of land containing 4½ acres lying at Trendle Wood, a piece of land containing 5 roods called Stony Land, a piece of land containing 5 roods lying in the South Field, 4 acres of land called Knots Hedge, a close called Sheephouse Close, 3 roods of meadow lying in the Mickle Meadow, a close called the Ox Pasture with hedges and ditches there, a piece of land containing 6 acres called Godelards Land, 10 acres of land parcel of Guspers Field, the herbage of a meadow in Small Brook, a curtilage formerly Robetels with ½ acre of land formerly of William Payne, 2 acres of land formerly of Robert Fornham near Godelards Land next to the land formerly of William Payne and 1 rood of land at Willow Mere formerly of Adam Pitlake, 2 acres 2 roods of land recently of Walter Dennis remaining in the lord's hands abutting upon Hundred Mere, the herbage of a piece of meadow \5s./ called Turfpit Acre, a piece of land called the Hulver, 12 acres of land next to Nether Haugh, a close called Burchards Close, 18 acres of land lying in Burchards Croft, a piece of land in High Hall Croft, a close called High Hall Close, a piece of land called Nether Haugh, a piece of land called Seventeen Acres, 18 acres of land called Blunts Land, 12 acres of land at Allwood Green recently leased to Robert Payne and for farm of a tenement formerly of John Syre at East End with the liberty of a fold by an indenture leased to him for a term of 10 years, this year is the last, 103s. 4d.

From the same John for Paynes tenement lying in East End of the lord's bondage granted to him by court roll, 13s. 6d.

From John Fuller for 1 rood of meadow recently of John Ermitt lying in the Mickle Meadow this year, 12d.

From Richard Poyken for a messuage, once with a house, formerly of Alice Rampley granted to him and his heirs by court roll this year, 6d.

Sum £18 16s. 8d.

Perquisites of court For perquisites of two courts held there this year, 77s. 10d.

Sum 77s. 10d.

Farm of a mill with the sale of stock From the miller for the farm of a windmill leased to him this year, 23s. 4d.

Sum 23s. 4d.

Works and customary services sold – For 15 qrs 1 bus. 1¾ peck of oats from rent sold as elsewhere, price per qr 2s. 8d., 40s. 5½d. and half a ¼d.

For 4 capons sold as elsewhere, 10d.

For 111½ hens from rent sold as elsewhere, price per head 1½d., 14s. 0¾d.

For 621½ eggs from custom sold as elsewhere, price per 120 4d., 20¾d.

For ½lb of cumin sold as elsewhere, 1½d.

For ½lb of pepper sold as elsewhere, 5d.

For 18 ploughing services sold as elsewhere, price per ploughing service 6d., 9s.

For 6 Ploughales from customary works sold as elsewhere, 3s.

For 723¾ winter works sold as elsewhere, price per work ½d., 30s. 1¾d. and half a ¼d.

For 7 carrying services sold as elsewhere, 7d.

For 5½ carryings of manure from services sold as elsewhere, price per carrying service 2d., 11d.

For 138 hoeing works sold as elsewhere, price per work ½d., 5s. 9d.

For 25¼ mowing works sold as elsewhere, price per work 1½d., 4s. 4¾d. and half a ¼d.

For 523¼ harvest works sold as elsewhere, price per work 2d., £4 8s. 0½d.

For 113 harvest boonworks from services sold as elsewhere, price per work 2d., 18s. 10d.

Sum £10 18s. 3¾d. and half a ¼d.

Sale of underwood From Richard Taylor for 1 rood of underwood sold to him in Lady's Wood this year, 16d.

From Peter Poye for 1 rood of underwood there, 16d.

From John Page for ½ acre of underwood there, 2s. 8d.

From Thomas Murrell for 1 rood of underwood there, 16d.

From John Fletcher for ½ rood of underwood there, 8d.

From John Tiptot for 38 perches of underwood there, 15d.

From John Tiptot for a parcel of underwood there, 4d.

From Robert Frances for a parcel of underwood there, 4d.

From Robert Lewkin for 37 perches of underwood there, 14½d.

From Cecil Bigge for ½ rood of underwood there, 8d.

From John Baker for ½ rood of underwood there, 8d.

From Robert Pepper for 1 rood of underwood there, 16d.

From John Ringbell for two white poplars blown down by the wind and sold to him, 2s.

From John Smith for two white poplars blown down by the wind, 16d.

From William Potenger, chaplain for an oak tree sold to him, 2s. 8d.

<16s. 5½d.>⁵⁶ Sum 20s. 1½d.

Foreign receipts nil.

Sum nil.

Sales at the audit From things sold at the audit, nothing this year.

Sum nil.

<Sum of receipts £51 2s. 8d. and two parts of ¼d.>⁵⁷

Sum total of receipts £51 2s. 7½d. and two parts of ¼d.

Rent resolute with decays From which in allowed rent, works and services reckoned in money for the tenement of Margaret Tuddenham in the office of reeve and for a fine of 2 marks for the said office not carried out 5s. 9½d. and half a ¼d.

From which in allowed rent, works and services reckoned in money for the tenement of Katherine Dinglove⁵⁸ in the office of hayward this year for a fine of 13s. 4d. for the said office not carried out [*illeg.*] 5d.

Item reckoned in rent resolute for the hall of Thelnetham of 2s., nothing because it is outside the lord's hands.

Item the hall of Rickinghall p.a., 3s. 1½d.

Item paid for castle ward of Norwich p.a., 16s.

Item paid to John Margery p.a. 1½d.

Item in allowance of rent for various tenements in the lord's hands both for this manor and for High Hall 52s. 5¼d. and half a quarter of ¼d. and two parts of ¼d., of which for High Hall 15s. 11¾d.

Item paid to the hall of Ashfield for castle ward for High Hall p.a., 17d.

Item paid to the same hall for rent p.a., 2d.

Item paid to the castle of Eye twice this year, 18d.

---

⁵⁶ Marginal note.

⁵⁷ Marginal note.

⁵⁸ Women, in theory, could serve as reeve or hayward but usually paid the fine instead.

Item for hundred suit released p.a. for Burchards, 16d.

Item paid to Helimot and for ward for Burchards p.a., 9d.

Item in rent resolute for Sir William Bardwell for 1 acre of meadow at Turf Pits purchased by the lord from John Rampley, chaplain, 4d.

Item in allowance of rent on 4 acres of land remaining in the lord's hands by John Syre, 18d. and three quarters of ¼d. and a third part of ¼d.

Item in allowance of the tenement formerly of John Spilman granted to John Bertram free by charter, 10s. 7¼d. and half a quarter of ¼d.

Item in allowance on ½ acre of land of the tenement Coppelowes granted to him in the same way, 6d.

Item in allowance on 1½ acres of land formerly of John Page granted to him, 6½d.

Item in allowance on a piece of land of the tenement of John Fuller granted to him in the same way, 7d.

Item in allowance on ½ acre of land recently leased to Thomas Bonde of the tenement Goslings from the lord's demesne granted to him in the same way, 3d.

Item in allowance on the tenement Gorys and for a parcel of the tenement Master Johns granted to him in the same way, 3¾d.

Item in allowance of a tenement formerly of John Syre because the lord has all the profits of the same tenement at farm as above, 5½d. with the price of a hen sold above.

In allowed rent of the tenement Paynes taken into the lord's hands and at farm as above, 15s. 4d. and a quarter of a ¼d.

Item allowed on a messuage formerly built in Church Street formerly of Alice Rampley taken into the lord's hands, 13d.

Sum 116s. 3d.

Cost of the buildings with pardons and allowances In the stipend of John Frances, thatcher, and his servant for one day's work thatching the barn at East End, 7d.

Item price allowed for one cart of hay carried as far as Bury on the instructions of the lord, 5s.

Item paid for straw bought for thatching a building at the manor and for thatching the said straw, 2s. 4d.

Sum 7s. 11d.

Cost of the mill In the stipend of John Manser, carpenter, for three days' work mending the *Wyndewhow* of the mill by carpentry, per day 4d., 12d.

Item in board bought for the same, 11d.

Item paid to John Smith for iron nails bought for the same and for mending the rind of the same mill, 7d.

Sum 2s. 6d.

Minute expenses In the stipend of Thomas Murrell for 6 days' work making hedges and mending the gaps at Lady's Wood per day 4d., 2s.

Item in the stipend of the same Thomas for 3 days' work mending and making hedges for the park [*pco*] at the manor, 12d.

Item paid for cutting underwood for the same there, 4d.

Item in the stipend of William Syre for 3 days piecework making hedges at Burchards Wood and at Luchesdell, 12d.

Item in the stipend of Richard Taylor for one day's piece-work making hedges at North Haugh Launde, 4d.

168

In parchment bought for writing court rolls and accounts, 8d.

Sum 5s. 4d.

Weeding and mowing In weeding corn, nothing and in mowing the meadow, nothing this year.

Sum nil.

Foreign expenses with steward's expenses In the expenses of John Bertram and the steward and others supervising there for two courts held this year, 14s. 0½d. Item paid for one quarter of a 15th to the lord king this year, 2s. 6d.

Sum 16s. 6½d.

Wages and stipends In the wages of the bailiff reckoned this year with his clothing, 40s.

In wages of the clerk of the roll and the clerk of the court, including clothing, 20s. <60s.>[59]

Sum 60s.

Cash delivered Delivered to John Bertram for rents and farms this year for one term, £17.

Sum £17.

Sum of all expenses and payments £27 8s. 6d.

And he owes, £23 14s. 1d. and 2 parts of ¼d.

[*Reverse*]

Walsham Account of works and customary services there in the 18th year of Henry VI.

Multure at the mill For the farm of one windmill leased this year to certain millers within for money and usually leased for 10 qrs of multure to the miller.

Sum nil.

Heriots For heriots, nil.

Sum nil.

Oats For rent of the lord's tenants at the Feast of St Edmund King and Martyr, 20 qrs and two parts of half of a bus. and half a peck [*torn*].

Sum 20 qrs and 2 parts of half a bus. and half a peck [*torn*]

From which, in allowance for various tenements in the lord's hands both for this manor and for High Hall this year, 4 qrs 5½ bus. and 2 parts of half a bus. and 2 parts of a peck of oats. In sales within, 15 qrs 1 bus. 1 peck and 2 quarters of half a peck of oats.

Sum as above.   It balances.

Capons For rent of the lord's tenants there at Easter, 8 capons.

Sum 8 capons.

---

[59] Marginal note.

169

From which in allowance for various tenements in the lord's hands, 4 capons. In sales within, 4.

Sum as above.   It balances.

Hens and cockerels For rent of the lord's tenants at Christmas, 141¾ hens and cockerels of which two are cockerels.

Sum 141¾ hens and cockerels.

From which, in allowance for various tenements in the lord's hands both for this manor and for High Hall, 28¼ hens.
Delivered to the bailiff of Westhorpe by the hand of Richard Sewell tenant of High Hall in Westhorpe, one.
In sales within, 112½ hens.

Sum as above.   It balances.

Eggs For rent of the lord's tenants there at Easter, 825 eggs.

Sum 825 eggs.

From which in allowance for various tenements in the lord's hands both for this manor and for High Hall, 203½ eggs. In sales within, 621½.

Sum as above.   It balances.

Dovecote For the issues on one dovecote, nothing this year because the lord did not stock it and none came.

Sum nil.

Cumin For rent from the Prior of Bricett p.a. ½lb of cumin.

Sum shown. And sales within. It balances.

Pepper For pepper rent from John Frances for the tenement formerly of John Pinfold pertaining to High Hall, ½lb pepper.

Sum shown. And sales within.   It balances.

Ploughing services For the issues of [*blank*] customary greater tenures this year, providing [*blank*] ploughteams this year, 9 ploughing services taken at the seasons of winter and Lent, each whole ploughteam doing 5 ploughing services receiving for each plough 6 loaves of mixed grain, at 20 to the bushel, and allowed two winter works.
For the issues of [*blank*] other customary tenants that provide [*blank*] ploughteams this year, 8 ploughing services of which each ploughteam shall do 3 ploughing services and receive from the lord 6 loaves of the same grain and said weight, no allowance of works.
For the issues of customary tenants of High Hall, nothing because none here.
For customary services bought from William Hore received from the tenement Patches at the winter season, one ploughing service.

Sum 18 ploughing services. And sales within.   It balances.

Ploughales For the services of customary tenants who join this year, 6 ploughing services.

Sum 6 ploughing services. And sales within.   It balances.

Winter and summer works For the services of customary tenants for half days, 962 and a third part of a winter work.

170

Sum 962 and 3 parts of a winter work.

From which in allowance for various tenements in the lord's hands both for this manor and for High Hall, 238¼ and a third part of a winter work. In sales within, 723 and a third part of a winter work.

Sum as above.   It balances.

Carrying works For the issues of customary tenants for 7 carrying services at the will of the lord by custom, price per work, 1d.

Sum 7 carrying works. And sales within.   It balances.

Carrying of manure For the services of customary tenants without resumption, 9 carryings of manure and allowed to them for carrying manure, one winter work, price per carry, 2d.

Sum 9 carryings.

From which in allowance for various tenements in the lord's hands, 3½ carrying services. In sales within, 5½.

Sum as above.   It balances.

Weeding works For the services of customary tenants, 175 and three quarters of half a weeding work.

Sum 175 and three quarters of half a weeding work.

From which in allowance for various tenements in the lord's hands both for this manor and for High Hall, 37¾ of a weeding work. In sales within, 138 works.

Sum as above. It balances.

Mowing works For the services of customary tenants for half days, 42¼ mowing works.

Sum 42¼ mowing works.

From which in allowance for various tenements in the lord's hands, 7 mowing works. In sales within, 35¼ mowing works.

Sum as above.   It balances.

Carrying of hay For the services of customary tenants that have carts without resumption and without meadow work, nothing this year because they were respited.

Sum nil.

Haymaking works For the services of customary tenants as many as the lord requires for lifting, turning and stacking all the hay without resumption, nothing this year.

Sum nil.

Harvest works For the services of customary tenants for whole days with food provided by the lord, reaping, tying and stacking, 754 works of which each shall receive from the lord at noon and for his supper 2 loaves of mixed grain, at 20 to the bushel, and 4 herrings, price per work 2d.

Sum 754 works.

From which, in allowance for various tenements in the lord's hands both for this manor and for High Hall, 225¼ harvest works. In sales within, 528¼ harvest works.

Sum as above.   It balances.

171

Harvest boonworks For the services from custom this year 139 harvest boon-works, of which each free man shall have for his food at noon and for his supper one loaf of wheat, at 20 to the bushel. And each customary tenant shall have for his food at noon as for the free tenants and for his supper a loaf of mixed grain, at 20 to the bushel, and one herring, price per work 2d.

Sum 139 works.

From which in allowance for various tenements in the lord's hands both for this manor and for High Hall, 26 boonworks. In sales within, 113 boonworks.

Sum as above.   It balances.

Document 14: Walsham manorial account,
28 September 1440 to 28 September 1441[60]

SA/B HA504/3/12

Walsham

Account of Robert Lester, bailiff there, from the eve of St Michael the Archangel in the 19th year of Henry VI until the eve of the same St Michael next coming in the 20th year of the same Henry for one whole year.

Arrears [*blank*]

Rents of assize The same accountant answers for £13 11s. 5d. half a ¼d. and two parts of a ¼d. from rents of assize there from both free and villein tenants for both this manor and for High Hall excluding rent in Westhorpe with ward of High Hall paid at Christmas, Easter and the Nativity of St John the Baptist and St Michael by equal portions.

And for 5d. from new rent received from John Robwood for a piece of land lying at Ulveswell this year.

And for 6d. from new rent received from John Margery for a piece of land called Gorommes Way this year.

And for 1d. from new rent received from Robert Margery for a garden of the tenement Goslings.

And for 3d. from new rent received from Nicholas Brond of Gislingham for a piece of land lying in the aforesaid vill next to the land of William Goddard on the north and the land of the Templars of Gislingham on the south.

And for 2d. from new rent received from Robert Carpenter of Langham for a piece of land lying next to the land of the parson of Langham this year.

And for 2d. from new rent received from Katherine Dinglove for a piece of land lying in Mill Field this year.

And for 2d. from new rent received from Robert Warde for a piece of land lying next to Calf Pightle this year.

And for 7s. 6d. from new rent received from John Page for land and a tenement formerly Coppelowes granted to him and his heirs by court roll.

---

[60] The first court of the new lord of Walsham manor, William de la Pole, Duke of Suffolk, and Alice his wife, was held on 9 February 1441, and the handwriting and presentation of the roll are immaculate. Sixty tenants made fealty and another twelve were distrained to make fealty at the next court: SA/B HA504/1/12.23.

And for 2s. 4d. from new rent received from John Robhood for a tenement called East End tenement [*Esthedtenement*] and two messuages formerly of Nicholas Dennis granted to him by court roll.

And for 20d. from new rent received from John Ringbell for 3 acres 1 rood of pasture parcel of New Hall Pasture granted to him and his heirs by court roll.

And for 5s. 10d. from new rent received from William Syre for a cottage with a curtilage called Walpoles Croft, 1 acre of land near the sheepfold of the Prior of Ixworth and 1 acre of land next to Gurrys Croft granted to him and his heirs by court roll.

And for 2s. 10d. from new rent received from the same William for a close next to his dwelling house granted to him and his heirs by court roll.

Sum £14 13s. 4d. half a ¼d. and two parts of a ¼d.

Castle ward And for 11s. 2d. from castle ward received from the manor of Wyken for the terms of Christmas, Easter, Nativity of St John the Baptist and St Michael by equal portions.

And for 2s. 10d. from castle ward received from the manor of Ixworth this year by equal portions.

Sum 14s.

Farms And for £6 14s. 8d.[61] from the lease of the manor called Walsham Hall with all the buildings situated in the said manor with a certain close called Park Yard within the manor buildings, a sheep-fold next to Conyger Close, a piece of land containing 42 acres called Old Toft, a close called Little Meadow containing 17 acres of meadow, and all the pasture called Cow Pasture pertaining to the aforesaid manor with a small Launde on the north side of North Haugh Wood with leafy willows growing in the said pasture there, a close called Conyger Close containing 12 acres and another close called the Conyger next to the aforesaid sheepfold, a piece of land called Dovehouse Wong containing by estimate 16 acres, a piece of land called Cocks Dirt containing 18 acres, a piece of land called Brooms Wong containing 20 acres, a piece of land in the Hall Croft containing 16 acres, a piece of land near there called the Eleven Acres, a piece of land at Childerwell containing 14 acres, a close called the Launde containing 14 acres on the north side of North Haugh Wood, a piece of land above the New Close containing 10 acres, a piece of land next to Summer Way containing 11 acres, a piece of land next to Hall Green containing 18 acres, a piece of land on the west side of Fishpond Field containing 16 acres and a close called the Calk Pightle with 1 acre of land at Fishpond Field recently in farm to Adam Blayer with the liberty of a fold of up to 300 sheep, thus granted to John Fuller this year.

And for 20s. from John Ringbell for the farm of 33½ acres of land and pasture lying in a close called New Close with leafy trees growing there granted to him this year.

And for 9d. from William Potenger chaplain for 1½ acres of land parcel of New Close towards his close granted to him and his heirs by court roll.

And for 8s. from George Hawes chaplain for a piece of land containing 42 acres called the Hatchmere and 1½ acres of land lying in the Bottom formerly of Walter Terwald granted to him this year.

---

[61] John Fuller is now the farmer of this package of leases, paying £6 14s. 8d. instead of £6 6s. 8d. that William Fuller paid for the same land in the previous year.

And for 8s. 4d. from Robert Vincent for a piece of land containing 42 acres called Fishpond Field with the liberty of a fold of up to 80 sheep this year, granted to him, recently in farm to William Hawes for 8s.

And for 20s. from the bailiff for a piece of meadow called Broad Dole containing 4½ acres sold to various men this year.

And for 6s. from Robert Lester for a piece of land at Mickle Meadow and a piece of land at West Mill and 2 acres of land called Nunns Land granted to him and his heirs by court roll.

And for 12d. from Thomas Bonde for 4 acres 1 rood of land abutting upon Harts Haugh formerly of Nicholas Denys, 1½ acres of land called the Butts of the tenement Osbern at Rickinghall Willows, 2 acres of land of the tenement Cranmer next to the land formerly of Nicholas Tiptot at Rickinghall Willows next to the land formerly of John Man and the Market Mere and 2 acres of land of the tenement Burchards on the west side of Burchards Wood granted to him this year.

And for 8s. from John Cooper for two pieces of land containing 22 acres called Doucedeux, 6 acres of land called Walpoles Croft, a pightle called Jacks Yard and ½ acre of land abutting upon the land of the Prior of Ixworth granted to him and his heirs by court roll.

And for 2s. from John Robwood senior for Sheepcote Yard and 1½ acres of land at Clay Hill, two pieces of land near there of the tenement Paynes, 1½ roods of land of the tenement Dennis abutting upon the Brook, 1 acre 3 roods of land at Willow Mere of the tenement Paynes recently in farm to Alice Morton granted to him this year.

And for 2s. 8d. from the same John for 6 acres of land and pasture called Home Stall and 1½ roods of land at Burchards Wood granted to him this year.

And for 4s. 8½d. from the same John for a piece of land and pasture containing 7 acres called Howes Toft per acre 8d. granted to him this year.

And for 18d. from the same John for 1½ acres of land of the tenement Paynes, a curtilage, 3 roods of land formerly of William Payne, 2 roods of land of the tenement of William Payne with three parts of a way called Outgoing towards Westhorpe and 1 acre of land in two pieces abutting upon Hundred Mere granted to him this year.

And for 2s. 4d. from the same John for 16 acres 1 rood of land parcel of Guspers Field granted to the same John this year.

And for 5s. from Robert Lester for the Launde in Lady's Wood granted to him this year.

And for 2s. 6d. from John Swift for 1½ acres of land of the tenement Paynes next to Market Way, 5 acres of land of the tenement Paynes, 1 acre of land of the tenement Robbys abutting upon Harts Haugh, ½ acre of land at Frances Row of the tenement Robbys, 2 acres of land at Brook Pits granted to him and his heirs by court roll this year.

And for 8d. from John Robwood for 4 acres of land next to Paynes recently in the farm of William Grocer leased to him this year.

And for 4d. from the same John for land recently in the farm of the said William leased to him this year.

And for 4d. from the same John for 2 acres of land abutting upon Helpes Wood leased to him this year.

And for 2s. 4d. from the same John for 16 acres of land at Guspers Field leased to him this year.

For [blank] received last year for the farm of 4 acres of land lying next to the close of the said William Grocer on the east side, nothing because it is in poor condition this year.

Thus received for [*blank*] 15d. from John Tiptot senior for 5 acres of land parcel of Guspers Field leased to him this year.

And for 8s. <7s. 11d.> from George Hawes chaplain for 7 acres of land parcel of Guspers Field of which one head abuts upon Harts Haugh, two pieces of land containing 4 acres in the field of Angrave of the tenement formerly of Agnes de Angerhale and for the herbage of a piece of meadow at Harts Haugh with pasture at the head of the same granted to him by court roll this year.

And for 2s. from John Ringbell for a close lying at Hall Gate on the north side of his messuage granted to him this year.

And for 10d. from John Deye for Godfreys Yard with 1½ acres of land of the same tenement leased to him this year.

And for 8s. from the bailiff reckoned for 7 roods of meadow lying in Mickle Meadow in two pieces of meadow leased to various tenants of the lord this year and last year the price received was 9s.

And for 9d. from Katherine Dinglove for 1 acre of land of the tenement Cranmer at Hulkes Bridge and 3 roods of land of the tenement Kebbils recently leased to John Cook granted to her and her heirs by court roll.

And for 12d. from John Fletcher for 3½ acres of land in various pieces of the tenement Kebbils leased to him this year.

And for 2s. from George Hawes chaplain for 18 acres of land called Blunts Hall leased to him this year.

And for 3s. 4d. from John Swift for 8 acres in Long Wheat in one piece, 4 acres of land of the said tenement lying at the end of the croft of Thomas Bonde granted to him and his heirs by court roll.

And for 3d. from John Fletcher for 1 acre of land of the tenement Robbys lying on the south side of Trendle Wood leased to him this year.

And for 4½d. from John Robwood for 1½ roods of land of the tenement Paynes at the head of the croft of the said John recently Martins Croft and 1 rood of land at the north head of the same recently in farm to Alice Morton leased to him this year.

And for 2d. from John Ermitt for ½ acre of land next to the Green Way formerly of John son of Oldenhog [*sic*] of the tenement Man leased to him this year.

And for 2d. from William Fuller for 1 acre of land abutting upon Wood Way of the same tenement at Pedders Path, ½ acre of land of the tenement Ratches lying at the Dales recently leased for 7d.

And for 6d. from John Robwood for 3 roods of land lying in the croft of Godfreys of the tenement of William Payne leased to him this year.

And for 3d. from Thomas Wells for 1 acre of land of the tenement Clevehog above the Brook leased to him this year.

And for 12d. from John Fletcher for a messuage and 2½ roods of land lying in the croft recently of Walter Denys remaining in the lord's hands by Robert Osbern granted to him and his heirs by court roll.

And for 2s. from Thomas Fletcher for 5 acres of land on the east side of Fishpond Field next to the land of Robert Sare and 2 acres of land lying next to Trendle Wood granted to him this year.

And for 18d. from Thomas Wells for 3 acres of land of the tenement Paynes, 6 acres of land formerly of Nicholas Dennis lying at New Hall granted to him this year.

And for 2d. from Robert Carpenter for 1½ roods of land in three parcels in the field of Langham recently leased to John Margery leased to him this year.

And for 5s. 10d. from John Tiptot junior for two headlands containing 1 rood parcel of the tenement of Peter Painter at Harts Haugh pasture of Painters Yard, 1 acre 3 roods of land in two pieces of the tenement of Peter Painter recently leased to Robert Bray, 5 acres 3 roods of land in six pieces of the same tenement of which 3 acres in three pieces lie in the field of Ashfield and 2 acres 3 roods of land in three pieces at the Brook recently leased to John Brook, 1 acre 1 rood of land abutting upon the Brook towards the east of the same tenement recently leased to Robert Man, 3 roods of land in one piece of the same tenement next to Ashfield Way recently leased to John Ermitt, ½ acre of land at Brook Bridge of the same tenement recently leased to Robert Man, 2 acres of land of the tenement Pudding lying at Procession Way abutting upon Hundred Mere, 1 rood of land of the said tenement next to Stubbing Way next to the land formerly of Richard Qwalm, 3 acres of land of the same tenement near East Mill in three pieces recently leased to Walter Frances granted to him and his heirs by court roll.

And for 3s. from John Fuller for a close recently of Robert Cokerell lying next to Lady's Wood leased to him this year.

And for 106s. 8d.[62] from John Robwood for the farm of a close called Katherines Croft with hedges and ditches there, a piece of land containing by estimate 6 acres with leafy willows there called Gurrys Croft, two pieces of land containing 4½ acres lying at Trendle Wood, a piece of land containing 5 roods called Stony Land, a piece of land containing 5 roods lying in South Field, 4 acres of land called Knots Hedge, a close called Sheephouse Close, 3 roods of meadow lying in Mickle Meadow, a close called Ox Pasture with hedges and ditches there, a piece of land containing 6 acres called Godelards Land, 10 acres of land parcel of Guspers Field, with the herbage of a meadow in Small Brook, a curtilage formerly Robetels with ½ acre of land formerly of William Payne, 2 acres of land formerly of Robert Fornham near Godelards Land next to the land formerly of William Payne and 1 rood of land at Willow Mere formerly of Adam Pitlake, 2 acres 2½ roods of land recently of Walter Dennis remaining in the lord's hands abutting upon Hundred Mere, the herbage \5s./ of a piece of meadow called Turfpit Acre, a piece of land called the Holner, 12 acres of land next to Nether Haugh, a close called Burchards Close, 18 acres of land lying in Burchards Croft, a piece of land lying in High Hall Croft, a close called High Hall Close, a piece of land called Nether Haugh Close, a piece of land called Seventeen Acres, 18 acres of land called Blunts Land, 12 acres of land at Allwood Green [*Aldel Grene*] recently leased to Robert Payne and for the farm of a tenement formerly of John Syre at East End the liberty of a fold leased to him this year and last year it was leased to the said John for 103s. 4d.

And for 13s. 6d. from the same John for Paynes tenement lying in East End of the lord's bondage granted to him by court roll.

And for 16d. from John Fuller for 1 rood of meadow recently of John Ermitt lying in Mickle Meadow leased to him this year and in the preceding year it was in farm to him for 12d.

And for 6d. from Richard Poyken for a messuage, once with a house, formerly of Alice Rampley granted to him and his heirs by court roll.

Sum £19 15s. 6d.

176

Perquisites of court And for 20s. 2d. from perquisites of one general court held there on Thursday next before the Feast of St Scolastice the Virgin in the 19th year of the king for the same roll.

And for 3s. 3d. from perquisites of another court held there on Monday next after the Feast of the Nativity of the Blessed Virgin Mary in the 20th year of the king within the time of this account as shown by this roll.

Sum 23s. 5d.

Farm of the mill And for 20s. from [*blank*] for the farm of a windmill leased this year and in the preceding year leased for 23s. 4d.

Sum 20s.

Works and customary services sold – And for 40s. 5½d. and half a ¼d. from 15 quarters 1 bushel 1¾ peck of oats from rent sold as elsewhere, price per quarter 2s. 8d.

And for 10d. from 4 capons from rent sold as elsewhere, price per capon 2½d.

And for 14s. 0¾d. from 111½ hens from rent sold as elsewhere, price per head 1½d.

And for 20¾d. from 621½ eggs from rent sold as elsewhere, price per 120 4d.

And for 1½d. from ½lb cumin from rent sold as elsewhere.

And for 5d. from ½lb pepper from rent sold as elsewhere.

And for 9s. from 18 ploughing services from services sold elsewhere, price per ploughing 6d.

And for 3s. from 6 Ploughales from services sold as elsewhere.

And for 30s. 1¾d. from 723¾ winter works from services sold as elsewhere, price per work ½d.

And for 7d. from 7 carrying works from services sold as elsewhere.

And for 11d. from 5½ carryings of manure from services sold as elsewhere, price per work 2d.

And for 5s. 9d. from 138 weeding works from services sold as elsewhere, price per work ½d.

And for 4s. 4½d. and quarter of half a ¼d. from 35¼ mowings from services sold as elsewhere, price per work 1½d.

And for £4 8s. 0½d. from 528¼ harvest works from services sold as elsewhere, price per work 2d.

And for 18s. 10d. from 113 harvest boonworks from services sold as elsewhere, price per work 2d.

Sum £10 18s. 3¾d.

Sales of wood and underwood From wood and underwood sold there this year, nothing because it was used by the lord and for hospitality at Westhorpe.

Sum nil.

Issues of the dovehouse From profits of the proceeds of the pigeons in the dovecote within the manor there, nothing because the farmer received them as part of the terms of his lease. Sum nil.

Foreign receipts Nil.

Sum nil.

Sales at the audit Nil.

Total sum of receipts £48 4s. 7d. and two parts of ¼d.[63]

Rent resolute with decays From which allowed to Thomas Wells reeve there for services and works of his tenure for the sake of his office this year, 6s. 2¾d.

And allowed to John Tiptot junior, hayward there for works and services now of him for the sake of his office released this year, 4s. 11d.

Item reckoned in rent resolute for the hall of Thelnetham of 2s., nothing because it is outside the lord's hands.

Item the hall of Rickinghall p.a., 3s. 1½d.

Item paid for castle ward of Norwich p.a., 16s.

Item paid to John Margery p.a. 1½d.

Item in allowance of rent for various tenements in the lord's hands both for this manor and for High Hall 52s. 5¼d. and half a quarter of ¼d. and two parts of ¼d., of which for High Hall 15s. 11¾d.

Item paid to the hall of Ashfield for castle ward for High Hall p.a., 17d.

Item paid to the same hall for rent p.a., 2d.

Item paid to the castle of Eye twice this year, 18d.

Item for hundred suit released p.a. for Burchards, 16d.

Item paid to Helimot and for ward for Burchards p.a., 9d.

Item in rent resolute for Sir William Bardwell for 1 acre of meadow at Turf Pits purchased by the lord from John Rampley, chaplain, 4d.

Item in allowance of rent on 4 acres of land remaining in the lord's hands by John Syre, 18d. and three quarters of ¼d. and a third part of ¼d.

Item in allowance of the tenement formerly of John Spilman granted to John Bertram free by charter, 10s. 7¼d. and half a quarter of ¼d.

Item in allowance on ½ acre of land of the tenement Coppelowes granted to him in the same way, 6d.

Item in allowance on 1½ acres of land formerly of John Page granted to him, 6½d.

Item in allowance on a piece of land of the tenement of John Fuller granted to him in the same way, 7d.

Item in allowance on ½ acre of land recently leased to Thomas Bonde of the tenement Goslings from the lord's demesne granted to him in the same way, 3d.

Item in allowance on the tenement Gorys and for a parcel of the tenement Master Johns granted to him in the same way, 3¾d.

Item in allowance of a tenement formerly of John Syre because the lord has all the profits of the same tenement at farm as above, 5½d. with the price of a hen sold above.

In allowed rent of the tenement Paynes taken into the lord's hands and at farm as above, 15s. 4d. and a quarter of a ¼d.

Item paid to the castle of Eye this year once, 9d.

And in the following year paid twice, that is 18d.

Item allowed for a messuage formerly built in Church Street formerly of Alice Rampley taken into the lord's hands, 13d.

Sum 118s. 3d.

Cost of the buildings And in the cost of various buildings made this year as a parcel shown in a bill upon this account indicated and examined and not noted in this account and other adjoining accounts, 79s.

---

[63] No wood or underwood was sold, although there were transfers to the lord's residence at Westhorpe Hall: perhaps it was being improved and renovated.

Sum 79s.

Cost of the mill And in various costs made upon the lord's mill this year as a parcel shown in the said bill upon this account indicated, examined and proved and not noted as above, 6s. 1d.

Sum 6s. 1d.

Minute costs None this year.

Sum nil.

Weeding and mowing – In weeding corn, nothing this year. And in mowing the meadows, nothing this year.

Sum nil.

Foreign expenses with expenses of the steward of the court
Thus the aforesaid accountant seeks allowances for the expenses of his horse going from Walsham towards Norwich for certain reasons touching the lord's money there and delivering it to the general receiver of the lord <there>, 12d.
And in the expenses of the steward of the lord's court and other expenses there being for the abovesaid court held there all reckoned in money, 10s. 9d.

Sum 11s. 9d.

Annuities And paid to John Belleys for his annuity 20 marks, because the lord and lady granted it both for his lease shown and through a letter issued to the receiver, farmer, bailiff, collector of the said manor who is therefore directed to make this payment and shall be audited and allowed within the account the same allowances, as dated on the last day of April in the 19th year of the king paying at the terms of the Nativity of St John the Baptist, Michaelmas, Christmas and Easter by equal portions. That is, for the terms of the Nativity of St John the Baptist and Michaelmas within the terms of this account taken for one acquittance for the aforesaid John Belleys, £6 13s. 4d.

Sum £6 13s. 4d.

Wages of the bailiff And in the wages of the said bailiff reckoned, nothing because he had from the lord certain land and tenement by an adjoined bill for having the office of bailiff.

Sum nil.

Cash delivered And delivered to Simon Braillis, clerk, Receiver General of the lord's money for part of an acquittance paid on the first day of May in the 19th year of Henry VI, £10.
And delivered to the same Simon, Receiver General of the lord's money, for one acquittance paid on the last day of June in the said 19th year, £6.
S. Braillis. Sum £16.

Total sum of expenses and payments, £33 8s. 5d., 2 parts of a ¼d. And thus owed to the lord, £14 16s. 2d. [*illeg.*]

[*The account ends here*]

Document 15: Walsham account, 29 September 1441 to 29 September 1442

SA/B HA504/3/13

Walsham

Account of John Robwood, farmer[64] there, from the Feast of St Michael the Arch-angel in the 20th year of Henry VI to the Feast of St Michael the Archangel in the 21st year of the same king, that is for one whole year.

Arrears The same is charged and answers for 30s. 0¼d. half and two parts of ¼d. from the arrears of the last account, as is contained there.

Sum 30s. 0¼d. half and two parts of ¼d.

Rents of assize For £14 13s. 4d. half a ¼d. and two parts of ¼d. p.a. from rents of assize with the farm of land, as in the account of the preceding year, nothing because it pertains to the said farmer by the terms of his lease.

Sum nil.

Castle ward For 14s. from castle ward p.a., nothing here because it pertains to the said farmer by the terms of his lease.

Sum nil.

Perquisites of court For perquisites of court, nothing because aforesaid.[65]

Sum nil.

Farm of the mill For 20s. recently received from the farm of a windmill, nothing because aforesaid.

Sum nil.

Works and services sold For £10 18s. 3½d. and half a ¼d. from works and services sold, nothing because aforesaid.

Sum nil.

Sales of underwood Nothing this year.

Sum nil.

Profits on the dovecote Nothing because it pertains to the said farmer by the terms of his lease.

Sum nil.

Farm of the manor The same answers for £44 from the farm of the manor of Walsham and the manor called High Hall, alias Wildcats, with all their appurte-

---

[64] The manor is now leased in its entirety. John Robwood is the 'farmer', meaning the lessee, who receives all the income due to the manor, including the proceeds of the manorial court. He also runs the demesne, which is partially stocked, and has the option to utilise or (more likely) commute the labour services. As a result, he is solely responsible for the account.

[65] Often the lord retained direct control over the manor court and the receipt of its income when the rest of the manor was leased, but here the court revenues are included in the lease. The summary of the terms of the lease of the manor makes clear that the lord's steward will continue to preside over the court, thus retaining control over the jurisdictional aspects of the manor, including the lord's rights.

nances in the county of Suffolk, [with] ward, marriage fines, reliefs, escheats, woods, underwood, and the advowson of the church excepted.[66] Thus leased to the said John Robwood and his attorney for the term of five years by an indenture which is dated 28th day of October in the 20th year, this year is the first, paying at Easter and Michaelmas by equal portions. And paying, making and bearing all other charges of the said manor with appurtenances during the aforesaid term, except the repair of the [demesne] houses and the mill which are supported by the lord. Providing always that all who take any lands and tenements [leased] for a term of years shall be included in his contract paying to the said farmer. The same farmer shall have underwood for maintaining the closes as above and other offices of the lord. And the court of the lord there shall be held by the steward and the counsel of the lord according to custom.[67] And the expenses of the said farmer with submitted claims are to be presented 15 days after the said feast for default of payment of arrears etc. The same farmer shall have for his clothing each year, such that general clothing[68] [general' vestura] is given, and he is allowed 6s. 8d. for the said gift.

Sum £44.

Sum total of receipts with arrears £45 10s. 0¼d. half and two parts of a ¼d.

Rent resolute with decays From 118s. 3d. from rent resolute with decays p.a. as shown in the account for the preceding year, nothing here because paid by the farmer by the terms of his lease.

Sum nil.

Cost of the buildings From that accountant, because he paid for a load of straw bought for thatching the south side of the barn, also on the hall and the bakehouse, 6s. 8d.
And in nails bought, 2d.
And in the stipend of John Frances, thatcher, for thatching upon the said building in defective places for 9 days, taking per day with his servant 7d. per day, 5s. 3d.
And in the stipend of John Bonde, thatcher, thatching for one day with his servant by task, 7d.
And in the stipend of John Frances similarly for 1½ days with his servant, 10½d.
And in the stipend of John Manser, carpenter with his servant, hired for one day to make a middle row [medellwowe] in the long stable and two trestles for a table within the hall, 8d.

Sum 14s. 2½d.

Cost of the mill house And in the stipend of John Manser, carpenter, hired to make a new mill house for 22 days, per day 4d., 7s. 4d.

---

66 The lease of the manor is clearly distinguishing the core physical resources of the manor – land, buildings, etc. – contained within the lease from its core jurisdiction rights, including the right to appoint the priest to the parish church, which are excluded.

67 The status of the manorial court is often unclear when manors were leased in their entirety. This lease is unequivocal that the lord continues to run the court – not the lessee – with his own officials, which explains why the rolls of the court continued to be recorded to a high standard and were retained among the muniments of the manor.

68 Seigniorial officials were often provided with the livery clothing of their lord as part of their remuneration package. This reference is rather obscure, but suggests that the farmer was being given an allowance for clothing generally rather than issued with clothing depicting the livery of the lord.

181

And paid for fitting laths and daubing the same house, altogether 3s.
And paid for thatching the same house, altogether 4s.
And in straw bought for thatching the said house, 6s.
And paid for cutting down timber with carriage of the same, 12d.
And in iron bands with nails bought from John Smith for tying the mill sail, 2s. 1d.

Sum 23s. 5d.

Minute costs And paid for cleaning the common water-course next to Mickle Meadow by order of the lord's steward, 8s.
And in the stipend of a labourer hired for 2½ days cutting underwood around the lord's wood, 10d.
And in the stipend of John Frances cutting down and making 140 perches of [blank] in [torn] wood, altogether 6s.
And in the stipend of one labourer stopping up gaps in defective places for 2 days, 10d.

Sum 15s. 8d.

Weeding and mowing Nothing, because pertaining to the farmer.

Sum nil.

Foreign expenses Nil.

Sum nil.

Expenses of the steward of the court Nothing, because pertaining to the farmer.

Sum nil.

Annuities Thus in the annuity of John Belley esq. [torn] granted 20 marks p.a. paid at the Feast of the Nativity of St John the Baptist, St Michael the Archangel, Christmas [torn] by equal portions viz: at the terms of Christmas, Easter, Nativity of St John and Michaelmas within the account here.
This allowance is authorised through a letter issued by the lord and lady to the receiver, farmer, bailiff and the collector of rents and farms of the said manor of Walsham who is therefore directed to do this for the duration of the life of the said John Belley to be paid and audited by the account of the aforesaid manor who for the time of the lease is commanded to pay the sum in money for which payment he ought to be allowed [against this account]. Wherefore the certain letter is dated on the last day of April in the 29th year of the reign of Henry VI. And paid during the period of the account through the hands of John Wareyn, attorney of the said John Belley, by the same John Wareyn etc., £13 6s. 8d.

Sum £13 6s. 8d.

Bailiff's wages Nothing this year.

Sum nil.

Cash delivered And delivered to John Squire, clerk, Receiver General of the lord for the arrears of Robert Lester, recently bailiff there at Haughley [Haghley] on 26th day of October [torn], 22s. 1d.
And delivered to the same receiver by a bill given at [torn] day of April, £11 6s. 8d.
And delivered to the same receiver at Walsham on the 32nd [sic] day of October in the 21st year of the same king, in the presence of the accountant at the audit of the account, £7 6s. 8d.

182

And delivered to the same receiver on the 23rd day of June, 66s. 8d.

And delivered to the same receiver at Ipswich on the 3rd day of December, as the same receiver acknowledged etc., 46s. 8d.

And delivered to the same receiver by the hand of John Joyntour, clerk, as the same receiver acknowledged etc., 33s. 4d.

Sum £27 2s. 1d.

Sum of all expenses and payments £43 2s. 0½d.

And thus he owes 47s. 11¾d. half and two parts of a ¼d., which is carried forward to the following account.

Of which, on Robert Lister bailiff there in the preceding year, 7s. 11¼d. half a ¼d., and two parts of a ¼d. And on John Robhood, farmer there this year, 40s. 0½d.

[*Reverse*]

Walsham

Account there from the Feast of St Michael [*torn*] … Henry [*torn*] … 21st by John Robhood, farmer there.

[*blank*]

Document 16: Walsham account, 29 September 1443 to 29 September 1444

SA/B HA504/3/14

Walsham

Account of John Robwood, farmer there, from the Feast of St Michael the Archangel in the 22nd year of Henry VI until the Feast of St Michael the Archangel in the 23rd year of the same king, that is for one whole year.

Arrears The same is charged and answers for £7 9¾d. half a ¼d. and two parts of a ¼d. from arrears of the last account, as contained there.

Sum shown.

Rents of assize For £14 13s. 4d. half a ¼d. and two parts of a ¼d. from rents of assize with the farm of the lands p.a. as in the account of the 4th year past, nothing because it pertains to the said farmer by the terms of his lease.

Sum nil.

Castle ward For 14s. from castle ward p.a., nothing this year because it pertains to the said farmer by the terms of his lease.

Sum nil.

Perquisites of court For perquisites of court, nothing because aforesaid.

Sum nil.

Farm of the mill For 20s. recently received from the farm of a windmill, nothing because aforesaid.

Sum nil.

Works and services sold For £10 18s. 3¾d. and half a ¼d. from works and services sold, nothing because aforesaid.

Sum nil.

Sales of wood and underwood Nothing this year.

Sum nil.

Profits of the dovecote Nothing because it pertains to the farmer by the terms of his lease.

Sum nil.

Farm of the manor The same answers for £44 from the farm of the manor of Walsham and the manor called High Hall, alias Wildcats, with all its appurtenances in the county of Suffolk, with ward, marriage fines, reliefs, escheats, woods, underwood, and the advowson of the church excepted. Thus leased to the said John Robwood and his attorney for the term of 5 years by an indenture, this year is the 3rd paying as shown in the preceding account.

Sum £44.

Sum total of receipts with arrears £51 0s. 9¾d. half a ¼d. and two parts of a ¼d.

Rent resolute From 118s. 3d. from rent resolute with decays p.a. as shown in the account four years ago, nothing because it was absorbed by the farmer by agreement of his lease.

Sum nil.

Cost of the buildings Thus the aforesaid accountant paid for a load of wheat and rye straw bought from the said accountant with carriage for thatching the wall next to the gate of the manor, 2s.
And in the stipend of John Frances for one day and Thomas Bonde, thatchers, for 1½ days thatching the said wall taken per day between them 4d. by task, 10d.
And in the stipend of their servants hired for the same time to work on the said thatch, 7½d.
And paid for collecting pegs for thatching [*sprengell*], broaches [*broches*] and bands for the same work, 2d.

Sum 3s. 7½d.

Cost of the mill And in 4 iron bands bought from John Smith for tying the axle and sailyard of the mill, 2s.
And in nails bought for the same work, 2d.
And in the stipend of John Mollows, carpenter hired for 2 days to work on a new sailyard of the mill, taken per day 5d. by task, 10d.
And in the stipend of Andrew Hawes, carpenter working upon the same work for 3 days, taken per day 4d. by task, 12d.
And in the stipend of John Manser, carpenter making cogs and staves for the mill trundle-wheel for 4 days, per day 5d., 20d.

Sum 5s. 8d.

Minute costs And in the stipend of John Frances cutting underwood and making hedges around the woods called Burchards and Luchesdell for 16 days, taken per day 4d. by task, 5s. 4d.

And paid to Thomas Murrell, labourer, stopping up small openings in wood hedges in the most defective places for 3 days, taken per day 4d. by task, 12d.

Sum 6s. 4d.

Annuities And in an annuity of John Belley esq. this year, nothing here because it was paid by the receiver.

Sum nil.

Weeding and mowing Nothing because pertaining to the said farmer.

Sum nil.

Foreign expenses Nothing.

Sum nil.

Wages of the bailiff Nothing this year.

Sum nil.

Cash delivered The aforesaid accountant delivered to John Squire clerk, general receiver of the lord's money, by the hand of John Dolet as the same receiver there acknowledged in the above account, £22.

Sum £22.

Sum of all expenses and payments £22 15s. 7½d.

And thus owed to the lord, £28 5s. 2¼d.

From which, in allowances of the same accountant £7, which was delivered to the receiver for the cost of 20 bullocks as received there, acknowledged upon the account.

And allowed to the same £6 12d., which was delivered to the said receiver at Eye on the 24th day of October in the 23rd year upon account, of which by the hand of John Dolet 21s.

And allowed to the same 62s. 1d., which was delivered to the said receiver by the hand of John Dolet as in money paid of which ?*quarryour* etc.

And thus owed to the lord, £11 13s. 1¼d. half and two parts of a ¼d.

Of which, on Robert Lester, bailiff there in the 4th year past, 7s. 11¼d. half a ¼d. and two parts of a ¼d.

On John Robwood, farmer there this year, £11 5s. 2d.

Document 17: Walsham account, 29 September 1444 to 29 September 1445

SA/B HA504/3/15 m.7

Walsham

Account of William Fuller, farmer there, from the Feast of St Michael the Archangel in the 23rd year of Henry VI until the feast of St Michael the Archangel in the 24th year of the same king, that is for one whole year.

Arrears The same is charged and answers for £11 13s. 1¼d. a half and two parts of a ¼d. from arrears of the last account thus contained there.
Sum £11 13s. 1¼d. a half and two parts of a ¼d.

Rents of assize For £14 13s. 4d. half a ¼d. and two parts of a ¼d. from rents of assize with the farm of the land p.a. as in the account of the last year there recorded and itemised, not documented here because it pertains to the said farmer by the terms of his contract.
Sum nil.

Castle ward For 14s. from castle ward p.a. received, nothing here because it pertains to the said farmer by the terms of his contract.
Sum nil.

Perquisites of court For perquisites of court, nothing here because aforesaid.
Sum nil.

Farm of the mill For 20s recently received from the farm of a windmill, nothing because aforesaid.
Sum nil.

Works and customary services For £10 18s. 3¾d. and half a ¼d. from works and customary services sold, nothing because aforesaid.
Sum nil.

Sale of wood and underwood For this, nothing this year.
Sum nil.

Profits on the dovecote For profits on the same, nothing received here because it pertains to the said farmer by the terms of his contract.
Sum nil.

Farm of the manor The same answers for £44 from the lease of the manor of Walsham, with the manor called High Hall alias Wildcats, with all their appurtenances in the county of Suffolk, with ward, marriage fines, relief, escheats, woods, underwood and the advowson of the church excepted and reserved to the lord. Thus granted to the said William Fuller and his attorney for the term of [*blank*] years by an indenture of the lord, this year is the first, paying:
Sum £44.

Sum total of receipts with arrears £55 13s. 1¼d. half a ¼d. and two parts of a ¼d.

Rent resolute From 118s. 3d. from rent resolute with decays p.a. as shown in the account of the last year, nothing because it was paid by the farmer by agreement of his contract.
Sum nil.

Cost of the buildings and walls As in the aforesaid account shown allowed for the stipend of John Tolcent, carpenter, hired for one day to make two trestles and to put bars [*legges*] and boards of poplar on the manor gate there by task, 4d.

And in the stipend of Peter Umfrey, carpenter, working upon the aforesaid task for the same time, 4d.

And in the stipend of John Manser, carpenter, working upon the same task for the said time, 4d.

And in two boards of poplar with nails bought for the same task, 5d.

And in four cartloads of straw bought for thatching one building called the Long-house with 4d. for carriage of the same, 3s. 10d.

And in the stipend of Thomas Bonde, thatcher, thatching upon the said building for 5 days together with the stipend of a labourer hired to serve the same, taken per day between them 7d. by task, 2s. 11d.

And on one cartload of straw bought from John Robwood for thatching a barn at Wildcats with carriage of the same, 14d.

And in the stipend of John Frances, thatcher, thatching upon the said barn for 2 days with the stipend of his servant, taken per day between them 8d. by task, 16d.

And in the stipend of William Syre, labourer, hired for one day to throw clay for ramming the barn there by task, 4d.

And in the stipend of the same William and Thomas Murrell hired for 2 days to ram plaster on the barn there by task, 16d.

Sum 12s. 4d.

Minute expenses And in the stipend of the said Thomas Murrell, labourer, hired for 3 days to make hedges and stop up gaps around the lord's wood called Lady's Wood, taken per day 4d. by task, 12d.

Sum 12d.

Annuities And in an annuity of John Belley esq., nothing here because it was paid by the receiver.

Sum nil.

Weeding and mowing [blank]

Foreign expenses And of these nothing this year.

Wages of the bailiff [blank]

Sum nil.

Cash delivered[69] Thus delivered to John Squyre, clerk, receiver general of the lord's money in part payment of the arrears of John Robwood, recently farmer there, without a bill in the presence of John Baron of Bildeston [Bilston] as the same receiver acknowledges upon this account, 40s.

And the same receiver for part of a fine of William Fuller, farmer, accounts for 40s. by the hand of John Dolet on the first occasion; for 26s. 8d. by the hand of the same John on the second occasion on 16th September; and for 18s. by the hand of the same John Dolet on the third occasion at Eye on 11th November in the 24th year, as the same receiver acknowledges upon this account, £4 4s. 8d.

And the same receiver by the hand of John Belley Esquire [armiger] by a bill dated 16th April in the 23rd year as the same acknowledges, £6 13s. 4d.

---

[69] The entire 'Cash delivered' section is bracketed in the margin with the words 'received J Squyre'.

And the same receiver by his own hand at Eye on 11th November in the 24th year before the auditors upon the account, £8.

Sum £21 18s.

Sum of all payments and deliveries £21 11s. 4d.

And thus owed to the lord, £34 21¼d. half a ¼d. two parts of a ¼d.

[70]Of which, allowed to the same farmer on account, 8s. 8d. following the advice and counsel of the lord, because he did not repair the windmill there this year.

And allowed to John Robwood recently the farmer there, 30s. because he delivered the same to the receiver general on [*blank*] day [*blank*] 24th year of the aforesaid king by the hand of John Dolet, as the same receiver acknowledged upon the account.

And thus owed to the lord, £32 3s. 1¼d. half a ¼d. two parts of a ¼d.

From which, allowed to the same accountant £9, because he delivered to the said receiver general after the account by the hand of John Dolet of Westhorpe, as the same receiver acknowledged on the date of the account.

And allowed to the same, 53s. 4d. because he delivered to the same receiver general at Westhorpe on the 7th February in the said 24th year and the same receiver acknowledged it.

And the same accountant, 66s. 8d. because he delivered the same to the receiver general by a bill dated 9th March in the said 24th year by the hand of the said John Dolet, as the same receiver acknowledges upon the date of the account.

And thus owed to the lord finally, £17 3s. 1¼d. half a ¼d. two parts of a ¼d.

Of this, on Robert Lester, bailiff there in the year now last past, as shown in the preceding account, 7s. 11¼d. half a ¼d. two parts of a ¼d.

On John Robwood, farmer there in the year last past, for arrears of his lease, £7 15s. 2d.

On William Fuller, the current farmer, to clear his debt, £9.

Document 18: Walsham account, 29 September 1445 to 29 September 1446

SA/B HA504/3/15 m.10

Walsham

Account of William Fuller, farmer there, from the Feast of St Michael the Archangel in the 24th year of Henry VI until the Feast of St Michael in the 25th year of the same king for one whole year.

Arrears The same is charged and answers for £17 3s. 1¼d. half a ¼d. and two parts of a ¼d. from arrears of the last account thus contained there.

Sum £17 3s. 1¼d. half a ¼d. and two parts of a ¼d.

Rents of assize For £14 13s. 4d. half a ¼d. and two parts of a ¼d. from rents of assize with the farm of the land p.a. as in the account of two years now past there recorded and itemised, nothing received here because it pertains to the said farmer by the terms of his lease.

Sum nil.

---

[70] Marginal note, 'Received John Squyre'.

Castle ward For 14s. from castle ward p.a. received, nothing this year because it pertains to the said farmer by the terms of his lease.
Sum nil.

Perquisites of court For perquisites of court, nothing this year because aforesaid.
Sum nil.

Farm of the mill For 20s. recently received from the farm of a windmill, nothing because aforesaid.
Sum nil.

Works and services sold For £10 18s. 3¾d. and half a ¼d. from works and services sold, nothing because aforesaid.
Sum nil.

Sale of wood and underwood For the same, nothing this year.
Sum nil.

Profits of the dovecote For profits of the same, nothing this year because it pertains to the said farmer by the terms of his lease.
Sum nil.

Farm of the manor Thus received from £44 from the farm of the manor of Walsham and the manor called High Hall, alias Wildcats, with all their appurtenances in the county of Suffolk, ward, marriage fines, reliefs, escheats, woods, underwood and advowson of the church excepted and reserved. Thus granted to the said William Fuller and his attorney for the term of [*blank*] years by an indenture of the lord, this year is the second, paying:
Sum £44.

Sum total of receipts with arrears £61 3s. 1½d.

Rent resolute The same accounts for rent resolute with decays viz: 118s. 3d. p.a. as shown in the above-said account, nothing here because by the said farmer.
Sum nil.

Costs of the manor buildings and the tenement called Syres Thus the accountant paid for a load of straw bought from John Bene by estimate 8 cartloads with carriage of the same from the rectory to the manor, altogether 9s.
And in a load of straw bought from William Fuller this is reckoned at 4 cartloads with carriage, price 3s. 4d.
And in the stipend of John Frances, thatcher for 22½ days thatching the stables \11 days/ and the cowshed [*illeg.*] and the kitchen \2½ days/ in the same manor with the stipend of a servant in service for the same time, taken per day 7d. by task, 13s. 1½d.
And in the stipend of Peter Umfrey, carpenter hired for half a day to make a screen with the placing [*impoc'*] of the same and shingles [*sindul*] upon the said kitchen, 2½d.
And in one load of straw bought for thatching the said tenement Syres with carriage of the same, 5s. 10d.

189

And in the stipend of Thomas Bonde, thatcher hired for 9 days to thatch the said tenement called Syres in the east end of the same with the stipend of one servant hired for the same time to help the same, taken per day between them 7d., by task, 5s. 3d.

And in the stipend of one man hired for one day to gather broaches and bindings for the same work, 4d.

And in the stipend of Peter Umfrey, carpenter hired for 3½ days to mend various carpentry defects in the same tenement, taken per day [blank], 13½d.

And in nails bought for the said work, 2d.

Sum 38s. 4½d.

Cost of the mill And in the stipend of [blank] hired with his cart to carry a mill-stone from Ipswich to the mill in the same vill [i.e. Walsham] through a certain contract, 4s.

And in the stipend of John Fish, carpenter hired with his servant for 8½ days to make a new trundle-wheel, laths, sail openings and shrouds[71] [shrowdes] for the sailyard of the said mill and to make the wyndwoghe with the new lower cog wheel [keggyng rote inferior] and other work, taken per day between them 9d. by task, 6s. 4½d.

And in the stipend of Peter Umfrey and Thomas Page, sawyers hired for 2 days to saw planks of the lord's timber for the sail openings of the said mill, 12d.

And in 100 feet of planks bought from John Manser for the said wyndwough with the making of the same, 22d.

And in nails bought for the said work, 2d.

And in 2 bands bought from John Smith for tying the said trundle-wheel, 10d.

And paid to the same for mending the spindle of the same and the rynds, 4d.

And in a support[72] [bolstyr] bought from the same for the same mill, 6d.

And in the stipend of John Miller of Wattisfield hired to dress [verberand'] and raise the said millstone by agreement, 2s.

Sum 17s. 2½d.

Annuities And paid to John Belley esq. for his annuity of 20 marks p.a. which lord William de la Pole and Alice his wife have granted to the aforesaid John for the term of his life, levied from the issues and profits of this manor of Walsham for the terms of Easter, Christmas, Nativity of St John the Baptist and Michaelmas equally divided, paid by the hand of the receiver, collector and farmer there as shown in a letter patent of the lord and Alice, made with the same John, dated 29th April in the 19th year of the aforesaid king and enrolled with this account.[73] That is, by payment to him on the said terms within the said time of this account, which has been done [accidentur], £13 6s. 8d.

Sum £13 6s. 8d.

Cash delivered And in cash delivered to John Squire clerk, receiver general of the lord's money, by the hand of the said farmer for his arrears from the previous year by a bill delivered on 17th May in the 25th year, £9.

---

71 The millstone was probably one imported from Germany. The shrouds were a protective addition to the sails.

72 The support was probably the neck bearing.

73 The letter is copied onto the reverse of the account, and is translated below.

And paid to the same receiver by the hand of the said farmer from this year's issues, that is on 17th May in the same year 30s., and on 11th October in the 24th year £13 10s., including £6 by the hand of John Dolet, total £15.

And to the same receiver by the hand of the same farmer from issues of his office upon production of this account, 53s. 4d.

Sum of cash delivered £26 13s. 4d.

Sum of allowances and deliveries £42 15s. 7d.

And thus he owes, £18 7s.

[74]Of which, allowed to him £10 4s. 5d., as paid to the said receiver by the hand of the said accountant this year by a bill dated at Walsham 14th February in the said 25th year, which the said farmer had retained until the settling [*determinac'*] of this account.

And allowed to him £4 14s. 6d., paid to the receiver by the hand of John Robwood, recently lessee there, for his arrears as acknowledged by the said receiver at the settling of the account.

And allowed to him 11s. 2d. from the arrears of the same John, recently the farmer, paid for the keep and the expenses of the said receiver and auditors of the lord with William Gimbald, when they were at London for 9 days in March of the said 24th year as mandated by the lord for examining both the minister's account from the year before, and also for the account of the receiver of the lord in the 24th year, hearing and settling the same in order to ascertain the state and the value of the lands [*pro statu valorum terrarum*] and tenements of the lord for the same year. And the lord there has cleared the account [*et dominus ibidem declara'*].

And allowed to him 24s. from the arrears of the same recent farmer, paid for the keep of the lord's auditors incurred in the month of August of the said 24th year and to ride from the same to the lady and the lord in the county of York there to hear and to settle. Also with his keep when travelling from Blythburgh \said receiver to Alderton[75]/ to London \and of the said auditors/ aforesaid in total for six days for each of them, by a detailed bill.

And allowed to him 12s. from the arrears of the same late farmer, paid for keep and expenses of the said auditors expended for three [*sic*] from London to Westhorpe for hearing the account of the said receiver for this year, and to please the lord [*et dominus adolariand'*]; and for their keep returning to London by horse with the keep of the same auditor travelling \for 6 [*two other words illegible*]/ by a detailed bill, etc.

And 13s. 6d. for the same period for diverse upkeep of houses, buildings and mills there, expended but not allowed.

And he owes 7s. 11½d., which is in the following account.

On Rober [*torn*], late bailiff there, for his arrears, 7s. 11½d.

---

74 'Received John Squyre' in the margin.
75 John Squire, the receiver general of monies for de la Pole's East Anglian estates, was the parson of Alderton, which is the obvious explanation for the detour en route to London. On 4 August 1450, during the breakdown of law and order in the Cade rebellion following the death of de la Pole, Squire was dragged from the rectory at Alderton by a mob and beheaded. See Harvey, *Jack Cade's rebellion*, p. 120. Such extreme violence reflects how closely Squire was associated with de la Pole.

[*Reverse*]
Walsham
Account there in the 25th year of Henry VI – William Fuller farmer there [*blank*]

In different hand half way down the manuscript

To all present and through this letter, William de la Pole earl of Suffolk and Alice wife of the same, greetings in lordship [*salutem in domino*]. Know that for good and laudable service by John Belley we bestow, grant, and by this document gift to the same John a certain annuity rent of 20 marks sterling during his life from and in our manor of Walsham in the county of Suffolk with appurtenances by the hand of the receiver, bailiff, collector or farmer of the aforesaid manor at the time at the terms of the Feast of the Nativity of St John the Baptist, St Michael the Archangel, Christmas and Easter levied by equal portions.

On condition that if it should happen that the aforesaid annuity rent of 20 marks should fall in arrears in part or in full after any of those said terms when it ought to be paid, then it shall be permitted for the aforesaid John and his attorneys to take from the aforesaid manor any manner of item to distrain and in distraint, thereby to drive cattle, to lead them out and impound, and to keep them for himself until the said annuity rent and his arrears are fully settled to his satisfaction. And this as often as shall be necessary for the life of the said John.

And we the said earl and our wife and our heirs hereby guarantee the aforesaid annuity rent of 20 marks to the aforesaid John during against all people [*contra omnes gentes*] by this document. For nominal seisin and possession of the said annuity rent we pay to the aforesaid John 4d. silver on the day of the present date. Witnessed in the court of the king and with our ducal seal affixed on the 29th day of April in the 19th year of Henry VI.[76]

Document 19: Walsham account, 29 September 1446 to 29 September 1447

SA/B HA504/3/15 m.11

Walsham
Account of William Fuller, farmer there, from the Feast of St Michael the Archangel in the 25th year of Henry VI until the Feast of St Michael the Archangel in the 26th year of the same king for one whole year.

Arrears The same is charged and answers for 7s. 11½d. from arrears of the last account as contained there.

Sum 7s. 11½d.

Rents of assize For £14 13s. 4d. half a ¼d. and two parts of a ¼d. from rents of assize with the farm of the land p.a. as in the account for the 7th year now past there recorded and itemised, nothing received because it pertains to the said farmer by the terms of his aforesaid lease.

Sum nil.

---

[76] April 1441.

Castle ward For 14s. from castle ward p.a. received, nothing this year because it pertains to the said farmer by the terms of his aforesaid lease.

Sum nil.

Perquisites of court For perquisites of court, nothing this year because as aforesaid.

Sum nil.

Farm of the mill For 20s. recently received from the farm of a windmill, nothing because as aforesaid.

Sum nil.

Works and services sold For £10 18s. 3¾d. and half a ¼d. from works and services sold, nothing because as aforesaid.

Sum nil.

Sale of wood and underwood Nothing this year.

Sum nil.

Profits of the dovecote For profits of the same, nothing this year because it pertains to the said farmer by the terms of his lease.

Sum nil.

Farm of the manor Thus received £44 from the farm of the manor of Walsham and from the manor called High Hall, alias Wildcats, with all their appurtenances in the county of Suffolk, with ward, marriage fines, reliefs, escheats, woods, underwood and the advowson of the church excepted and reserved. Thus granted to the said William Fuller and his attorney for a term of [*blank*] years by an indenture of the lord paying, this year is the 3rd, paying:

Sum £44.

Sum total of the aforesaid lease with arrears £44 7s. 11½d.

Rent resolute – The same accounts for rent resolute with decays viz: 118s. 3d. p.a. as shown in the abovesaid account, nothing this year because by the said farmer.

Sum nil.

Cost of the manor buildings The accountant paid John Manser hired for 1 day to mend a half part of the door of the barn by task, 4d.
And in a plank bought from the same John for the same work, price 5d.
And in 60 nails bought for the same work, 2d.
And in a plate with an iron pike bought for the same work, 2d.
And in wheat and rye straw bought from John Bene for thatching the building called the Sheep Pen [*le Shepene*], price 3s.
And in the stipend of John Thaxter hired for 6 days to thatch the said building with the stipend of Alice Bene hired for the same time to mend the same, taken between them per day 7d. by task, 3s. 6d.

Sum 7s. 7d.

Cost of the mill And in the stipend of John Frances hired for 1 day to cut and fell an oak at the lord's wood in Westhorpe at Woodbites for the mill axle by task, 4d.
And in the stipend of Peter Umfrey, carpenter, hired for 1 day to trim and shape the said oak for a cart by work, 4d.
And in the stipend of John Rampley hired with his cart to carry the said mill axle by piecework towards the mill, 6d.
And in the stipend of John Fish, millwright [*millewrygthe*], hired to prepare the said mill axle in placing the same in the mill, 6s. 8d.
And in the expenses of various men there that is to help lift the said mill axle, in all expenses, 3d.
And in the stipend of the same John Fish hired for 1 day to make a bridge-tree below the millstone by task, 4d.
And in the stipend of John Manser, \millwright/ and his servant hired to make cogs and staves for the said mill for one day <8d.>
And paid to John Smith, blacksmith hired to mend an iron collar to lie around the mill axle, 4d.
And paid to the same John for mending the mill spindle, 2½d.
And in nails bought to attach a band on the mill axle, price 2d.
And in a millstone bought for the mill from Thomas Dennis of Ipswich, price 46s. 8d.

Sum 55s. 7d.

Cost of closes with minute [*expenses*] And in the stipend of John Hill and others hired to make 74 perches of new hedge around the wood of the lord called Lady's Wood in Walsham, both on the north and west sides, per perch ½d., 3s. 0½d.
And in the stipend of Thomas Murrell hired for 1 day to stop up and mend various holes around the said wood of the lord called Lady's Wood, by task, 4d.
And in the stipend of Thomas Murrell and Thomas Potenger hired together to clean out a pond in the manor for water for the animals there, by task <2s. 16d.>

Sum 3s. 5d.

Annuities And paid to John Belley esq. for his annuity of 20 marks p.a. which lord William de la Pole and Alice his wife have granted to the aforesaid John for the term of his life, levied from the issues and profits of this manor of Walsham for the terms of Easter, Christmas, Nativity of St John the Baptist and Michaelmas equally divided, paid by the hand of the receiver, collector and farmer there as shown in a letter patent of the lord and Alice, made with the same John, dated 29th April in the 19th year of the aforesaid king, as enrolled with the account of the previous. That is, by payment of the same annuity on the said terms [*torn*] to the said John Belley paid beyond the account, £13 6s. 8d.

Sum £13 6s. 8d.

Money allowed And in money [*torn*] … clerk general, receiver of the lord's money from his part of rent this year by a bill dated 9th [*torn*] by the hands of Richard Wright and William Sewal, £4 6s. 8d.
And in money [*torn*] by the said William Fuller bailiff of the account paid for various expenses of the household and [*torn*] of Westhorpe in March in the 25th year of the king by the time of parliament held at [*torn*] shown in a bill indented upon this accounted delivered, £8 17d.

194

And in [*torn*] part of his rent this year by a bill dated 12th December [*torn*] as the same receiver acknowledged upon this account.

And [*torn*] part of his rent this year without a bill received money for [*torn*] at Westhorpe as the same receiver acknowledged upon this account, £9 [*torn*]

Sum of all allowances and deliveries £44. And so owes 7s. 11½d. which is charged in the account 'Deye' on Robert Lester, recently bailiff there, for his arrears of 7s. 11½d.

[*On the reverse of this account is one account for the manors of Westhorpe and Cotton, by John Dolet the farmer, and another account of Nicholas Hill, farmer of a tenement with appurtenances called Stubcroft in Stradbroke.*]

Document 20: Walsham account, 29 September 1449 to 29 September 1450

SA/B HA504/3/15 m.9

Walsham

Account of William Fuller bailiff there from the Feast of St Michael in the 28th year of Henry VI until now.

Arrears The same accountant answers for 7s. 11½d. from arrears of the last account.
Sum 7s. 11½d.

Rents of assize with castle ward And for £14 13s. 4¼d. and two parts of a ¼d. \ of which from free rents 60s. 3¼d./ from rents of assize there p.a.
And for 14s. from castle ward there p.a., that is from the manor of Wyken p.a. 11s. 2d. and from the manor of Ixworth 2s. 10d.
Sum £15 7s. 4¼d. and two parts of a ¼d.

Farm of land, pasture and meadow And for <£18 9s. 7½d.> \£18 4s. 9½d./ from the farm of land, meadow and pasture leased there by the lord to various persons for [*blank*] as shown by a bill there.
Sum £18 4s. 9½d.

Farm of the mill And for 17s. from the farm of a mill there this year to John Miller.
Sum 17s.

Sale of works and services And for £10 18s. 3¾d. and half a ¼d. received from works and services there p.a. as shown in the previous account of the 10th year.
Sum – £10 18s. 3¾d. and half a ¼d.

Sales of underwood And for 6s. 8d. received from persons cutting down underwood in a certain grove there called Luchesdell this year.
And for 3s. 4d. from cutting down underwood in a wood there called Lady's Wood sold to Thomas Dunning this year.
And for 2s. from cutting down underwood in a wood [*illeg.*] sold to Robert Pepper this year.
Sum 12s.

Perquisites of court And for 15s. 5d. from perquisites of one court held there this year as shown by the same roll.

Sum 15s. 5d.

Sum total of receipts with arrears £47 2s. 10d. and three parts of ¼d.

[*Reverse*]
Rent resolute And in rent resolute for the ward of Norwich p.a. as in the account of the 10th year, 16s.

And in rent resolute for John Margery p.a. as in the said account, 1½d.

And in rent resolute for the hall of Ashfield p.a. as in the said account, 19d.

And in rent resolute for the castle of Eye p.a. as in the said account, 20d. \in the 30th year 10d. at the Feast of the Annunciation of the Blessed Virgin Mary, and in the next year owes 20d. at the Feast of the Apostles Andrew and James at Blackbourn/ And paid for hundred suit released p.a. for Burchards, sum [*damaged*]

And in rent resolute \for allowance of the same hundred/ for ward of Helimot for Burchards p.a., 9d.

And in rent resolute for the heirs of William Bardwell esq. on 1 acre of meadow called Turf Pits purchased by the lord from John Rampley chaplain as in the aforesaid account, 4d.

And in rent resolute for the hall of Rickinghall p.a., 3s. 1½d.

[*torn, two lines missing*]

Sum £13 16s. 8d.

Making hedges And in money paid to John Frances and John Hill hired to make 68 perches of new hedge [*damaged ...*] on the west part of a wood called High Hall Wood, taken for each perch ½d., 2s. 9½d.

And in the wages of John Frances hired for one day to stop up and mend the hedge around a wood called Burchards Wood, 4d.

And in the wages of Thomas Murrell for one day to stop up and mend the hedge around the wood called Ladys Wood, 4d.

Sum 3s. 5½d.

Steward's expenses And in the expenses of the steward and other supervisors for the court held this year as shown by the roll of the same court upon this present account, 5s.

Sum 5s.

Necessary expenses[77]
And paid for various costs and expenses of John Harleston esquire and George Wiseman[78] and others being at Walsham <Hall> this year to support [*consortand'*] the lord's tenants <there> and to watch over the lordship there, in order to place

---

[77] This paragraph is difficult to read in places, a function of a worn and torn paper manuscript, small and untidy handwriting, and various deletions. I am grateful to Nick Amor for helping me to decipher its meaning: we are confident that the sense of the translation is accurate. The background is sketched in the Introduction, pp. xxxii–xxxiii.

[78] Neither Harleston nor Wiseman appear in the fifteenth-century Walsham court rolls, so they were both outsiders. They were members of the local gentry within the de la Pole affinity. The Wiseman family were from Thornham Magna. See Richmond, 'East Anglian politics', pp. 189, 196 fn. 34.

[*ponend'*] it in good governance as testified at the auditing of the account, as shown and authorised by a detailed schedule, 3s. 7d.

And paid for the costs and expenses imposed as a penalty on the tenants of the <lord> lady forfeited [*fact' super tenentes domine puntes*] with <c> the said [*next three words are illegible*] pigs and livestock afterwards in the hedges of Thomas Porrett being there \unjustly/ seized [*next three words faded and illegible ... ?and driven away and delivered*] into the hands of the Duke of Norfolk [*in manu ducu' Norff'*] et cetera, 18d.[79]

And paid to John Jermyn, sheriff of the county of Suffolk, for three writs supersedeas[80] [*supersedior'*] from his office for 33[81] tenants <of> of the lordship of Walsham who were harassed by writ at the suit of Robert <Walsall> Walsam alias Wyldekattes[82] <this year for unrecovered [*exannalis*] debts>, also the costs of George Wysman, John Seggebrook,[83] William <Fol> Fuller and three other servants of the lady riding <from> to Bury and staying for one day and one night to obtain from the said sheriff the said three writs of supersedeas and for copies of the writs of prosecution for debt against the said tenants, of which 20d. are the expenses of the clerk [*viro scriptorum*] of the said sheriff, 13s. 4d.[84]

Sum 18s. 5d.

Stipend of the accountant – And in the stipend of the same accountant because he occupied the office of bailiff there p.a. And in clothing of the same accountant p.a., 6s. 8d. because he was not given clothing to wear.

Sum 40s.

Payment of money And in money delivered to Andrew Wriggs, the receiver general,[85] by the hand of the said accountant from the profits of his office by a bill dated 21st April in the 28th year of Henry VI.

By the same Simon Dale, 10s. by a bill dated 14th May in the same year, the 28th.

By a bill dated 8th September in the 29th year by the hand of the said Simon Dale as shown by a bill signed by the same receiver upon the account, £17 6s. 8d.

---

79 These first two paragraphs indicate the following chain of events. The death of de la Pole in May 1450 led to a summer of disorder, including attacks on his East Anglian properties by members of the affinity of his rival, the Duke of Norfolk. Some animals belonging to Walsham tenants had been driven off, and Harleston and Wiseman travelled to Walsham to provide support and maybe protection. See Introduction, p. xxxii.

80 A writ 'supersedeas' was a writ to halt legal proceedings temporarily.

81 Manuscript worn, the figure could be 28.

82 So one Robert Walsam, alias Wildcats, had issued a writ against a number of Walsham tenants for what appear to be old debts. Neither the timing – the fall of de la Pole, and the involvement of the Duke of Norfolk – nor Robert's surname and alias Wildcats, the alternative name for High Hall, can be a coincidence: he is either the heir of whoever sold High Hall to William de Elmham in the 1380s or a former tenant claiming debts against a group of tenants. This is clearly a ploy to put pressure on Alice de la Pole as part of the disorder and posturing in the summer.

83 Sedgebrook does not appear in the fifteenth-century court rolls of Walsham, so he was another outsider.

84 This passage indicates that Wiseman, Sedgebrook and Fuller responded to Robert W's issue of writs for debt against the tenants of Walsham by travelling to Bury St Edmunds and paying for a counter writ to halt the proceedings, and to obtain copies of those writs against them from the sheriff's scribe: almost certainly so that they could discover what exactly was the case against them. The original writs probably related to the county court.

85 John Squire is no longer the receiver general of the de la Pole estates following his murder in August 1450.

Sum of money delivered, £17 16s. 8d.
Sum of all allowances and deliveries [*blank*].
And he owes [*blank*]

Document 21: Walsham account, 29 September 1451 to 29 September 1452

SA/B HA504/3/15.12 and 15.13

Walsham
Account of William Fuller bailiff there from the Feast of St Michael in the 30th year of Henry VI until the same feast next coming in the 31st year of the same, that is for one whole year as within.

Arrears The same accountant answers for £13 15s. 4d. from arrears of the last account, as shown in the last account at the foot of the same account.
Sum £13 15s. 4d.

Rents of assize And for £14 13s. 4¼d. two parts of ¼d. from fixed rents there p.a., with 51s. 3¼d. from free rents there p.a., paid at the terms of Easter and Michaelmas equally, that is for the same terms within the said time of this account.
Sum £14 13s. 4¼d. and two parts of a ¼d.

Sale of works and services with castle ward And for £10 18s. 3¾d. half a ¼d. from works and services there p.a.
And for 14s. from castle ward received there from the manor of Wyken \11s. 2d./ and the manor of Ixworth \2s. 10d./ equally at the aforesaid feasts.
Sum £11 12s. 3¾d. half a ¼d.

Farm of meadow and pasture leased And for 20s. from the farm of a close called New Close leased to Robert Fuller this year.
And for 26s. 8d. from the farm of a piece of meadow called Broad Dole containing 4½ acres to the said accountant this year.
And for 9s. from the farm of 7 roods of meadow from High Hall lying in various places leased to various people this year by the oath of the accountant.
And for 4s. from the farm of a meadow called Turf Pit containing 1 acre leased to the said accountant this year.
And for 5s. from the farm of a close there called Lady's Wood Launde leased to the said accountant this year.
And for 3s. from the farm of a close called Lady's Wood Close lying next to the aforesaid close leased to the said accountant this year.
And for 4s. from the farm of various pieces of pasture containing by estimate 12 acres leased to the rector of the church of Wattisfield by court roll.
And for 5s. 6d. from the farm of a piece of pasture called Guspers Field with a certain pasture called Small Brook leased to John Tiptot this year.
And for 15d. from the farm of 5 acres of pasture, parcel of the said Guspers Field leased to the said John Tiptot p.a. and his heirs by court roll.
And for 20d. from the farm of 3 acres 1 rood of pasture, parcel of Nether Haugh leased to John Ringbell and his heirs p.a. by court roll.
And for 10d. from the farm of a croft there called Godfreys Yard and 1½ acres of meadow of the same tenement leased to John Deye this year.

And for 4s. from the farm of a close of pasture called Sheepcote Close leased to John Robwood son of Marion Robwood lately 8s. for arable land charged in the title of the farm of the land.

And for 8s. for the farm of a close called Burchards Close containing [blank] acres of land leased to John Robwood junior son of John Robwood senior this year lately 24s. 4d. from the farm of arable land in the tenement of the same John as shown in the said title of the farm of the land.

And for 26s. 8d. from the farm of a close called High Hall Close containing [blank] acres with a certain close called Katherines Croft containing 8 acres leased to John Robwood this year.

And for 17s. 2½d. from the farm of 12 acres of pasture lying next to Allwood Green, 18 acres of pasture \3d./ called Blunts Land, 8 acres of pasture \12d./ next to a close recently of William Grocer, 4 acres of pasture \8d./ there called Sadds Land recently pertaining to the tenement of Robert Payne, 2 acres of pasture \5d./ lying at Helpes Wood, 14 acres of pasture \2s. 4d./ parcel of a field called Guspers Field, 6 acres of land of the tenement Syres lying at the end of the said field, 10 acres of pasture \20d./ lying at Willow Mere, 2 acres of pasture \4d./ lying next to the said 10 acres, 6 acres 1 rood of pasture in various pieces of land lying in the field called Home Stall Field and in the field called Clay Field with 1 acre lying on the west side of the stream and 7 acres of pasture \2s. 4d./ of the tenement Sadds leased to John Robwood senior this year, lately 5s. from the farm of various pieces of arable land in the same tenement charged in the said title of the farm of the land.

And for 6s. 8d. from the farm of a pightle called Calk Pightle \3s. 4d./ containing [blank] acres and a close called Camping Close[86] \3s. 4d./ containing [blank] acres leased to John Becon p.a. and his heirs by court roll lately 8s. 4d. from the farm of a close of arable land called Old Toft recently leased together for 15s. p.a.

And for 4s. from the farm of 5 acres of pasture lying at Walpoles Croft and a pightle called Jack's Yard containing [blank] acres leased to Cecily Cooper and her heirs p.a. lately 4s. from the farm of arable land leased together to the same for 8s.

And for 8d. from the farm of 4 acres of pasture called [blank] leased to John Rampley this year.

Sum £7 8s. 1½d.

Farm of leased land And for 4s. 4d. from the farm of arable land called Howes Toft containing 8 acres of land by estimate leased to Thomas Dennis and his heirs by court roll in the preceding year.

And for 2s. from the farm of various pieces of arable land cont. by estimate 7 acres leased to the rector of Wattisfield recently 4s. paid for the farm of various pieces of pasture cont. by estimate 12 acres above in the title of the farm of meadow and pasture charged to him together leased by court roll for 6s. p.a.

And for 9s. from the farm of a piece of arable land containing 42 acres called Fish-pond Field leased to Isabel Vincent this year.

And for 8s. from the farm of a piece of land containing 42 acres by estimate called Hatchmere leased to James Hawes by court roll.

---

[86] Camping was an early form of contact sport, popular in eastern England. See D. Dymond, 'A lost social institution: the camping close', *Rural History* 1 (1990), pp. 165–92; and D. Dymond, 'The game of camping in eastern England', *The Local Historian* 51 (2021), pp. 2–16.

And for 2s. from the farm of a piece of arable land called Boynhall containing 12 acres by estimate leased to the same James by court roll.

And for 2d. from the farm of ½ acre of land lying next to Brook Way leased to John Tiptot this year.

And for 6s. 4d. from the farm of a piece of land called Home Stall cont. by estimate 9 acres leased to Thomas Bonde this year.

And for 2s. from the farm of a close of arable land lying next to Hall Gate cont. by estimate 2½ acres leased to Robert Fuller by court roll.

And for 9d. from the farm of 1 acre of land of the tenement Cranmer at Hulkes Bridge and 3 roods of land from the tenement Kebbils leased to John Kirton by court roll.

And for 2s. from the farm of 3½ acres of land lying in various pieces there leased to [torn] Fletcher by court roll.

And for 3s. 4d. from the farm of 8 acres of arable land lying in Long Wheat and 4 acres [torn] land at the end of the croft of Thomas Bonde leased to John Swift and his heirs by court roll.

And for 8s. from the farm of 6 acres of land called Godelards Land, a pightle of arable land called Stony Land and a close of arable land called Trendle Wood leased to John Robwood son of Marion Robwood this year is the last, 4s. from the farm of a close of pasture called Sheepcote Close above in the title of the farm of meadow and pasture charged together leased to the same John by court roll.

And for 25s. 4d. from the farm of 18 acres of land lying in Burchards Croft, a piece of land called High Hall Croft, a piece of land called Nether Haugh otherwise called Seventeen Acres and a piece of land lying at Ulveswell leased to John Robwood junior son of John Robwood senior lately 8s., a close called Burchards above in the title of the farm of meadow and charged to him together leased to the said John for 36s. 8d.

And for 5s. 5d. from the farm of 4 acres \8d./ of arable land called Knots Hedge, 6 acres \18d./ of arable land there, 1 acre \8d./ of arable land called Stony Land, 2 acres \10d./ of arable land lying between the land recently of John Cooper and the land of the tenement Paynes, ½ acre \3d./ of land called Saddes tenement and 3 acres \18d./ of arable land lying in the field called South Field called Stony Land leased to John Robwood senior this year is the last, 17s. 2½d. from the farm of various pieces of pasture above in the title of the farm of meadow and pasture charged together leased at farm to the same John for 22s. 7½d. p.a.

And for 8s. 4d. from the farm of a close there called Old Toft containing 20 acres leased to John Becon and his heirs by court roll lately 6s. 8d. from the farm of a pightle and a close of pasture above in the said title charged together leased to the same John and his heirs by court roll for 15s. p.a.

And for 3s. 4d. from the farm of 7 acres of arable land parcel of [torn] William Fuller and his heirs by court roll.

And for 4s. from the farm of two pieces of land [torn] containing 22½ acres of arable land abutting upon the land of the Prior and Convent of Ixworth [torn] Cecily Cooper and her heirs by court roll lately 4s. from the farm of 6 acres of pasture at Walpoles Croft and a pightle of pasture called Jacks Yard above in the said title charged at 4s. together leased to the same Cecily and her heirs by court roll for 8s. p.a.

Sum £4 14s. 4d.

Farm of the manor site And for £6 from the farm of the manor there called Walsham Hall with various closes and arable land adjacent to the same and pertaining, as in the account in the preceding year, leased to John Bene p.a. paying at the terms of Easter and Michaelmas equally within the aforesaid time as appears more fully.
Sum £6.

Profits of the mill there For the farm of a windmill there recently granted for 17s. p.a. for the aforesaid time, nothing received because it lies ruined in the lady's hands because no one wanted to hire it.
Sum nil.

Sales of underwood And for 36s. 8d. from the sale of 5½ acres of underwood in the lady's wood there called Lady's Wood this year cut down and sold to the persons below, 6s. 8d. per acre, that is to William Smith 1 rood, Thomas Parker 1 rood, John Baye 1 rood, Andrew Hawes 1 rood, John Fletcher 1 rood, Thomas Fletcher 1 rood, Thomas Dunning 2 roods, Richard Page 1 rood, Robert Pepper 1 rood, Thomas Smith 1 rood, Thomas Berne 1 rood, John Becon 3 roods, Richard Neale 1 rood, John Miller and Nicholas Fuller 1 rood, Robert Fuller 1 rood, sold this year by oath of the said accountant upon the account.
[*Torn, but must be 12s.*] from the sale of 2 acres of underwood in the lady's wood there called North Haugh this year cut down and sold, that is to Nicholas [*torn*], John Page 1 rood, Robert Potenger 1 rood, William Vincent 1 rood, John Bonde 1 rood, John Margery [*torn*] 2 roods.
And for 4s. 6d. from the sale of 3 roods of underwood in the lady's wood there called High Hall this year cut down and sold to John Swift 1 rood, John Bray 1 rood, John Dinglove and Thomas Rose 1 rood, sold for 18d. per rood.
Sum 53s. 2d.

Perquisites of court And for 40s. for certain fines from the tenants there for the office of reeve and reap-reeve there not undertaken this year.
And from 49s. 8d. from perquisites of two general courts held there this year, of which from a fine for entry to lands 23s. 4d., fine for a suit 6d. and from small perquisites 25s. 10d. as shown on the roll.
Sum £4 9s. 8d.

Total received from profits £51 10s. 11¾d.

Sum total of receipts with arrears £65 6s. 3¾d. From which:

Rent resolute In rent resolute for castle ward of Norwich p.a., 16s.
And in rent resolute for castle ward of Eye this year twice, 20d.
And in the year next following owed once paid thus, 10d.
And in [*torn*] for the manor of Rickinghall p.a., 3s. 1½d.
And in rent resolute for the manor of [*torn*] p.a., 19d.
And in money to the bailiff of Blackbourne Hundred and suit of the same hundred this year released for the tenement Burchards, 16d.
And in money paid to Helimot from castle ward for the said tenement Burchards, 9d.
And paid to the heirs of Sir William Bardwell for 1 acre of meadow [...]

[*Manuscript HA504/3/15.12 ends abruptly here, because the lower half of the original has become detached. The final section of the original survives as HA504/3/5.13. Here we have reunited the two surviving sections rather than present the bottom section as a separate document. However, one panel of the original manuscript, containing the rest of the expenses, has been completely lost.*]

[...]

Sum of money allowed £42 11s. 11d.

Sum of allowances and payments £48 7s. 4d.
And owing, £16 18s. 11¾d.
From which, 7s. previously charged as arrears by various persons now raised for debt examined and sworn by the said accountant upon this account. And owing, £16 11s. 11¾d.

Respites
And he is respited 75s. 3d., of which 37s. 7½d. charged above within arrears and 37s. 7¾d. \part of £10 18s. 4¾d./ charged above against the works and services of tenants there p.a., because the said accountant says he did not raise all of the same works and services, except £9 16s. 0½d. \p.a./; and because 15s. 4d. is charged as above under the heading Sale of works and services on Robert Payne for his tenement, as contained in the rental examined upon this account; also it is alleged that the said tenement came into the possession of the lady in the preceding year and the said John Robwood with other land, meadow and pasture for 22s. 1½d., as charged above under the heading Farms of land.
And he is respited 12s. 9d. charged as above against arrears of rent \6d./ and works \2s. 8d./ from the tenement held by John Margery in the preceding year for his election to the office of reeve; and for works \4s. 1d./ from the tenement held by Simon Margery for the preceding year for his election to the office of hayward, because they are quit of the rent for occupying the same office, just as was the case in the preceding year and as it is said.
And he is respited 9s. 8d. charged as above against the rent, works and services of the tenement of John Bene \4s. 3d./ who is elected to the office of reeve and of the tenement of Nicholas Smith \5s. 5d./ elected to the office of hayward there for this year, because they claim to be quit of the same having inspected the old account rolls from the time when the demesne there was being exploited directly [*de tempore quo dominicum ibidem fuit in appriamento*].
Sum respited £4 17s. 8d., of which from issues 47s. 3½d.
And remaining beyond the respites, £11 14s. 3¾d.
Of which, on Robert Lynster, recently bailiff there, for his arrears, 7s. 11½d.
On John Miller, lessee of the mill there in the last year, from the arrears of the same lease, 17s. \he ought to be allowed this because <made> vacant as established at the audit/
On the said accountant for his arrears for the aforesaid time, £10 9s. 4¼d.

[*The manuscript continues with short accounts of Wyverstone, Wattisfield and Stubbecroft.*]

Document 22: Walsham account, 29 September 1470 to 29 September 1471

SA/Ipswich, HD1538/411/4 mm.2 and 3[87]

Walsham

Account of John Hawe, reeve and bailiff there, for the tenement Spylmann in the tenure of the said John, and of William Rosyer, hayward there, for the tenement Vannoys in the tenure of the same William which are liable for the said offices from the Feast of St Michael Archangel in the 10th year of the reign of Edward IV to the same Feast in the 11th year of the same for one whole year as elsewhere.

Arrears Item, he is charged for £41 6s. 5½d. for the arrears of the last year, just as appears at the foot of the same.

Sum £41 6s. 5½d.

Rents of assize And for £14 13s. 4d. two parts of ¼d. from fixed rents there owed p.a., with 51s. 3¼d. paid at the terms of Easter and Michaelmas equally, that is for the same terms within the said time of this account.

Sum £14 13s. 4d. and two parts of a ¼d.

Castle ward And for 14s. from castle ward there per annum, that is from the manor of Wyken 11s. 2d. and from the manor of Ixworth 2s. 10d. equally at the aforesaid feasts, that is for the said ward due from this manor.

Sum 14s.

Sale of works and services

And for £10 18s. 2½d. half a ¼d. from the sale of works and services there p.a. as detailed in a certain rental made in respect therefore, updated and in possession of the said accountant.

Sum £10 18s. 2½d. half a ¼d.

Farm of meadow and pasture leased And for 23s. 4d. from the lease of one close there called New Close leased to John Shepherd and Isabella his wife, their heirs and assignees by the rolls of the court this year.[88] And for 20s. from the lease of one meadow there called Broad Dole containing 5 acres, as sold this year for 4s. per acre, compared with the 13th year preceding[89] [*when it was leased*] for 26s. 8d. And for 9s. 8d. for the lease of various parcels of meadow of *Haggehalle* lying in diverse places thus leased one acre to Walter Judde \4s./, half an acre to John Howlyn \2s./,

---

[87] This document comprises three bound leaves of parchment. The first two cover the manors of Westhorpe, Wyverstone, Stubcroft and Braiseworth in Cotton, and the second half of the second manuscript and third comprises the Walsham account. The beginning of the Walsham account has various brief notes in a later hand.

[88] The court held on 3 December 1470 recorded the grant of this land at fee farm, i.e. it was not a fixed-term lease but granted in perpetuity to them and their heirs: SA/B 504/1/13.30. Hence the use of the words 'farm' and 'lease' in the account is slightly misleading, because they imply leasehold when the tenure is in fact more secure. Similar loose wording is deployed in other entries in this section, where the mention of heirs indicates a heritable right to the land. The reference to the rolls of the court signals that they are the definitive source of the title to this land, not the account.

[89] Cross-references to earlier accounts usually referred to the regnal year, yet this cannot be the 13th year of Edward IV's reign but could be the 13th year of Henry VI's reign. It probably refers to the account 13 years ago, i.e. 1457–8.

1 rood to Thomas Smyth \12d./, 1 rood to Hugo Loyde \20d./, and 1 rood and third part of a rood to William Fuller \12d./ thus leased to these people this year by the oath of the accountant. And for 3s. 4d. from the lease of one acre of meadow called Turfpit thus leased to William Fuller this year, lately leased at 4s. per annum. And for 8s. from the lease of two closes there, of which one is called *Ladeyswodelond* and the other is called Lady's Wood Close thus leased to William Fuller to hold to him his heirs and assignees. And for 5s. 9d. from the lease of 5 parcels of land containing 16 acres of unfree [*nat'*] land as leased in the account 17 preceding. And for 5s. 6d. from the lease of one piece of land, a parcel of Guspers Field, as leased in the account 13 preceding. And for 15d. from the lease of 3 acres 1 rood of pasture as leased in the preceding account. And for 20d. from the lease of 3 acres 1 rood of pasture there as leased in the preceding account. And for 20d. from the lease of one croft called *Godfrayesyerd* as leased in the preceding account. And for 8s. from the lease of 3 parcels of land and pasture there as leased in the preceding account. And for 36s. 8d. from the lease of 9 parcels of land and pasture there as was lately in the tenure of John Robhood junior by the court rolls. And for 36s. 8d. from the lease of one close called *Haggehalclose* containing [*blank*] acres and one close called *Catleciscrofte* containing 8 acres thus leased to Richard Day, cooper, in the court rolls of last year to him and his heirs. And for 8s. 5d. from the lease of 11 acres of pasture thus leased to John Bekton this year. And for 4s. from the lease of 6 acres of pasture there lying at Walpoles Croft thus leased this year. And for 10s. from the lease of the tenement Syres and Sadds thus leased to Thomas Rose this year. And for 2s. 8d. from the lease of one piece of land containing 8 acres lying next to Aldwodegrene thus leased. And for 9s. 4d. from the lease of one parcel of land containing 28 acres of land thus leased to Thomas Hermyte this year. And for 6s. 8d. from the farm of one pightle there called Calk Pightle thus leased this year. And for 16d. from the farm of two parcels of demesne there containing four acres, thus leased this year.

Sum £10 4s. 2d.

Farm of the demesne land And for 71s. 7d. \½d./ for the leases of various demesne lands there as detailed in the account of the 16th year preceding all together [*unacium*], including 12s. 10½d. for the lease of four acres of arable in the tenure of John Robwood senior with leases to various people by the rolls of the court for them and their heirs, as in the preceding account and also in a certain rental made in respect thereof, and examined at the audit and in the possession of the accountant.

Sum 71s. 7½d.

Farm of the manor of High Hall And for £6 15s. for the lease of the site of the manor there with lands and tenements pertaining to the same manor, as leased to various people 7d. \½d./ for the leases of various demesne lands there, as detailed in the account \of/ the 17th year preceding all together, including 36s. 8d. for the lease of a certain meadow called *Lytilmedow* thus leased to various people this year.

Sum £6 15s.

Profit of the mill And the lease of the windmill there, lately leased for 16s. per annum, is available to any person for their profit, but for the time aforesaid nothing received because it lies ruinous in the lands of the lord and no one wishes to hire it for want of repairs to the same.

Sum nothing.

Profits of the woods of the lady there And for 5s. 1d. received for the price of 3 roods 2 perches of underwood cut and thrown down in the wood of the lady called Lady's Wood, as sold to various people at 5s. 6d. per acre, in the preceding account. And for 3s. 9d. received for the price of underwood cut and thrown down in the wood of the lady called *Newhawode*, as sold to various people according to an appraisal at 6s. per acre, as in the preceding accounts. And for 2s. 3d. received for the price of 1½ roods and 4 perches of underwood cut and thrown down in the wood of the lady called High Hall Wood, as sold to various people according to an appraisal at 5s. 6d. per acre, as in the preceding account. And for the price of other underwood cut and thrown down in the wood there of the lady called *Lyrchesdalwode*, that is nothing received for the time aforesaid because there were no sales \ there/ this year on the oath of the accountant.
Sum 11s. 6d.

Perquisites of court And for 40s. for certain fines from the tenants there for the office of reeve and reap-reeve there not undertaken this year. And from 69s. 2d. from the perquisites of two general courts held there this year, just as appears on the rolls of the same and examined at the audit.
Sum 109s. 2d.

Sum total of receipts with arrears £97 3s. 7d.
From which:

Payments and allowances of rent In rent resolute for castle ward of Norwich p.a., 16s.
And in rent resolute for castle ward of Eye paid this year at the Feast of the Annunciation of the Blessed Virgin Mary, 10d. And in the year next following it ought to be paid in two instalments totalling 20d., that is equally at the Feasts of St Andrew and St James apostles.
And in rent resolute to the manor of Ashfield p.a., 19d.
And in money paid to castle ward for the said tenement Burchards, 9d. And in money to the bailiff of Blackbourne Hundred and suit of the same hundred this year released for the tenement Burchards, 16d.
And in rent resolute for the heirs of William Bardwell esq. on 1 acre of meadow called *Thiftalpitts* purchased by the lord from [*blank*] Rampley chaplain as in the aforesaid account, 4d.
And in rent resolute of John Margery p.a., 1½d.
And in rent resolute of the manor of Rickinghall p.a., 3s. 1½d.
And in allowance of rent, works and services on the tenement Spylman \4s. 10¾d./ in the tenure of John Hawe, elected this year into a certain office of collector, and of the rent, works and customs there of the tenement Vannoy \4s. 10¾d./ in the tenure of William Rosyer elected this year into a certain office of hayward there, just as appears in the court rolls aforesaid, and so for the same rents and farms, 9s. 6d.
Sum 33s. 7d.

[*m.3*]

Wages of the accountant with the expenses of the steward And in the wages of the accountant, because he occupied the office of bailiff there this year, 40s.[90] And in the expenses of the steward, the clerk of the court, and of others attending the courts aforesaid this year, just as appears in the rolls of the court which were examined at the audit, 14s. 9d.

Sum 54s. 9d.

Costs of enclosing the woods of the lady And paid for making 135 perches of hedge around the enclosure of the woods of the lady, that is in Northawe 12, Lyrchesdale 34, Lady's Wood 50, and High Hall Wood 39 perches, that is for each perch ½d., 5s. 7½d. Item, in the wages of one labourer hired for 2½ days to make good various ditches and hedges of the aforesaid woods in those places most in need of repair, taking 4d. per day, 10d.

Sum 6s. 5½d.

Payments of money And in money paid to William Stanley, esq., Receiver of the lady in the county aforesaid, by the hand of the accountant from the issues of office in this year as follows, that is on 15 January in the 11th year of the king by a bill for £8; on 9 July in the same year by another bill for £4; on the 27th day of the same month for £12 19s.; and from the same at the audit 18d., as recognised by the said Receiver at the audit.

Sum of payments of money, £45 0s. 6d.

Sum of allowances and payments £49 15s. 3½d.
And owing, £47 8s. 3¾d.
From which allowed to him, 2s. charged on him above in respect of the rent and lease of one cottage lately in the tenure of John Maunser and taken into the hands of the lord because it is ruinous and decayed, and no profits were raised from it for the time aforesaid by the oath of the accountant. And allowed to him, 13s. charged above within the perquisites of the court aforesaid, for the remission of part of the fine of William Fuller for the sale of land to John Howchen, as recorded in the court rolls in the 8th year of the king, for non-payment and non-observance of his responsibility detailed in the court roll, because he had surrendered the said land according to custom, therefore he does not need to pay other than a small fine, that is 2s. out of the fine of 15s.[91] And allowed to him, 9¾d. for his keep when coming to Wingfield on two occasions to render this account and various other requirements. And he owes £6 12s. ½d. This total to be charged in the following account.

---

90 The office of reeve was, of course, elected and unpaid, other than receiving remission of rent for the year; hence the need to explain why John Hawe is in receipt of wages for his work this year.

91 An entry fine was invariably due on the transfer of unfree land from one person to another, and the level of the fine payable varied according to a variety of factors and local customs. Clearly the actors in this transaction felt the charge was too high, given that the land had been transferred in accordance with custom: consequently, the fine was substantially reduced, thus reducing the charge on the bailiff whose responsibility it was to collect.

Document 23: Walsham account, with Church House,
29 September 1558 to 29 September 1559

SA/B HA504/3/17

[*In English*]
The manor and parsonage of Walsham in Suffolk
The account of George Creme of the said manor and parsonage[92] for one whole year ended at the Feast of St Michael the Archangel 1559 the first year of Queen Elizabeth.

Arrears
Firstly in arrears as in the foot of the preceding account appear being discharged by the lord, nil.

Demesne and tithes
Item of the said George Creme for the lease of the said manor and parsonage with all the houses and barns and all manner of tithes and oblations pertaining to the same, except all those pastures, lands and feedings late in the lord's hands and now in the tenure of Thomas Seman; and all manner of free and copyhold rents and all other rents belonging to the same manor and parsonage; and the profits of the court by year, £14.
Item of Thomas Seman for the closes and pastures in Walsham, parcel of the manor and parsonage, with the stock of Cortes Reve to the value £30, so to him devised by indenture for term of years by year, £17.

Rents and courts
Item the rents of assize of the said manor and parsonage by year, £3 5s. 7d.
Item for the profits of the court there holden on St Margaret's day in years Philip and Mary 3rd and 5th, 59s. 5d.

And of the court holden the 12th April in the 1st year of Elizabeth, £3 6s. 7d., £6 6s.
£40 11s. 7d.
Sum total £40 11s. 7d.

Deductions
Firstly, paid to the executors of Robood for tenements and pieces of land lying within the closes and pasture in the tenure of Thomas Seman containing [*blank*] acres, nil.
Item for rent to Walsham now allowed, nil.
Sum of deductions, nil.   And so remaining clear.

Livery money
Firstly, paid by Thomas Seman in his reckoning made the 13th day of September 1559, £17.

---

92 Church House had been leased by the lords of Walsham for much of the fifteenth century, and therefore managed as if it was a permanent element of Walsham manor. The freehold had been acquired sometime between the dissolution of Ixworth priory in 1538 and this account. See Introduction, p. xxii.

Item discharged by the said George Creme the said sums of £14 and £3 5s. 7d., for these he stand bound by obligation for the payment of the same and other arrears, £17 5s. 7d.

Item paid to Austen Curtis every year for the profits of the court holden on St Margaret's day <the 12th of April> year Philip and Mary 3rd and 5th these sums, viz: of Clarke 23s. 8d., of Parker 5s., of Robood 15s. 8d., of Thomas Lacy 15s. 1d.: in full, 59s. 5d.

[*in later hand*] my husband hath an obligation for this same this 59s. 5d. is ? into three in my book.

Sum of livery money, £37 5s.

Upon various presents for the profits of the rest holden the 12th April 1st year of Elizabeth viz: Francis Rookwood 6d., Vincent 20d., Mourton 16s. 4d., Parker 13d., Payne 48s., in all £3 6s. 7d. Sum of debts.

[The document continues with an account of the manor of Mellis.]

Section Five

Indentures of receipts of payments, 1447 to 1451
Documents 24 to 33[1]

Document 24: Indenture of receipt of payment, 22 April 1447

SA/B HA504/3/15.8

Know all men by this present document that I, John Belley esq., have received and had at the day of the making of this document from my venerable lord, William de la Pole earl and marshal of Suffolk and Pembroke, 30s. 4d. sterling from a certain fee of 60s. 8d. p.a. for the office of parker of Huntingfield. That is, for 2d. a day to me the aforesaid John for the term of my life granted by the aforesaid, my venerable lord, to be taken annually from the revenues and profits of the manor of Hunting-field at the terms of Christmas, Easter, the Nativity of St John the Baptist and St Michael the Archangel, in equal portions. Of which, a certain 30s. 4d. for the terms of Christmas and Easter last past before the date of the document I acknowledge myself to be paid by the hands of John Burghard, bailiff of Huntingfield, and so my said venerable lord, his heirs and his executors are to be quit by the document. In witness of which, I have affixed my seal to this document. Made the 22nd day of April in the 25th year of the reign of King Henry VI after the conquest.
Signed J. Belley

Document 25: Indenture of receipt of payment, 20 April 1447

SA/B HA504/3/15.9

Know all men by this present document that I, John Belley esq., have received and had at the day of the making of this document from my venerable lord, William de la Pole earl and marshal of Suffolk and Pembroke, £6 13s. 4d. sterling from a certain annuity of 20 marks p.a. granted to me, the aforesaid John, for the term of my life by the aforesaid my venerable lord to be taken annually from the revenues and profits of the manor of Walsham at the terms of Christmas, Easter, the Nativity of St John the Baptist and St Michael the Archangel by equal portions. From which, a certain £6 13s. 4d. for the terms of Christmas and Easter last past, at the present date I acknowledge myself to be paid by the hand of William Fuller, farmer of Walsham, and so the said venerable lord, his heirs or executors are to be quit by the document. In witness whereof, I have affixed my seal to this document. Made the 20th day of April in the 25th year of King Henry VI after the conquest.
Signed J. Belley

---

[1]   See Introduction, pp. xxxiv–xxxv.

Document 26: Indenture of receipt of payment, 1450

SA/B HA504/3/16 m.1

Bill indented for Andrew Griggs, receiver general of lord William Duke of Suffolk in the counties of Suffolk, Norfolk and Essex, received from William Fuller farmer of Walsham, from the issues of his lease for the term of Easter in the 28th year of the reign of H[*enry VI*], £6 6s. 8d.

Document 27: Indenture of receipt of payment, 8 September 1450

SA/B HA504/3/16 m.2

By this indented document made at Walsham on 8th September in the 29th year of Henry VI it is testified that William Fuller, bailiff of Walsham aforesaid, paid Simon Dale £10.

Document 28: Indenture of receipt of payment, 21 April 1450

SA/B HA504/3/16 m.3

By this indented document made at Walsham 21st April in the 28th year of Henry VI it is testified that William Fuller, bailiff of Walsham aforesaid, paid Simon Dale £5.

Document 29: Indenture of receipt of payment, 6 October 1450

SA/B HA504/3/16 m.4

[*In English*] Be it known to all manner of men that I, John Belley, have received from William Fuller of the manor of Walsham for my quarter of a year the fee owed to me at the feast of Michaelmas in the 29th year of Henry VI last past, five marks. For this sum of 66s. 8d. I hold me well content and paid, my witness whereof I set to my sign manual for 6th October 29th year of aforesaid king.
John Belley

Document 30: Indenture of receipt of payment, 10 May 1450

SA/B HA504/3/16 m.5

[*In English*] This bill witnesseth that I, John Belley, have received from William Fuller, farmer of the manor of Walsham, £6 13s. 4d. for my half year ending at Easter last past. For which sum of £6 13s. 4d. I hold me well paid and content. In witness whereof I set my sign manual for 10th May 28th year of Henry VI.
John Belley

Document 31: Indenture of receipt of payment, 9 July 1450

SA/B HA504/3/16 m.6

[*In English*] Know all men by this present writing that I, John Belley, have received and have from William Fuller, farmer of the manor of Walsham, for my quarter year ending at Michaelmas last past 6 marks. For which sum of 66s. 8d. I hold me

well paid, in witness whereof I have set to my sign manual for 9th July 28th year of Henry VI.
John Belley

Document 32: Indenture of receipt of payment, 1450–1

SA/B HA504/3/16 m.7

[*The document begins with a petition from Hugh Jolyff, farmer of Wyverstone, not translated here.*]

Walsham
From William Fuller farmer there from the feast of Michaelmas in the 29th year.
For the lease of the manor, £44.
From which, allowed to him 20 marks per year.
John Belley received by three bills, £17 6s. 8d.
And he owes £13 6s. 8d.
Of which, allowed for a customary close of wood as [*recorded*] in the book, 3s. 5½d.
Item allowed for receipt from John Rookwood senior for the allowance of the price of 5 quarters of wheat for the lady's guests at Westhorpe, as in the book, 25s.
Item allowed to him 18s. 5d., which was paid for [*blank*].
And he owes £10 19s. 9½d.
Of which, allowed to him, 60s.
And allowed to him 12d., for the carriage of a bed from Bury towards Westhorpe, the lady's guests being there.[2]
And allowed to him 22d., for 20 [*blank*] which the lady bought at Westhorpe as in a bill.
And allowed to him, 17d.
Thus owing, £7 15s. 6½d.

Document 33:[3] Indenture of receipt of payment, undated

SA/B HA504/3/16 m.8

And allowed to him for delivery to the aforesaid receiver by the hand of John Rookwood senior as for the price of 5 qr of wheat delivered for the lady's hospitality at Westhorpe, as delivered to the gate-house this year by the hand of the said accountant.
As for all the money paid for the carriage of a bed \12d./ from Bury towards Westhorpe, the lord's guests being there, for the carriage of wheat \17d./ towards the mill, and for expenses incurred [*estusfur*'] travelling from Bedingfield [*Benningfeld*] to Wingfield, and for 20 [*blank*] \22d./ for the lady's use bought at Westhorpe and delivered there.

---

2 In the aftermath of de la Pole's death, some use was clearly made of the residence at Westhorpe. Alice Chaucer was probably touring her East Anglian estates in the summer of 1451 and stayed briefly during her progress. She was certainly there in July 1452. See next footnote.

3 A fragment of an account for another de la Pole manor, contained within HA504/3/15.13, notes the expenses incurred while the lady was at Westhorpe in July 1452.

And allowed to him 40s. for the loss made to him by a transgression in [*blank*] term. For consideration [*blank*] lord, both for his costs and his profits of one court held this year [*blank*] said farmer [*blank*] for his [*blank*] this year and five years aforesaid for one year.

GLOSSARY

Note: arcane and exceptional English and Latin words are explained in the body of the text rather than included in this glossary.

account (*compotus*): annual statement prepared by the bailiff or reeve (or another manorial official) of all money, stock and labour services ('works') received or charged, and expended or discharged, on the lord's behalf.

acre: the principal unit of land measurement, equivalent to 4,047 square metres or approximately 40 per cent of a hectare.

affeerer: official of a manorial court with responsibility for assessing the level of fines and amercements in individual cases.

amercement: penalty in money or in kind for an offence against the lord or the manor court.

attachment: seizure of a person's possessions to ensure compliance with the lord's, or the manorial court's, orders.

bailiff: salaried officer of the lord, responsible for the day-to-day management of one or more manors, which included the collection of rents and the preparation of the accounts.

balance/it balances: accounting device, usually a statement added at the audit, confirming that the auditors are satisfied that the stock or works due during the period covered by the account have been properly accounted for.

boonwork: seasonal labour service owed by free or unfree tenants, for whom the lord provides food.

brosty: a young calf

bullimong: an equal mix of peas and oats.

bushel: a dry measure of eight gallons (four pecks), especially used for grain.

capon: a castrated and fattened cockerel.

chaff: the protective husks around the seed of grain.

collector: official responsible for collecting fines, rents and other monies for the lord, and for keeping the tallies of expenditure.

common land: land over which tenants had certain rights, such as pasturing animals, collecting fuel, etc.

commutation: payment of money in lieu of performing some kind of service, whether a labour service on the lord's demesne or military service. The amount payable was seldom negotiated, but instead was fixed by custom.

crone: old or weak animal.

customs of the manor: a framework of practices, rules and expectations relating to activities within the manor, particularly associated with land and property tenure.

default: failure to perform an obligatory duty, usually to attend court, but could be another requirement laid down by a court.

demesne: the land within a manor allocated to the lord for his (or occasionally her) own use.

distrain: temporary confiscation of land or goods to enforce a court's decision or to recover a debt; **distraint**: the action of distraining.

dues and customs: tenurial obligations owed to the lord of the manor.

ell: measure of cloth, around 45 inches.

ewes: mature female sheep, i.e. in their third year and above.

faggots: bundles of wood cut from trees, especially branches, and bound for use as fuel.

farm: fixed sum paid annually in money or kind, without any other services, often for leasing land or for exercising an office.

fee farm: a form of tenure: a heritable grant of unfree land for a fixed annual cash sum, entry fine and suit of court.

feoffee: holder of a fief or 'fee'.

fief: hereditary land held from a superior lord.

fine: payment made to the lord in return for a specific concession, e.g. entry to unfree land.

fold: movable enclosure of land for keeping animals, usually sheep, by night; **liberty of fold**: right to keep a fold in a specified area.

frond: green leaves removed from trees, for example to feed animals or to use as bedding.

full age: age at which heirs were able to enter their inheritance.

furlong: a sub-division of open, strip, fields, not usually a fixed area of land.

gimmer: female sheep in its second year.

gudgeon: the pin or spindle forming part of a hinge.

heaped measures: the practice of heaping grain measures, such as bushels and quarters.

hogget, hogg: male sheep in their second year.

homage: body of persons who owed allegiance in the manor court.

labour services: part of the rent package of the landholding peasantry, and of holders of unfree land in particular, comprised working on the lord's demesne for a certain number of days each year. The lord could require these works to be performed bodily or could opt to commute them for a set cash sum.

leet: territorial and jurisdictional sub-unit of the hundred, which might have its own court to assess infringements against the king's peace, adjudged through the system of 'view of frankpledge'.

livery: clothing and/or food issued to a lord's paid officials and/or servants.

love bedripe: a seasonal labour service.

mark: unit of monetary value equivalent to two-thirds of a pound, i.e. 13s. 4d.

maslin: a mixture of different types of grain.

messuage: a plot of land with a dwelling house.

mixture: *see* maslin.

mollond: a base form of free tenure.

multure: the grains collected as toll through suit of mill. *See* suit of mill.

murrain: generic term for disease in livestock.

neif: person who is personally unfree; a hereditary serf.

peck: a dry measure equal to a quarter of a bushel, especially used for measuring grain.

pelt: the skin of a sheep that had died soon after shearing.

perch: one-fortieth of a rood.

pightle: an enclosed parcel of land, typically in a residential area and perhaps used as a garden or to keep poultry/livestock.

pledge: a guarantor held legally responsible by a court for ensuring that the person being guaranteed adhered to its orders.

ploughdale: a labour service ploughing on the demesne with sustenance provided for the workers.

pound: enclosure in which stray animals and those taken in distraint were penned.

poundage: the action or right of impounding stray or trespassing animals; also used to refer to the charge levied upon the owner of the animals which had been impounded.

presentment: incontestable accusation brought by a sworn jury or tithing group.

Purification: the feast day of the Purification of the Blessed Virgin Mary, 2nd February, also known as Candlemas.

quarter: a dry measure equal to eight bushels, used for measuring grain.

receiver: a senior estate official responsible for the collection and custody of monies from across the estate and answerable directly to the lord.

recognition: acknowledgement of a debt.

recovery: taking impounded goods or animals, attached or distrained, without seigniorial permission.

remit: formal renunciation of a claim to land.

rent of assize: the core standing rents of the manor, paid in cash annually by the long-established free and unfree lands and tenures.

rent resolute: rent which the lord of the manor owed to others, and therefore appears on the charge/expenditure section of the account.

rod: symbol of the lord's authority when ratifying transfers of land. Land held 'by the rod' was held at the lord's will.

rood: quarter of an acre.

seisin: possession of land.

serjeant: *see* bailiff.

sheriff: the principal officer of the Crown in a county, appointed annually by the Crown.

sheriff's aid: annual and ancient payment from some free tenants to the sheriff to help defray the expenses of the office. Sometimes called sheriff's silver.

stallage: fee charged by the lord for the rent of stalls.

steward: a senior manorial or estate administrator, responsible for a number of manors and answerable directly to the lord.

stot: a small draught horse.

submit: to place oneself in a position of submission or compliance to the court.

suit: the act of suing in a court of law, a legal prosecution.

suit of court: customary obligation of a tenant to attend the court of his lord.

suit of mill: customary obligation to mill grain at the lord's mill, for which the lord extracted a toll fixed by custom. *See* multure.

suitor: an individual attending the court to meet his customary obligation.

tenement/*tenementum*: a parcel of land held from the lord, usually including a house and an associated enclosure. The composition and size were not standardised (i.e. *tenementum* A would not be exactly the same size and layout as *tenementum* B), but the tenement itself was fixed (i.e. *tenementum* A did not vary over time).

term: an agreed period by which a tenant held a tenement or other holding or parcel of land from the lord.

tithe: tenth of profits and income on certain types of produce due to be paid to the rector of the parish for the upkeep of the priest and the chancel of the church.

trespass: a transgression committed against another person or their property.

vill: local unit of civil administration, particularly for taxation purposes.

ward: castle ward, an obligation on free tenants to perform some kind of military duty at the castle of their superior lord, such as joining the castle's garrison for a specific period. Sometimes called ward silver.

wether: a castrated adult male sheep, over three years old.

wong: signifying an area of open field.

works: *see* labour services.

BIBLIOGRAPHY

PRIMARY SOURCES

Rentals

1327 SA/B HA504/5/1 (1) and (2)

Accounts

1327–8 SA/B HA504/3/1b
1373–4 SA/B HA504/3/1c
1390–1 SA/B HA504/3/3
1396–7 SA/B HA504/3/4
1402–3 SA/B HA504/3/5a
1406–7 SA/B HA504/3/5b
1426–7 SA/B HA504/3/15 m.1
1427–8 SA/B HA504/315 m.2
1428–9 SA/B HA504/3/15 m.3
1429–30 SA/B HA504/3/6
1430–1 SA/B HA504/3/15 m.4
1431–2 SA/B HA504/3/7
1432–3 SA/B HA504/3/8
1433–4 SA/B HA504/3/9
1434–5 SA/B HA504/3/10
1436–7 SA/B HA504/3/15 m.5
1437–8 SA/B HA504/3/15 m.6
1439–40 SA/B HA504/3/11
1440–1 SA/B HA504/3/12
1441–2 SA/B HA504/3/13
1443–4 SA/B HA504/3/14
1444–5 SA/B HA504/3/15 m.7
1445–6 SA/B HA504/3/15 m.10
1446–7 SA/B HA504/3/15 m.11
1449–50 SA/B HA504/3/15 m.9
1451–2 SA/B HA504/3/15 mm.12 and 13
1470–1 SA/I HD1538/411/4 mm.2 and 3
1558–9 SA/B HA504/3

Indentures

1447–52 SA/B HA504/3/15 m.8
SA/B HA504/3/16 mm.1 to 9

SECONDARY SOURCES

Amor, N., 'Riding out recession: Ixworth and Woolpit in the later Middle Ages', *PSIAH* 40 (2002), pp. 127–44

Amor, N., *Keeping the peace in medieval Suffolk* (Stanningfield, 2021)

M. Bailey, *A marginal economy? East Anglian Breckland in the later Middle Ages* (Cambridge, 1989)

Bailey, M., 'Sand into gold. The foldcourse system in west Suffolk, 1200–1600', *Agricultural History Review* 38 (1990), pp. 40–57

Bailey, M., ed., *The bailiffs' minute book of Dunwich 1403 to 1430*, Suffolk Records Society 34 (1992)

Bailey, M., ed., *The English manor c.1200 to c.1500* (Manchester, 2002)

Bailey, M., *Medieval Suffolk. An economic and social history 1200 to 1500* (Woodbridge, 2007)

Bailey, M., 'The form, function and evolution of irregular field systems in Suffolk, 1300 to 1550', *Agricultural History Review* 57 (2009), pp. 15–36

Bailey, M., 'Villeinage in England: a regional case study', *Economic History Review* 62 (2009), pp. 430–57

Bailey, M., *The decline of serfdom in late medieval England. From bondage to freedom* (Woodbridge, 2014)

Bailey, M., 'The transformation of customary tenures in southern England, c.1350 to c.1500', *Agricultural History Review* 62 (2014), pp. 210–30

Bailey, M., *After the Black Death. Economy, society and the law in fourteenth-century England* (Oxford, 2021)

Bailey, M., 'Servile and gender migration in late medieval England: the evidence of manorial court rolls', *Past and Present* 261 (2023), pp. 47–85

Belcher, J., *The foldcourse and East Anglian agriculture and landscape, 1100–1900* (Woodbridge, 2020)

Britnell, R.H., '*Advantagium mercatoris*: a custom in medieval English trade', *Nottingham Medieval Studies* 27 (1983), pp. 37–50

Britnell, R.H., 'Minor landlords in England and medieval agrarian capitalism', in T.H. Aston, ed., *Landlords, peasants and politics in medieval England* (Cambridge, 1987), pp. 227–46

Campbell, B.M.S., 'The agrarian problem in the early fourteenth century', *Past and Present* 188 (2005), pp. 3–70

Campbell, B.M.S., and Bartley, K., *England on the eve of the Black Death: an atlas of lay lordship, land and wealth, 1300–49* (Manchester, 2006)

Copinger, W.A., *The manors of Suffolk: volume III* (London, 1909)

Dodd, K.M., ed., *The field book of Walsham-le-Willows 1577*, Suffolk Records Society 17 (1974)

Dymond, D., 'A lost social institution: the camping close', *Rural History* 1 (1990), pp. 165–92

Dymond, D., 'The game of camping in eastern England', *The Local Historian* 51 (2021), pp. 2–16

Eldridge, L., *Law and the medieval village community. Reinvigorating historical jurisprudence* (Abingdon, 2023)

Farmer, D.L., 'Marketing the produce of the countryside 1200 to 1500', in E. Miller, ed., *The agrarian history of England and Wales, volume III, 1348–1500* (Cambridge, 1991), pp. 324–430

Fisk, J., 'The lordship, structure, and evolution of the manor of Laxfield in Suffolk, 1066 to 1410' (University of East Anglia, MA by Research thesis, 2022)

Harriss, G.L., *Shaping the nation: England 1360 to 1461* (Oxford, 2005)

Harvey, I.M.W., *Jack Cade's rebellion of 1450* (Oxford, 1991)

Harvey, P.D.A., 'Agricultural treatises and manorial accounting in medieval England', *Agricultural History Review* 20 (1972), pp. 170–82

Harvey, P.D.A., ed., *Manorial records of Cuxham Oxfordshire, c.1200–1359*, Oxfordshire Records Society 50 (1976)

Harvey, P.D.A., *Manorial Records* (British Records Association, Archives and the User, No. 5, 1984)

Hatcher, J., 'The Great Slump of the mid fifteenth century', in R.H. Britnell and J. Hatcher, eds, *Progress and problems in medieval England. Essays in honour of Edward Miller* (Cambridge, 1996), pp. 237–72

Hatcher, J., *The Black Death. An intimate history* (London, 2008)

Hervey, F., ed., *The Pinchbeck Register relating to Bury St Edmunds abbey, volume II* (Brighton, 1925)

Kosminsky, E.A., *Studies in the agrarian history of thirteenth-century England* (Oxford, 1956)

Lock, R., 'The Black Death in Walsham le Willows', *PSIAH* 37 (1992), pp. 316–36

Lock, R., ed., *The court rolls of Walsham le Willows 1303–50*, Suffolk Records Society 41 (1998)

Lock, R., ed., *The court rolls of Walsham le Willows 1351–99*, Suffolk Records Society 45 (2002)

Martin, E., *Great Bricett manor and priory* (Suffolk Institute of Archaeology and History, 2021)

Martin, E., and Satchell, M., *Where most enclosures be. East Anglian fields, history, morphology and management*, East Anglian Archaeology 124 (2008)

Oschinsky, D., ed., *Walter of Henley and other treatises on estate management and accounting* (Oxford, 1971)

Page, W., ed., *Victoria History of the County of Suffolk, volume II* (London, 1907)

Powell, E., *A Suffolk Hundred in the year 1283* (Cambridge, 1910)

Pribyl, K., *Farming, famine and plague. The impact of climate in late medieval England* (Cham, 2017)

Rackham, O., *The history of the countryside* (London, 1986)

Richmond, C., 'East Anglian politics and society in the fifteenth century', in C. Harper-Bill, ed., *Medieval East Anglia* (Woodbridge, 2005), pp. 183–208

Taxatio Ecclesiastica Angliae et Walliae Auctoritate P. Nicholai IV Circa A.D.1291 (London, 1802)

Virgoe, R., 'The murder of James Andrew: Suffolk faction in the 1430s', *PSIAH* 34 (1980), pp. 263–8

West, S.E., and McLaughlin, A., *Towards a landscape history of Walsham le Willows, Suffolk*, East Anglian Archaeology 85 (1998)

INDEX OF PEOPLE AND PLACES

The numerous names of fields, woods etc in Walsham are indexed all together under Walsham le Willows.

INDEX OF SUBJECTS

235

THE SUFFOLK RECORDS SOCIETY

For over sixty-five years, the Suffolk Records Society has added to the knowledge of Suffolk's history by issuing an annual volume of previously unpublished manuscripts, each throwing light on some new aspect of the history of the county.

Covering 700 years and embracing letters, diaries, maps, accounts and other archives, many of them previously little known or neglected, these books have together made a major contribution to historical studies.

At the heart of this achievement lie the Society's members, all of whom share a passion for Suffolk and its history and whose support, subscriptions and donations make possible the opening up of the landscape of historical research in the area.

In exchange for this tangible support, members receive a new volume each year at a considerable saving on the retail price at which the books are then offered for sale.

Members are also welcomed to the launch of the new volume, held each year in a different and appropriate setting within the county and giving them a chance to meet and listen to some of the leading historians in their fields talking about their latest work.

For anyone with a love of history, a desire to build a library on Suffolk themes at modest cost and a wish to see historical research continue to thrive and bring new sources to the public eye in decades to come, a subscription to the Suffolk Records Society is the ideal way to make a contribution and join the company of those who give Suffolk history a future.

THE CHARTERS SERIES

To supplement the annual volumes and serve the need of medieval historians, the Charters Series was launched in 1979 with the challenge of publishing the transcribed texts of all the surviving monastic charters for the county. Since then, twenty-two volumes have been published as an occasional series, the latest in 2023.

The Charter Series is financed by a separate annual subscription leading to receipt of each volume on publication.

CURRENT PROJECTS

Volumes approved by the Council of the Society for future publication include *The Incorporated Hundreds of Suffolk* edited by John Shaw, *The First World War Diaries of George Punchard from Ipswich* edited by Paul Botwright; and in the Charters Series, *Bury St Edmunds Town Charters* in two volumes edited by Vivien Brown, and *Rumburgh Priory Charters* edited by Nicholas Karn. The order in which these and other volumes appear in print will depend on the dates of completion of editorial work.

MEMBERSHIP

Membership enquiries should be addressed to Mrs Tanya Christian, 8 Orchid Way, Needham Market, IP6 8JQ; e-mail: suffolkrecordssociety@gmail.com

The Suffolk Records Society is a registered charity, No. 1084279.